Deposit Insurance around the World

Deposit Insurance around the World

Issues of Design and Implementation

Edited by Aslı Demirgüç-Kunt, Edward Kane, and Luc Laeven

The MIT Press
Cambridge, Massachusetts
London, England

MIT Press books may be purchased at special quantity discounts for business or sales promotional use. For information, please e-mail special_sales@mitpress.mit.edu or write to Special Sales Department, The MIT Press, 55 Hayward Street, Cambridge, MA 02142.

This book was set in Palatino on 3B2 by Asco Typesetters, Hong Kong and was printed and bound in the United States of America.

Library of Congress Cataloging-in-Publication Data

Deposit insurance around the world : issues of design and implementation / edited by Aslı Demirgüç-Kunt, Edward J. Kane, and Luc Laeven.
    p.   cm.
Includes bibliographical references and index.
ISBN 978-0-262-04254-3 (hbk. : alk. paper)
1. Deposit insurance. I. Demirgüç-Kunt, Aslı, 1961– II. Kane, Edward J. (Edward James), 1935– III. Laeven, Luc.
HG1662.A3D474   2008
368.8'54—dc22   2007049245

10 9 8 7 6 5 4 3 2 1

Contents

Contributors

Thorsten Beck   World Bank

Modibo K. Camara   International Finance Corporation

Aslı Demirgüç-Kunt   World Bank

Kalina Dimitrova   Bulgarian National Bank

Stephen Haber   Stanford University

Patrick Honohan   World Bank

Harry Huizinga   Tilburg University

Edward Kane   Boston College

Baybars Karacaovali   Fordham University

Randall S. Kroszner   Board of Governors of the Federal Reserve System

Luc Laeven   World Bank and CEPR

William R. Melick   Kenyon College and Federal Reserve Bank of Cleveland

Fernando Montes-Negret   World Bank

Nikolay Nenovsky   Bulgarian National Bank

Preface

Explicit deposit insurance (DI) systems are multiplying rapidly in the developing world. The number of countries offering explicit deposit guarantees surged from twenty in 1980 to eighty-seven by the end of 2003. Although many recent adopters were transition countries of Eastern Europe seeking to comply with the European Union Directive on Deposit Insurance, adopters can be found in every region of the world. This book argues that this is an alarming trend that should not be interpreted as evidence that designing and operating an efficient system are straightforward tasks. To the contrary, the analysis presented in this book confirms that officials in many countries would do well to delay the installation of a deposit insurance system. The message is timely because despite the rise of deposit insurance over the last decades, holdouts—particularly among low-income countries with poor institutional development—still outnumber DI adopters.

One reason for this surge is that having an explicit deposit insurance scheme has come to be seen as one of the pillars of modern financial safety nets. Establishing explicit deposit insurance has become a principal feature of policy advice on financial architecture that outside experts give to countries undergoing reform. Starting in the 1990s, IMF crisis management advice recommended erecting DI as a way of either containing crisis or winding down crisis-generated blanket guarantees. The World Bank has also actively supported the adoption of DI and provided adjustment loans for initial capital of deposit insurance funds in a number of countries. This book challenges the wisdom of encouraging countries to adopt DI without first remedying observable weaknesses in their institutional environment.

An extensive body of economic theory analyzes the benefits and costs of deposit insurance and explores how balancing these benefits and costs can produce an optimal deposit insurance system. Starting from the premise that the main benefit of deposit insurance is to prevent wasteful liquidations of bank assets caused by deposit runs, the theoretical debate centers on the question of how effectively hypothetical variations in deposit insurance arrangements can curtail voluntary risk taking (i.e., moral hazard). In contrast, cross-country empirical evidence on the efficiency of existing deposit insurance systems has been scarce and analysis has been limited to developed country experiences. Due to lack of data, there has been very little empirical evidence on what factors determine DI adoption and design, or the impact of DI and its design on bank stability, market discipline, and financial development.

This book brings together a unified collection of papers that mitigates some of the existing weaknesses in the literature by (1) constructing and analyzing a broad cross-country dataset on deposit insurance, and (2) assessing the impact of DI and its design in individual developing countries.

Deposit insurance is strong medicine. Whether it benefits or harms a country depends on how well it is designed and administered. For countries in the process of adopting DI, this volume provides advice that identifies six guiding principles of good design: limited insurance coverage, compulsory membership, private-sector participation in overseeing the scheme, appropriate pricing, restrictions on the ability of the fund to shift losses to the taxpayer, and assigning explicit responsibility for bank insolvency resolution.

In the summer of 2007, bank runs on loss-making banks in Germany and in the United Kingdom underscored inadequacies in European safety nets and in arrangements for supporting securitized loans. Delays in verifying and resolving the insolvency of Northern Rock and other troubled banks revealed worldwide defects in credit ratings and gaps in the enforceability of securitized bank liabilities. The unanticipated return to bank balance sheets of loss exposures that such liabilities were designed to transfer to others pushed the issues of deposit insurance coverage and safeguards back to the center of debates on regulatory policy in both developing and industrialized countries. The guiding principles identified in this book can contribute mightily to this debate.

The book is aimed at academics working in the area of finance, development, and international economics along with public policy professionals working at international institutions, central banks, and ministries of finance. We sincerely believe that this book belongs on the bookshelf of every policymaker who hopes to contribute to a national and cross-country debate on the wisdom of adopting or the need to redesign a deposit insurance system.

Acknowledgments

This volume is the fruit of a research project sponsored by the World Bank's Research Department and Financial Sector Vice Presidency. We are grateful to Cesare Calari, Gerard Caprio, and Alan Winters for their intellectual guidance and support.

Many colleagues helped by providing valuable input or comments at various stages of the project: Thorsten Beck, Gerard Caprio, Stijn Claessens, James Hanson, David Hoelscher, Patrick Honohan, Ross Levine, Fernando Montes-Negret, Augusto de la Torre, as well as three anonymous referees for MIT Press. Many thanks are due to the authors for their contributions to this volume.

Guillermo Noguera and Baybars Karacaovali provided excellent research assistance. We are also grateful to Polly Means and Agnes Yaptenco for their help in producing the manuscript.

Last but not least, our warmest thanks go to our families, for permitting us to devote so much of our time to our research.

This book was written while Luc Laeven was at the World Bank; he is currently at the International Monetary Fund. The findings, interpretations, and conclusions of this book are those of the authors and do not necessarily reflect the views of the World Bank, its executive directors, or the countries they represent.

I   Introduction

1 Deposit Insurance Design and Implementation: Policy Lessons from Research and Practice

Aslı Demirgüç-Kunt, Edward Kane, and Luc Laeven

1.1 Introduction

Deposit insurance can be explicit or merely implicit. Explicit insurance coverages are contractual obligations; implicit coverages are only conjectural. Implicit insurance exists to the extent political incentives that influence a government's reaction to large or widespread banking problems make taxpayer bailouts of insolvent banks seem inevitable. Every country offers implicit insurance because, during banking crises, the pressure on government officials to rescue at least some bank stakeholders becomes difficult to resist. While still far from universal, explicit deposit insurance (DI) systems are multiplying rapidly. Countries explicitly guaranteeing deposits surged from twenty in 1980 to eighty-seven by the end of 2003 (see figure 1.1).

One reason for this surge is that having an explicit deposit insurance scheme has come to be seen as one of the pillars of modern financial safety nets. Establishing explicit deposit insurance has become a principal feature of policy advice on financial architecture that outside experts give to countries undergoing reform. Starting in the 1990s, IMF crisis management advice recommended erecting DI as a way of either containing crisis or winding down crisis-generated blanket guarantees (Folkerts-Landau and Lindgren 1998; Garcia 1999). The World Bank has also actively supported the adoption of DI and provided adjustment loans for initial capital of deposit insurance funds in a number of countries.[1]

Table 1.1 lists countries that have adopted DI since 1995. Although many recent adopters were transition countries of Eastern Europe seeking to comply with the European Union (EU) Directive on Deposit Insurance, adopters can be found in every region of the world.

Total number of explicit deposit insurance systems established

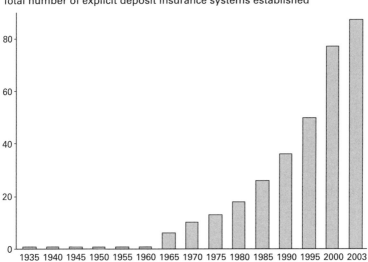

Figure 1.1
The rise of deposit insurance around the world, 1935–2003

Table 1.1
Recent establishment of deposit insurance schemes

Year adopted	Countries that have established an explicit scheme
2003	Malta, Paraguay, Russia, Zimbabwe
2002	Albania
2001	Nicaragua, Serbia and Montenegro, Slovenia
2000	Cyprus, Jordan, Vietnam
1999	Bahamas, Ecuador,* El Salvador, Guatemala, Honduras, Kazakhstan (Cameroon, Central African Republic, Chad, Equatorial Guinea, Gabon, Republic of Congo: deposit insurance law ratified by two out of these six CEMAC countries)
1998	Bosnia and Herzegovina, Estonia, Gibraltar, Indonesia,* Jamaica, Latvia, Malaysia,* Ukraine
1997	Algeria, Croatia, Thailand*
1996	Belarus, Korea, Lithuania, Macedonia, Romania, Slovak Republic, Sweden
1995	Brazil, Bulgaria, Oman, Poland

* Blanket coverage

Countries with and without DI at year-end 2003 are mapped in figure 1.2. Holdouts outnumber DI adopters. China and most African countries do not offer explicit deposit insurance. In the developed world, Australia, New Zealand, and Israel stand out as important exceptions.

Trends in DI adoption should not be interpreted as evidence that designing and operating an efficient system are straightforward tasks. On the contrary, system personnel are tasked with conflicting objectives that make both jobs exceedingly difficult. Conflict comes from differences in the size and distribution of costs and benefits. The central challenge of deposit insurance management is to strike an optimal balance between the benefits of preventing crises and the costs of controlling bank and customer risk taking. Protecting against crises and shocks absorbs considerable resources and can easily end up subsidizing bank risk taking. When such subsidies exist, they foster imprudent banking practices and support inefficient borrower investments in real resources.

Given the difficulties policymakers face in designing and operating a country's safety net, they typically look to experts to help them decide whether to adopt explicit deposit insurance and, if so, how to design a workable system. Cost-benefit analysts should want to conduct a careful review of cross-country econometric evidence as well as to collect and examine testimony from practitioners in individual countries.

This study adds some new data points to the evidence available to guide decisions about deposit insurance adoption, design, and implementation. The next section summarizes the dimensions of the data set and highlights cross-country differences in deposit insurance design. Section 1.3 reviews cross-country econometric evidence on the costs and benefits of deposit insurance. Section 1.4 develops practical lessons from individual country experiences. Section 1.5 distills both kinds of evidence into a set of principles of good design.

1.2   Deposit Insurance around the World

Banking crises are painful and disruptive. During a crisis, liquidity typically dries up. Customers lose access to bank balances, and some worthy borrowers and equity issuers find that financial markets cannot accommodate their need for funding. Working-class and retired households may be forced into a hand-to-mouth existence. Severe crises derail macroeconomic stabilization programs, slow future growth, and increase poverty. Solid businesses may lose access to credit and be

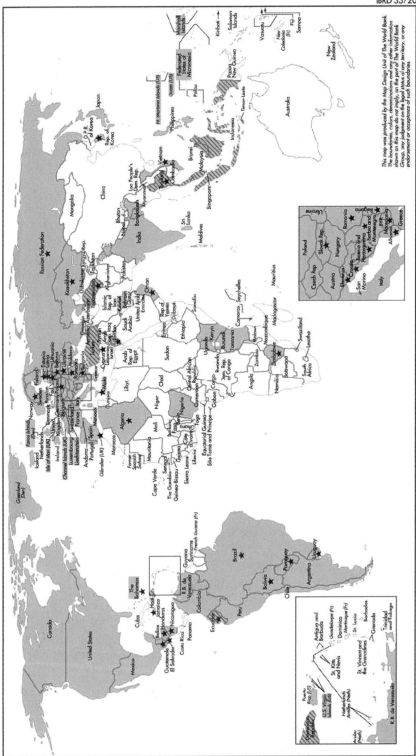

EXPLICIT DEPOSIT INSURANCE AROUND THE WORLD

The World Bank

EXPLICIT DEPOSIT INSURANCE

ISSUED UNLIMITED GUARANTEE

NO EXPLICIT DEPOSIT INSURANCE

★ RECENT ADOPTERS OF EXPLICIT DEPOSIT INSURANCE (SINCE 1995)

Data as of end 2003.

Figure 1.2
Adoption of deposit insurance around the world (as of 2003)

forced into bankruptcy. Diminished confidence in domestic financial institutions may fuel a panicky flight of foreign and domestic capital that not only closes down institutions but generates a currency crisis.

To minimize pain and disruption, policymakers erect a financial safety net. The net seeks simultaneously to make crises less likely and to limit the harm suffered when insolvencies occur. Implicit and explicit deposit insurance are critical components of national safety nets.

Deposit insurance guarantees appeal to policymakers for multiple reasons. One reason is that their costs are less immediately visible than their benefits. In the short run, installing explicit deposit insurance can actually lower reported budget deficits. This is because accountants can book premium revenue paid by banks without fully recording on the other side of the government's income statement the incremental value of the financial obligations that DI guarantees generate. Such one-sided accounting paints deposit insurance as a costless way of reducing the threat of bank runs. More lasting benefits include protecting unsophisticated depositors and improving opportunities for small and opaque domestic banks to compete with larger and more transparent domestic and foreign institutions. Also, when adopted as part of a program of privatization or postcrisis restructuring, cutting back the maximum size of balances covered by government guarantees becomes an important goal. Explicit deposit insurance can formally curtail the size of guarantees previously conveyed to banks that were government-owned or granted emergency blanket coverage.

To document differences in deposit insurance systems, the authors assembled a cross-country and time-series database covering 181 countries. This database provides comprehensive information on the existence and timing of deposit insurance adoption, design features installed, and any changes in features made over time. Chapter 11 describes the sample in detail.[2]

Table 1.2 shows that 75 percent of high-income countries offer DI, but only 16 percent of low-income countries do. DI is widespread in Europe and Latin America, but less common in the Middle East (29 percent) and sub-Saharan Africa (11 percent).

Figures 1.3 and 1.4 display trends in the adoption of DI by size of per capita income and by region, respectively. The frequency of adoption varies markedly across regions and per capita income classes. Except in the low-income category, countries have been adopting DI at an increasing rate. Regionally, Europe, Central Asia, and the Latin-Caribbean region show accelerated adoption activity.

Table 1.2
Proportion of countries with explicit deposit insurance to total by category (in percent, as of 2003)

	Proportion based on		
Category	Number of countries	GDP	GDP per capita
By income level			
High-income	75.00	96.35	83.45
Upper-middle-income	60.71	86.20	63.26
Lower-middle-income	58.82	57.56	64.25
Low-income	16.39	78.11	17.26
*By geographical region**			
Asia and Pacific	38.46	48.76	53.78
Europe and Central Asia	74.07	97.24	93.40
Latin America and Caribbean	66.67	98.34	71.11
Middle East and North Africa	28.57	16.36	42.84
Sub-Saharan Africa	10.87	17.12	3.63

*Regional breakdown excludes high-income countries.

The database indicates that deposit insurance design features vary widely across countries. For example, account coverages range from unlimited guarantees to tight coverage limits. Whereas Mexico, Turkey, and Japan promise 100 percent coverage, Chile, Switzerland, and the United Kingdom limit individual depositor reimbursements to amounts less than their nation's per capita GDP.

Table 1.3 summarizes how selected design features vary across different income groups and regions. Besides setting a maximum level of guarantees, countries limit their *coverages* in several other ways. First, some countries insist that accountholders "coinsure" a proportion of their balances. However, coinsurance provisions remain relatively rare and are particularly infrequent in low-income countries. Second, countries do not always cover deposits denominated in foreign currency. Finally, although most schemes exclude interbank deposits, a disproportionally large number of countries in the low- to middle-income categories choose to guarantee such deposits.

Deposit insurance obligations are *funded* in diverse ways. Most are advance funded, commonly from a blend of government and bank sources. To enable managers to build and maintain a dedicated fund of reserves against loss exposures, insurers usually assess client banks an annual user charge. Premiums are typically based on the amount of

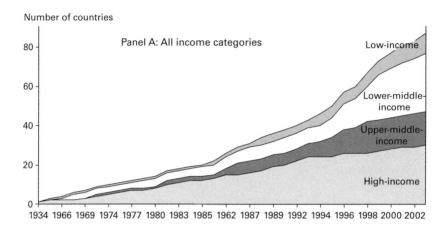

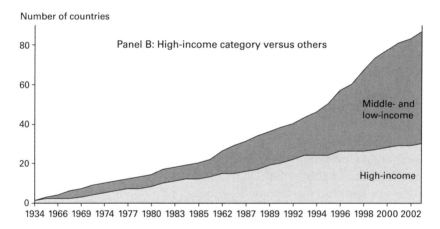

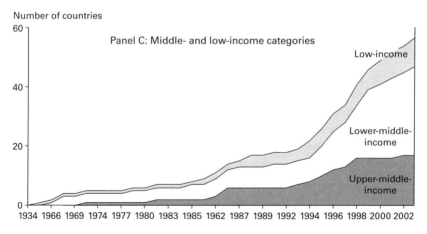

Figure 1.3
Trends in the adoption of explicit deposit insurance by income level

Number of countries

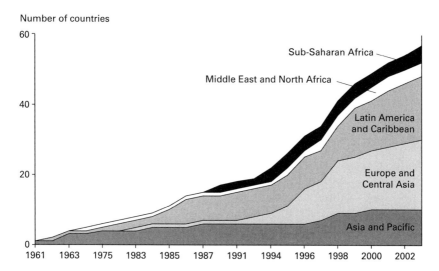

Figure 1.4
Trends in the adoption of explicit deposit insurance by region
Note: High-income countries are excluded from the analysis.

insured deposits, but efforts to tie premiums to individual bank risk exposures have gained momentum in recent years. Risk rating is a difficult task. Assessing risk requires a sophisticated staff and access to reliable balance sheet information from client banks. Difficulties in meeting staff and informational requirements help to explain why flat rate systems predominate among low-income adopters.

Insurance schemes are typically *managed* by a government agency or by a public-private partnership. Only a few countries (such as Argentina, Germany, and Switzerland) manage their schemes privately. Finally, in many countries, *membership* is compulsory for chartered banks. Here, too, Switzerland is a notable exception.

When countries are grouped by regions, similarities emerge. Compulsory membership is less common in Asia and the Pacific, and management is almost always official. Sub-Saharan African countries cover interbank deposits much more frequently than other countries.

Precisely because combinations of design features are so diverse, the value of the database lies in allowing investigators to compare and contrast the ways in which different features work in different environments. Section 1.3 summarizes what econometric analysis of this database can tell us about how individual features work in various circumstances.

Table 1.3
Design features of explicit deposit insurance schemes: Proportion of countries with each feature in a given category (as of 2003, in percent)

By income level

Feature	High-income	Upper-middle-income	Lower-middle-income	Low-income	Proportion in all countries
Foreign currency deposits covered	73	80	82	57	76
Interbank deposits covered	7	7	29	43	18
Coinsurance exists	27	44	21	0	25
Payment per depositor	77	94	72	78	79
Scheme is permanently funded	63	94	97	100	84
Premiums are risk-adjusted	20	19	39	0	25
Membership is compulsory	93	100	82	100	91
Source of funding:					
Private	50	7	42	14	36
Joint	50	87	58	86	63
Public	0	7	0	0	1
Administration:					
Official	47	63	70	75	60
Joint	30	31	26	13	27
Private	23	6	4	13	12

By region*

Feature	Asia and Pacific	Europe and Central Asia	Latin America and Caribbean	Middle East and North Africa	Sub-Saharan Africa
Foreign currency deposits covered	71	100	75	25	40
Interbank deposits covered	57	5	19	25	75
Coinsurance exists	0	45	18	25	0
Payment per depositor	75	80	82	75	80
Scheme is permanently funded	86	100	94	100	100
Premiums are risk-adjusted	33	35	29	0	0
Membership is compulsory	50	95	94	100	100

Table 1.3
(continued)

By region*

Feature	Asia and Pacific	Europe and Central Asia	Latin America and Caribbean	Middle East and North Africa	Sub-Saharan Africa
Source of funding:					
Private	33	26	33	25	0
Joint	67	74	60	75	100
Public	0	0	7	0	0
Administration:					
Official	100	63	71	50	60
Joint	0	37	18	50	20
Private	0	0	12	0	20

*Regional breakdown excludes high-income countries.

1.3 Deposit Insurance: Empirical Evidence

An extensive body of economic theory analyzes the benefits and costs of deposit insurance and explores how balancing these benefits and costs can produce an optimal deposit insurance system. Foundational studies include Merton 1977, 1978; Buser, Chen, and Kane 1981; Diamond and Dybvig 1983; Chari and Jagannathan 1988; Kane 1995, 2000; Calomiris 1996; Bhattacharya et al. 1998; and Allen and Gale 1998. Starting from the premise that the main benefit of deposit insurance is to prevent wasteful (i.e., value-destroying) liquidations of bank assets caused by deposit runs, the theoretical debate centers on the question of how effectively hypothetical variations in deposit insurance arrangements can curtail voluntary risk taking (i.e., moral hazard).

Empirical evidence on the actual operation and design of deposit insurance systems is relatively scarce and limited in geographic coverage. An adequate body of cross-country econometric research is just emerging. Empirical research addresses five questions about the design and effectiveness of individual country deposit insurance systems and about the circumstances that might lead a country to establish an explicit scheme. These questions are:

• How does deposit insurance affect bank stability?

• How does deposit insurance affect market discipline?

• How does deposit insurance impact financial development?

• What role does deposit insurance play in managing crises?

• What factors and circumstances influence deposit insurance adoption and design?

The answer to the first four questions is "It depends." Chief among the items on which outcomes depend are the factors and circumstances that influence DI adoption and design decisions.

1.3.1 Deposit Insurance and Banking Crises

Economic theory indicates that, depending on how it is designed and managed, deposit insurance can either increase or decrease banking stability. On the one hand, credible deposit insurance can enhance financial stability by making depositor runs less likely. On the other hand, if insured institutions' capital positions and risk taking are not supervised carefully, the insurer tends to accrue loss exposures that undermine bank stability in the long run. Economists label insurance-induced risk taking as "moral hazard." Moral hazard occurs because sheltering risk takers from the negative consequences of their behavior increases their appetite for risk. The importance of controlling moral hazard in banking has been stressed by academics, but disparaged by many policymakers.

Demirgüç-Kunt and Detragiache (2002) are the first to use a cross-county database to study the link between deposit insurance and financial crises. Their model of banking crisis uses 1980–1997 data from sixty-one countries. After controlling for numerous other determinants, they find that weaknesses in deposit insurance design increase the likelihood that a country will experience a banking crisis. More precisely, deposit insurance significantly reduces banking stability in countries whose contracting environment is poorly developed, but in stronger environments deposit insurance schemes have little significant effect on stability. Sensitivity tests indicate that this finding is not driven by reverse causality.[3] Investigation of individual design features shows that deposit insurance proves troublesome in countries where coverage is extensive, where authorities amass a large fund of explicit reserves and earmark it for insolvency resolution, and where the scheme is managed by government officials rather than administered in the private sector.

An overriding theme that emerges from research on financial crises concerns the adverse influence defects in bank transparency and in mechanisms for enforcing counterparty obligations exert on the quality of a country's regulatory regime. A large and growing body of evidence supports the hypothesis that the more effectively the private and public contracting environment serves to control incentive conflict, the more readily prudential regulation and supervision can rein in the moral hazard incentives that deposit insurance might otherwise generate.

1.3.2 Deposit Insurance and Market Discipline

In high-transparency environments, depositors discipline banks that engage in excessive risk taking by demanding higher deposit interest rates and/or moving balances to safer institutions. Because and to the extent that deposit insurance reduces a depositor's stake in monitoring and policing bank capital and loss exposures, it shifts responsibility for assuring transparency and controlling bank risk taking to the regulatory system.

Of course, even if a country's safety net covered all bank balances, depositors would remain at risk for the opportunity costs of claiming and reinvesting the amounts they are due and for costs occasioned by delays in receiving deposit insurance disbursements. This means that government guarantees never completely extinguish market discipline. Still, stability can be undermined if deposit insurance managers displace more discipline than they are able to exert.

Using a bank level dataset covering forty-three countries over 1990–1997, Demirgüç-Kunt and Huizinga (2004) study depositor discipline by modeling deposit interest rates. They show that explicit insurance does lower a bank's interest expense and does make interest payments less sensitive to individual bank risk and liquidity.

It is important to investigate how particular DI design characteristics affect bank risk-taking incentives. Statistical research establishes that, although market discipline increases with institutional development, particular deposit insurance design features consistently strengthen or weaken market discipline. On the one hand, market discipline is enhanced by coinsurance provisions covering accounts denominated *Strengthen* in foreign currency, and involving private managers in the insurance enterprise. On the other hand, significant amounts of private market discipline is displaced by setting high coverage limits, extending coverage to interbank deposits, establishing an ex ante fund of reserves, *weaken* granting the insurer direct access to government resources, or insisting on public management.

Although deposit insurance displaces some market discipline even in advanced countries, the net effect DI has on stability need not be negative. At the margin, stability is improved if DI is accompanied by appropriate regulation and supervision. This conclusion further clarifies the link between insurance and banking crises.

A complementary body of research explores the risk-shifting incentives that one can infer from the behavior of estimates of safety net subsidies imbedded in individual bank stock prices (e.g., Hovakimian, Kane, and Laeven 2003). These studies show that countries with poor private and public contracting environments are less apt to design their DI system well. This implies countries with weak contracting environments are apt to suffer adverse consequences from installing a DI scheme.

1.3.3   Deposit Insurance and Financial Development

Individual countries adopt deposit insurance for different reasons. In developing countries, a common goal is to expand the reach of the formal banking system and to increase the flow of bank credit by minimizing depositor doubts about the banking system's ability to redeem depositor claims when funds are needed. To the extent that deposit insurance bolsters depositors' faith in the stability of a country's banking industry, it mobilizes household savings and allows these savings to be invested in more efficient ways. A considerable body of research shows that financial development does indeed improve the productivity of real investment and sustain higher levels of aggregate economic growth (e.g., Levine 1997).

The quality of a nation's contracting environment limits the contribution that variations in regulatory structure can make to economic development and macroeconomic growth. Recent adopters of deposit insurance include African and Latin American countries with low levels of financial development and government accountability. Using time-series data for fifty-eight countries, Cull, Senbet, and Sorge (2005) find that explicit deposit insurance favorably impacts the level and volatility of financial activity only in the presence of strong institutional development. In institutionally weak environments, deposit insurance appears to undermine the productivity of real investment and retards, rather than promotes, sustainable financial development.

1.3.4   Deposit Insurance and Crisis Management

Crisis management entails a number of difficult policy trade-offs between recovery speed, economic efficiency, and distributional fairness. Due to deficiencies in prior disaster planning, it has become common practice to issue blanket guarantees to arrest a banking crisis. Countries adopting this strategy include Sweden (1992), Japan (1996), Thailand (1997), Korea (1997), Malaysia (1998), and Indonesia (1998). Turkey tried to halt its financial panic in 2000 by guaranteeing not just bank depositors, but all domestic and foreign nondeposit creditors of Turkish banks.

Advocates of using blanket guarantees to halt a systemic crisis argue that sweeping guarantees can be immediately helpful—if not essential—in stopping a spreading flight to quality. However, because blanket guarantees create an expectation of their future use in similar circumstances, they undermine market discipline and may prove greatly destabilizing over longer periods. Although countries can formally scale back explicit DI coverages when a crisis recedes, it is very difficult to eliminate conjectural coverages in a credible manner.

Honohan and Klingebiel (2003) analyze the impact of blanket guarantees and other crisis management strategies on the full fiscal costs of resolving banking system distress. Their analysis of forty separate crises experienced in 1980–1997 indicates that unlimited deposit guarantees, open-ended liquidity support, and capital forbearance significantly increase the ultimate fiscal cost of resolving a banking crisis. Moreover, the data show no trade-off between fiscal costs and the speed of economic recovery. In their sample, depositor guarantees and regulatory forbearance failed to reduce significantly either the length of a country's crisis or the size of the crisis-induced decline in aggregate real output the crisis induced.

Providing liquidity support for economically insolvent institutions appears to prolong a crisis. It does this by distorting bank incentives: disposing bank managers to favor risky longshot investments over less risky projects. Bank-level gambles for resurrection delay healthy adjustments and tend to generate further declines in aggregate output.

1.3.5 Determinants of Deposit Insurance Adoption and Design

Our review of the literature indicates that introducing explicit deposit insurance into weak private and public contracting environments tends to undermine market discipline in ways that reduce bank stability, destroy real economic capital, and sidetrack economic development. To understand and counter this threat, one must examine the factors that dispose a country to adopt deposit insurance and influence its design. Demirgüç-Kunt, Kane, and Laeven (chapter 2) investigate this question using 1960–2003 data covering 170 countries.

Their goal is to assemble a comprehensive dataset with which to determine whether and how outside influences, economic circumstances, crisis pressures, and political institutions affect deposit insurance adoption and design. To study this sample robustly, the authors use three complementary regression strategies: limited dependent-variable regression, hazard analysis, and Heckman selection models. They estimate adoption and design decisions simultaneously and control for the influence of economic and political characteristics, disruptive events (such as macroeconomic shocks), occurrence and severity of crises, and the nature of the contracting environment. They find that outside pressure to emulate developed-country regulatory frameworks and political arrangements that facilitate intersectoral deal making dispose a country toward adopting a DI scheme. Another strong and robust conclusion is that countries design their schemes especially poorly when they install DI in response to a financial crisis. In Demirgüç-Kunt, Kane, and Laeven (2007), the authors further investigate the impact of the source and impact of external pressures. They find that while external pressures indeed make a country more likely to adopt deposit insurance, expert advice that sometimes accompanies this pressure (from international financial institutions, the European Union, and the like) is also more likely to lead to prudent design.

To summarize, research on the first four questions suggests that, to install DI successfully, weaknesses in a country's contracting environment must be identified so that design features can be adapted to them. Decisions to install DI during and after a crisis must not proceed hastily. Policymakers must make a concerted effort to appreciate that preexisting weaknesses in transparency, government accountability, and private contract enforcement limit the kinds of reforms they may advantageously pursue.

1.4   Lessons from Country Experiences

This section reviews a few instructive examples of good and bad experience with deposit insurance. The United States was the first country to establish nationwide deposit insurance. It did so in 1934 in response to the Great Depression as Kane and Wilson (1998) explain. Kroszner and Mellick review U.S. experience in chapter 5. Initially, the coverage limit was set at $2,500, but rose quickly to $5,000. The limit has been increased many times since then: to $10,000 in 1950, $15,000 in 1966, $20,000 in 1969, $40,000 in 1974, and to $100,000 in 1980. Legislation passed in 2006 indexes coverage limits for inflation and extends coverage for retirement accounts to $250,000.

In chapter 2, Demirgüç-Kunt, Kane, and Laeven show that outside influences and crisis pressures are major determinants of deposit insurance adoption and design. Many countries installed DI countries during times of banking crisis. To stop bank runs quickly and to forestall civil unrest, organizations such as the IMF and the World Bank often advise the prompt introduction of sweeping government guarantees of bank deposits.

During financial crises, response speed is important, but authorities must not allow it to become the only consideration. Guaranteeing the liabilities of deeply insolvent banks is invariably a mistake. This is because insolvent banks have strong incentives to book risk exposures that abuse government guarantees. Even though broad coverages—including blanket guarantees—can stem bank runs, they adversely constrain a nation's future policy options (Kane and Klingebiel 2004). After issuing broad guarantees, countries typically find themselves forced to support sweeping coverages for many years after the crisis has receded. When guarantees are issued abruptly without prior planning (as in Turkey in 2000), it becomes particularly difficult to scale back the guarantees when the emergency ends. After its 1986 banking crisis, Mexico covered deposit balances in full for more than a decade.

Haber (chapter 6) reviews Mexico's experience with deposit insurance over the last 120 years. During the period 1884–1982, Mexico did not have explicit deposit insurance. Potentially imprudent behavior by insiders was mitigated by arrangements that served simultaneously to promote good corporate governance and to limit competition by controlling the entry of new banks. The resulting banking system proved stable and profitable, but attracted extremely low levels of deposits. Supplemental activity by government development banks generated a large number of inefficient public-sector enterprises. During the period 1991–2004, Mexico introduced deposit insurance, but because the scheme countenanced minimal bank regulation and weak corporate governance, it led to reckless lending, high borrower default rates, and a taxpayer-financed bailout of various bank stockholders.

Among more recent adopters, Russia has received considerable attention. Russia is a large country that has experienced financial crisis and taken nearly ten years to finalize its decision to introduce deposit insurance. Camara and Montes-Negret (chapter 9) review Russian experience with deposit insurance planning. Partly because of poor licensing policies, during Russia's post-Soviet transition, authorities had to cope with a number of very weak banks. Many institutions were severely underdiversified, having had to limit their lending activity to enterprises operating within an assigned business group.

Russia suffered a major banking crisis in 1998. A unilateral restructuring of government debt resulted in depositor runs and a collapse of the payments system. In the absence of formal deposit insurance, officials rescued many households by transferring their deposits from privately owned banks to the government-owned Sberbank. The collapse of several private banks and the resulting expansion of loanable funds allowed Sberbank to transform itself from a savings bank to a universal bank. Sberbank now holds 75 percent of the country's retail deposits and roughly 25 percent of banking assets overall.

In the wake of these events, government-sponsored deposit insurance was seen as a way both to increase trust in the payments system and to create a level playing field between the state-owned Sberbank and the private banks. Legislation providing for a system of deposit insurance was adopted at the end of 2003.

In this instance, because the regulatory and supervisory framework of Russia was seen as weak, the international community cautioned against DI adoption. Possibilities and incentives for depositors to exert market discipline on banks were limited and had been further undermined by the government's willingness to protect well-connected bank owners from the consequences of the 1998 crisis. Incentives for additional risk taking established by deposit insurance could easily increase financial fragility and slow financial and economic development. It seemed wiser to consolidate and restructure the banking sector and establish a competitive balance between Sberbank and the private banks before deposit insurance was implemented. In this way, authorities could build trust by enforcing bank rules and regulations effectively, by delicensing fragile banks, and by allowing only sound and relatively transparent financial institutions to operate. This would give private creditors and investors the ability to monitor banks and an incentive to exert market discipline.

However, the Russian government chose a different path. It put deposit insurance into effect in early 2004. In the hopes of mitigating moral hazard, the new scheme covered only balances in household accounts up to Rb 100,000 (around US$3,400). This limit was roughly the same as the country's per capita GDP. Excluding corporate deposits from the scheme lessened the participation of banks that were connected to business groups. Membership in the scheme required approval from the Central Bank of Russia so that distressed banks could in principle be excluded from the scheme. A special state guarantee on deposits in the state-owned Sberbank was scheduled to be phased out by January 2007.[4]

Apart from crises, efforts to integrate national financial markets exert strong extraterritorial influence on deposit insurance design. For example, the EU Directive on Deposit Insurance dictates that each member state insure individual accounts up to at least 20,000 euros. In low–income countries, this minimum has generated inefficiently high coverage. Nenovsky and Dimitrova (chapter 8) show that efforts by EU accession countries in Central and Eastern Europe to comply with the EU Directive produced deposit insurance coverages that are inordinately high relative both to bank capital and to GDP per capita. Nenovsky and Dimitrova argue that the overinsurance in accession countries has increased moral hazard by distorting the incentives of their poorly capitalized domestic banks. Huizinga (chapter 7) also shows that the high coverage limits of the EU Directive is more in line with the preferred policies of the higher income EU-15, and that overinsurance is visible in several new members in Eastern Europe.

Financial integration also led six Francophone African countries that had previously established a common central bank to plan for deposit insurance: Cameroon, Central African Republic, Chad, Equatorial Guinea, Gabon, and Republic of Congo. Together, these countries form the Communité Économique et Monétaire de l'Afrique Centrale (CEMAC), an organization that plans to install explicit deposit insurance in all six member countries. As in the EU case, large differences in the level of GDP per capita exist across member states and these differences make it difficult to negotiate a common level of deposit insurance coverage for all member states. The result is that, although proposed in 1999, so far the DI plan has only been ratified by two of the six CEMAC countries.

Although it is unusual for a country to revoke explicit deposit insurance once it is in place, a few exceptional cases exist. Argentina provides a recent example. Before 1979, deposits in Argentina were unconditionally guaranteed by the Argentinean government. In 1979, a deposit insurance scheme was installed by the military government. The scheme provided full coverage for an accountholder's first million pesos (about $640) and 90 percent coinsurance thereafter. In 1991, this scheme was abolished and replaced by a system that intensified the supervision of Argentine banks. However, after supervisors suspended the operations of five private banks in April 1995, deposit insurance was reintroduced. Current accounts, savings accounts, and time deposits are now covered up to $30,000.

Other countries have considered and rejected explicit deposit insurance. Namibia is a case in point. Spurred by neighboring South Africa's debate on whether or not to adopt deposit insurance, the Central Bank of Namibia formally investigated the desirability and feasibility of installing deposit insurance in Namibia. The Namibian banking system is dominated by a few South African banks. The study concluded that domestic banks were too small and too few to warrant an insurance scheme.

Yet other countries, such as Malaysia, have made a conscious decision to restructure their financial system before undertaking a deposit insurance program. For many years, China has been studying the wisdom of DI adoption. Although burdened by a large proportion of nonperforming loans, the Chinese have developed one of the deepest banking systems in the world and done so without introducing deposit insurance or other kinds of formal guarantees. Chinese authorities are now proposing a deposit insurance scheme that would combine a high threshold for complete coverage of individual accounts with a low coinsurance rate for balances that exceed the ceiling. In chapter 10, Honohan examines some of the benefits and costs of this proposal. The potential benefit is that, by relieving pressure on the Chinese central bank to rescue insolvent banks, a well-designed scheme could improve regulatory incentives. However, without a prior restructuring to assign definitely the losses imbedded in state banks, deposit insurance is likely—rather than to correct bank and regulator incentives—to introduce further distortions.

1.5 Principles of Good Design

Cross-country empirical research and individual country experiences confirm that, for at least the time being, officials in many countries would do well to delay the installation of a deposit insurance system. Explicit insurance can help to develop a robust financial system. But it does so only when it is carefully designed and introduced into a country whose public and private contracting environment includes reliable institutions of loss control. The difficulty is one of sequencing. Where financial controls are poor, explicit deposit insurance can spur financial development only in the very short run. Although formal guarantees make banks more eager to lend, they also undermine longstanding patterns of bank bonding and depositor discipline. Over longer periods, the displacement of preexisting private discipline can encourage patterns of lending that increase financial fragility and deter financial development. In this case, excessive risk taking leads to financial and nonfinancial insolvencies that destroy real economic capital.

[handwritten margin note: need a resolution regime.]

The downside of installing explicit insurance is that it reduces incentives for depositors to monitor the riskiness of their banks. Depositors are prepared to tolerate aggressive bank lending whenever they believe that, even if borrowers cannot repay the bank, their deposit claims will be paid by the deposit insurer. Unless the insurer can effectively replace the (private) monitoring that government guarantees displace, aggressive banks can fund a portfolio of risky loans at a deposit interest rate that lies far below the yield at which the resulting exposure to loss deserves to be funded. In institutionally weak environments, effective deposit insurance design is often blocked by political obstacles that end up intensifying rather than reducing the probability and depth of future crises.

For countries that have already installed or are in the process of designing an explicit deposit insurance scheme, cross-country empirical research identifies six commonsense principles of good design. No government can afford to neglect these principles. Even in the strong institutional environments, weaknesses in deposit insurance design and distortionary political pressures that support them can fuel financial fragility and lessen the discipline that banks receive from private counterparties. To control and offset these effects, six design features have proved themselves useful.

The most straightforward principle entails setting enforceable coverage limits. Insurers' first priority must be to assure that official supervision complements private monitoring. To accomplish this, the scheme must be designed and managed in ways that convince large depositors, subordinated debtholders, and correspondent banks that their funds are truly and inescapably at risk. Maintaining strong incentives for private parties to bond and police bank risk exposures is especially important in contracting environments where accounting transparency and government accountability are deficient.

[handwritten margin note: X]

A second principle is to make membership in the deposit insurance system compulsory. This increases the size of the insurance pool and prevents strong institutions from selecting out of the pool whenever the fund needs an injection of new capital.

[handwritten margin note: ✓]

A third principle supported by cross-country evidence is to make the public and private sectors jointly responsible for overseeing the scheme. A public-private partnership establishes checks and balances that improve management performance.

The fourth principle is to limit the fund's ability to shift losses and loss exposures to the general taxpayer. Whether or not the insurer holds a formal fund of reserves, it must be crystal clear that except, in truly catastrophic circumstances, funds to cover bank losses will come principally from the pool of surviving banks. Access to taxpayer assistance should be legally impeded by statutory provisions that can be relaxed only in extraordinary circumstances and by following extraordinary procedures.

The fifth principle is to price deposit insurance services appropriately. Laeven (chapter 3) shows that countries have typically underpriced deposit insurance because banks in many developing countries cannot afford to pay actuarially fair premiums. He describes several methods for pricing deposit insurance accurately but his results suggest that many of these countries cannot afford deposit insurance.

The sixth and final principle is that deposit insurers must actively involve themselves in decisions about when and how to resolve individual bank insolvencies. Because deposit insurers are responsible for paying off insured depositors, they have a strong interest in assuring the prompt and speedy resolution of insolvent banks. Beck and Laeven (chapter 4) argue that deposit insurers are more efficient than courts because banking supervisors better understand bank risk-taking incentives and how to remedy them. Using data for over large number of banks in over fifty countries, they show that banks are more stable and less likely to become insolvent in countries where the deposit insurer has responsibility for intervening failed banks and the power to revoke membership in the deposit insurance scheme.

Deposit insurance is strong medicine. Whether it benefits or harms a country depends on how well it is designed and administered. It can be a useful part of a country's overall system of bank regulation and financial markets, but cross-country research stresses the importance of promptly identifying and eliminating individual bank insolvencies, fostering informative accounting standards, and establishing reliable procedures for contract enforcement before adopting explicit deposit insurance. Research also underscores the need to build in a capacity to adapt dynamically to financial changes. Managers must be empowered and incentivized to upgrade their loss controls to disable unforseeable loopholes that regulation-induced financial innovation will inevitably open in their system.

Notes

1. A World Bank report (OED) found that, during the period 1993–2004, the World Bank concerned itself in a total of sixty instances with reforms in the deposit insurance schemes of thirty-five countries.

2. This database updates and extends an earlier database by Demirgüç-Kunt and Sobaci (2001).

3. The experience of countries that introduce deposit insurance as a result of a crisis does not contribute to these results; in fact, observations for each country's crisis period are dropped from the sample. To double check this issue, the authors also analyze a two-stage model that first estimates the probability of adopting explicit deposit insurance and then inserts this estimated variable into a second-stage crisis equation. The first-stage results indicate that sample countries decide to adopt deposit insurance because other countries adopt it as it becomes perceived to be best practice. In the second stage, the influence of deposit insurance variables becomes even more significant, indicating that allowing for reverse causality does not alter the results.

4. Sberbank's DI premia were to be maintained in a separate account until its share of household deposits fell below 50 percent or until January 1, 2007, whichever came first. The funds accumulated in this account could only be used for payouts on Sberbank deposits.

References

Allen, Franklin, and Douglas Gale. 1998. Optimal Banking Crises. *Journal of Finance* 53: 1245–1284.

Bhattacharya, Sudipto, Arnoud W. A. Boot, and Anjan V. Thakor. 1998. The Economics of Bank Regulation. *Journal of Money, Credit and Banking* 30: 745–770.

Buser, Stephen A., Andrew H. Chen, and Edward J. Kane. 1981. Federal Deposit Insurance, Regulatory Policy, and Optimal Bank Capital. *Journal of Finance* 36: 51–60.

Calomiris, Charles, W. 1996. Building an Incentive-Compatible Safety Net: Special Problems for Developing Countries. Mimeo., Columbia University.

Chari, Varadarajan V., and Ravi Jagannathan. 1988. Banking Panics, Information, and Rational Expectations Equilibrium. *Journal of Finance* 43: 749–761.

Cull, Robert, Lemma W. Senbet, and Marco Sorge. 2005. Deposit Insurance and Financial Development. *Journal of Money, Credit and Banking* 37: 43–82.

Demirgüç-Kunt, Aslı, and Enrica Detragiache. 2002. Does Deposit Insurance Increase Banking System Stability? An Empirical Investigation. *Journal of Monetary Economics* 49: 1373–1406.

Demirgüç-Kunt, Aslı, and Harry Huizinga. 2004. Market Discipline and Deposit Insurance Design. *Journal of Monetary Economics* 51: 375–399.

Demirgüç-Kunt, Aslı, and Edward J. Kane. 2002. Deposit Insurance around the Globe: Where Does It Work? *Journal of Economic Perspectives* 16: 175–195.

Demirgüç-Kunt, Aslı, Edward J. Kane, and Luc Laeven. 2007. Determinants of Deposit-Insurance Adoption and Design. Forthcoming in *Journal of Financial Intermediation*.

Demirgüç-Kunt, Aslı, and Tolga Sobaci, 2001. Deposit Insurance around the World: A Database. *World Bank Economic Review* 15: 481–490.

Diamond, Douglas, and Philip Dybvig. 1983. Bank Runs, Deposit Insurance and Liquidity. *Journal of Political Economy* 91: 401–419.

Folkerts-Landau, David, and Carl-Johan Lindgren. 1998. Toward a Framework for Financial Stability. International Monetary Fund, Washington, D.C.

Garcia, Gillian. 1999. Deposit Insurance: A Survey of Actual and Best Practices. IMF Working Paper no. 99/54, International Monetary Fund, Washington, D.C.

Honohan, Patrick, and Daniela Klingebiel. 2003. Controlling Fiscal Costs of Banking Crises. *Journal of Banking and Finance* 27: 1539–1560.

Hovakimian, Armen, Edward J. Kane, and Luc Laeven. 2003. How Country and Safety-Net Characteristics Affect Bank Risk-Shifting. *Journal of Financial Services Research* 23 (3): 177–204.

Kane, Edward J. 1995. Three Paradigms for the Role of Capitalization Requirements in Insured Financial Institutions. *Journal of Banking and Finance* 19: 431–459.

Kane, Edward J. 2000. Designing Financial Safety Nets to Fit Country Circumstances. Policy Research Working Paper no. 2453, The World Bank, Washington, D.C.

Kane, Edward J., and Berry K. Wilson. 1998. A Contracting-Theory Interpretation of the Origins of Federal Deposit Insurance. *Journal of Money, Credit, and Banking* 30: 573–595.

Kane, Edward J., and Daniela Klingebiel. 2004. Alternatives to Blanket Guarantees for Containing a Systemic Crisis. *Journal of Financial Stability* 1 (September): 31–63.

Levine, Ross. 1997. Financial Development and Economic Growth: Views and Agenda. *Journal of Economic Literature* 35: 688–726.

Merton, Robert. 1977. An Analytical Derivation of the Cost of Deposit Insurance and Loan Guarantees. *Journal of Banking and Finance* 1: 3–11.

Merton, Robert. 1978. On the Cost of Deposit Insurance When There Are Surveillance Costs. *Journal of Business* 51: 439–452.

World Bank. 2004. Deposit Insurance—Reforms Supported by the World Bank during the Period 1993–2004. Mimeo., Operations Evaluation Department. The World Bank, Washington, D.C.

II   Deposit Insurance: Adoption, Pricing, and Linkages with Insolvency Resolution

2 Adoption and Design of Deposit Insurance

Aslı Demirgüç-Kunt, Edward Kane, and Luc Laeven

2.1 Introduction

Every country offers implicit deposit insurance, no matter how strongly top officials may deny it. This is because whenever a large or widespread banking insolvency occurs, even if no explicit deposit insurance system is in place, pressure for governmental relief of at least some bank stakeholders becomes politically too intense to resist. Adopting a system of explicit deposit insurance does not eliminate implicit guarantees. It supplements them with formal obligations that contractually link the capitalization of a country's private banks to the credit and tax-collecting capacity of their chartering government.

The 1990s saw a rapid spread of explicit deposit insurance schemes (EDIS) in the developing world. In January 1995 only forty-nine countries had an EDIS. However, by year-end 2003, this number had surged to eighty-seven countries, an increase of almost 80 percent. Although a significant share of the surge can be attributed to transition countries of Eastern Europe that were "encouraged" to adopt deposit insurance by the EU directive on deposit insurance (European Commission 1994), recent adopters can be found in all continents of the world.

This chapter views the crafting of a country's financial safety net as an exercise in incomplete contracting in which the counterparties are major sectors of a nation's economy. Including an EDIS in the net allocates to each sector a mix of contingent subsidies and burdens. Our statistical analysis seeks to determine what factors influence safety net design, focusing on a country's decision to adopt an EDIS and whether and how these same factors affect risk-shifting controls. Our study constructs and examines a 1960–2003 dataset on deposit insurance design covering 170 countries. Besides reducing sample selection bias, our goal is to use a simultaneous equations framework to model how internal and external institutional and political factors affect a country's decision to adopt deposit insurance and various follow-on decisions it makes about safety net design.

Cross-country differences in political arrangements are bound to affect both kinds of decisions. The presence and design of an EDIS affect many constituencies, especially banks, depositors, creditors, specialized bureaucracies, and taxpayers. Because individual constituencies have conflicting interests, the political process governing adoption and design decisions can be complex. Moreover, we fear that the spread of explicit deposit insurance schemes across countries has been based in part on a presumption that an EDIS is a hallmark of regulatory best practice. We hypothesize that, in some countries, the restraining influence of internal economic and political pressures may have been overcome by domestic and foreign pressure to "emulate" developed country safety net arrangements without adequately tailoring the design features to differences in public and private contracting environments. To test this hypothesis, we estimate models of deposit insurance adoption and design that enter proxies for outside pressure alongside a battery of domestic determinants of regulatory decisions.

Starting in the 1990s, IMF crisis management advice recommended erecting an EDIS as a way either of containing crises or of formally winding down crisis-generated blanket guarantees (Folkerts-Landau and Lindgren 1998; Garcia 1999). The World Bank and European Union have endorsed EDIS as well. This leads us to test the narrower hypothesis that outside international pressure—namely, an emulation effect—might adversely influence design decisions in countries that experience a systemic crisis.

Economists presume that political dealmaking serves both public and private interests. Public interest rationales for deposit insurance focus on protecting small, uninformed depositors and assuring the stability of the banking system (Diamond and Dybvig 1983). Purely private interest theories portray the public interest as a distracting fiction. Between these extremes, theories of incentive-conflicted intervention conceive of regulatory decisions as the outcome of interest group competition, in which well-organized or powerful groups compete with voters to pressure public-spirited, but opportunistic politicians and regulators for regulatory interventions that authorize sponsoring groups to capture rents from other sectors (Stigler 1971; Peltzman 1976; Becker 1983).[1] For example, Calomiris and White (1994) argue that federal deposit insurance benefited predominantly smaller and poorly diversified unit banks and that, had not the Great Depression reduced confidence in the banking system as a whole, their pleas for federal insurance could not have overcome the opposition of politically stronger large banks. Kane and Wilson (1998) show that, in the face of the Great Depression, large banks' wish list changed and that large-bank share prices benefited greatly from introducing deposit insurance precisely because depositors had lost confidence in banks of all sizes.

Deposit insurance benefits banks that are prepared to exploit weaknesses in supervisory risk control to extract net subsidies from taxpayers and safer banks. Safety net subsidies may be defined as implicit risk capital that the government administers in helping to recapitalize banks when they become deeply insolvent.

It is natural to hypothesize that differences in political systems would influence safety net design. Financial institutions regularly lobby for "reforms" that promise to increase their franchise value (Kroszner and Stratmann 1998). The more a country's political system allows sectors to share power, the better banking interests can make their concerns heard.

In testing this hypothesis, candidate economic control variables include macroeconomic conditions and variation in the ownership structure of the banking system (as proxied by state-owned banks' market share). As robustness tests, we experiment with different statistical methods and alternative indices of economic, political, and cultural influences.

A long literature analyzes the benefits and costs of explicit deposit insurance and explores theoretically the challenges of designing an optimal deposit insurance system.[2] This chapter summarizes an emerging body of complementary body of empirical research. Using much smaller cross-country datasets, Demirgüç-Kunt and Detragiache (2002) and Demirgüç-Kunt and Huizinga (2004) show that EDIS design features affect banking system fragility and market discipline. Demirgüç-Kunt and Kane (2002), Hovakimian, Kane, and Laeven (2003), and Laeven (2002) show that weak institutional environments undermine deposit insurance design. Cull, Senbet, and Sorge (2005) produce evidence that, in weak institutional environments, an EDIS retards financial development rather than fosters it. Looking specifically at crisis countries, Honohan and Klingebiel (2003) and Kane and Klingebiel (2004) show that blanket deposit insurance guarantees—when adopted as a crisis management strategy—increase the fiscal cost of resolving distress without reducing either the cumulative output loss or the duration of crisis pressures.

Laeven (2004) studies how political arrangements affect coverage levels across countries. Our more comprehensive dataset lets us model simultaneously decisions about adoption and system design. The novelty of our paper is twofold: (1) using a simultaneous equation model to generate cross-country evidence on the determinants of EDIS adoption and design; and (2) updating and extending the deposit insurance dataset developed in earlier studies and tracking changes in EDIS design across time in each country.

High-income, institutionally advanced countries and those undergoing financial crisis are more likely to adopt an EDIS. Controlling for income and institutional quality, external pressures and internal politics play significant roles. Outside influences prove especially important in the adoption decision, particularly during crisis. The more contestable a country's political system, the more likely it is both to install an EDIS and to adopt inadequate risk controls. Risk controls are weaker if adoption occurs either during or in the wake of a crisis. Finally, the more surprising the selection model finds the adoption decision to be, the more likely it is that the scheme chosen incorporates design features that subsidize bank risk taking. In a companion paper, Demirgüç-Kunt, Kane, and Laeven (2007), we explore in greater detail both the sources and the impact of external pressure on deposit insurance design. We still find that external pressure pushes more countries to adopt. However, to the extent expert advice from international financial institutions is provided, the insurance system tends to incorporate better design features.

The rest of the chapter is organized as follows. Section 2.2 reviews our dataset and the sources used to construct it. It also presents summary statistics for all included variables. Section 2.3 explores single-equation models of the adoption decision. Section 2.4 incorporates a baseline adoption equation into simultaneous models of safety net design. Section 2.5 summarizes our findings and explains their policy implications.

2.2 Sampling Frame

Our goal is to investigate the extent to which regression methods can explain whether and when a country installs a system of explicit deposit insurance and, if so, how well that system is designed. To this

Table 2.1
Distribution of countries with and without explicit deposit insurance by income quartile at year-end 2003

Income group	Number of countries	Number of countries with explicit deposit insurance	Number of countries with merely implicit deposit insurance
High-income	41	32	9
Upper-middle-income	28	16	12
Lower-middle-income	51	29	22
Low-income	61	10	51
Total	181	87	94

Note: This table tallies countries with and without explicit deposit insurance at year-end 2003. The data are compiled by the authors. We refer to the data section of this chapter for details about the data sources and variable definitions. The total number of countries included is 181. Blanket guarantees are coded as explicit deposit insurance.

end, we construct a unique dataset covering all countries that have adopted explicit deposit insurance through year-end 2003, relying on official country sources and information provided by World Bank country specialists. We also carried out a survey of deposit insurance agencies or related institutions to enrich available data on coverage levels. Chapter 11 provides a more detailed list of the sources of the deposit insurance data we collected.

We extend the Demirgüç-Kunt and Sobaci (2001) database in two ways: first, we update the endpoint to 2003 to include data on recent adopters; second, we create a time series dataset of individual country design features. We compile data on coverage, not only for the year 2000 (as in Demirgüç-Kunt and Sobaci 2001) but for every year in which an EDIS existed. For example, coverage levels in the United States have been revised five times: from US$5,000 at adoption in 1934, to US$10,000 in 1950, to US$15,000 in 1966, to US$20,000 in 1969, to US$40,000 in 1974, and to US$100,000 since 1980.

Table 2.1 partitions 181 sample countries for which we have per capita income data into four income groups and shows that the propensity to adopt an EDIS rises with income. Table 2.2 lists adopting countries and the year their EDIS was installed.

Table 2.3 lists the design features our dataset covers and the country characteristics our regression experiments employ. The unit of observation is a country-year. The table presents summary statistics for all

Table 2.2
Explicit deposit insurance systems at year-end 2003

Country	Date enacted	Unlimited guarantee (1 = Yes; 0 = No)	Coverage limit in 2003 (in US$)	GDP per capita in 2003 (in 1999 US$)	Coverage limit-to-GDP per capita in 2002	Coverage ratio adjusted for coinsurance in 2002	Maximum coinsurance (in percent) in 2002	Coverage limit-to-deposits per capita in 2002
Albania	2002	0	6,568	914	3.3	3.0	15[a]	n.a.
Algeria	1997	0	8,263	1,592	4.2	4.2	0	n.a.
Argentina	1979	0	10,327	8,076	3.6	3.6	0	16.0
Austria	1979	0	25,260	32,049	0.8	0.7	10	0.9
Bahamas	1999	0	50,000	13,485	n.a.	n.a.	0	4.4
Bahrain	1993	0	39,894	10,593	3.5	3.5	0	4.4
Bangladesh	1984	0	1,021	358	5.0	5.0	0	14.6
Belarus	1996	0	1,000	1,347	0.8	0.7	20[b]	5.8
Belgium	1974	0	25,260	29,889	0.8	0.7	10	0.9
Bosnia and Herzegovina	1998	0	3,228	1,551	1.8	1.8	0	n.a.
Brazil	1995	0	6,925	4,486	2.6	2.6	0	8.9
Bulgaria	1995	0	9,686	1,453	2.4	2.4	0	8.5
Canada	1967	0	46,425	22,174	1.7	1.7	0	2.6
Chile	1986	0	3,764	5,146	0.8	0.7	10[c]	2.1
Colombia	1985	0	7,192	2,268	4.3	3.2	25	18.0
Croatia	1997	0	16,343	4,943	2.5	2.5	0	4.1
Cyprus	2000	0	25,260	13,467	2.5	2.2	10	2.0

Czech Republic	1994	0	31,575	5,207	3.6	3.2	10	5.3
Denmark[d]	1988	0	40,296	37,500	1.2	1.2	0	2.5
Dominican Republic	1962	1	Full	1,946	n.a.	n.a.	0	n.a.
Ecuador	1999	1	Full	1,660	n.a.	n.a.	0	n.a.
El Salvador	1999	0	4,720	1,756	3.1	3.1	0	63.3
Estonia	1998	0	8,058	4,148	0.5	0.4	10	1.4
Finland	1969	0	31,863	30,332	0.9	0.9	0	1.9
France	1980	0	88,410	29,133	2.7	2.7	0	4.2
Germany	1966	0	25,260	31,773	0.8	0.7	10	0.8
Gibraltar	1998	0	25,260	n.a.	n.a.	n.a.	0	n.a.
Greece	1993	0	25,260	12,652	1.5	1.5	0	1.7
Guatemala	1999	0	2,487	1,549	1.3	1.3	0	6.3
Honduras	1999	0	9,297	695	n.a.	n.a.	0	n.a.
Hungary	1993	0	14,429	5,136	0.6	0.6	0	1.5
Iceland	1985	0	29,455	29,984	0.7	0.7	0	1.5
India	1961	0	2,193	453	4.2	4.2	0	8.1
Indonesia	1998	1	Full	980	n.a.	n.a.	0	n.a.
Ireland	1989	0	25,260	25,497	0.6	0.5	10	0.8
Isle of Man	1991	0	35,694	n.a.	n.a.	n.a.	25	n.a.
Italy	1987	0	130,457	20,302	4.8	4.8	0	8.7
Jamaica	1998	0	4,957	2,149	2.1	2.1	0	4.9
Japan	1971	0	93,371	43,818	2.5	2.5	0	2.1
Jordan	2000	0	14,104	1,591	7.8	7.8	0	8.0
Kazakhstan	1999	0	2,774	1,342	0.8	0.8	0	5.3

Table 2.2
(continued)

Country	Date enacted	Unlimited guarantee (1 = Yes; 0 = No)	Coverage limit in 2003 (in US$)	GDP per capita in 2003 (in 1999 US$)	Coverage limit-to-GDP per capita in 2002	Coverage ratio adjusted for coinsurance in 2002	Maximum coinsurance (in percent) in 2002	Coverage limit-to-deposits per capita in 2002
Kenya	1985	0	1,313	337	3.2	3.2	0	9.5
Korea	1996	0	41,925	12,174	4.0	4.0	0	4.8
Kuwait	1982	0	Full	13,792	n.a.	n.a.	0	n.a.
Latvia	1998	0	5,545	2,476	1.4	1.4	0	5.2
Lebanon	1967	0	3,317	2,929	0.9	0.9	0	0.4
Liechtenstein	1992	0	25,260	n.a.	n.a.	n.a.	0	n.a.
Lithuania	1996	0	16,293	2,215	3.1	2.8	10[e]	14.1
Luxembourg	1989	0	25,260	53,013	0.4	0.4	10	0.1
Macedonia	1996	0	25,260	2,441	10.3	9.2	10[f]	46.0
Malaysia	1998	1	Full	4,541	n.a.	n.a.	0	n.a.
Malta	2003	0	25,260	9,812	n.a.	n.a.	n.a.	n.a.
Marshall Islands	1975	0	100,000	1,593	50.3	50.3	0	n.a.
Mexico	1986	0	2,871,337	3,621	n.a.[g]	n.a.[g]	0	n.a.[g]
Micronesia	1963	0	100,000	1,674	52.7	52.7	0	121.2
Netherlands	1979	0	25,260	30,389	0.7	0.7	0	0.7
Nicaragua	2001	0	20,000	n.a.	27.4	27.4	0	74.9
Nigeria	1988	0	366	250	1.3	1.3	0	5.7

Country								
Norway	1961[h]	0	299,401	37,369	6.0	6.0	0	11.3
Oman	1995	0	52,016	5,766	6.5	4.9	25[i]	20.6
Paraguay	2003	0	10,500	1,820	n.a.	n.a.	0	n.a.
Peru	1992	0	19,773	2,305	9.2	9.2	0	36.0
Philippines	1963	0	1,800	1,133	2.0	2.0	0	3.8
Poland	1995	0	28,418	3,536	3.6	3.5	10[j]	14.3
Portugal	1992	0	31,575	12,499	1.9	1.9	0	2.1
Romania	1996	0	3,842	1,451	1.6	1.6	0	13.9
Russia	2003	0	6,098	2,255	n.a.	n.a.	n.a.	n.a.
Serbia and Montenegro	2001	0	87	n.a.	0.1	0.1	0	n.a.
Slovak Republic	1996	0	25,260	4,180	2.8	2.8	10	4.8
Slovenia	2001	0	26,931	11,160	1.6	1.6	0	3.0
Spain	1977	0	25,260	16,824	1.2	1.2	10	1.4
Sri Lanka	1987	0	1,034	863	1.2	1.2	0	3.5
Sweden	1996	0	34,364	30,286	1.0	1.0	0	n.a.
Switzerland	1984	0	24,254	45,680	0.5	0.5	0	0.4
Taiwan	1985	0	29,420	15,023	2.3	2.3	0	n.a.
Tanzania	1994	0	235	185	1.0	1.0	0	5.7
Thailand	1997	1	Full	2,721	n.a.	n.a.	0	n.a.
Trinidad and Tobago	1986	0	7,937	4,951	1.1	1.1	0	2.7
Turkey	1983	1	Full	2,887	n.a.	n.a.	0	n.a.
Uganda	1994	0	1,550	345	6.9	6.9	0	44.2
Ukraine	1998	0	281	840	0.3	0.3	0	1.6

Table 2.2
(continued)

Country	Date enacted	Unlimited guarantee (1 = Yes; 0 = No)	Coverage limit in 2003 (in US$)	GDP per capita in 2003 (in 1999 US$)	Coverage limit-to-GDP per capita in 2002	Coverage ratio adjusted for coinsurance in 2002	Maximum coinsurance (in percent) in 2002	Coverage limit-to-deposits per capita in 2002
United Kingdom	1982	0	19,611	21,616	2.0	1.8	10[k]	n.a.
United States	1934	0	100,000	30,956	2.8	2.8	0	8.7
Venezuela	1985	0	6,258	3,260	2.3	2.3	0	16.5
Vietnam	2000	0	1,948	351	4.5	4.5	0	n.a.
Zimbabwe	2003	0	3,640	665	n.a.	n.a.	n.a.	n.a.

Note: This table lists the countries that adopted explicit deposit insurance systems by year-end 2003. The data are compiled by the authors. We refer to the data section of this paper for details about the data sources and variable definitions. GDP and bank deposits per capita are from International Financial Statistics (IFS). The following "nonadopting" countries are included in our sample: Afghanistan, Angola, Armenia, Australia, Azerbaijan, Barbados, Belize, Benin, Bhutan, Bolivia, Botswana, Brunei, Burkina Faso, Burundi, Cambodia, Cameroon, Cape Verde, Central African Republic, Chad, China, Comoro Islands, Costa Rica, Côte d'Ivoire, Cuba, Djibouti, Egypt, Equatorial Guinea, Eritrea, Ethiopia, Fiji, Gabon, Gambia, Georgia, Ghana, Grenada, Guinea, Guinea-Bissau, Guyana, Haiti, Hong Kong (China), Iran, Iraq, Israel, Kiribati, Kyrgyz Republic, Laos, Lesotho, Liberia, Libya, Madagascar, Malawi, Maldives, Mali, Mauritania, Mauritius, Moldova, Mongolia, Morocco, Mozambique, Myanmar, Namibia, Nepal, New Zealand, Niger, Pakistan, Panama, Papua New Guinea, Qatar, Republic of Congo, Rwanda, Saudi Arabia, Senegal, Seychelles, Sierra Leone, Singapore, Solomon Islands, Somalia, South Africa, St. Lucia, Sudan, Suriname, Swaziland, Syria, Tajikistan, Togo, Tunisia, United Arab Emirates, Uruguay, Uzbekistan, Vanuatu, W. Samoa, Yemen, Zaire, Zambia. The total number of countries covered is 181.

Moldova adopted deposit insurance in 2004. While Bolivia does not have a formal deposit insurance system, it has a Financial Restructuring Fund set up in December 2001 that acts as deposit insurance. Uruguay established a deposit insurance system in 2002 (law on protection of bank deposits was enacted on December 27, 2002, creating a bank deposits collateral fund and a Superintendency of Bank Savings Protection), but it is not yet regulated. A proposal for explicit deposit insurance was drafted in 1999 by these six Francophone African countries but the proposal has only been ratified by two out of the six Communauté Économique et Monétaire de l'Afrique Centrale (CEMAC) countries: Cameroon, Central African Republic, Chad, Equatorial Guinea, Gabon, and the Republic of Congo.

a Coinsurance of up to 15 percent (up to 350,000 Lek full insurance, and from 35,000 to 700,000 insurance at 85 percent).

b The equivalent of US$2,000 (per person per bank) is fully covered by insurance. Eighty percent coverage is provided for the next US$3,000 (that is from US$2,000 to US$5,000). Amounts exceeding the equivalent of US$5,000 per person per bank are not insured.

c Full guarantee on time deposits; 90 percent coverage of savings deposits up to a limit of 120 Unidades de Fomento. (1 Unidad de Fomento = US$24).

d Banks in Greenland with Danish ownership are covered by the Danish deposit insurance scheme.

e Coverage of 100 percent up to LTL 10,000 and the balance at 90 percent.

f Coverage of 100 percent up to 10,000 euros; 90 percent next 10,000 euros.

g In Mexico, a blanket guarantee was in place until year-end 2002. The guarantee has been gradually removed and the coverage limit is to be reduced from 10,000,000 Investment Units (UDIs) in 2003 to 400,000 Investment Units (UDIs), or about US$110,000 at the current exchange rate, by the year 2005.

h In Norway, a private guarantee fund for savings banks with voluntary membership had been in place since 1921, with membership becoming obligatory in 1924. A private guarantee fund for commercial banks was first introduced in 1938. Both guarantee funds were not pure deposit insurance schemes but had wide mandates to support member banks in liquidity or solvency crisis.

i Coverage is RO20,000 or 75 percent of net deposits, whichever is less.

j Coverage is 100 percent of deposits up to 1,000 euros; and 90 percent from 1,000 to 18,000 euros.

k Coverage is 100 percent of the first £2,000, and 90 percent of the next £33,000.

Table 2.3
Summary statistics

Variable	Mean	Median	Standard deviation	Minimum	Maximum	Number of obser-vations
Endogenous						
Deposit insurance (EI)	0.17	0.00	0.37	0.00	1.00	7783
Coverage ratio	6.24	2.45	13.73	0.05	117.86	919
Administration	0.55	1.00	0.50	0.00	1.00	1249
Membership	0.14	0.00	0.35	0.00	1.00	1249
Foreign currency deposits	0.75	1.00	0.43	0.00	1.00	1255
Interbank deposits	0.24	0.00	0.43	0.00	1.00	1255
Coinsurance	0.74	1.00	0.44	0.00	1.00	1220
Permanent fund	0.83	1.00	0.38	0.00	1.00	1256
Funding	0.01	0.00	0.12	0.00	1.00	1243
Moral hazard composite	0.00	−0.04	1.00	−1.95	3.84	911
Explanatory						
Real interest rate	−0.88	1.33	12.36	−98.83	44.62	3962
Inflation	47.96	6.51	532.72	−31.91	26762.02	5788
GDP growth	3.64	3.89	5.82	−34.86	34.31	5811
Credit growth	20.38	14.91	27.24	−99.84	249.04	4821
Terms-of-trade change	0.46	0.00	12.79	−64.35	139.60	4346
GDP per capita	5.48	1.56	8.62	0.05	56.51	5748
External pressure	0.12	0.00	0.32	0.00	1.00	7783
World Bank loan	0.01	0.00	0.10	0.00	1.00	7783
EU directive	0.03	0.00	0.18	0.00	1.00	7783
EU candidacy	0.01	0.00	0.12	0.00	1.00	7783
Emulation	0.17	0.11	0.14	0.02	0.48	7783
Crisis dummy	0.07	0.00	0.25	0.00	1.00	7783
Postcrisis adoption	0.10	0.00	0.30	0.00	1.00	7783
Fiscal cost/GDP	0.56	0.00	4.13	0.00	55.10	7501
Government ownership	54.31	53.08	34.98	0.00	100.00	3128
Bank deposits/ GDP	0.34	0.25	0.34	0.00	7.78	4149
Executive constraints	3.88	3.00	2.34	1.00	7.00	5563
Polity score	−0.19	−3.00	7.64	−10.00	10.00	5563

Table 2.3
(continued)

Variable	Mean	Median	Standard deviation	Minimum	Maximum	Number of obser-vations
Political competition	4.88	3.00	3.77	1.00	10.00	5563
Bureaucracy	2.15	2.00	1.22	0.00	4.00	2464
Corruption	3.23	3.00	1.39	0.00	6.00	2464
Democratic accountability	3.58	4.00	1.64	0.00	6.00	2464
Law and order	3.65	4.00	1.56	0.00	6.00	2464

Note: This table presents summary statistics for the endogenous and explanatory variables used in the regressions. See the appendix for a detailed explanation of variables and data sources.

variables. For each variable, detailed definitions and sources are provided in the appendix.

In studying deposit insurance adoption and design, the number of country-years to be sampled is an element of research strategy. One natural starting point is 1934, when the U.S. Federal Deposit Insurance Corporation opened its doors. If we begin in 1934, the maximum sample size is $181 \times 40 = 7,240$. Later starting dates are more attractive because we want to examine whether and how the occurrence of a financial crisis might influence deposit insurance adoption and design. As it happens, a World Bank cross-country dataset on crises compiled by Caprio et al. (2005) begins in 1970, although it is thought to be more reliable after 1975. If we begin in 1975, the maximum sample size is $181 \times 29 = 5,249$. For the adoption models we fit, coefficient estimates prove much the same whether we start the clock at 1934, 1970, or even 1980. Of course, because observations are missing for some explanatory variables in many countries, the number of usable observations is much less than these maximum values. The usable sample increases markedly when we restrict the determinants of EDIS adoption and design to measures of inflation, per capita GDP, and GDP growth.

The first column of the first panel of table 2.3 lists a series of endogenous deposit insurance design features. The mean value of the EDIS indicator variable, *Deposit insurance*, states the proportion of country-years in which the countries in our sample included explicit deposit guarantees in their safety net. This turns out to be 17 percent, since many countries adopted EDIS relatively recently. The mean value of indicator variables for specific design characteristics tells us what proportion of *Installed schemes* incorporates each particular characteristic. All variables are coded so that higher values indicate an increased exposure to risk shifting. Higher values indicate that, according to the empirical literature, moral hazard is less effectively controlled by that particular design feature. Indicator variables take the value one: if the administration is publicly managed (*Administration*), if membership is voluntary (*Membership*), if foreign currency deposits and interbank deposits are covered (*Foreign currency deposits* and *Interbank deposits*), if there is no coinsurance (*Coinsurance*), if a permanent fund exists (*Permanent fund*), and if funding comes from only public sources (*Funding*). The last two endogenous variables are (1) the EDIS coverage ratio (*Coverage ratio*), which we define as the ratio of the maximum insured value of individual account balances to per capita GDP, and (2) a proposed overall "moral hazard index" (*Moral hazard*), which we represent by the first principal component of the variance-covariance matrix for the coverage ratio and indicator variables for the six other features.

We represent outside influences in several different ways. *External pressure* is a dummy variable that takes the value one for the years 1999 on. In 1999, the IMF published a best-practice paper on deposit insurance and its design, recommending explicit deposit insurance for developing countries. The World Bank also recommended explicit deposit insurance for specific developing countries during the sample period. *World Bank loan* is an indicator variable that moves from zero to one for individual countries starting in the year the World Bank began an adjustment lending program that entailed EDIS installation. European Union directives also encouraged deposit insurance adoption. To capture this effect, we deploy two indicators: *EU directive* and *EU candidacy*. In 1994, the EU's directive encouraging countries to adopt deposit insurance came into force. For EU member countries, *EU directive* is set to one from 1994 on, but is zero otherwise. Since the directive was aimed at candidate countries, *EU candidacy* takes the value of one from 1994 on for EU candidate countries only and is zero otherwise. Finally, we introduce a variable, *Emulation*, which is the interpretive name we assign to the nonlinear trend that tracks the proportion of countries having EDIS systems at each point in time. As more and more countries adopt an EDIS, *Emulation* increases in value. We interpret this ratio as a proxy for the extent to which deposit insurance is believed to be a universal best practice. Reported regressions feature

External pressure as the main measure of outside influence, but in most models the *World Bank* and *EU dummies* work at least equally well.

We also investigate whether and how the occurrence and fiscal cost of a financial crisis might affect the timing and character of deposit insurance decisions. *Crisis dummy* moves from zero to one for countries that are experiencing a crisis in a given year. *Postcrisis adoption* variable is an indicator variable that identifies countries that adopted EDIS up to three years after a crisis. *Fiscal cost/GDP* expresses the fiscal cost of resolving a banking crisis as a percentage of GDP. This variable lets us explore how crisis severity might influence safety net decisions.

To characterize the political environment of a country, we focus on *Executive constraints*. This index measures the extent to which institutionalized constraints on the decision-making powers of the country's chief executive create other "accountability groups." The index ranges from 1 to 7. Higher values indicate increased restriction on executive authority. Because other researchers have used *Polity score*, *Political competition*, and *Democratic accountability*, we experiment with these alternative indicators as well. *Polity score* ranges from −10 to 10, with negative scores assigned to countries that are autocracies and positive values to democracies. *Political competition* ranges from 1 to 10, with higher scores representing increased political competition. Finally, *Democratic accountability* measures how responsive the government is to its people and whether changes occur peacefully or violently. It ranges from 0 to 6, with values increasing with the extent of democracy.

To control for differences in the economic environment, we include the following macroeconomic variables: *Real interest rate*, *Inflation*, *GDP growth*, *Terms of trade change*, and *Credit growth*. Movement in these variables captures the extent of internal and external macroeconomic shocks the countries experience. *Real interest rate* and *Inflation* are defined as the annual rates of real interest and inflation, respectively. *GDP growth* is the growth rate in real GDP, and *Credit growth* is the growth rate in the amount of real credit extended to the private sector by financial intermediaries. *Terms-of-trade change* states the annual percentage change in terms of trade.

To explore whether cross-country variation in direct government control of the banking system matters, we include a government-ownership ratio. *Government ownership* states the percentage size of government's ownership stake in the banking system. The importance of banks in the economy is represented by *Bank deposits/GDP*, which

Table 2.4
Correlation matrix

	Deposit insurance	Coverage ratio	Moral hazard composite	Real interest rate	Inflation	GDP growth	Credit growth	Terms-of-trade change	GDP per capita	External pressure	World Bank loan	EU directive	EU candidacy	Emulation	Crisis dummy	Postcrisis adoption	Fiscal cost/GDP	Government ownership	Polity score
Coverage ratio	0.10*																		
Moral hazard	0.65*	-0.05																	
Real interest rate	0.01	-0.04	-0.01																
Inflation	-0.03*	-0.01	0.06	-0.43*															
GDP growth	-0.02	0.02	0.02	-0.02	-0.14*														
Credit growth	-0.04*	-0.05	0.04	-0.41*	0.45*	0.18*													
Terms-of-trade change	0.00	0.02	0.03	0.00	-0.01	0.03	0.00												
GDP per capita	0.41*	-0.26*	-0.41*	0.09*	-0.08*	-0.11*	-0.26*	-0.04											
External pressure	0.27*	-0.10*	-0.08*	0.08*	-0.05	-0.04	-0.08*	0.04	-0.07*										
World Bank loan	0.15*	-0.04	-0.04	0.04	-0.01	0.02	0.03	-0.01	-0.17*	0.21*									
EU directive	0.34*	-0.15*	-0.37*	0.04	-0.05	0.00*	-0.09	-0.01	0.28*	0.23*	0.07*								
EU candidacy	0.16*	-0.08*	-0.15*	0.00	0.03	0.00	0.10*	0.01	-0.17*	0.19*	0.35*	0.39*							
Emulation	0.37*	-0.11*	-0.12*	0.08*	-0.04	-0.07*	-0.03	0.03	-0.05	0.80*	0.23*	0.35*	0.23*						
Crisis dummy	0.10*	-0.01	0.09*	-0.04	0.13*	-0.12*	0.02	-0.02	-0.14*	-0.04	-0.04	-0.13*	-0.02	0.03					
Postcrisis adoption	0.06*	-0.05	-0.03	0.00	-0.01	-0.01	0.08*	0.01	-0.29*	0.15*	0.23*	0.07*	0.22*	0.20*	0.25*				
Fiscal cost/GDP	0.12*	-0.03	0.03	-0.04	0.07*	-0.15*	0.03	-0.03	-0.05	0.09*	-0.05	-0.10*	-0.05	0.12*	0.78*	0.18*			
Government ownership	-0.24*	0.27*	-0.04	-0.08*	0.11	0.07	0.25*	0.03	-0.42*	-0.10*	0.03	-0.13*	0.15*	-0.10*	0.05	0.03	-0.05		
Polity score	0.41*	-0.22*	-0.24*	0.16*	-0.03	-0.20*	-0.26*	-0.06	0.46*	-0.02	0.01	0.26*	0.10*	-0.04	-0.18*	-0.06	-0.04	-0.19*	
Executive constraints	0.10*	-0.23*	-0.27*	0.14*	-0.03	-0.19*	-0.26*	-0.06	0.47*	-0.02	0.00	0.28*	0.14*	-0.04	-0.17*	-0.02	-0.04	-0.22*	0.96*

Notes: This table shows the bivariate correlation between the variables used in the regressions and the significance level of each correlation coefficient. * indicates significance at the 5 percent level.

expresses total deposits in banks as a share of GDP. When bank deposits represent a larger share of GDP, banks might have more clout and be better able to lobby for deposit insurance subsidies.

As measures of institutional development, we use *GDP per capita*, and indices for *Bureaucracy, Corruption*, and *Law and order*. *Bureaucracy* ranges from 0 to 4, increasing in the strength and quality of the bureaucracy. *Corruption* measures how well bribery is controlled in the country. It ranges from 0 to 6, with low scores indicating high levels of corruption. *Law and order* expresses the quality of country's legal system and rule of law. It ranges from 0 to 6, where high scores indicate a high level of law and order.

Table 2.4 reports the correlation matrix of deposit insurance variables and country characteristics across the years and countries for which data are available for both members of each pair of variables. The presence of explicit deposit insurance is positively associated with economic development (as measured by *GDP per capita*), external pressure indicators, crisis experience, and constraints on executive authority. For countries with explicit insurance, we find that coverage levels and exposures to moral hazard are higher when per capita GDP and constraints on executive authority are low and during periods of increased external pressure. Coverage levels prove higher in countries where government ownership of banks is more extensive.

Because we expect the same variables to influence adoption and design, design decisions must be modelled simultaneously with adoption. Because it ignores potential selection bias, table 2.4 probably overstates the bivariate correlation of deposit insurance characteristics with country variables. To avoid selection bias, regressions seeking to explain design decisions are estimated simultaneously with an EDIS adoption equation whose relatively parsimonious specification is based on evidence generated by first fitting alternative single equation models of the adoption decision.

2.3   Empirical Results of the Adoption Decision

2.3.1   Logit Models of the Adoption Decision
Tables 2.5 through 2.9 report on stepwise regression experiments aimed at developing a benchmark model of the adoption decision. The first-cut model appears in column (1) of table 2.5. It relates the indicator variable, *Deposit insurance*, to six macroeconomic variables: *Real interest rate, Inflation, GDP growth, Credit growth, Terms-of-trade change,*

Table 2.5
Alternative logit models of deposit insurance adoption

	(1)	(2)	(3)	(4)	(5)	(6)	(7)	(8)	(9)	(10) Marginal effects
Real interest rate	0.026** (0.012)	0.008 (0.008)	0.019* (0.011)	0.018* (0.011)	0.012 (0.010)	0.010 (0.009)	0.004 (0.008)			-0.000 (0.000)
Inflation	0.014** (0.006)	0.011* (0.006)	0.014** (0.006)	0.012* (0.007)	0.012* (0.007)	0.009 (0.007)	0.007 (0.007)	-0.000 (0.000)	-0.001 (0.001)	-0.000 (0.000)
GDP growth	-0.023 (0.014)	-0.009 (0.016)	-0.021 (0.015)	-0.024 (0.018)	-0.021 (0.019)	-0.006 (0.019)	0.002 (0.023)	-0.004 (0.013)	-0.039* (0.023)	-0.000 (0.002)
Credit growth	0.001 (0.003)	0.002 (0.003)	0.003 (0.003)	0.002 (0.003)	0.004 (0.003)	0.003 (0.003)	0.003 (0.003)			
Terms-of-trade change	-0.001 (0.002)	-0.002 (0.003)	-0.002 (0.003)	0.001 (0.003)	-0.000 (0.003)	-0.001 (0.003)	0.002 (0.004)			
GDP per capita	0.098*** (0.020)	0.125*** (0.026)	0.110*** (0.022)	0.069*** (0.021)	0.084*** (0.025)	0.086*** (0.024)	0.102*** (0.025)	0.078*** (0.020)	0.045*** (0.015)	0.010*** (0.003)
External pressure			1.476*** (0.227)		1.557*** (0.245)	1.422*** (0.234)	1.244*** (0.215)	1.579*** (0.197)	0.813*** (0.339)	0.292*** (0.041)
Executive constraints				0.263*** (0.081)	0.255*** (0.087)	0.268*** (0.089)	0.260*** (0.091)	0.325*** (0.070)	0.240*** (0.058)	0.042*** (0.010)
Observations	3091	3091	3091	2831	2831	2517	1958	4685	3733	4685
Number of countries	136	136	136	123	123	123	122	147	144	147
Percent correct	78.62	78.58	78.55	77.71	79.90	79.02	77.57	84.27	78.23	84.27
Model χ^2	32.61	238.87	60.12	45.15	66.71	64.00	71.54	112.13	41.33	112.13
Pseudo R^2	0.15	0.24	0.19	0.18	0.22	0.23	0.24	0.25	0.07	0.25

Notes: This table uses logit regressions to explain the adoption of explicit deposit insurance. The endogenous variable is the explicit deposit insurance indicator. The regression in column (2) includes year dummies (not shown). Regression (3) is the same as 1 but includes the external pressure variable. Regression (4) is the same as regression (1) but adds the *Executive constraints* variable. Regression (5) adds the *Executive constraints* variable to regression (3). Regression (6) reestimates model (5), restricting the sample to the post-1970 era. Regression (7) fits model (5) to the post-1980 era. Regression (8) fits model (5) and increases the sample size by excluding three macroeconomic explanatory variables. Regression (9) reestimates model (8) but drops observations after deposit insurance is adopted in the country. Regression (10) presents the marginal effects and their standard errors of regression (8). An intercept is used but not shown. White standard errors are shown in brackets. The standard errors are adjusted for clustering at the country level. *, **, and *** indicate significance at the 10 percent, 5 percent, and 1 percent level, respectively.

and *GDP per capita*. This experiment establishes the baseline extent to which macroeconomic variables alone can explain the presence or absence of explicit deposit guarantees. Consistent with our preliminary analysis, *GDP per capita* shows the strongest influence. Column (2) shows that, except for *GDP per capita* and *Inflation*, the estimated influence of macroeconomic forces becomes negligible when year dummies are introduced. This experiment also confirms that individual-country adoption decisions are significantly influenced by the spread of these schemes across countries.

Column (3) steps in the *External pressure* indicator. This variable proxies encouragement from international entities to install explicit insurance. As expected, *External pressure* earns a significant and positive coefficient. The probability of adopting an EDIS increases after the IMF endorsed such schemes as best practice.

Columns (4)–(10) make use of our preferred political variable, *Executive constraints*. The results indicate that political systems that more strongly constrain their executive are more likely to adopt an EDIS. Column (5) includes *Executive constraints* with *External pressure* and shows that both are significant. Columns (6) and (7) show that coefficient values and significance patterns found for the *GDP per capita*, *External pressure* and *Executive constraints* are virtually unaffected by moving the starting date of the study forward either to 1970 or 1980.

Column (8) drops three consistently insignificant macrovariables whose spotty availability constrains the usable size of our sample. This relatively parsimonious model also serves as the "benchmark" model for subsequent regression experiments. This experiment indicates that inflation loses significance in the enlarged sample, while the coefficients of *GDP per capita*, *External pressure*, and *Executive constraints* remain much the same and model performance is enhanced.

The logit models estimated in columns (1)–(8) assume that a country makes a decision each year about changing its deposit insurance status.[3] However, once explicit insurance is in place, countries rarely jettison it. In column (9), we investigate—by dropping all postadoption observations—how much including the period after the adoption decision biases estimates. Coefficients of interest remain significant, but their magnitude declines.

To communicate the economic significance of these findings and to sharpen their interpretation, it is helpful to calculate the marginal influence each regressor has on the probability of adoption. Using the mean of each explanatory variable in regression (8), column (10) reports each variable's marginal effect (and standard error). For example, GDP per capita is expressed in thousands of U.S. dollars. Its coefficient in column (10) implies that, on average, a US$1000 increase in GDP per capita brings about a 0.01 increase in adoption probability. It is particularly instructive to calculate the marginal effect of a one standard deviation increase in each regressor. This exercise shows that one standard deviation increases in *GDP per capita*, *Executive constraints*, and *Emulation* have similar impacts on adoption probability. A one standard deviation increase in GDP per capita (or US$8660) is associated with a 0.08 increase in the probability of deposit insurance adoption; a one standard deviation increase in emulation (or 0.32) is associated with a 0.09 increase in the probability of deposit insurance adoption; and a one standard deviation increase in executive constraints (2.34) is associated with a 0.10 increase in the probability of deposit insurance adoption. Relative to the 0.22 mean value the deposit insurance variable in the column (10) sample, these incremental effects are substantial.

Table 2.6 introduces alternative proxies for external pressure. Panel A shows that whatever measure we use—*World Bank loan*, *EU directive/candidacy*, *Emulation*—outside forces significantly influence adoption decisions. Indeed, the last column shows that, when entered together, *IMF, World Bank loan*, and *EU directive* influences are each significant.[4] Panel B replicates these results, controlling for a linear time trend. Even in the presence of this uninterpreted trend, pressure from the three multinational organizations significantly influences adoption decisions. In specifications that include the trend, *World Bank loan* and *EU directive* remain significant at conventional levels, while *External pressure* and *Emulation* prove marginally significant at 10 percent.

Table 2.7 investigates whether and how financial crisis experience, bank ownership, institutional quality, and bank dependence affect the adoption decision. The experiment depicted in the first column supports the hypothesis that countries that experience a crisis are more likely to adopt an EDIS. The second column confirms the hypothesis that an EDIS is likely to be adopted as a way of *unwinding* a crisis, while the third column shows that the odds of adoption increase with the fiscal burden the particular crisis poses.[5]

Columns (4) and (5) of table 2.7 explore whether EDIS adoption and government ownership are substitute ways of protecting depositors. The datasets used to generate the ownership data cover a much smaller number of countries. *Privatization*, but not *Government ownership* is

Table 2.6
Robustness experiments investigating alternative external pressure variables

Panel A. Without time trend

	(1)	(2)	(3)	(4)	(5)	(6)	(7)	(8)
Inflation	-0.000	-0.000	-0.000	-0.001	-0.000	-0.000	-0.000	-0.000
	(0.000)	(0.001)	(0.001)	(0.001)	(0.000)	(0.000)	(0.000)	(0.000)
GDP growth	-0.004	-0.007	-0.008	-0.008	-0.004	-0.005	-0.004	-0.005
	(0.013)	(0.012)	(0.012)	(0.012)	(0.013)	(0.013)	(0.013)	(0.013)
GDP per capita	0.078***	0.074***	0.065***	0.075***	0.080***	0.074***	0.081***	0.075***
	(0.020)	(0.018)	(0.018)	(0.018)	(0.020)	(0.020)	(0.020)	(0.020)
External pressure	1.579***				1.491***	1.476***	1.526***	1.401***
	(0.197)				(0.193)	(0.205)	(0.196)	(0.200)
World Bank loan		2.082***			1.569***			1.328**
		(0.486)			(0.570)			(0.593)
EU directive			2.221***			1.961***		
			(0.467)			(0.490)		
EU candidacy				1.645***			1.353**	
				(0.500)			(0.545)	
Executive constraints	0.325***	0.325***	0.294***	0.306***	0.319***	0.291***	0.303***	0.288***
	(0.070)	(0.066)	(0.066)	(0.066)	(0.070)	(0.071)	(0.071)	(0.071)
Observations	4685	4685	4685	4685	4685	4685	4685	4685
Number of countries	147	147	147	147	147	147	147	147
Model χ^2	112.13	72.06	93.46	71.34	113.18	119.85	114.28	123.11
Pseudo R^2	0.25	0.22	0.24	0.22	0.26	0.27	0.26	0.28

Panel B. With a linear time trend

	(1)	(2)	(3)	(4)	(5)	(6)	(7)	(8)
Inflation	-0.001	-0.000	-0.000	-0.000	-0.001	-0.001	-0.001	-0.000
	(0.001)	(0.000)	(0.001)	(0.001)	(0.001)	(0.001)	(0.001)	(0.001)
GDP growth	0.017	0.009	0.014	0.016	0.016	0.014	0.016	0.013
	(0.013)	(0.013)	(0.013)	(0.013)	(0.013)	(0.012)	(0.013)	(0.013)
GDP per capita	0.086***	0.088***	0.088***	0.087***	0.088***	0.083***	0.088***	0.084***
	(0.023)	(0.023)	(0.023)	(0.023)	(0.023)	(0.023)	(0.023)	(0.023)
External pressure				0.325*				0.301
				(0.197)				(0.199)
World Bank loan					1.147**			0.994*
					(0.497)			(0.524)
EU directive						1.232***		1.169**
						(0.474)		(0.474)
EU candidacy							0.749	
							(0.516)	
Executive constraints	0.320***	0.316***	0.318***	0.320***	0.315***	0.295***	0.305***	0.293***
	(0.077)	(0.077)	(0.077)	(0.078)	(0.078)	(0.078)	(0.079)	(0.079)
Time trend	0.085***		0.053*	0.078***	0.083***	0.078***	0.083***	0.070***
	(0.016)		(0.028)	(0.017)	(0.016)	(0.015)	(0.016)	(0.016)
Emulation		6.556***	2.630					
		(0.975)	(1.769)					
Observations	4685	4685	4685	4685	4685	4685	4685	4685
Number of countries	147	147	147	147	147	147	147	147
Model χ^2	77.83	87.05	82.16	85.03	82.22	93.36	81.79	104.06
Pseudo R^2	0.31	0.31	0.31	0.31	0.31	0.31	0.31	0.32

Notes: This table compares alternative logit regressions seeking to explain the adoption of explicit deposit insurance. The endogenous variable is the explicit deposit insurance indicator. An intercept is used but not shown. White standard errors are shown in brackets. The standard errors are adjusted for clustering at the country level. *, **, and *** indicate significance at the 10 percent, 5 percent, and 1 percent level, respectively.

Table 2.7
Robustness experiments focused on the effects of crisis experience, government ownership of banks, and quality of institutions

	(1)	(2)	(3)	(4)	(5)	(6)	(7)	(8)	(9)
Inflation	-0.000	-0.000	-0.001	-0.000	-0.000	-0.000	-0.000	-0.000	-0.000
	(0.000)	(0.001)	(0.001)	(0.000)	(0.000)	(0.000)	(0.000)	(0.000)	(0.000)
GDP growth	0.007	-0.002	-0.005	-0.044*	-0.007	0.006	0.010	0.007	-0.021
	(0.013)	(0.013)	(0.015)	(0.026)	(0.017)	(0.018)	(0.017)	(0.017)	(0.017)
GDP per capita	0.084***	0.087***	0.078***	0.049*	0.058***	0.068***	0.112***	0.085***	0.076***
	(0.021)	(0.022)	(0.020)	(0.027)	(0.019)	(0.025)	(0.025)	(0.023)	(0.025)
External pressure	1.640***	1.604***	1.565***	0.266	1.753***	1.078***	0.853***	1.040***	1.582***
	(0.214)	(0.210)	(0.216)	(0.275)	(0.227)	(0.190)	(0.232)	(0.183)	(0.220)
Executive constraints	0.330***	0.306***	0.361***	0.246**	0.283***	0.260***	0.336***	0.287***	0.259***
	(0.071)	(0.071)	(0.073)	(0.116)	(0.080)	(0.088)	(0.090)	(0.088)	(0.083)
Crisis dummy	1.234***								
	(0.279)								
Postcrisis adoption		0.867**							
		(0.387)							
Fiscal cost/GDP			0.043***						
			(0.017)						
Privatization				1.729***					
				(0.345)					
Government ownership					0.003				
					(0.005)				
Bureaucracy						0.269			
						(0.191)			
Corruption							-0.270*		
							(0.143)		

Law and order							0.043 (0.123)	
Bank deposits/GDP								0.334 (0.713)
Observations	4685	4439	1851	2513	2081	2081	2081	3527
Number of countries	147	147	47	85	125	125	125	132
Model χ^2	116.39	105.87	56.49	83.49	67.26	85.56	72.68	85.28
Pseudo R^2	0.27	0.28	0.24	0.21	0.24	0.25	0.24	0.23

Notes: This table compares alternative logit regressions seeking to explain the adoption of explicit deposit insurance. The endogenous variable is explicit deposit insurance indicator. An intercept is used but not shown. White standard errors are shown in brackets. The standard errors are adjusted for clustering at the country level. *, **, and *** indicate significance at the 10 percent, 5 percent, and 1 percent level, respectively.

significant; including these variables reduces the coefficient assigned to per capita GDP. Although *Government ownership* is itself a trend variable in many countries,[6] the size and significance of the *External pressure* coefficient prove greater in this specification than in the benchmark model.

Columns (5)–(7) of table 2.7 further explore the impact of institutional quality. By institutional quality, we mean contractual enhancements generated by the institutional environment in which banks and customers contract. Our benchmark specifications begin with *GDP per capita*, which is a widely recognized correlate of institutional quality. We insert *Bureaucracy*, *Corruption*, and *Law and order* into the model to investigate whether variation in these indices affects the adoption decision. We find weak evidence that more corrupt countries are more likely to adopt deposit insurance, but none of the other institutional variables enters significantly. *External pressure* and *Executive constraints* remain positive and significant even after controlling for institutional quality.

Finally, column (8) controls for the importance of banks in the economy by introducing *Bank deposit/GDP*. One might suppose that, when banks play a more important role, risky banks might promote their interests more effectively. This hypothesis is rejected. The relevant coefficient is insignificant and its inclusion does not affect the significance levels of other regressors.

Table 2.8 introduces alternative proxies for political power sharing. Columns 2 and 3 replace *Executive constraints* with two alternative measures: *Polity score* and *Political competition*. Both variables come out of the University of Maryland's INSCR Program. The INSCR program covers more countries than the third index featured in the table, which comes from the International Country Risk Guide (ICRG) database. Both INSCR variables show a similar effect: countries with effective systems of political checks and balances are more likely to adopt an EDIS than countries in which political power is more concentrated. Each variable shows a positive and significant impact on the adoption decision. Introducing either one of them reduces the *GDP per capita* coefficient by about a standard error, but has a negligible effect on the coefficient of *External pressure*. The last column introduces the ICRG's measure of *Democratic accountability*. This measure also enters significantly and reduces the *external pressure* and *per capita GDP* coefficients more than the INSCR indices.

Table 2.8
Robustness experiments investigating alternative political variables

	(1)	(2)	(3)
Inflation	−0.000	−0.000	−0.000
	(0.000)	(0.000)	(0.000)
GDP growth	−0.005	−0.006	0.007
	(0.013)	(0.013)	(0.016)
GDP per capita	0.078***	0.078***	0.068***
	(0.020)	(0.019)	(0.019)
External pressure	1.530***	1.482***	1.069***
	(0.203)	(0.206)	(0.177)
Polity score	0.103***		
	(0.021)		
Political competition		0.201***	
		(0.039)	
Democratic accountability			0.454***
			(0.115)
Observations	4685	4685	2275
Number of countries	147	147	133
Model χ^2	118.28	118.97	84.17
Pseudo R^2	0.26	0.25	0.23

Notes: This table compares alternative logit regressions seeking to explain the adoption of explicit deposit insurance. The endogenous variable is the explicit deposit insurance indicator. An intercept is used but not shown. White standard errors are shown in brackets. The standard errors are adjusted for clustering at the country level. *, **, and *** indicate significance at the 10 percent, 5 percent, and 1 percent level, respectively.

Table 2.9 uses the baseline model to investigate how much the impact of *External pressure* and *Executive constraints* varies across regions and country types. The first three columns investigate whether the European Union requirement that member countries adopt an EDIS might be responsible for the significance of *External pressure*, *Executive constraints*, and *GDP per capita*. Although the coefficients of *GDP per capita* and *External pressure* decline when EU countries are excised from the sample, their effects remain sizeable and significant. *Executive constraints* shows a slightly larger effect in this sample. Columns 4 to 6 show that deleting very small countries (where intersectoral conflict may be easier to resolve) from the sample increases the coefficients of these three variables. Finally, the last three columns establish that introducing a fixed effect for each continent virtually halves the effect of variation in *GDP per capita*, intensifies the effect of *External pressure*, and lessens the effect of *Executive constraints*.

Table 2.9
Robustness experiments focused on the influence of region and population size

	Excluding EU members			Excluding countries with population < 1 million			With dummies by continent		
	(1)	(2)	(3)	(4)	(5)	(6)	(7)	(8)	(9)
Inflation	-0.000	-0.000	-0.000	-0.000	-0.000	-0.000	-0.001	-0.001	-0.001
	(0.000)	(0.000)	(0.000)	(0.001)	(0.000)	(0.000)	(0.001)	(0.001)	(0.001)
GDP growth	-0.006	-0.002	-0.000	-0.011	-0.008	-0.002	-0.015	-0.008	-0.008
	(0.009)	(0.009)	(0.013)	(0.010)	(0.011)	(0.013)	(0.010)	(0.011)	(0.014)
GDP per capita	0.083***	0.087***	0.065***	0.103***	0.110***	0.074***	0.057***	0.062***	0.059***
	(0.021)	(0.023)	(0.024)	(0.019)	(0.021)	(0.019)	(0.016)	(0.017)	(0.020)
External pressure		1.460***	1.347***		1.725***	1.577***		1.852***	1.803***
		(0.186)	(0.213)		(0.188)	(0.203)		(0.194)	(0.228)
Executive constraints			0.319***			0.344***			0.276***
			(0.077)			(0.071)			(0.080)
Observations	4757	4757	3958	4858	4858	4517	5609	5609	4541
Number of countries	145	145	124	143	143	140	170	170	143
Model χ^2	16.50	74.61	83.78	32.49	95.62	107.66	114.41	170.91	168.30
Pseudo R^2	0.08	0.12	0.19	0.15	0.20	0.26	0.22	0.27	0.32

Notes: This table compares alternative logit regressions seeking to explain the adoption of explicit deposit insurance. The endogenous variable is the explicit deposit insurance indicator. Regressions in columns (1) and (2) exclude current European Union members. Regressions in columns (3) and (4) exclude countries with fewer than one million inhabitants. Regressions in columns (5) and (6) include dummies by continent. An intercept is used but not shown. White standard errors are shown in brackets. The standard errors are adjusted for clustering at the country level. *, **, and *** indicate significance at the 10 percent, 5 percent, and 1 percent level, respectively.

These regression experiments strongly support a role for *External pressure* and *Executive constraints* in EDIS adoption decisions. This finding is robust to numerous changes in specification, such as introducing proxies for crisis pressures, macroeconomic shocks, institutional quality, population size, and regional differences in culture. *GDP per capita*—a frequently used proxy for economic and institutional development—remains significant in alternative specifications and does not eliminate the significance of *External pressure* and *Executive constraints*. The next section demonstrates that these conclusions are robust to the use of an alternative statistical method.

2.3.2 Hazard Models of the Adoption Decision

Another way to analyze the timing of adoption decisions would be to regress the duration of a country's stay in the non-EDIS state (state N) against subsets of the determinants we used in the logit models. The difficulty with this approach is that countries that are in state N at year-end 2003 would give incomplete (i.e., downward-biased or right-censored) data on the length of their stay.

Hazard models surmount this problem by focusing instead on the transitional probability of staying in state N for a spell of exactly t years, where results for $t > 43$ can be extrapolated from the transitions observed. The hazard rate $\lambda(t)$ may be interpreted as the probability of country's leaving state N in year t, given that it was in state N when the year began. The logit models estimated in the previous section imply that this probability λ is a function of country characteristics as well as time.

As a robustness test, table 2.10 fits a series of hazard rate models that let us examine how different factors affect a country's probability of transitioning to an EDIS. The first three columns of the table estimate each of three widely used hazard models, using only the benchmark macrodeterminants identified in table 2.5. The Cox procedure models the hazard rate as

$$\lambda^i(t) = \lambda(t)\exp(\beta'x_i), \tag{1}$$

where x is any specified vector of potential explanatory variables. The exponential procedure imposes on (1) the restriction that $\lambda(t) = \lambda$. Finally, the Weibull model specifies that $\lambda(t)$ in (1) evolves as

$$\lambda(t) = \lambda\alpha t^{\alpha-1}. \tag{2}$$

Table 2.10
Hazard models of deposit insurance adoption

	Cox (1)	Exponential (2)	Weibull (3)	Weibull (4)	Weibull (5)	Weibull (6)	Weibull (7)	Weibull (8)	Weibull (9)
Inflation	-0.001 (0.001)	-0.000 (0.000)	-0.001 (0.001)	-0.002 (0.001)	-0.002 (0.002)	-0.002 (0.002)	-0.002 (0.002)	-0.002 (0.002)	-0.002 (0.002)
GDP growth	-0.007 (0.020)	-0.021 (0.018)	-0.001 (0.020)	-0.019 (0.025)	-0.005 (0.024)	-0.005 (0.024)	-0.010 (0.025)	-0.012 (0.024)	-0.014 (0.024)
GDP per capita	0.072*** (0.011)	0.068*** (0.011)	0.069*** (0.011)	0.048*** (0.013)	0.058*** (0.012)	0.058*** (0.012)	0.062*** (0.012)	0.059*** (0.012)	0.059*** (0.012)
Executive constraints				0.224*** (0.064)	0.219*** (0.064)	0.219*** (0.064)	0.205*** (0.064)	0.181*** (0.064)	0.177*** (0.064)
Crisis dummy					1.246*** (0.271)	1.247*** (0.284)	1.129*** (0.267)	1.158*** (0.279)	1.128*** (0.278)
External pressure						0.007 (0.377)			
World Bank loan							1.869*** (0.344)		
EU directive								1.221*** (0.277)	
EU candidacy									1.286*** (0.265)
Observations	4567	4567	4567	3730	3730	3730	3730	3730	3730
Number of countries	166	166	166	145	145	145	145	145	145
Number of adopting countries	74	74	74	68	68	68	68	68	68
Evolutionary parameter		4.48	4.48	4.49	4.26	4.00	4.00	4.05	4.02
α (p-value)		(0.00)	(0.00)	(0.00)	(0.00)	(0.00)	(0.00)	(0.00)	(0.00)

Notes: This table compares alternative hazard regressions seeking to explain the hazard rate of adopting explicit deposit insurance over the period 1934–2003. The model considers the adoption of deposit insurance as a "transforming event." The endogenous variable is the number of years between 1934 and the adoption date. Column 1 uses a proportional Cox hazard model (1972). Columns (2)–(9) estimate other parametric survival models. The assumed distributions of the hazard function in column (2) is exponential and in columns (3)–(9) Weibull. The coefficients reported are the logarithms of the underlying relative hazard coefficients. The number of adopting countries is the number of countries that have adopted deposit insurance during the observation period. An intercept is used but not shown. Lin and Wei standard errors (1989) are shown in brackets. The standard errors are adjusted for clustering at the country level. *, **, and *** indicate significance at the 10 percent, 5 percent, and 1 percent level, respectively.

The evolutionary parameter α determines whether the hazard rate is increasing ($\alpha > 1$), decreasing ($\alpha < 1$), or constant ($\alpha = 1$) over time. High and significant values of α (which emerge in all of our Weibull specifications) denote positive duration dependence and can be interpreted as evidence of external influence or emulation. Because our dataset reduces to a cross section of durations when employing duration model techniques, we compare alternative specifications of the hazard model (focusing specifically on the values of α) to investigate the presence of external influence rather than estimating a time trend or including *Emulation* as an explanatory variable.

Because explanatory variables enter exponentially, the coefficients reported in table 2.10 are the logarithms of the underlying relative hazard coefficients. The relative hazard coefficients can be calculated as the antilog of the reported coefficients. The exponent of each coefficient estimate shows the proportional increase in the hazard rate that occurs when the focal explanatory variable increases by one unit. Regression (3) may serve as an example.

GDP per capita is denominated in thousands of U.S. dollars. The results show that: if *GDP per capita* increases by one unit (i.e., by $1,000), then the hazard rate for adopting deposit insurance increases by $\exp(0.069) = 1.071$ fold (or an increase of about 7 percent). This tells us that countries with higher *GDP per capita* are more likely to adopt sooner. On the other hand, countries with higher *Inflation* or more rapid *GDP growth* are likely to delay deposit insurance adoption, although these restraining effects are not statistically significant.

In regression (3), the estimated value of α is 4.49 (positive and significant). This tells us that the hazard function for adopting deposit insurance is increasing rapidly over our sample period 1934–2003. To see just how quickly, we can compare the hazard rates for the years 1980 and 2003. Focusing on the estimate of α in column (3), we find that for a typical country

$$\frac{\lambda(Year\ 2000) = \lambda(66) = \lambda\alpha(\lambda66)^{\alpha-1}}{\lambda(Year\ 1980) = \lambda(46) = \lambda\alpha(\lambda46)^{\alpha-1}} = (66/46)^{\alpha-1} = (66/46)^{4.49-1} = 3.53.$$

This tells us that such a country is 3.5 times more likely to adopt deposit insurance in 2000 than in 1980. This nonlinear trend approximates the *emulation* effect that we estimate in our logit specifications.

The first three columns of table 2.9 indicate that all three procedures for estimating the hazard rate assign similar roles to the benchmarked macrovariables, but only *GDP per capita* shows a significant effect. In unreported regressions, we included additional macroeconomic variables (including proxies for the real interest rate, credit growth, and the terms of trade) but none of these variables entered significantly and the main results were unaltered.

Columns (4)–(9) use the Weibull procedure and expand the set of variables to include measures of government power sharing and crisis experience. The significant positive values of α in the Weibull models support our contention that external influence is important: the likelihood of adoption (the "transforming event") at time t, conditional upon duration up to time t, increases over time. Table 2.10 investigates additional external influence variables and shows that *World Bank loan*, *EU directive* and *EU candidacy* are still significant and positive confirming earlier results. *External pressure* loses significance but as in the case of *Emulation*, its impact is actually captured by the evolutionary trend α.

The significance of the *Crisis dummy* confirms the hypothesis that EDIS is more likely to be adopted during crisis. Finally, the significantly positive sign captured by the government power sharing variable *Executive constraints* and the fact that its inclusion reduces the impact of *GDP per capita* indicate that social capital plays an important role in adoption decisions: democratic countries are more likely to adopt an EDIS, confirming again our initial findings. The results are similar when using the Cox model rather than the Weibull procedure, except that the Cox model excludes the possibility of time variation in the hazard rate.

Table 2.11 reports out-of-sample predictions of the year of adoption for countries that had no deposit insurance by year-end 2002—the end of our sample period. These estimates are based on the Weibull duration model in column (6) of table 2.10. We also report estimates of the number of years until each country without an EDIS can be expected to adopt deposit insurance given year 2002 circumstances. For a large number of countries, particularly poor countries in Africa, the model predicts adoption not until more than a decade from now. For example, for Zimbabwe the model predicts adoption in the year 2021. (In reality, Zimbabwe adopted deposit insurance "prematurely" in the year 2003.) Based on our model, one would have expected several other countries to already have adopted deposit insurance (for example, rich countries like Australia and New Zealand, but also China). A better interpretation is to say that these nonadopting countries must have seriously debated adoption for many years and rejected it for substitute

Table 2.11
Predicted year of adoption for countries that have not adopted deposit insurance as of year-end 2002

Country	Predicted adoption year	Predicted years until adoption (from 2002)
Australia	1981	−21
New Zealand	1985	−17
Singapore	1989	−13
China	1993	−9
Mauritius	1996	−6
Botswana	1996	−6
South Africa	1996	−6
Costa Rica	1996	−6
Paraguay*	1998	−4
Bolivia*	1999	−3
Papua New Guinea	1999	−3
Lesotho	1999	−3
Panama	1999	−3
Moldova*	1999	−3
Mongolia	2000	−2
Fiji	2000	−2
Senegal	2002	0
Ghana	2003	1
Namibia	2004	2
Russia*	2004	2
Guyana	2005	3
Madagascar	2006	4
Côte d'Ivoire	2006	4
Armenia	2006	4
Guinea-Bissau	2006	4
Central African Republic	2006	4
Georgia	2006	4
Benin	2006	4
Niger	2006	4
Zambia	2007	5
Sierra Leone	2007	5
Mali	2007	5
Iran	2009	7
Kyrgyz Republic	2010	8
Cambodia	2010	8
Malawi	2010	8
Tajikistan	2011	9

Table 2.11
(continued)

Country	Predicted adoption year	Predicted years until adoption (from 2002)
Mozambique	2011	9
Morocco	2013	11
Egypt	2013	11
Djibouti	2013	11
Syria	2013	11
Guinea	2014	12
Nepal	2014	12
Gabon	2014	12
Mauritania	2014	12
Haiti	2014	12
Ethiopia	2014	12
Laos	2014	12
Burkina Faso	2014	12
Burundi	2015	13
Tunisia	2016	14
Equatorial Guinea	2017	15
Swaziland	2017	15
Republic of Congo	2018	16
Cameroon	2018	16
Togo	2018	16
Pakistan	2018	16
Gambia	2018	16
Angola	2018	16
Bhutan	2018	16
Azerbaijan	2019	17
Rwanda	2019	17
Yemen	2019	17
Eritrea	2019	17
Chad	2019	17
Liberia	2020	18
Zimbabwe*	2021	19
Sudan	2023	21
Uzbekistan	2024	22

Notes: Predicted year of adoption based on the Weibull duration model in column (6), table 2.10, for countries with no deposit insurance in 2002. We also report estimates of the number of years until each country without an EDIS can be expected to adopt deposit insurance under year 2002 circumstances (the last year of our sample period). We could not estimate the expected adoption year for the following countries due to missing information for some of the model variables: Afghanistan, Barbados, Belize, Brunei, Cape Verde,

Table 2.11
(continued)

Comoro Islands, Cuba, Democratic Republic of Congo, Grenada, Hong Kong, Iraq, Israel, Kiribati, Libya, Maldives, Malta, Myanmar, Qatar, Saudi Arabia, Seychelles, Solomon Islands, Somalia, St. Lucia, Suriname, United Arab Emirates, Vanuatu, and Western Samoa. Countries that have adopted deposit insurance since 2002 are marked with an asterisk. Paraguay, Russia, and Zimbabwe have adopted deposit insurance in 2003. Moldova has adopted deposit insurance in 2004. Bolivia has set up a Financial Restructuring Fund in December 2001 that acts as deposit insurance. A proposal for explicit deposit insurance was drafted in 1999 by six Francophone African countries (Cameroon, Central African Republic, Chad, Equatorial Guinea, Gabon, and Republic of Congo) but the proposal has only been ratified by two out of the six countries that together form the Communauté Économique et Monétaire de l'Afrique Centrale (CEMAC). To our knowledge, several countries have considered (or are considering) the adoption of deposit insurance: Australia, New Zealand, Singapore, China, South Africa, Namibia, and Pakistan.

arrangements that, in their particular environments, promised to resolve intersectoral conflict in a more satisfactory way.

2.4   Explaining Deposit Insurance Design

A credible EDIS builds and maintains depositor confidence even in dangerously fragile and broken banks. For this reason, the fairness and efficiency of a country's safety net design may be measured by the extent to which design features promise to preserve the system's financial integrity without either subsidizing or penalizing bank risk taking. Theories of interest group interaction suggest that, in almost every country, society may count on bank clout and lobbying activity to curtail unfair and inefficient restrictions on bank risk taking. However, these same theories suggest that, in many environments, weak and risky banks can use their clout to persuade authorities to subsidize risk (Laeven 2004).

In table 2.12, controlling for macroshocks, crisis experience, and institutional development, we investigate how outside pressure and the political system influence the generosity of system design. By the "generosity" of a design feature, we mean the extent to which empirical evidence summarized in Demirgüç-Kunt and Kane (2002) indicates that its presence or size promotes bank risk taking (i.e., moral hazard). We investigate decisions about the coverage ratio separately because (1) coverage limits are particularly important in controlling moral hazard, and (2) compared to other design features, time series data on coverage are of better quality. However, to recognize that the particular

Table 2.12
Heckman two-step selection model for deposit insurance coverage and other design features

Second stage: Design	Coverage ratio	Coverage ratio adjusted for coinsurance	Coverage limit to deposits	Moral hazard	Moral hazard without coverage
	(1)	(2)	(3)	(4)	(5)
Inflation	−0.004***	−0.004***	−0.003***	−0.002***	−0.001**
	(0.001)	(0.001)	(0.001)	(0.001)	(0.000)
GDP growth	−0.018*	−0.016	−0.021*	0.006	0.006
	(0.010)	(0.010)	(0.013)	(0.010)	(0.010)
GDP per capita	−0.000	0.002	−0.020	0.012	0.013
	(0.011)	(0.011)	(0.015)	(0.011)	(0.010)
External pressure	0.174	0.216	0.358	0.449**	0.465**
	(0.218)	(0.223)	(0.308)	(0.217)	(0.187)
Executive constraints	0.061	0.071	0.059	0.089*	0.088*
	(0.054)	(0.055)	(0.075)	(0.054)	(0.051)
Crisis dummy	0.605***	0.676***	0.564***	0.631***	0.702***
	(0.155)	(0.158)	(0.207)	(0.154)	(0.153)
Postcrisis adoption	0.207	0.190	0.452**	0.191	0.149
	(0.154)	(0.157)	(0.212)	(0.154)	(0.134)
Heckman Lambda	0.980***	1.053***	1.410***	1.037***	1.023***
	(0.346)	(0.353)	(0.482)	(0.349)	(0.310)
First stage: DI					
Inflation	−0.001***	−0.001***	−0.001**	−0.001**	−0.000*
	(0.001)	(0.001)	(0.000)	(0.001)	(0.000)
GDP growth	−0.001	−0.001	−0.004	−0.002	0.001
	(0.006)	(0.006)	(0.006)	(0.006)	(0.005)
GDP per capita	0.050***	0.050***	0.048***	0.051***	0.054***
	(0.003)	(0.003)	(0.003)	(0.003)	(0.003)
External pressure	0.949***	0.949***	0.943***	0.932***	0.931***
	(0.069)	(0.069)	(0.070)	(0.070)	(0.068)
Executive constraints	0.178***	0.178***	0.181***	0.177***	0.183***
	(0.013)	(0.013)	(0.013)	(0.013)	(0.013)
Crisis dummy	0.488***	0.488***	0.472***	0.476***	0.618***
	(0.087)	(0.087)	(0.089)	(0.088)	(0.080)
Postcrisis adoption	0.510***	0.510***	0.515***	0.507***	0.441***
	(0.073)	(0.073)	(0.074)	(0.073)	(0.072)
Number of observations	4,492	4,492	4,435	4,484	4,600
Number of censored observations	3,665	3,665	3,665	3,665	3,665

Table 2.12
(continued)

Notes: This table reports a series of Heckman two-stage selection regressions for design features. The endogenous variable in the first-stage regression (selection equation) is the explicit deposit insurance indicator. The endogenous variable in the second stage (design equation) is the logarithm of the indicated deposit insurance coverage ratio. Coverage ratio is the ratio of coverage limit per person to GDP per capita. Coverage ratio adjusted for coinsurance is the ratio of the effective coverage per person (i.e., adjusting the coverage limit for the percentage of coinsurance) to GDP per capita, where effective coverage is calculated by adjusting the coverage limit by the amount of coinsurance. Coverage limit to deposits is the ratio of coverage limit per person to bank deposits per capita. Moral hazard is an index based on the first principal component of the following design features: *Coverage ratio, Administration, Membership, Foreign currency deposits, Interbank deposits, Coinsurance, Permanent fund*, and *Funding*. All design features have been transformed to standardized variables (with mean zero and standard deviation of one) for the principal component calculations. Moral hazard without coverage is an alternative moral hazard index variable that focuses on design features excluding the coverage ratio. We report Heckman's two-step efficient estimates (1979). Standard errors are shown in brackets. *, **, and *** indicate significance at the 10 percent, 5 percent, and 1 percent level, respectively.

combination of features chosen might mute or reinforce the impact of some of the others, we introduce a variable we call *Moral hazard*, defined as the first principal component of the covariance matrix of the eight individual features listed in section 2.2. We also explore an alternative *Moral hazard without coverage* variable that focuses on design features excluding coverage. In constructing the covariance matrix, all design features are standardized to have a mean of zero and a standard deviation of one.

We estimate decisions about features in a two-stage Heckman selection framework. The first stage is an EDIS selection model, using regressors that represent forces whose significance was established in sections 2.2 and 2.3. We report Heckman's two-step estimates.[7] Although not constrained to be the same across features, first-stage coefficients are virtually identical in all columns. Second-stage regressions incorporate a regressor (an inverse measure of adoption probability called the Heckman Lambda) that accounts for the sample selection bias that would emerge if a single-equation estimator were used and also measures how "surprising" it would be for each country to adopt or not adopt an EDIS. This regressor proves positive and significant for all specifications, confirming that the latent characteristics that make adoption surprising also encourage generosity in design. Wherever they are significant, the second-stage coefficients for determinants of particular features always show the same sign.

The first three specifications in table 2.12 explain (the logarithm of) coverage ratios, while the last two model the moral hazard composites. These regressions show that *External pressure* is a significant determinant of EDIS adoption and the two moral hazard composites. *External pressure* does not have a significant impact on the coverage ratio.[8]

Executive constraints exerts a positive influence on the moral hazard composites, although this effect is marginally significant (at the 10 percent level). This means that countries with more democratic political systems prove not only more likely to adopt an EDIS, but also more likely to install design features that entail substantial moral hazard. Again, the effect on coverage ratios is not significant.

Crises dispose a country to design a more generous EDIS. This is indicated by the positive and significant coefficients the *Crisis dummy* receives in both stages. These results provide further evidence that systems adopted in crises tend to be poorly designed (Hovakimian, Kane, and Laeven 2003).

Among the strictly economic variables, we find that *GDP per capita* increases the probability of adoption, but—except through its incorporation in Heckman's Lambda—has no significant impact on design. Interestingly, *Inflation* proves significant in both stages, and it is the only determinant that seems both to restrain adoption and to promote better design.

Table 2.13 reports predicted coverage ratios for nonadopting countries at year-end 2002. These predictions come from the Heckman two-step model in column (1) of table 2.12. The predicted coverage ratios for this subset of countries ranges from 0.41 for Angola to 1.33 for China, well below the world average of actual coverage ratios of existing deposit insurance schemes, which stood at 2.45 at year-end 2002. This predicted reluctance to provide generous coverage supports the hypothesis that banks in nonadopting countries find it hard to negotiate with other sectors a contract that would prove more advantageous to them than the implicit system that the nonadopting country has in place.

2.5   Summary and Implications

Because banks play a key role in pricing and constraining risk taking in other sectors, a well-regulated banking sector may be characterized as a cornerstone of a well-functioning national economy. Regulatory systems are asked to establish and enforce efficient standards for bank

Table 2.13
Predicted coverage ratios for countries that have not adopted deposit insurance as of year-end 2002

Country	Predicted coverage ratio (2002)
Angola	0.41
Zimbabwe*	0.57
Uzbekistan	0.57
Sudan	0.61
Chad	0.64
Liberia	0.64
Azerbaijan	0.65
Eritrea	0.66
Rwanda	0.67
Bhutan	0.67
Yemen	0.69
Tajikistan	0.69
Mozambique	0.70
Pakistan	0.71
Swaziland	0.72
Cameroon	0.73
Gabon	0.73
Iran	0.73
Laos	0.74
Republic of Congo	0.74
Togo	0.74
Armenia	0.74
Gambia	0.74
Burundi	0.74
Equatorial Guinea	0.75
Burkina Faso	0.75
Tunisia	0.75
Morocco	0.76
Guinea	0.77
Mauritania	0.77
Egypt	0.78
Mali	0.78
Syria	0.78
Ethiopia	0.78
Singapore	0.79
Djibouti	0.81
Cambodia	0.81
Haiti	0.82
Malawi	0.82
Russia*	0.82
Zambia	0.83

Table 2.13
(continued)

Country	Predicted coverage ratio (2002)
Sierra Leone	0.83
Nepal	0.84
Georgia	0.84
Benin	0.85
Ghana	0.85
Namibia	0.87
Central African Republic	0.87
Niger	0.88
Kyrgyz Republic	0.89
Moldova*	0.91
Fiji	0.92
Mongolia	0.92
Guyana	0.93
Côte d'Ivoire	0.94
Senegal	0.95
Mauritius	0.96
Lesotho	0.96
Costa Rica	0.97
South Africa	0.98
Australia	0.98
Botswana	0.98
Panama	0.98
New Zealand	0.99
Guinea-Bissau	0.99
Bolivia*	1.01
Papua New Guinea	1.06
Paraguay*	1.06
Madagascar	1.10
China	1.33

Notes: Predicted coverage ratio based on the Heckman two-step model in column (1), table 2.12, for countries with no deposit insurance in 2002. We could not estimate the expected coverage ratio for the following countries due to missing information for some of the model variables: Afghanistan, Barbados, Belize, Brunei, Cape Verde, Comoro Islands, Cuba, Democratic Republic of Congo, Grenada, Hong Kong, Iraq, Israel, Kiribati, Libya, Maldives, Malta, Myanmar, Qatar, Saudi Arabia, Seychelles, Solomon Islands, Somalia, St. Lucia, Suriname, United Arab Emirates, Vanuatu, and Western Samoa. Countries that have adopted deposit insurance since 2002 are marked with an asterisk. Paraguay, Russia, and Zimbabwe have adopted deposit insurance in 2003. Moldova has adopted deposit insurance in 2004. Bolivia has set up a Financial Restructuring Fund in December 2001 that acts as deposit insurance. A proposal for explicit deposit insurance was drafted in 1999 by six Francophone African countries (Cameroon, Central African Republic, Chad, Equatorial Guinea, Gabon, and Republic of Congo) but the proposal has only been ratified by two out of the six countries that together form the Communauté Économique et Monétaire de l'Afrique Centrale (CEMAC).

behavior. Deposit insurance is an important and potentially construc-tive element of a country's financial safety net.

To study the spread of explicit deposit insurance systems and deter-minants of decisions about adoption and design during recent decades, this chapter reduces selection bias by using data for 170 countries. This more comprehensive sample confirms that richer and more institution-ally developed countries prove more likely to adopt explicit deposit insurance, but also shows that such countries better manage the choice of design features. Among economic control variables, only inflation plays a restraining role.

Analysis also focuses on how outside influences and internal politi-cal factors feed into the intersectoral contracting process. Our results indicate that democratic political processes and external pressure to emulate developed-country regulatory frameworks promote adoption and dispose a country toward generous design. Adoption proves more likely during or after a crisis, presumably because representatives for sectoral interests find it easier to negotiate regulatory reform during distressed times. Unhappily, crisis pressures are likely to result in design features that inadequately control moral hazard. Robustness tests show that these findings are insensitive to the use of different sta-tistical methods, different control variables, and differences in sample coverage.

Overall, the policy lesson is not that deposit insurance is to be avoided, but that it has effective substitutes and takes many forms. Democratic systems—which allow sectoral interests to negotiate more openly with one another—prove more likely to adopt deposit insur-ance and (at least initially) to design it poorly. Ceteris paribus, systems installed in crisis circumstances and in response to external pressures to emulate other countries are especially apt to be poorly designed. Econometrically, recognizing that deposit insurance selection and de-sign decisions are simultaneously determined implies that cross-country studies seeking to determine how the presence or absence of an EDIS affects the performance of a country's financial sector and na-tional economy ought to imbed their performance assessment equation in a larger multiple-equation system of safety net design.

Appendix

Table 2A.1 provides detailed definitions and sources of the variables used in this chapter.

Table 2A.1
Variable definitions and data sources

Variable	Definition	Source
Deposit insurance	Dummy that equals 1 if the country has explicit deposit insurance (including blanket guarantees) and 0 if it has implicit deposit insurance.	Authors' calculation
Coverage ratio	Coverage limit of the EDIS in local currency divided by GDP per capita. Missing for countries with full coverage.	Authors' calculation
Coverage ratio adjusted for coinsurance	Coverage limit of the EDIS adjusted for coinsurance divided by GDP per capita. Missing for countries with full coverage.	Authors' calculation
Coinsurance	Maximum coinsurance percentage of the EDIS. Zero for countries with full coverage.	Authors' calculation
Coverage limit to deposits	Coverage limit of the EDIS in local currency divided by bank deposits per capita. Missing for countries with full coverage.	Authors' calculation
Moral hazard	Principal component of the variables coverage ratio, administration, membership, foreign deposits, interbank deposits, coinsurance, permanent fund, and funding. All variables are standardized with mean of zero and standard deviation of one before conducting the principal component analysis.	Authors' calculation
Moral hazard without coverage	Principal component of the variables administration, membership, foreign deposits, interbank deposits, coinsurance, permanent fund, and funding. All variables are standardized with mean of zero and standard deviation of one before conducting the principal component analysis.	Authors' calculation
Administration	Equals 0 if the administration of the EDIS is private or joint, 1 if it is public, and missing otherwise.	Authors' calculation
Membership	Equals 0 if membership to the EDIS is compulsory to all banks, 1 if it is voluntary, and missing otherwise.	Authors' calculation

Table 2A.1
(continued)

Variable	Definition	Source
Foreign currency deposits	Equals 0 if foreign deposits are not covered by the EDIS, 1 if they are covered, and missing otherwise.	Authors' calculation
Interbank deposits	Equals 0 if Interbank deposits are not covered by the EDIS, 1 if they are covered, and missing otherwise.	Authors' calculation
Coinsurance	Equals 0 if EDIS has coinsurance, 1 if it has no coinsurance, and missing otherwise.	Authors' calculation
Fund	Equals 0 if EDIS but no permanent fund, 1 if permanent fund, and missing otherwise.	Authors' calculation
Funding	Equals 0 if source of funding of the EDIS is private or joint, 1 if it is public, and missing otherwise.	Authors' calculation
Real interest rate	Real interest rate (in percent) equals nominal interest rate minus inflation rate.	IFS (nominal interest rate is the treasury, discount, or deposit rate depending on availability—lines 60c, 60, or 60l) and WDI (inflation rate is the change in the consumer price index)
Inflation	Inflation, GDP deflator (annual percent).	WDI
GDP growth	Real GDP growth rate (in percent).	WDI
Credit growth	Real private credit growth rate (divided by GDP deflator) (in percent).	IFS (private credit is line 32d) and WDI (GDP deflator)
Terms-of-trade change	Percentage change in terms of trade.	WDI
GDP per capita	GDP per capita (constant 1995 thousands of US$).	WDI
External pressure	Dummy variable that takes a value of one for the years 1999 and onwards, the year 1999 being the year that the IMF endorsed deposit insurance by publishing a paper on best practices and guidelines in deposit insurance.	Garcia 2000

Variable	Description	Source
World Bank loan	Dummy variable that takes the value of one during and following the year that the World Bank started an adjustment lending program with the country for reforms to establish deposit insurance (in addition to possibly other objectives), and zero otherwise. This variable takes a value of one for the following countries and periods (between brackets): Albania (2002 and onward), Bolivia (1998 and onward), Bosnia-Herzegovina (1996 and onward), Croatia (1995 and onward), El Salvador (1996 and onward), Jordan (1995 and onward), Lithuania (1996 and onward), Nicaragua (2000 and onward), Poland (1993 and onward), Romania (1996 and onward), Russia (1997 and onward), Ukraine (1998 and onward).	World Bank 2004
EU directive	Dummy variable that takes a value of one for the years 1994 and onwards for EU member countries only (the EU-15), and zero otherwise. The year 1994 was the year when the EU Directive on Deposit Insurance came into force.	EU 1994
EU candidacy	Dummy variable that takes a value of one for the years 1994 and onwards for EU candidate countries only (i.e., Bulgaria, Cyprus, Czech Republic, Estonia, Hungary, Latvia, Lithuania, Malta, Poland, Romania, Slovak Republic, Slovenia), and zero otherwise. The year 1994 was the year when the EU Directive on Deposit Insurance came into force.	EU 1994
Emulation	Proportion of countries with explicit deposit insurance at a given year (in percent).	Authors' calculation
Crisis dummy	Systemic banking crisis dummy equals 1 if the country experiences a systemic crisis in that year and 0 otherwise, from 1976 to October 2003.	Caprio et al. 2005
Postcrisis adoption	Equals 1 if DIS was adopted between zero and three years following a crisis, and 0 otherwise	Caprio et al. 2005
Fiscal cost/GDP	Fiscal cost of banking crisis resolution (as percent of GDP), values reported during the crisis period and 0 otherwise	Caprio et al. 2005

Table 2A.1
(continued)

Variable	Definition	Source
Government ownership	Government ownership of banks in 1970 used for 1970 to 1994 and in 1995 onwards (in percent).	La Porta, Lopez-de-Silanes, and Shleifer 2002
Privatization	Bank privatization dummy equals 1 if first state-owned bank privatization took place.	Boehmer, Nash, and Netter 2005
Bank deposits/GDP	Demand, time and saving deposits in deposit money banks as a share of GDP, calculated using the following deflation method: $\{(0.5) * [D_t/Pe_t + D_{t-1}/Pe_{t-1}]\}/[GDP_t/Pa_t]$, where D is demand and time and saving deposits, Pe is end of period CPI, and Pa is average annual CPI, and t is year t.	Beck, Demirgüç-Kunt, and Levine 2000, Financial Structure Database. Raw data are from the electronic version of the IMF's International Financial Statistics (IFS lines 24 and 25). Data on GDP in local currency (lines 99) and annual CPI (line 64).
Polity score	Index combining democracy and autocracy scores. It ranges from −10 to 10, where negative scores are assigned to countries under autocracies and positive values to countries under democracies and −10 and 10 are the extreme cases of these two systems. Autocracies sharply restrict or suppress competitive political participation. Their chief executives are chosen in a regularized process of selection within the political elite, and once in office they exercise power with few institutional constraints. Democracy is conceived as three essential, interdependent elements. First is the presence of institutions and procedures through which citizens can express effective preferences about alternative policies and leaders. Second is the existence of institutionalized constraints on the exercise of power by the executive. Third is the guarantee of civil liberties to all citizens in their daily lives and in acts of political participation.	Polity IV, INSCR Program, CIDCM, University of Maryland, College Park

Term	Description	Source
Executive constraints	Index measuring the extent of institutionalized constraints on the decision-making powers of chief executives. Such limitations may be imposed by any accountability group. The index ranges from 1 to 7, where 1 represents unlimited authority and 7 executive parity or subordination.	Polity IV, INSCR Program, CIDCM, University of Maryland, College Park
Political competition	Index combining regulation of participation and competitiveness of participation scores. It ranges from 1 to 10, where higher scores represent more political competition. Participation is regulated to the extent that there are binding rules on when, whether, and how political preferences are expressed. One-party states and Western democracies both regulate participation but they do so in different ways, the former by channeling participation through a single party structure, with sharp limits on diversity of opinion; the latter by allowing relatively stable and enduring groups to compete nonviolently for political influence. The polar opposite is unregulated participation, in which there are no enduring national political organizations and no effective regime controls on political activity. In such situations political competition is fluid and often characterized by recurring coercion among shifting coalitions of partisan groups. The competitiveness of participation refers to the extent to which alternative preferences for policy and leadership can be pursued in the political arena.	Polity IV, INSCR Program, CIDCM, University of Maryland, College Park
Bureaucracy	Index measuring the institutional strength and quality of the bureaucracy. It ranges from 0 to 4. High scores are given to countries where the bureaucracy has the strength and expertise to govern without drastic changes in policy or interruptions in government services. In these low-risk countries, the bureaucracy tends to be somewhat autonomous from political pressure and to have an established mechanism for recruitment and training. Countries that lack the cushioning effect of a strong bureaucracy receive low scores because a change in government tends to be traumatic in terms of policy formulation and day-to-day administrative functions.	International Country Risk Guide (ICRG)

Table 2A.1
(continued)

Variable	Definition	Source
Corruption	Index measuring the extent to which bribery is present within the political system. Forms of corruption considered are related to bribes in the areas of exchange controls, tax assessments, police protection, loans, and licensing of exports and imports. It ranges from 0 to 6, where low scores indicate high levels of corruption.	International Country Risk Guide (ICRG)
Democratic accountability	Index measuring how responsive government is to its people, on the basis that the less responsive it is, the more likely it is that the government will fall, peacefully in a democratic society, but possibly violently in a nondemocratic one. It ranges from 0 to 6, where 0 is assigned to autarchies and 6 to alternating democracies.	International Country Risk Guide (ICRG)
Law and order	Index measuring a country's legal system and rule of law. It ranges from 0 to 6, where a high score indicates high level of law and order. Law and order are assessed separately, with each subcomponent comprising zero to three points. The law subcomponent is an assessment of the strength and impartiality of the legal system while the order subcomponent is an assessment of popular observance of law.	International Country Risk Guide (ICRG)

Note: Whenever we indicate the data source as "Authors' calculation," we refer to the data section of this chapter.

Acknowledgments

We are grateful to Thorsten Beck, Stijn Claessens, Mark Flannery, Patrick Honohan, Ozer Karagedikli, and Loretta Mester for comments. For additional suggestions, we also want to thank seminar participants at the Reserve Bank of New Zealand, Victoria University of Wellington, the FDIC Center for Financial Research's Fifth Annual Banking Research Conference, and the 2005 AFA meetings in Philadelphia. We thank Baybars Karacaovali and Guillermo Noguera for helping to construct the new database and for providing excellent research assistance, and we thank numerous colleagues at the World Bank for providing input for the deposit insurance database.

Notes

1. Kroszner and Strahan (2001) review competing political economy views of deposit insurance.

2. See for example, Diamond and Dybvig 1983, Ronn and Verma 1986, Pennacchi 1987, Chari and Jagannathan 1988, Cooperstein, Pennacchi, and Stevens 1995, Kane 1995, Wheelock and Wilson 1995, Calomiris 1996, Bhattacharya, Boot, and Thakor 1998, Allen and Gale 1998, and Pennacchi 2006.

3. However, we do allow for correlation among errors for each country by estimating logit using clustered errors at the country level.

4. Because *Emulation* and *External pressure* are very highly correlated at 80 percent, we exclude *Emulation* from column (8).

5. Demirgüç-Kunt and Detragiache (2002) show that bank crisis probabilities increase with the adoption and generous design of an EDIS. Their results are robust to (1) restricting the sample to countries that only adopted deposit insurance previous to crises and excluding crisis periods, and (2) estimating a two-equation model where *Emulation* serves as the instrument for the first stage adoption model. Thus, while EDIS is more likely to be adopted as a result of crises, adoption directly increases fragility.

6. In 1970, twenty-nine countries out of ninety-two (31.5 percent) had more than 90 percent government ownership of banks. In 1995, eleven countries out of ninety-two (12.0 percent) had more than 90 percent government ownership of banks. In 1970, only one country (India) of the twenty-nine countries with more than 90 percent government ownership of banks had an explicit deposit insurance system in place. In 1995, two of the eleven countries with more than 90 percent government ownership of banks had an EDIS.

7. We obtain qualitatively similar results when using maximum likelihood to estimate the Heckman selection model.

8. See Demirgüç-Kunt, Kane, and Laeven 2007 on how external pressure from different sources affects system design.

References

Allen, Franklin, and Douglas Gale. 1998. Optimal Banking Crises. *Journal of Finance* 53 (4): 1245–1284.

Beck, Thorsten, Aslı Demirgüç-Kunt, and Ross Levine. 2000. A New Database on the Structure and Development of the Financial Sector. *World Bank Economic Review* 14 (3): 597–605. Updated versions available at econ.worldbank.org/programs/finance.

Becker, Garry S. 1983. A Theory of Competition among Pressure Groups for Political Influence. *Quarterly Journal of Economics* 98: 371–400.

Bhattacharya, Sudipto, Arnoud W. A. Boot, and Anjan V. Thakor. 1998. The Economics of Bank Regulation. *Journal of Money, Credit and Banking* 30 (4): 745–770.

Boehmer, E., R. Nash, and J. Netter. 2005. Bank Privatization and Developing and Developed Countries: Cross-Sectional Evidence on the Impact of Economic and Political Factors. *Journal of Banking and Finance* (August–September): 1981–2013.

Calomiris, Charles. 1996. Building an Incentive-Compatible Safety Net: Special Problems for Developing Countries. Mimeo., Columbia University.

Calomiris, Charles, and Eugene White. 1994. The Origins of Federal Deposit Insurance. In *The Regulated Economy: A Historical Approach to Political Economy*, ed. Claudia Goldin and Gary Libecap, 145–188. Chicago: University of Chicago Press.

Caprio, Gerard, Daniela Klingebiel, Luc Laeven, and Guillermo Noguera. 2005. Banking Crisis Database. In *Systemic Financial Crises: Containment and Resolution*, ed. Patrick Honohan and Luc Laeven, 307–340. New York: Cambridge University Press.

Chari, Varadarajan V., and Ravi Jagannathan. 1988. Banking Panics, Information, and Rational Expectations Equilibrium. *Journal of Finance* 43: 749–761.

Cooperstein, Richard, George Pennacchi, and Redburn Stevens. 1995. The Aggregate Cost of Deposit Insurance: A Multiperiod Analysis. *Journal of Financial Intermediation* 4 (3): 242–271.

Cox, David. 1972. Regression Models and Life Tables (with Discussion). *Journal of the Royal Statistical Society*, Series B 34: 187–220.

Cull, Robert, Lemma Senbet, and Marco Sorge. 2005. Deposit Insurance and Financial Development. *Journal of Money, Credit and Banking* 37 (1): 43–82.

Demirgüç-Kunt, Aslı, and Enrica Detragiache. 2002. Does Deposit Insurance Increase Banking System Stability? An Empirical Investigation. *Journal of Monetary Economics* 49: 1373–1406.

Demirgüç-Kunt, Aslı, and Harry Huizinga. 2004. Market Discipline and Deposit Insurance. *Journal of Monetary Economics* 51: 375–399.

Demirgüç-Kunt, Aslı, and Edward Kane. 2002. Deposit Insurance around the World: Where Does It Work? *Journal of Economic Perspectives* 16: 175–195.

Demirgüç-Kunt, Aslı, Edward J. Kane, and Luc Laeven. 2007. Determinants of Deposit-Insurance Adoption and Design. Forthcoming in *Journal of Financial Intermediation*.

Demirgüç-Kunt, Aslı, and Tolga Sobaci. 2001. A New Development Database. Deposit Insurance around the World. *World Bank Economic Review* 15: 481–490.

Diamond, Douglas, and Philip Dybvig. 1983. Bank Runs, Deposit Insurance and Liquidity. *Journal of Political Economy* 91: 401–419.

European Commission. 1994. *Directive 94/19/EC of the European Parliament and of the Council of 30 May 1994 on Deposit-Guarantee Schemes.* O.J., L135, 5–14.

Folkerts-Landau, David, and Carl-Johan Lindgren. 1998. Toward a Framework for Financial Stability. Mimeo., International Monetary Fund, Washington, D.C.

Garcia, Gillian G. 1999. Deposit Insurance: Actual and Best Practices. IMF Working Paper no. 99/54, International Monetary Fund, Washington D.C.

Garcia, Gillian G. 2000. Deposit Insurance: Actual and Good Practices. Occasional Paper no. 197, International Monetary Fund, Washington D.C.

Heckman, James. 1979. Sample Selection Bias as a Specification Error. *Econometrica* 47 (1): 153–161.

Honohan, Patrick, and Daniela Klingebiel. 2003. The Fiscal Cost Implications of an Accommodating Approach to Banking Crises. *Journal of Banking and Finance* 27 (8): 1539–1560.

Hovakimian, Armen, Edward Kane, and Luc Laeven. 2003. How Country and Safety-Net Characteristics Affect Bank Risk-Shifting. *Journal of Financial Services Research* 23: 177–204.

Kane, Edward J. 1995. Three Paradigms for the Role of Capitalization Requirements in Insured Financial Institutions. *Journal of Banking and Finance* 19 (3–4): 431–459.

Kane, Edward J., and Daniela Klingebiel. 2004. Alternatives to Blanket Guarantees for Containing a Systemic Crisis. *Journal of Financial Stability* 1: 31–63.

Kane, Edward J., and Berry K. Wilson. 1998. A Contracting-Theory Interpretation of the Origins of Federal Deposit Insurance. *Journal of Money, Credit, and Banking* 30: 573–595.

Kroszner, Randall S., and Philip Strahan. 2001. Obstacles to Optimal Policy: The Interplay of Politics and Economics in Shaping Bank Supervision and Regulation Reforms. In *Prudential Supervision: What Works and What Doesn't*, ed. Frederick S. Mishkin, 233–273. Chicago: University of Chicago Press.

Kroszner, Randall S., and Thomass Stratmann. 1998. Interest Group Competition and the Organization of Congress: Theory and Evidence from Financial Services' Political Action Committees. *American Economic Review* 88: 1163–1187.

La Porta, Rafael, Florencio Lopez-de-Silanes, and Andrei Shleifer. 2002. Government Ownership of Banks. *Journal of Finance* 57: 265–301.

Laeven, Luc. 2002. Bank Risk and Deposit Insurance. *World Bank Economic Review* 16: 109–137.

Laeven, Luc. 2004. The Political Economy of Deposit Insurance. *Journal of Financial Services Research* 26 (3): 201–224.

Lin, Danyu and Lee-Jen Wei. 1989. The Robust Inference for the Cox Proportional Hazards Model, *Journal of the American Statistical Association* 84: 1074–1078.

Peltzman, Sam. 1976. Toward a More General Theory of Regulation. *Journal of Law and Economics* 19: 109–148.

Pennacchi, George, 1987. A Reexamination of the Over- (or Under-) Pricing of Deposit Insurance. *Journal of Money, Credit, and Banking* 19 (3): 340–360.

Pennacchi, George. 2006. Deposit Insurance, Bank Regulation, and Financial System Risks. *Journal of Monetary Economics* 53 (1): 1–30.

Ronn, Ehud I., and Avinash K. Verma. 1986. Pricing Risk-Adjusted Deposit Insurance: An Option-Based Model. *Journal of Finance* 41: 871–895.

Stigler, George J. 1971. The Theory of Economic Regulation. *Bell Journal of Economics and Management Science* 2: 3–21.

Wheelock, David C., and Paul W. Wilson. 1995. Explaining Bank Failures: Deposit Insurance, Regulation, and Efficiency. *Review of Economics and Statistics* 77 (4): 689–700.

World Bank. 2004. Deposit Insurance—Reforms Supported by the World Bank during the Period 1993–2004. Mimeo., Operations Evaluation Department, The World Bank, Washington, D.C.

3   Pricing of Deposit Insurance

Luc Laeven

3.1   Introduction

Recently, many countries have implemented deposit insurance schemes and many more countries are planning to do so. The design of this part of the financial safety net differs across countries, especially in account coverage. Countries that introduce explicit deposit insurance make many decisions: which classes of deposits to insure and up to what amount, which banks should participate, who should manage and own the deposit insurance fund, and at what levels premiums should be set. When countries elect not to introduce explicit deposit insurance, insurance is implicit. In either case, the benefits banks gain depend on how effective the government is at managing bank risk shifting.

Explicit deposit insurance schemes appeal increasingly to policymakers. First, an explicit scheme supposedly sets the rules of the game regarding coverage, participants, and funding. Second, an explicit scheme is appealing to politicians because it protects small depositors without immediate impact on the government budget. One should, however, not ignore the potential cost of deposit insurance. Deposit insurance reduces the incentives for (large) depositors to exert market discipline on banks, and encourages banks to take on risk. This form of moral hazard has received a lot of attention in the deposit insurance literature.[1]

In this chapter, we investigate how different design features of deposit insurance schemes affect the price of deposit insurance. Questions abound: What is a "fair" price of deposit insurance and how to estimate it? How costly is deposit insurance? Who is to pay for bank losses and bank systemic risk? How does financial regulation, including risk-based capital requirements, change the way deposit insurance is priced? Should the existence of a reserve fund change the price of deposit insurance? Can deposit insurance be priced for banks lacking publicly traded securities? Should the design and effectiveness of bank resolution affect deposit insurance? The goals of the chapter are three-fold: (1) to present several methodologies that can be used to set benchmarks for the pricing level of deposit insurance in a country; (2) to quantify how specific design features affect the price of deposit insurance; and (3) and to assess whether premiums of current deposit insurance pricing schemes are adequate to cover costs.

Throughout the chapter we refer to the funding of deposit insurance as the actual contributions by banks to cover deposits and to the pricing of deposit insurance as the actuarially fair price of deposit insurance. Actual contributions can be made on an ex ante basis, in which case contributions are typically accumulated towards a deposit insurance fund or reserve, or on an ex post basis, in which case banks pay deposit insurance premiums or levies only after bank failures occur. Actual contributions by banks can differ substantially from estimates of the actuarially fair price of deposit insurance for several reasons. First, deposit insurance can be over- or underpriced. Second, the estimate of the fair price of deposit insurance may be biased. Third, the government may contribute funds or issue guarantees on certain bank liabilities. And fourth, actual contributions are not always smoothed over time, unlike fair premiums that are typically calculated as annual annuities. For instance, many countries establish target fund levels. Once the fund achieves its target level, contributions may be (close to) zero. Also, countries may decide to set contributions high initially in order to quickly reach a certain minimum fund size.

The academic foundations for measuring the value of deposit insurance lie in Merton (1977), who models deposit insurance as a put option on the value of the bank's assets. Most of the empirical literature on deposit insurance has either focused on the issue of over- or underpricing of deposit insurance or on how different design features affect the effectiveness of deposit insurance. No study thus far has systematically investigated how the different design features affect the value of deposit insurance, and therefore its pricing.

In countries with explicit deposit insurance, deposit insurance is underpriced (overpriced) if the deposit insurer actually charges less (more) for its services than the estimated opportunity cost value of these services. Underpricing of deposit insurance services is a sign that banks extract deposit insurance subsidies. Marcus and Shaked (1984)

use Merton's (1977) theoretical model of deposit insurance to estimate the actuarially "fair" value of deposit insurance. By comparing
these implicit premiums with the official insurance premiums for U.S.
banks they test empirically whether deposit insurance is over- or
underpriced.[2]

The effectiveness of deposit insurance has been shown to be country-
specific. Demirgüç-Kunt and Huizinga (2004) offer empirical evidence
that explicit deposit insurance introduces a trade-off between the benefits of increased depositor safety and the costs of reduced creditor discipline. Demirgüç-Kunt and Detragiache (2002) find cross-country
evidence that explicit deposit insurance increases the probability of
banking crises in countries with weak institutional environments.
Kane (2000) argues that the design of a country's financial safety net
should take country-specific factors into account, in particular differences in informational environments and the enforceability of private
contracts. Demirgüç-Kunt and Kane (2002) argue that explicit deposit
insurance should not be adopted in countries with a weak institutional
environment: "In any country, explicit deposit insurance threatens to
displace more private discipline than official oversight can generate. In
strong contracting environments, officials usually manage to avoid this
result." This literature also argues against prefunding deposit insurance in a weak institutional environment, as the evidence suggests
that losses will be high in this case. In countries with weak institutions,
these funds can literally be looted. This chapter does not challenge
this view, but rather argues that for countries that have adopted or
are adopting deposit insurance and have decided to prefund it, pricing it as accurately as possible is important. Consistent with this literature, we find that many countries cannot afford fairly priced deposit
insurance.

Laeven (2002b) investigates how country-specific and bank-specific
features contribute to the opportunity cost value of deposit insurance
services, with a special focus on the comparison of the opportunity
cost value of deposit insurance services in countries with explicit deposit insurance and countries without explicit deposit insurance.
Laeven (2002b) finds that the opportunity cost value of deposit insurance services is higher in countries with explicit deposit insurance. The
detrimental impact of explicit deposit insurance is largely offset in
countries with high-quality and well-enforced legal systems, and the
value of deposit insurance is found to be higher for banks with concentrated ownership. Hovakimian, Kane, and Laeven (2003) investigate

the effectiveness of private and governmental controls on bank risk-shifting incentives across a large sample of countries. Their results show that significant portions of the variation in the effectiveness of risk control are explained by differences in contracting environments. On balance, explicit deposit insurance expands risk-shifting opportunities in poor contracting environments, but this effect is reduced in systems that impose appropriate combinations of loss-sharing rules, risk-sensitive premiums, and coverage limits. They also find that recent adopters of explicit insurance have done a particularly poor job of replacing the private discipline that explicit insurance displaced.

Political economy factors cannot be ignored when analyzing financial safety net design. After all, the process underlying the adoption and design of deposit insurance is a complex interplay of various political constituencies with often conflicting interests. The pricing of deposit insurance not only affects banks' depositors, but also banks' other stakeholders, such as shareholders, creditors, bank managers, the deposit insurance agency, the government, and taxpayers. Each of these groups will pursue their own interests that need not be aligned with the public interest. For example, banks will lobby the government for subsidized (underpriced) deposit insurance. The public interest motives for adopting deposit insurance typically include the provision of protection for small depositors and the enhancement of public confidence in the banking system and systemic financial stability. These goals come at large costs, both direct costs in the form of a tax and indirect costs due to increased moral hazard in the behavior of banks.

External pressure can also affect the decision to adopt deposit insurance (cf. chapter 2). The European Union (EU) accession countries of Central and Eastern Europe were politically motivated to adopt deposit insurance because of the EU Directive on Deposit Insurance of 1994, which imposes minimum standards on national deposit insurance policies in the EU member countries, including a minimum covered amount of €20,000 per individual. All countries in Central and Eastern Europe have since adopted deposit insurance (Hungary being the first in 1993, and Moldova being the last in 2004), even those countries that are not EU candidate countries. The EU accession countries of Central and Eastern Europe have been "encouraged" to raise their coverage levels to a minimum of €20,000 in preparation for full membership in the EU.[3] The drive to comply with EU standards is clearly a politically motivated external factor that has led to coverage levels of deposit insurance that are relatively high for some of these countries if compared to their income levels.[4] Many of these countries now face the problem that the risk embedded in their banking systems and the stipulated coverage levels demand excessively high deposit insurance premiums that most banks in these countries simply cannot afford to pay on the basis of their income, and as a result the premature, high levels of coverage have led to underpricing of deposit insurance in a number of EU accession countries (see also section 3.4). Outside Europe, many countries have adopted deposit insurance because they were advised to do so by international financial institutions, such as the International Monetary Fund (IMF).[5] A full review and analysis of how political economy factors affect the pricing and design of deposit insurance is beyond the scope of this chapter. We refer to Kroszner 1998, Kroszner and Stratmann 1998, and Laeven 2004 for a more detailed discussion of these issues.

The chapter is organized as follows. Section 3.2 describes several methods to price the value of deposit insurance. Section 3.3 presents several examples and case studies on how different design features of deposit insurance affect its pricing structure. Section 3.4 investigates whether deposit insurance is underpriced around the world. Section 3.5 summarizes our findings, translates some of our findings in good practices for deposit insurance, and concludes.

3.2   Deposit Insurance Pricing Methods

Several methods exist to price deposit insurance. Central to any deposit insurance pricing method is a methodology to estimate the risk of the value of a bank's assets. To estimate bank risk and set deposit insurance premiums, regulators typically use (a combination of) qualitative indicators collected from on-site and off-site bank examinations, together with accounting-based indicators, such as CAMEL-type indicators.

In the academic literature, several methods have been developed that make use of market-based indicators. Most of these methods are based on Merton's (1977) option pricing model that models deposit insurance as a put option on the bank's assets. This model is attractive from an academic point of view, because it is based on a theoretical framework that establishes a direct link between the value of the deposit insurance contract and the value of the bank's assets, and because it uses the market's assessment of the value of the bank's equity and assets rather than accounting values. The basic model in Merton 1977 has been extended by several authors to include different design features of the deposit insurance contract and to deal with several practical estimation problems when implementing the model. We will discuss each of these models in the following section.

Another approach of pricing deposit insurance is known as "expected loss pricing." This credit risk modeling approach is centered around the expected default probability of a bank, which can be estimated using fundamental analysis and/or market analysis. Fundamental analysis is typically based on CAMEL-type ratings, and thus on accounting values. Market analysis is typically based on interest rates or yields of uninsured bank debt, such as certificates of deposits (CDs), interbank deposits, subordinated debt, and/or debentures. Default probabilities are generally estimated on the basis of a credit risk model for banks with traded debt instruments or credit ratings.

If markets are efficient, market prices reflect their true value, meaning that all relevant and ascertainable information is reflected in asset prices.[6] Therefore, in countries with well-developed capital markets, market-based models are to be preferred over accounting-based models of deposit insurance. However, the application of market-based models of deposit insurance is limited. First, market-based models may give poor estimates of asset risk in countries with underdeveloped (illiquid) capital markets. Second, market-based information is not available for all banks. For example, market value of equity are only available for listed banks, and debenture yields are available only for banks that have issued debentures. For these reasons, practical models of pricing deposit insurance typically embed both market-based and accounting-based information.[7]

In the next sections, we introduce the Merton (1977) option pricing model of deposit insurance (and several of its implementations and extensions) and the expected loss pricing approach to pricing deposit insurance.

3.2.1 Merton's (1977) Limited-Term Put Option Model of Deposit Insurance

In this section we describe Merton's (1977) model of deposit insurance that can be used to calculate the implicit value of deposit insurance, and the implementations of the model by Ronn and Verma (1986). Merton (1977) shows that the payoff of a perfectly credible third-party guarantee on the payment to the bondholders of a firm where there is no uncertainty about the obligation of the guarantee being met is identical to that of a put option, where the promised debt payment corresponds to the exercise price, and the value of the firm's assets V corresponds to the underlying asset.[8]

In applying this model to a bank, Merton substitutes corporate debt for bank deposits and interprets deposit insurance as a third-party guarantee on deposits, where there is no uncertainty about the obligation of the guarantee being met. He shows that the payoff structure to the bank of this guarantee is identical to that of a put option on the value of the bank's assets with exercise price equal to the bank's deposits. Because most deposits are due on demand, the maturity of deposit debt is very short. Customarily, the maturity of the option is conceived as the time until the next audit of the bank's assets. Two more assumptions are made in the Merton model. First, it is assumed that deposits equal total bank debt and that principal and interest are both fully insured and therefore riskless. In reality, bank liabilities typically include not only insured deposits but also uninsured deposits and other liabilities. Second, the bank's asset value is assumed to exhibit geometric Brownian motion

$$d \ln V_t = \mu \, dt + \sigma \, dW_t, \tag{1}$$

where V is the value of assets, μ is the instantaneous expected return on assets, σ is instantaneous expected standard deviation of assets returns, and W indicates a standard Wiener process. This allows us to use the Black and Scholes (1973) option pricing model to value the deposit insurance per unit of deposits

$$g = \Phi(\sigma\sqrt{T-t} - h_t) - \frac{(1-\delta)V_t}{D}\Phi(-h_t), \tag{2}$$

where $h_t = \left(\ln\left(\frac{(1-\delta)V_t}{D}\right) + \frac{\sigma^2}{2}(T-t) \right) \Big/ \sigma\sqrt{T-t}$,

g is the value of the deposit insurance guarantee per dollar of insured deposits, Φ is the cumulative normal distribution function, T is the time until maturity of the bank debt, t is time, D is the face value of the bank debt, and δ is the annualized dividend yield.

To apply the model, values have to be assigned to two unobservable variables: the bank's asset value V and the volatility parameter σ. Ronn and Verma (1986) generate proxy values for these unknowns from two identifying restrictions. The first restriction comes from modeling the directly observable equity value of the bank as a call option on the bank's assets with a strike price equal to the value of bank debt

$$E_t = V_t\Phi(d_t) - D\Phi(d_t - \sigma\sqrt{T-t}), \tag{3}$$

where $d_t = \left(\ln\left(\dfrac{V_t}{D}\right) + \dfrac{\sigma^2}{2}(T - t) \right) \bigg/ \sigma\sqrt{T - t}.$

Ronn and Verma (1986) model equity as being dividend protected and therefore dividends do not appear in the equation (3). Note that if dividends are zero, that $h_t = d_t$.

The relationship between the equity and asset volatility implied by the call valuation becomes the second restriction

$$\sigma = \frac{\sigma_E E_t}{V_t \Phi(d_t)}, \tag{4}$$

where σ_E is the standard deviation of equity returns.[9] Since the market value of equity is observable and the equity volatility can be estimated, two nonlinear restrictions are now in place for identifying two unknowns.

Data on total debt, bank equity, and equity volatility allow equations (3) and (4) to be solved simultaneously for the value of the bank's assets, V, and the volatility of asset returns, σ. From these two values, the value of deposit insurance per unit of deposits can be calculated using equation (2).[10] The Ronn and Verma (1986) method uses the sample standard deviation of daily stock returns as an estimator for instantaneous equity volatility. Duan (1994) points out that this is not an efficient estimator for instantaneous equity volatility. When using the Ronn and Verma (1986) method, it is therefore recommended to use high frequency data to improve the efficiency of the estimator.

Thus far, we have assumed that the next audit of the bank will take place in one year, and that the debt matures at the audit date. We have thus modeled deposit insurance as a limited-term contract. Since it is likely that the government will give the bank some forbearance after it finds out that the bank is undercapitalized modeling deposit insurance as a one year contract is restrictive. It is clear that the value of insurance is higher if the audit indicates that a bank is undercapitalized and the government gives the bank forbearance instead of forcing it to immediately increase its capital ratio.

Ronn and Verma (1986) incorporate capital forbearance by the bank regulators by permitting asset values to deteriorate to a certain share of debt value, $\rho < 1$, before the option kicks in. More specifically, Ronn and Verma (1986) assume a closure rule of $V \leq \rho D$, where V is the value of the bank's assets, D is the value of the bank's debt, and ρ is the regulatory forbearance parameter. In essence, the Ronn and Verma (1986) specification transfers $(1 - \rho)$ times the bank's expected debt repayment as risk capital to stockholders, irrespective of the bank's financial status.[11] With the $V \leq \rho D$ closure rule, the modified model is

$$E_t = V_t \Phi(d_t') - \rho D \Phi(d_t' - \sigma\sqrt{T-t}), \tag{5}$$

where $d_t' = \left(\ln\left(\dfrac{V_t}{\rho D}\right) + \dfrac{\sigma^2}{2}(T-t) \right) \Big/ \sigma\sqrt{T-t}$, and

$$\sigma = \frac{\sigma_E E_t}{V_t \Phi(d_t')}. \tag{6}$$

Ronn and Verma (1986) estimate instantaneous equity volatility by the sample standard deviation of daily equity returns and therefore impose equity volatility to be constant. Duan (1994, 2000) points out that such a premise is inconsistent with the underlying theoretical model of Merton (1977) where equity volatility is stochastic. Therefore, the Ronn and Verma (1986) estimator does not possess the properties such as consistency and efficiency normally expected from a sound statistical procedure. Duan (1994, 2000) has developed a maximum likelihood framework to estimate the value of the deposit insurance that allows equity volatility that is stochastic. The Duan (1994, 2000) method has been applied to a large sample of banks by Laeven (2002a). Duan (1994, 2000) maintains the assumption that the value of the bank's assets V follows Brownian motion. By this process, the one-period transition density of the unobserved values of the bank's assets can be characterized by $\ln(V_{t+1}/V_t) \sim N(\mu, \sigma^2)$. It follows that the log likelihood function for a sample of unobserved asset values V_t can be expressed as

$$L_V(V_t, t = 1, \ldots, n; \mu, \sigma)$$

$$= -\frac{n-1}{2} \ln(2\pi\sigma^2) - \sum_{t=2}^{n} \ln V_t - \frac{1}{2\sigma^2} \sum_{t=2}^{n} \left[\ln\left(\frac{V_t}{V_{t-1}}\right) - \mu \right]^2. \tag{7}$$

Using the call option formula in (3), one can write the log likelihood function for the observed sample of equity values as

$$L(E_t, t = 1, \ldots, n; \mu, \sigma) = -\frac{n-1}{2} \ln(2\pi\sigma^2) - \sum_{t=2}^{n} \ln(\hat{V}_t(\sigma)\Phi(\hat{d}_t))$$

$$- \frac{1}{2\sigma^2} \sum_{t=2}^{n} \left[\ln\left(\frac{\hat{V}_t(\sigma)}{\hat{V}_{t-1}(\sigma)}\right) - \mu \right]^2, \tag{8}$$

where $\hat{V}_t(\sigma)$ is the unique solution to (3) for any σ, and $\hat{d}_t$ corresponds to d_t with $\hat{V}_t(\sigma)$ in place of V_t. With the log likelihood function in (8), an iterative optimization routine can be used to compute the maximum likelihood estimates of $\hat{\mu}$ and $\hat{\sigma}$, which in turn can be used to solve for the value of the guarantee per dollar of deposits and its standard error. The asymptotic distribution of the estimator for the deposit insurance premium is reported in Duan 1994, 2000.

As an alternative to risk-based deposit insurance premiums, Kuester King and O'Brien (1991) consider a risk-adjusted examination schedule whereby riskier banks are examined more frequently with the possibility of closure or regulatory action following each examination. They show how Merton's (1977) framework can be used to derive such a risk-adjusted examination schedule. In essence, rather than setting different prices for deposit insurance, this approach sets different examination frequencies.

For several reasons, Merton's (1977) option pricing model of deposit insurance gives downward biased estimates of the benefits bank stockholders derive from the safety net. First, the basic model in Merton (1977) ignores the possibility of regulatory forbearance. Ronn and Verma (1986) incorporate capital forbearance by the bank regulators by permitting asset values to deteriorate to a given percentage of debt value before the option kicks in. However, the level of regulatory control is unknown ex ante which makes it difficult to incorporate the Ronn and Verma (1986) model. Moreover, as Laeven (2000b) points out, the level of forbearance is likely to vary across countries. It is likely that regulatory control is weaker in countries with weak banks, so that one would underestimate the value of deposit insurance to the most risky banks.

Second, by imposing prompt option settlement, Merton's (1977) single-period model of a limited-term option contract understates stockholder benefits from deposit insurance more than multiperiod models do. The counterfactual assumption of a limited-term option contract is that at the time of an audit the bank's insurance premium is adjusted to a new actuarially fair rate, as in a variable rate insurance scheme, and/or that the bank's capital ratio is adjusted back to its minimum required level. Merton (1978) extends the standard single-period model of deposit insurance to a multiperiod setting by treating deposit insurance as an infinite maturity put option. In Merton's model, the government randomly audits banks and closes banks if they become economically insolvent. We describe Merton's (1978) model in more detail in the next section. Pennacchi (1987a, 1987b) allows for unlimited term contracts and shows that the assumption of a limited-term contract in a single-period model can underestimate the value of deposit insurance.

Third, Kane (1995) argues that option pricing models suffer from treating banking risk as exogenous, from presuming the possibility of accurate risk measurement and ex ante pricing, and from modeling deposit insurance as a bilateral contract between the insurer and the bank, thereby ignoring the agency conflicts that arise from the difficulty of enforcing capitalization requirements in a multilateral nexus of contracts. In reality, there is no market for options in open–ended commitments if banking risk cannot be observed and controlled on a continuous basis, even in well-developed capital markets.

Ronn and Verma (1986) emphasize that the option-based approach lends itself more readily to cross-sectional comparisons of risks across banks rather than assessing under- or overpricing of deposit insurance. They find that the rank orderings of banks remain robust to changes in model specifications, such as periodicity of audit and degree of forbearance.

Application of the Merton (1977) Model   Next, we illustrate how deposit insurance premiums vary by input parameters in the theoretical model of Merton (1977). For simplicity we assume that dividends are zero, and that the time until the next audit (the maturity of the put option) equals one. In that case, it follows from equation (2) that the theoretical deposit insurance premium per unit of deposits (at time zero) depends only on the asset volatility, σ, and the financial leverage, D/V, of the bank. Panel A in table 3.1 presents the deposit insurance premium per U.S. dollar of deposits (in percentage points). For example, for a bank with asset volatility of 4 percent per annum and a value of bank assets equal to 105 percent of the value of bank debt, the deposit insurance premium equals 0.22 percent of total bank deposits. We find that as leverage increases, or as V/D decreases, that the per deposit premium of deposit insurance tends to increase. We also find that greater asset volatility increases the per deposit premium of deposit insurance.

To assess more precisely the sensitivity of the estimate of actuarially fair premiums to changes in financial leverage or asset volatility it can be useful to calculate the Delta (Δ) and the Vega of the deposit insurance put option contract. The Δ represents the rate of change of the

Table 3.1
Deposit insurance premiums in the Merton (1977) model Premiums are expressed in percentage points of deposits. Dividends are assumed zero. Time until the next audit (T) equals one. Time indicator (t) equals zero.

σ V/D	1%	2%	3%	4%	5%	10%	15%	20%	25%
0.90	10.00	10.00	10.00	10.00	10.03	10.71	12.02	13.59	15.27
0.95	5.00	5.00	5.05	5.18	5.39	6.89	8.67	10.52	12.40
1.00	0.40	0.80	1.20	1.60	1.99	3.99	5.98	7.97	9.95
1.05	0.00	0.00	0.07	0.22	0.45	2.06	3.95	5.91	7.89
1.10	0.00	0.00	0.00	0.01	0.06	0.95	2.50	4.29	6.19
1.15	0.00	0.00	0.00	0.00	0.00	0.39	1.52	3.06	4.81
1.20	0.00	0.00	0.00	0.00	0.00	0.15	0.89	2.15	3.71

deposit insurance premium with respect to the value of bank assets, and the Vega is the rate of change in the price of deposit insurance with respect to the volatility of bank assets. Assuming dividends are zero, a the time until maturity is one year $(T = 1)$, and keeping the value of deposits constant, Δ is given by

$$\Delta = \frac{\partial g}{\partial V} = \Phi(\tilde{h}_t) - 1,$$ (9)

and Vega is given by

$$Vega = \frac{\partial g}{\partial V} = V\Phi'(\tilde{h}_t) = \frac{V \exp(-\tilde{h}_t^2/2)}{\sqrt{2\pi}},$$ (10)

where $\tilde{h}_t = \left(\ln\left(\frac{V_t}{D}\right) + \frac{\sigma^2}{2} \right) / \sigma.$

Application of the Ronn and Verma (1986) Model The Merton (1977) model cannot be applied in practice, because its two parameters, the value of bank assets and asset volatility, are not observed. Next, we illustrate how deposit insurance premiums vary by input parameters when applying Ronn and Verma's (1986) practical implementation of Merton's (1977) model. We assume that dividends are zero, that the time until maturity equals one year, and that all bank debt is insured. In this case, it follows from equations (2)–(4a) that the price of deposit insurance can be expressed as a function of two observable variables: the equity volatility, σ_E, and the ratio of the market value of equity to the market value of bank debt, E/D.

Panel A in table 3.2 presents the Ronn and Verma (1986) deposit insurance premiums as a percentage of deposits assuming that there is no regulatory capital forbearance. Panel B follows the specification in Ronn and Verma (1986) model and assumes that there is capital forbearance of the degree $\rho = 0.97$, meaning that the bank is closed if the value of the bank's assets is less than or equal to 97 percent of the value of the bank's debt. Ronn and Verma (1986) take this level as a reasonable proxy for the level of regulatory forbearance in the United States. Although this level of forbearance seems reasonable in a number of other countries, the level of forbearance is likely to be higher in many other countries, such as most developing countries, where enforcement of regulation tends to be weak. Panel C assumes a larger degree of capital forbearance by setting the forbearance parameter ρ to 0.95. The range of premiums in panel C thus seems to be more applicable to most developing countries.

We find that the price of deposit insurance increases with the level of equity volatility. The relation between deposit insurance premiums and the inverse leverage ratio E/D is less straightforward, and depends on the assumed degree of regulatory forbearance, ρ. The reason is that the deposit insurance premiums are expressed as a percentage of deposits. The price of deposit insurance is also highly affected by the level of regulatory forbearance. In particular, going from $\rho = 1$ to $\rho = 0.97$ has a large, disproportionate impact on the premium. For example, given an equity volatility of 60 percent and an equity-to-debt ratio of 10 percent, such a increase in capital forbearance would require an increase in the premium from 13 bp to 39 bp of deposits, or a threefold increase. Indeed, Ronn and Verma (1986) show for a sample of U.S. banks that the rank ordering of premiums is less robust to changes in ρ than to changes in other model specifications. The reason is that a change in ρ has an impact on both the leverage and the estimate of asset volatility.

In the basic model of Ronn and Verma (1986), the time to maturity, T, is assumed to be one year. Merton (1977) interprets the maturity of the put option as the length of time until the next audit. Ronn and Verma (1986) experiment with the maturity by taking values from three months to five years. They find that increasing the maturity increases the deposit insurance premium, but that the ranking of the banks is not much affected.

Table 3.2
Ronn and Verma deposit insurance premiums (1986) as percent of deposits

σ_E E/D	10	20	30	40	50	60	70	80	90	100
Panel A: $\rho = 1$ (no capital forbearance)										
1	0.00	0.00	0.00	0.00	0.00	0.02	0.04	0.09	0.16	0.29
2	0.00	0.00	0.00	0.00	0.01	0.03	0.08	0.17	0.32	0.55
3	0.00	0.00	0.00	0.00	0.01	0.05	0.12	0.25	0.46	0.80
4	0.00	0.00	0.00	0.00	0.02	0.06	0.15	0.32	0.60	1.03
5	0.00	0.00	0.00	0.00	0.02	0.07	0.17	0.37	0.66	1.24
10	0.00	0.00	0.00	0.01	0.04	0.13	0.30	0.65	1.22	2.06
20	0.00	0.00	0.00	0.01	0.05	0.19	0.47	1.01	1.89	3.13
30	0.00	0.00	0.00	0.01	0.06	0.22	0.56	1.20	2.22	3.68
40	0.00	0.00	0.00	0.01	0.06	0.23	0.61	1.31	2.43	4.05
50	0.00	0.00	0.00	0.01	0.05	0.22	0.61	1.34	2.50	4.18
Panel B: $\rho = 0.97$ (capital forbearance)										
1	2.00	2.00	2.00	2.00	2.01	2.02	2.04	2.09	2.19	2.32
2	1.00	1.00	1.01	1.04	1.10	1.19	1.31	1.49	1.74	2.09
3	0.12	0.24	0.36	0.48	0.62	0.79	0.99	1.27	1.64	2.12
4	0.00	0.04	0.13	0.26	0.41	0.61	0.86	1.19	1.64	2.24
5	0.00	0.01	0.06	0.17	0.31	0.52	0.80	1.17	1.69	2.39
10	0.00	0.00	0.01	0.06	0.18	0.39	0.74	1.27	2.03	3.08
20	0.00	0.00	0.00	0.03	0.13	0.37	0.80	1.50	2.53	3.99
30	0.00	0.00	0.00	0.02	0.11	0.36	0.83	1.62	2.79	4.45
40	0.00	0.00	0.00	0.01	0.10	0.34	0.83	1.65	2.90	4.66
50	0.00	0.00	0.00	0.01	0.09	0.32	0.81	1.65	2.92	4.72
Panel C: $\rho = 0.95$ (capital forbearance)										
1	4.00	4.00	4.00	4.00	4.00	4.02	4.04	4.09	4.17	4.29
2	3.00	3.00	3.00	3.00	3.01	3.04	3.10	3.21	3.41	3.71
3	2.00	2.00	2.00	2.03	2.09	2.19	2.36	2.61	2.97	3.46
4	1.00	1.04	1.14	1.27	1.43	1.64	1.91	2.27	2.76	3.40
5	0.20	0.40	0.60	0.80	1.03	1.30	1.64	2.09	2.66	3.44
10	0.00	0.00	0.05	0.19	0.42	0.75	1.21	1.85	2.71	3.88
20	0.00	0.00	0.01	0.06	0.23	0.56	1.09	1.90	3.05	4.62
30	0.00	0.00	0.00	0.04	0.18	0.49	1.06	1.94	3.22	4.98
40	0.00	0.00	0.00	0.03	0.14	0.45	1.01	1.93	3.27	5.12
50	0.00	0.00	0.00	0.02	0.12	0.40	0.96	1.88	3.25	5.14

Note: Dividends are assumed zero. Time to maturity (T) equals 1. It is assumed that all bank debt is insured.

3.2.2 Merton's (1978) Unlimited-Term Put Option Model of Deposit Insurance

Merton (1978) models deposit insurance as an infinite maturity put. The model extends the limited-term model in Merton (1977) to an unlimited term model and takes into account explicitly surveillance or auditing costs and provides for random auditing. Several papers have built on this multiperiod perspective by incorporating a variety of features describing bank and regulator behavior, such as endogenous capital adjustments and regulatory forbearance.[12]

We present Merton's (1978) model without dividend payments. The government randomly audits banks and follows the no forbearance closure rule $V \leq D$. Let λ be the audit rate (in other words, $\lambda\,dt$ is the probability of an audit taking place over the next instant), K the audit costs, and, as before, let V equal the value of the bank's assets, D the value of the bank's deposits, and σ the volatility of the bank's asset returns.

Merton (1978) shows that, if there are no barriers to entry into banking, the equilibrium deposit insurance premium per dollar of deposits can be written as

$$p_1^*(x) = 1 - \frac{k^* - 1}{\delta^* + k^*} x^{-\delta^*}, \quad x \geq 1, \tag{11}$$

where $x = V/D$, $k^* = \frac{1}{2}\{1 - \delta^* + [(1 + \delta^*)^2 + \gamma]^{1/2}\}$, $\delta^* = 2\lambda K/\sigma^2$, and $\gamma \equiv 8\lambda/\sigma^2$.

Application of the Merton (1978) Model Next, we investigate how changes in the input parameters affect the deposit insurance premiums predicted by the Merton (1978) model. As in Saunders and Wilson (1995), we set audit costs per dollar of deposits, K, to 0.000134 (the U.S. historical equivalent) and the auditing frequency, λ, is set equal to 1. The resulting premium values, $p_1^*(x)$, are treated as lump sum perpetuities and multiplied by a yield rate to derive an equivalent annual payment amount. As yield rate we use either 4 percent (panel A in table 3.3) or 8 percent (panel B in table 3.3). The premiums are highly affected by the yield rate on Treasury bills. Basically, a doubling in the yield rate doubles the premium.

Unlike the premium in the Merton (1977) model, $p_1^*(x)$ is not a monotonically decreasing function of the assets-to-deposits ratio, V/D. The reason is that there are two sources of the deposit insurer liability

Table 3.3
Deposit insurance premiums in the Merton (1978) model

σ V/D	1%	2%	3%	4%	5%	10%	15%	20%	25%
1.00	0.10	0.09	0.11	0.13	0.15	0.28	0.41	0.53	0.65
1.05	0.58	0.22	0.16	0.16	0.17	0.28	0.41	0.53	0.65
1.10	0.98	0.34	0.22	0.19	0.19	0.29	0.41	0.53	0.65
1.15	1.32	0.44	0.27	0.22	0.21	0.29	0.41	0.53	0.65
1.20	1.61	0.54	0.31	0.25	0.23	0.30	0.41	0.53	0.65

Note: Deposit insurance premiums are expressed in percentage points of deposits. Premiums are calculated under the assumption that dividends equal zero. λ is set equal to one. $K = 0.000134$, and the Treasury yield (discount factor) equals 4 percent per annum. Premiums are calculated only for $V/D \geq 1$.

in the Merton (1978) model: (1) the guarantee of deposits which is a monotonically decreasing function of the assets-to-deposits ratio, as in the Merton (1977) model, and (2) the surveillance or audit cost which is a monotonically increasing function of the assets-to-deposits ratio. The latter increases even though the cost per audit is assumed constant because the expected number of audits prior to a "successful" audit where the bank is found to be insolvent is an increasing function of the assets-to-deposits ratio. In particular, we find that leverage does not affect the premium in case the asset return volatility is high.

3.2.3 Expected Loss Pricing

The option pricing methodology in Merton 1977, 1978 is limited to application to banks for which market valuations of the bank's net worth are available. In practical terms, this typically means that the put option approach to value deposit insurance is limited to application to banks that are listed on a stock exchange. However, Cooperstein, Pennacchi, and Redburn (1995) illustrate how a bank's net worth can be estimated from reported cash flows so that deposit insurance valuation can in principle be applied to all banks, and not just to those that are publicly traded.

Nevertheless, one should acknowledge the limitations of the option pricing methodology, in particular when applied to banks in countries that are not market oriented. In this section we introduce an alternative methodology to pricing deposit insurance known as expected loss pricing, which is based on a credit risk modeling approach. The advantage of this methodology is that is very general in setup and can therefore be adopted to fit country circumstances.

The principle of expected loss pricing is simple, and can be represented by the following equation:

Expected loss = Expected default probability ∗ Exposure

$$∗ Loss\ given\ default.$$

In this equation, *Expected loss* equals the size of the loss to the deposit insurer as a percentage of insured deposits, and thus measures the cost of deposit insurance. In order to breakeven in expectation, the deposit insurer should set a premium per insured deposit equal to the expected loss price. *Expected default probability* is the expected probability that the bank will default on its debt and can be estimated based on historical default data, when available, and using fundamental analysis, market analysis, or rating analysis. Fundamental analysis typically involves the use of CAMEL-like ratings. Market analysis, on the other hand, uses interest rates or yields on uninsured bank debt, such as interbank deposits, subordinated debt, and debentures. Rating analysis indicates the use of credit ratings of rating agencies, such as Moody's and Standard and Poor's. In principle, credit ratings can be based on both fundamental and market analysis, although they also tend to be affected by political considerations. Historical data on bank defaults in the United States for the period 1934–2001 as collected by the FDIC suggest an average default probability for U.S. banks of 0.24.[13]

Exposure is the liabilities that are to be covered in case of a bank failure. Typically, the exposure equals the amount of insured deposits, but in practice coverage is often also extended to uninsured deposits and other liabilities, particularly during episodes of systemic distress. In such cases, the defaulted exposure will exceed the amount of insured deposits.

Loss given default indicates is the size of the loss to the deposit insurer as a percentage of the total defaulted exposure and denotes the severity of the loss. The loss given default is calculated net of the present value of assets recovered from bank failure resolution. The higher the recovery rate on failed assets, the lower the actual loss given default. Good indicators for estimating the loss given default may include the business mix of bank, its loan concentration, the structure of bank liabilities, the efficiency of the bank failure resolution system, and the quality of the legal system more generally. Estimates of losses given default are typically also based on historical experience. Regulatory forbearance can be incorporated in estimates of the loss given default. The historical average loss rate in the United States as collected by the

FDIC equals 25 percent of bank assets.[14] In most countries, particularly developing countries without efficient and speedy bank failure resolution, recovery rates on bank assets tend to be much smaller than in the United States, and consequently, loss rates tend to be much higher. In developing countries, loss rates of 50 percent and up are typical. In net present value terms, loss rates tend to be even higher in most countries because of the high opportunity cost of recovery values resulting from slow asset recovery and high real interest rates. Speed is of the essence in bank failure resolution to keep down the cost of deposit insurance, particularly when the process of asset recovery takes many years and real interest rates are high.[15] A well-designed safety net thus cannot do without a well-functioning bank failure resolution. If the average country could double its recovery rate on failed bank assets, it could half the cost of deposit insurance.

Although all three components to the expected loss pricing formula (expected default probability, exposure, loss given default) are equally important in terms of estimating the expected of loss of a bank to the deposit insurance fund, the focus is typically on estimating the default probability of the bank, given that the other two components (exposure and loss given default) are relatively easy to measure given the availability of bank-specific information on the amount of uninsured deposits and historical information on the losses incurred by the deposit insurance fund given default.

In the following section we present how a credit risk modeling approach based on a bank's credit ratings or credit spreads on uninsured debt (such as interbank deposits or subordinated debt) can be used to estimate the expected default probabilities. We focus on the analysis of credit ratings and interest rates rather than on fundamental analysis, because fundamental analysis is more ad hoc and is not based on market principles. Nevertheless, in practice one may use fundamental analysis of expected default probabilities, either as a complement to the other two types of analyses to check for robustness, or in case the other types of analyses cannot be carried out due to the lack of data on either market rates or credit ratings. If deposit insurance has been in place for a while and historical data on losses of the deposit insurer are available, of course such data can and should also be used to forecast expected default probabilities going forward.

Credit ratings can be translated in expected default probabilities by using historical default probabilities. Both rating agencies like Moody's and Standard and Poor's have extensive time series on historical default rates for each of their rating categories. In the case of Moody's, these time series go back to the year 1920. For example, one can translate credit ratings on long-term bank deposits by using historical default rates on corporate bonds in the same rating category, and use these default rates as an estimate of the expected default probability of the bank. To reduce measurement error, it is advisable to estimate one-year default probabilities by taking the average cumulative default rate over several years. The optimal number of years depends on the specific situation. It should be large enough to reduce measurement error, but short enough in order not to use outdated information.

Market analysis of expected default probabilities is based on the principles of no arbitrage and risk-neutral pricing. Let r^f be the interest rate on riskless debt, r the interest rate on risky debt, and p the expected default probability. The principles of no arbitrage and risk-neutral pricing then imply that the payoff of US$1 invested in riskless debt should equal the expected payoff of US$1 invested in risky debt. In other words, $1 + r^f$ equals $(1 - p)(1 + r)$. This implies that the expected default probability can be calculated as

$$p = 1 - \frac{1 + r^f}{1 + r} = \frac{r - r^f}{1 + r}, \quad r \geq r^f. \tag{12}$$

When applying this methodology to uninsured deposits to estimate bank default probabilities, r equals the interest rate on uninsured deposits, and r^f equals the yield on zero coupon Treasury securities rate (with the same maturity). Uninsured deposits can include such deposits as interbank deposits. $r - r^f$ is the risk premium on uninsured deposits.[16]

This methodology to estimate bank default probabilities is only suitable for application to deposit premiums on uninsured deposits, not to deposit premiums on insured deposits. The reason is that risk premiums on insured deposits not only reflect the risk of the individual deposit-issuing bank (as do risk premiums on uninsured deposits), but are also affected by the credibility of deposit insurance, namely, the guarantor risk, which is difficult to estimate. Guarantor risk comprises both the risk of repudiation of the guarantee and the restitution costs borne by depositor when seeking restitution of his insured deposit losses. Because of the protection provided by deposit insurance, risk premiums on insured deposits tend to be lower than risk premiums on uninsured deposits. If deposit insurance were fully credible, depositors do not bear losses in case of bank failure, inducing a low risk premium on insured deposits. With imperfect credibility of deposit insurance, the risk premium on insured deposits is higher. By using data on uninsured deposits one avoids the problem of estimating the guarantor risk.

Since the previously mentioned methodology to estimate bank default probabilities requires the availability of data on deposit rates on uninsured deposits, it can not be applied to countries that insure all deposits. A more general problem with using deposit premiums to estimate default probabilities is that they are influenced by monetary policy and may therefore not only reflect default probabilities.

Given the problems associated with the use of deposit rates to estimate default probabilities, one may consider to use interest rates or yield data on marketable securities to estimate default probabilities, assuming that such data are available. In case of unsecured, risky debt, such as subordinated debentures, we can restate equation (12) as

$$p = 1 - \frac{1 + r^f}{1 + y} = \frac{y - r^f}{1 + y}, \qquad (12a)$$

where p is the one-year probability of default on the default risky debt, y is the yield on the one-year, zero coupon default risky debt (for example, subordinated debenture), r^f is the yield on the one-year, zero coupon, default risk free debt (e.g., Treasury bond), and $y - r^f$ is the yield spread. In case of simple, unsecured, subordinated debt with no call features, provisions or restrictions and no liquidity premiums, the yield spread equals the between the one-year, zero coupon yield on the subordinated debenture and the one-year, zero coupon yield on the Treasury security.

In case of zero coupon default risky debt with a maturity longer than one year, expected default probabilities for each year can be calculated if prices on zero coupon subordinated debentures and zero coupon Treasury bonds are available for every year until maturity (see, e.g., Iben and Litterman 1991). In this manner, a term structure of the bank's credit risk can be estimated.

The preceding analysis can only be applied to risky zero coupon bonds, not to risky coupon bonds. The reason for this is that, if the bank defaults on a coupon payment, then all subsequent coupon payments (and payments of principal) are also defaulted on. Thus, the default on one of the "mini" bonds associated with a given maturity is not independent of the event of default on the "mini" bond associated with a later maturity. In practice, single payment, zero coupon corporate bonds may not be traded, in which case it is more difficult to estimate the term structure of spreads. In such cases, and for more complex corporate debt instruments option pricing theory can be applied to price the risky debt and estimate default probabilities (Merton 1974).

The usefulness of using market rates on unsecured bank debt as a tool for estimating default probabilities not only relies on the liquidity of the unsecured debt market, but it also presumes that holders of such unsecured bank debt exercise market discipline, meaning that they monitor the bank and price the risk of the bank. The banking literature has provided ample evidence of the existence of market discipline in several markets.[17] Of course, the existence of market discipline may differ across countries and debt markets. This should be taken into account when applying the expected loss pricing methodology to price deposit insurance.

The expected loss pricing approach as discussed thus far generates actuarial premia that are calculated as the historical average of expected losses. Unlike the market-based Merton model discussed in the previous section, it does not consider the presence of a market premium to compensate for the market and liquidity risks borne by the deposit insurer. Duffie et al. (2003) suggest to apply a multiple to the historical default probably to account for market and liquidity risk.

Furthermore, deposit insurers are generally interested not only in the expected loss of the deposit insurance scheme, but also in the standard deviation of the expected loss (also known as the unexpected loss) and the potential loss of the scheme, and pricing should reflect this risk. In principle, similar techniques as discussed here can be adopted to estimate the loss distribution.[18] For the government, it is critical to know the loss distribution of its banking system when deciding on which part of the loss distribution is to be covered by the deposit insurer, on the extent of contingent financing made available to the deposit insurer in case of a shortfall of funds, and more generally on risk sharing arrangements of unexpected losses between the government and the private sector. Clearly, deposit insurance premiums should at least be able to cover the expected losses of the deposit insurance scheme. Most policymakers are of the opinion, however, that systemic risk arising from unexpected high losses can nor should not be covered in full by the deposit insurer but that rules should be adopted for risk sharing of unexpected losses between the government and the private sector. In fact, even the more than US$30 billion in current reserves of the U.S.

Deposit Insurance Fund would not be enough to cover unexpected high losses in the United States with certainty and may not even be large enough to cover the default of a single large bank (Kuritzkes, Schuermann, and Weiner 2002).

Application of Expected Loss Pricing   Next, we apply the methodology of expected loss pricing of deposit insurance to bank credit ratings and yields on subordinated bank debt. Table 3.4 shows the results for different scenarios. Panel A in table 3.4 highlights the expected loss pricing method using Moody's credit ratings. Panel B in table 3.4 highlights the expect loss pricing method using yield rates on subordinated debt. In principle, one can apply the methodology to any type of uninsured bank debenture, not just subordinated debt.

Column (1) in panel A of table 3.4 reports the broad classification of Moody's credit ratings. Moody's credit ratings range from Aaa to C, where Aaa indicates high credit rating and C indicates low credit rating. Column (1) in panel B reports the yield on a one-year, zero coupon Treasury bond. We set this yield equal to 3 percent for each scenario. Column (2) in panel A transforms the credit ratings into five-year average cumulative default rates. The average cumulative default rate over five years are calculated using historical default rates for the period 1920–1999 and are taken from exhibit 31 of Moody's Historical Default Rates of Corporate Bond Issuers, 1920–1999 (Moody's Investor Services 2000). Note that we use historical default rates on corporates rather than banks as estimate for the default rates of banks. Column (2) in panel B reports the spread of a one-year, zero coupon subordinated bank debt over the one-year, zero coupon Treasury bond. Column (3) in panel A reports the one-year default rate for each corresponding credit rating. The one-year default rate is calculated by dividing the average cumulative default rate over five years reported in column (1) by five. Column (3) in panel B reports the average one-year likelihood of default, which is calculated using risk-neutral pricing (see equation 12a). This means that the average one-year likelihood of default p equals $(y - r^f)/(1 + y)$, where $y - r^f$ is the spread of the one-year, zero coupon subordinated bank debt over the one-year, zero coupon Treasury bond and y is the yield on the one-year, zero coupon subordinated bank debt, which in this case can be calculated as the yield on a one-year, zero coupon Treasury bond r^f plus the spread of the one-year, zero coupon subordinated bank debt $y - r^f$. Column (4) in panels A and B reports the loss rate on assets. The loss rate is set equal to 8 percent of bank assets, which corresponds to the FDIC's historical loss rates on bank assets for banks with assets exceeding US$5 billion. Column (5) in panels A and B reports the expected one-year loss rate as a percentage of assets, which corresponds to the product of the one-year default rate and the loss rate on assets. Column (6) in panels A and B reports the share of deposits in total bank assets, and therefore indicates the loss exposure in terms of total assets. Column (7) in panels A and B reports the expected loss as a percentage of deposits, which corresponds to the quotient of the figures in column (4) and column (5). Column (8) in panels A and B reports the expected loss in basis points (bp) of deposits, and equals the product of 10,000 times the figure in column (6). The expected loss in basis points (bp) of deposits is an estimate of the assessment rate for deposit insurance.

3.3 Design Features and Pricing of Deposit Insurance

Deposit insurance premiums differ widely across countries, depending on the design features of the deposit insurance scheme of the respective countries and their institutional environment, among others. Table 3.5 presents country averages of actuarially fair deposit insurance premium estimates. These figures are taken from Hovakimian, Kane, and Laeven (2003), and are calculated by applying the Ronn and Verma (1986) method to a large sample of banks in different countries for the period 1991–1999. The premiums are expressed as a percentage of deposits, and are estimated either under the assumption of no regulatory forbearance ($\rho = 1$), or under the assumption of a regulatory forbearance parameter of $\rho = 0.97$, as in the original Ronn and Verma (1986) model. The estimates are based on calculations for listed banks and as such for a better-than-average sample of the banks in each country.

Without forbearance the country averages range from less than 0.001 percent of deposits in Australia, Austria, Germany, and Luxembourg to 1.93 percent of deposits in Russia, and average 0.18 percent of deposits. The premiums tend to be lower for developed countries. They average 0.04 percent for developed countries, but 0.32 percent for developing countries. These figures are underestimates of the actuarially fair price of deposit insurance, mainly because they ignore regulatory forbearance.

With a regulatory forbearance parameter of $\rho = 0.97$, the country averages range from 0.01 percent of deposits in Australia, Switzerland,

Table 3.4
Expected loss pricing

Panel A: Credit ratings

(1)	(2)	(3)	(4)	(5)	(6)	(7)	(8)
Credit rating	Five-year cumulative default rate	One-year default rate	Loss rate on assets	One-year loss rate (percent of assets)	Deposits/ assets	Expected loss (percent of deposits)	Expected loss (bp of deposits)
Aaa	0.20%	0.04%	8%	0.00	75%	0.00	0.43
Aa	0.36%	0.07%	8%	0.01	75%	0.01	0.78
A	0.55%	0.11%	8%	0.01	75%	0.01	1.18
Baa	1.97%	0.39%	8%	0.03	75%	0.04	4.21
Ba	12.88%	2.58%	8%	0.21	75%	0.27	27.47
B	30.16%	6.03%	8%	0.48	75%	0.64	64.33
Caa-C	43.37%	8.67%	8%	0.69	75%	0.93	92.52

Panel B: Subordinated bank debt

(1)	(2)	(3)	(4)	(5)	(6)	(7)	(8)
T-bond yield	Spread of subordinated debt over T-bond	One-year default rate	Loss rate on assets	One-year loss rate (percent of assets)	Deposits/ assets	Expected loss (percent of deposits)	Expected loss (bp of deposits)
3%	0.05%	0.05%	8%	0.00	75%	0.01	0.54
3%	0.10%	0.10%	8%	0.01	75%	0.01	1.03
3%	0.20%	0.19%	8%	0.02	75%	0.02	2.07
3%	0.40%	0.39%	8%	0.03	75%	0.04	4.13

3%	0.60%	0.58%	8%	0.05	75%	0.06	6.18
3%	0.80%	0.77%	8%	0.06	75%	0.08	8.22
3%	1.00%	0.96%	8%	0.08	75%	0.10	10.26
3%	1.20%	1.15%	8%	0.09	75%	0.12	12.28
3%	1.40%	1.34%	8%	0.11	75%	0.14	14.30
3%	1.60%	1.53%	8%	0.12	75%	0.16	16.32
3%	1.80%	1.72%	8%	0.14	75%	0.18	18.32
3%	2.00%	1.90%	8%	0.15	75%	0.20	20.32
3%	2.50%	2.37%	8%	0.19	75%	0.25	25.28
3%	3.00%	2.83%	8%	0.23	75%	0.30	30.19

Note: Panel A in table 3.4 highlights the expected loss pricing method using Moody's credit ratings. Panel B in table 3.4 highlights the expect loss pricing method using yield rates on subordinated debt. We set the yield on a one year, zero coupon Treasury bond equal to 3 percent for each scenario. The average cumulative default rate over five years are calculated using historical default rates for the period 1920–1999 and are taken from exhibit 31 of Moody's Historical Default Rates of Corporate Bond Issuers, 1920–1999 (Moody's Investors Service 2000). The loss rate is set equal to 8 percent of bank assets, which corresponds to the FDIC's historical loss rates on bank assets for banks with assets exceeding US$5 billion.

Table 3.5
Ronn and Verma deposit insurance premiums (1986) by country

Developing countries			Developed countries		
	Premium (percent of deposits)			Premium (percent of deposits)	
Country	$\rho = 1.00$	$\rho = 0.97$	Country	$\rho = 1.00$	$\rho = 0.97$
Argentina	0.361	0.579	Australia	0.000	0.005
Bangladesh	0.067	0.769	Austria	0.000	0.374
Brazil	0.923	1.701	Canada	0.013	0.143
Chile	0.003	0.018	Denmark	0.091	0.178
Colombia	0.039	0.107	Finland	0.010	0.109
Cyprus	0.043	0.097	France	0.004	0.105
Czech Republic	0.057	0.323	Germany	0.000	0.152
Ecuador	0.062	0.176	Greece	0.183	0.408
Hungary	0.078	0.422	Hong Kong	0.441	0.614
India	0.192	0.603	Ireland	0.002	0.018
Indonesia	0.466	0.798	Israel	0.001	0.093
Kenya	0.708	1.018	Italy	0.016	0.135
Korea, Republic of	0.280	0.853	Japan	0.090	0.417
Malaysia	0.350	0.618	Luxembourg	0.000	0.066
Morocco	0.002	0.042	Netherlands	0.003	0.030
Pakistan	0.078	0.403	Norway	0.002	0.174
Peru	0.350	0.670	Portugal	0.005	0.058
Philippines	0.408	0.623	Singapore	0.013	0.040
Poland	0.155	0.276	Spain	0.051	0.073
Russia	1.928	2.943	Sweden	0.021	0.214
South Africa	0.054	0.211	Switzerland	0.002	0.006
Sri Lanka	0.112	0.358	United Kingdom	0.011	0.092
Taiwan	0.020	0.059	United States	0.002	0.009
Thailand	0.780	1.189			
Zimbabwe	0.536	1.157			
Average developing countries	0.322	0.641	Average developed countries	0.042	0.153
Grand average	0.188	0.407	Grand average	0.188	0.407

and the United States to 2.94 percent of deposits in Russia, and average 0.41 percent of deposits. The premiums under forbearance also tend to be lower for developed countries. They average 0.15 percent for developed countries, but 0.64 percent for developing countries. It is, however, difficult to choose the level of regulatory forbearance a priori, particularly across countries.

This section investigates how several design features affect the price of deposit insurance, and vice versa. In particular, we focus on the relation between deposit insurance coverage and the price of deposit insurance, and how risk diversification and risk differentiation within a deposit insurance system can reduce the price of deposit insurance.

3.3.1   Coverage and Pricing of Deposit Insurance

Of all design features, the pricing of deposit insurance is of course most directly reflected in the premium system. As deposits are the entity that is insured, most systems use deposits as the base on which to levy premiums. In some cases, the premiums are levied only on insured categories of deposits or only on the amount actually covered. A few countries use a premium assessment base other than deposits, such as risk adjusted assets (see the appendix).

The premium can be the same for each bank, a so-called flat-rate premium system, or the premium can be differentiated by bank on the basis of bank-specific risks, a so-called risk-based system. The particular difficulties related to executing an equitable system of risk-adjusted premiums include (1) measuring bank risk; (2) access to reliable and timely data; (3) ensuring that rating criteria are transparent; and (4) examining the potential destabilizing effect of imposing high premiums on troubled banks (Financial Stability Forum 2001). The most commonly used measures of bank risk include capital adequacy, CAMEL ratings, and supervisory ratings. Some countries combine these measures to arrive at a composite measure for differentiating among banks. Thus far, only a few countries use more complex methods for assessing risk (such as Argentina and Canada). Currently, none of the countries uses the option pricing method or other market-based methods explored in this chapter to assess premiums (see the appendix). Despite the difficulties associated with implementing a risk-based deposit insurance system, an increasingly large number of countries have decided to do so. As of year-end 2000, risk adjusted premiums are used in 40.8 percent of countries with explicit deposit insurance.

Before the adoption of a deposit insurance scheme, its insurability should be assessed. The terms and conditions that need to hold for a risk to be insurable can be broadly summarized as fortuity of event, insurable interest of insured parties and indemnity basis of settlement. A more rigorous development of the limits of insurability of risks is given by Berliner (1982). He argues that the insurability of a risk is greater if (1) losses occur with a high degree of randomness; (2) the maximum possible loss is very limited; (3) the average loss amount upon loss occurrence is small; (4) losses occur frequently; (5) the insurance premium is high; (6) the possibility of moral hazard is low; (7) the coverage of the risk is consistent with public policy; and (8) the law permits the cover. With respect to deposit insurance, arguably only the latter two criteria are met. Bank failures are to some extent predictable and often do not occur independently. For example, during banking crises, many banks enter distress. Thus, deposit insurance losses do not occur with a high degree of randomness. Once losses occur, these losses tend to be large. The failure of a single large bank could in fact pose a systemic risk to the banking sector and have negative spillover effects to the corporate and household sectors. In addition, deposit insurance premiums tend to be set low for political reasons, and deposit insurance encourages extensive moral hazard. These insurability criteria should be taken into account at an early stage when considering the adoption of deposit insurance. If most of these criteria cannot be met at least partially, deposit insurance should not be adopted. Several of these criteria, in particular points (5) and (6) may be largely met through a well-designed deposit insurance scheme.[19]

Although chapter 1 identified several design features of deposit insurance that could curtail moral hazard, the practical design and implementation of a deposit insurance system needs to deal with several more complicated issues. The challenge is to implement a deposit insurance scheme that is incentive compatible for all parties involved.[20] An incentive compatible insurance system would provide incentives to banks to truthfully reveal the necessary information and thereby facilitate the efficient pricing of the risk shifted to the deposit insurer. As mentioned earlier, many countries are considering the introduction of risk-based insurance premiums in an effort to price deposit insurance more fairly and to give better incentives to banks. Although fair pricing of deposit insurance may eliminate inequitable wealth transfers, it need not lead to an efficient equilibrium that is incentive compatible.

For example, when banks have private information concerning the quality of the bank's assets, a risk-sensitive pricing policy is likely to provide banks with similar risk-taking incentives that is associated with a risk insensitive pricing arrangement.

Limiting the coverage of deposit insurance is the most common way to contain moral hazard, and therefore to reduce the cost of deposit insurance. For example, the cost of a deposit insurance system can be dramatically reduced by excluding certain types of deposits (such as large deposits, foreign currency deposits, interbank deposits, and/or government deposits) from deposit insurance coverage. Note that as long as all deposits have equal seniority and the asset composition of the bank (and with it the asset risk σ_V) does not change, excluding certain deposits from coverage does not affect the actuarially fair deposit insurance premium (expressed as percentage of insured deposits). In reality, however, a reduction in insurance coverage is likely to reduce moral hazard and thus reduce the asset risk of the bank and the actuarially fair deposit insurance premium. Since the per dollar insurance premium is higher with higher asset risk, limiting the coverage has a larger impact on reducing the total value of deposit insurance in countries with high bank asset risk than in countries with low bank asset risk.

Depending on the percentage of the value of total deposit covered by the deposit insurance fund, the premium expressed per insured deposits can differ substantially from the premium expressed per total deposits, as illustrated by table 3.6. For countries that do not report official premium as a percentage of insured deposits, but only as a percentage of total deposits, we use reported figures on the deposit coverage to translate the reported premiums in estimates of the premiums expressed as a percentage of insured deposits. Due to data limitations, we cannot calculate the official premiums as a percentage of insured deposits for all countries. Table 3.6 only includes those countries for which the premium as a percentage of insured deposits can be calculated. Column (2) in table 3.6 shows whether the insured deposits or total deposits (insured plus uninsured deposits) are the premium assessment base. Column (3) presents annual premiums for flat rate deposit insurance schemes as a percentage of the assessment base, and as reported by country authorities. Column (4) shows the value of deposit insurance coverage as a percentage of total deposits. Column (5) presents annual premiums as a percentage of insured deposits. The

Table 3.6
Premium per insured deposit

Country	Assessment base For premium	Premium Percent of assessment base	Deposit coverage Percent of value of total deposits	Premium Percent of insured deposits
Argentina	Insured deposits	0.66–1.02	40.0	0.66–1.02
Bahamas	Insured deposits	0.05	11.5	0.05
Bangladesh	Total deposits	0.01	31.0	0.02
Belgium	Insured deposits	0.02	n.a.	0.02
Brazil	Total deposits	0.30	43.0	0.70
Bulgaria	Insured deposits	0.50	<35.0	0.50
Canada	Insured deposits	0.04–0.33	35.9	0.04–0.33
Croatia	Insured deposits	0.80	68.0	0.80
Czech Republic	Insured deposits	0.50	n.a.	0.50
Denmark	Insured deposits	Max. 0.20	<50.0	Max. 0.20
Finland	Insured deposits	0.05–0.30	40.0	0.05–0.30
Germany	Insured deposits	0.01–0.11	n.a.	0.01–0.11
Guatemala	Insured deposits	1.00	n.a.	1.00
Hungary	Insured deposits	0.16–0.19	48.0	0.16–0.19
Iceland	Insured deposits	0.15	n.a.	0.15
India	Total deposits	0.05	72.0	0.07
Ireland	Insured deposits	0.20	n.a.	0.20
Jamaica	Insured deposits	0.10	33.5	0.10
Japan	Insured deposits	0.08	100.0	0.08
Kazakhstan	Insured deposits	0.13–0.38	n.a.	0.13–0.38
Kenya	Total deposits	0.15	16.0	0.94
Korea	Total deposits	0.05	100.0	0.05
Latvia	Insured deposits	0.30	18.7	0.30
Lithuania	Insured deposits	1.00	44.0	1.00
Macedonia	Insured deposits	0.01–0.03	99.0	0.01–0.03
Mexico	Total deposits	0.40–0.80	100.0	0.40–0.80
Nigeria	Total deposits	0.94	21.0	4.46
Peru	Insured deposits	>0.65	n.a.	>0.65
Portugal	Insured deposits	0.08–0.12	n.a.	0.08–0.12
Romania	Insured deposits	0.30–0.60	n.a.	0.30–0.60
Slovak Republic	Insured deposits	0.10–0.30	47.0	0.10–0.30
Spain	Insured deposits	0.10	60.0	0.10
Sweden	Insured deposits	Max. 0.50	n.a.	Max. 0.50
Taiwan	Insured deposits	0.05–0.06	45.0	0.05–0.06

Table 3.6
(continued)

Country	Assessment base For premium	Premium Percent of assessment base	Deposit coverage Percent of value of total deposits	Premium Percent of insured deposits
Tanzania	Total deposits	0.10	12.0	0.83
Trinidad and Tobago	Total deposits	0.20	34.1	0.59
Turkey	Insured deposits	1.00–1.20	100.0	1.00–1.20
Uganda	Total deposits	0.20	26.0	0.77
Ukraine	Total deposits	0.50	19.0	2.63
United Kingdom	Insured deposits	<0.30	n.a.	<0.30
United States	Insured deposits	0.00–0.27	65.2	0.00–0.27
Venezuela	Insured deposits	2.00	n.a.	2.00

Note: Column (2) presents the premium assessment base. Column (3) presents annual premiums for flat rate deposit insurance schemes as a percentage of the assessment base. Column (4) shows the value of deposit insurance coverage as a percentage of total deposits. Column (5) presents annual premiums as a percentage of insured deposits.

table illustrates that it is important to know the assessment base of the premiums, when looking at officially charged deposit insurance premiums.

Deposit insurance coverage differs substantially across countries. Coverage limits average US$20,660 per deposit for all countries, but range from as low as US$120 in the Ukraine to as high as US$243,520 in Norway. Insurance coverage tends to increase with the level of economic development of the country. Naturally, coverage levels are expected to be higher in countries with higher levels of economic development. When controlling for differences in the level of per capita GDP, there is less variation in coverage across countries. The coverage limit to per capita GDP ratio averages 3.19 for all countries, 1.98 for developed countries, and 3.78 for developing countries.

The higher coverage in developed countries would suggest that the price of deposit insurance is higher in these countries, unless these countries are more effective in controlling the moral hazard arising from a high level of coverage. For example, these countries may be more inclined to install risk-adjusted insurance premiums, coinsurance, and/or private funding and administration. In what follows we analyze in more detail whether countries with high insurance coverage tend to be countries with high income levels, and whether these countries are more inclined to implement design features of deposit insurance systems that tend to limit moral hazard, such as risk-adjusted insurance premiums, coinsurance, and/or private funding and administration.

First, we regress the insurance coverage limit on per capita GDP and several design features. The design features are the age of the deposit insurance scheme, a variable that indicates whether the scheme involves coinsurance or not, a variable that indicates whether premiums are risk-adjusted or not, a variable that indicates whether the source of funding is private or not, and a variable that indicates whether the fund administration is private or not. We include per capita GDP to control for the level of economic development. The sample includes all countries with explicit deposit insurance schemes as of year-end 2000. The results are presented in column (1) of table 3.7. The table also presents the correlation matrix of the design features.

The findings confirm that coverage limit tends to increase with per capita GDP. We also find that coverage tends to higher in countries where deposit insurance has been introduced a long time ago. However, the age of the deposit insurance fund is also strongly correlated with per capita GDP, suggesting that deposit insurance has been around for longer on average in rich countries than in poor countries. Next, we find that coverage tend to be higher in countries that have installed risk-adjusted premiums. Given the difficulty of implementing risk-adjusted premiums, one would expect that they tend to be more common in developed countries that in developing countries. However, the correlation matrix does not suggest such a relation. Private funding and administration are not significantly related to insurance coverage in the regression results, although the correlation between coverage limit and private fund administration is positive and significant.

Next, we use the deposit insurance coverage–to–per capita GDP ratio as dependent variable. Interestingly, we find that the coverage ratio is negatively associated with per capita GDP, suggesting that although coverage increases with per capita GDP, the rate of increase in coverage is lower than the rate of increase in per capita GDP. In other words, once we control for the level of economic development, we actually find that the insurance coverage is less generous in rich countries than in poor countries. We also find that countries with high coverage ratios tend to implement risk-adjusted premiums, suggesting that these countries try to curb the moral hazard arising from the generous level of insurance coverage. The other design features do not appear to be significantly associated with the coverage ratio.

We thus find that (1) deposit insurance coverage is higher in rich countries, but that (2) once one controls for the level of economic development, deposit insurance coverage is more generous in poor countries, and (3) that countries with generous levels of coverage tend to limit the cost of deposit insurance through adjusting insurance premiums for risk.

3.3.2 Risk Diversification, Risk Differentiation, and Pricing of Deposit Insurance

It is well known from investment portfolio theory that nonsystemic risk can be diversified away by pooling different assets into one portfolio (see, e.g. Markowitz 1952). The risk diversification value of an additional asset relates linearly to the covariance between the returns on the additional asset and the asset returns of the portfolio. The deposit insurance analogue to portfolio diversification is that, unless bank equity returns are perfectly correlated, the price of deposit insurance of a group of banks is lower than the sum of the price of deposit insurance for each individual bank. The risk diversification potential of a particular bank is greater if the correlation between its equity returns and the equity returns of the other banks in the group is lower.

More generally, the actuarial cost of insurance decreases with the pool of underlying assets. If default probabilities are not perfectly correlated, it is cheaper to insure a large pool of assets than a small pool of assets. A larger pool of assets is also more likely to be insurable, because losses occur with a higher degree of randomness and more frequently, and the average loss amount upon loss occurrence is smaller (see Berliner 1982).

The issue of potential diversification of nonsystemic risk is often overlooked when discussing appropriate pricing levels for deposit insurance in a country. Typically, the actuarially fair price of deposit insurance for a country is estimated by averaging estimated actuarially fair deposit insurance premiums of individual banks in the country. From the above, it follows that the cost of insuring the deposits of a banking system is lower than the sum of the cost of insuring each bank individually. The difference between the cost of insuring the system and the sum of the individual parts is greater if there is greater risk diversification potential in the country. Naturally, the potential for risk

Table 3.7
Coverage limit as a function of deposit insurance design features

Panel A: Regression results

	Coverage limit	Coverage limit to per capita GDP
	(1)	(2)
Per capita GDP	***1.546	***−0.098
	(0.466)	(0.028)
Age of the scheme	**0.594	0.004
	(0.293)	(0.027)
Coinsurance	−1.079	−0.668
	(7.657)	(0.663)
Risk-adjusted premiums	**13.366	**2.200
	(5.813)	(0.988)
Private funding	−23.668	0.179
	(14.960)	(0.650)
Private administration	15.135	0.214
	(12.661)	(0.735)
R^2	0.482	0.202
Number of observations	61	61

Panel B: Correlation matrix

	Coverage limit	Coverage ratio	Per capita GDP	Age of scheme	Coinsurance	Risk adjusted	Private funding	Private admin.
Coverage limit	1.00							
Coverage ratio	0.14	1.00						
Per capita GDP	***0.58	**−0.28	1.00					
Age of scheme	***0.43	−0.12	***0.45	1.00				
Coinsurance	0.02	−0.09	0.09	−0.09	1.00			
Risk-adjusted	**0.26	**0.27	0.11	0.03	−0.07	1.00		
Private funding	0.02	−0.17	***0.41	0.08	**0.31	−0.06	1.00	
Private administration	***0.40	−0.07	***0.47	**0.26	0.09	*0.21	**0.26	1.00

Notes: Panel A presents the regression results of coverage limit as a function of design features. Panel B presents the correlation matrix of several design features for countries with explicit deposit insurance as of year-end 2000. Dependent variable in column (1) is the coverage limit expressed in thousands of U.S. dollars. Dependent variable in column (2) is the coverage limit divided by per capita GDP, also referred to as the coverage ratio. Per capita GDP is expressed in thousands of U.S. dollars. Age of the scheme refers to the age of the deposit insurance scheme and is calculated as 2000 minus the year when deposit insurance was enacted. Coinsurance takes value of one if there is coinsurance, and zero if not. Risk adjusted premiums takes value of one if premiums are risk adjusted, and zero if not. Private funding takes value of one if the source of funding is private, and zero if not. Private administration takes value one if the fund administration is private, and zero otherwise. The data are presented in the appendix to chapter 3. The number of country observations is sixty-seven. Six countries are deleted from the sample due to lack of data on any of the regression variables. The remaining sample is sixty-one countries. The correlation matrix is based on the total sample of sixty-seven countries. A constant term was included, but is not reported. Heteroskedasticity constistent standard errors between brackets. * indicates significance at a 10 percent level. ** indicates significance at a 5 percent level. *** indicates significance at a 1 percent level.

diversification is larger in larger countries, in countries with many banks, and in countries with different types of banks (other things being equal). Therefore, the deposit insurance premium should be higher (or the insurance coverage smaller) in small countries, in countries with few banks, and in countries without substantial differentiation between banks (and their risk characteristics).

A more direct way to limit the risk of deposit insurance, and therefore its price, is to exclude risky banks from the insurance contract. Unless some of these banks have great diversification potential because of their covariance matrix structure, and exclusion of the risky banks from insurance can reduce the cost of deposit insurance significantly. Of course, the success of this risk differentiation approach depends on the technical ability and political will to differentiate between risky banks and not-so-risky banks.

In this section, we investigate the potential of risk diversification and risk differentiation of banks in the Republic of Korea. We compare Ronn and Verma (1986) estimates of actuarially fair deposit insurance premiums for individual banks with their equivalent for a group of listed banks in Korea. The reasons for focusing on Korea are threefold. First, to apply the Ronn and Verma (1986) methodology, we need data on bank equity returns. Most commercial banks in Korea are listed and data on their equity returns are readily available. Second, and most important, the majority of the Korean commercial banking system consists of listed banks, so that the portfolio of listed banks is a good proxy for the overall commercial banking system. Ideally, one would want to look at all banks in the country when assessing the potential of risk diversification in the country. Unfortunately, there is no country where all banks are listed. Korea is one of the best case studies from this perspective.

We collect daily market data and annual balance sheet data on all listed commercial banks in Korea for the year 1999 from Bankscope and Datastream. Data on the total commercial banking system come from the Korean Central Bank. A summary of the data is presented in table 3.8. We estimate annual equity volatility from weekly equity returns expressed in U.S. dollars, and we follow Fama's (1965) suggestion to delete days when the Korean stock exchange is closed. We also delete observations for days on which large jumps in share prices occur. Such observations may be due to restructuring or merger announcements. Inclusion of such observations would overestimate the volatility of equity returns.

Table 3.8 confirms that the group of listed banks comprises a large part of the total commercial banking system in Korea. In terms of total assets, the thirteen listed commercial banks in Korea account for 81.8 percent of total commercial banking system assets. The share of listed banks in total commercial bank deposits is even slightly higher with 82.5 percent. This means that the group of listed banks in Korea is a reasonable proxy for the entire commercial banking system in Korea, so that the risk diversification potential embedded in the group of listed banks (and the corresponding saving in the cost of deposit insurance) approximates the risk diversification potential of the country.

The average equity volatility weighted by equity market values is 80.1 percent, which is substantially larger than the equity volatility of the portfolio of stocks of the thirteen listed banks reported in table 3.8 of 56.2 percent. The total equity volatility is lower than the average equity volatility due to imperfect correlation of the equity returns of the sampled banks.

Table 3.9 presents the correlation matrix between the equity returns. The table shows that there is a large variation in the equity return correlations of different banks. Some equity return correlations are close to zero.[21] These correlations suggest that the potential for risk diversification among Korea banks is substantial.[22]

This is confirmed when we compare Ronn and Verma (1986) estimates of actuarially fair deposit insurance premiums for the individual banks with their equivalent for the total group of listed banks in Korea. Table 3.10 shows that the average actuarially fair premium for listed banks is 2.81 percent of deposits (weighted by total deposits), while the actuarially fair premium of insuring the portfolio of all banks is only 1.44 percent of deposits. The total value of deposit insurance drops from US$8.3 billion to US$4.2 billion. In other words, diversifying nonsystemic risk by insuring the deposits of all banks via the same contract (a typical explicit deposit insurance contract) almost halves the deposit insurance premiums, as compared to insuring banks via individual contracts.

In estimating actuarially fair deposit insurance premiums, we assume a forbearance parameter of 0.95. This is slightly lower than the corresponding figure of 0.97 in Ronn and Verma (1986). Our setup is intended to reflect the difference in the expected level of forbearance between the United States, the country under investigation in Ronn and Verma (1986), and Korea. The Republic of Korea recently experienced a financial crisis and has arguably a weaker level of government enforcement and greater fiscal weakness than the United States.

Table 3.8
Korean bank data as of end-1999

Bank name	(1) Total assets (mln US$)	(2) Deposits (mln US$)	(3) Total debt (mln US$)	(4) MV equity (mln US$)	(5) Equity volatility (percent)	(6) Dividend paid (mln US$)	(7) Debt-over-equity	(8) Deposits/(assets-deposits)
Chohung Bank	40,815	29,910	38,900	2,200	69.8	0	17.7	2.7
Daegu Bank	10,352	8,190	9,874	344	68.6	0	28.7	4.0
H&C Bank	42,495	31,418	40,615	3,126	68.3	58.8	13.0	2.5
Hana Bank	32,088	25,251	30,408	854	79.2	45.5	35.6	4.2
Hanvit Bank	63,581	55,371	61,245	2,941	90.4	0	20.8	6.3
Kookmin Bank	63,715	46,692	60,652	4,670	72.3	14.8	13.0	2.5
Koram Bank	19,991	15,454	19,119	736	73.6	0	26.0	3.5
Korea First Bank	24,794	18,972	23,937	741	120.0	0	32.2	3.3
Kwangju Bank	6,179	4,966	6,051	150	77.9	0	40.4	4.0
Kyongnam Bank	7,059	5,393	6,743	163	80.5	0	41.4	3.6
Pusan Bank	8,773	7,564	8,422	194	79.1	0	43.5	7.2
Seoul Bank	21,203	18,178	20,290	325	124.4	0	62.3	7.5
Shinhan Bank	37,223	26,598	34,673	2,646	72.6	0	13.1	2.5
Total (13) all listed banks	378,267	293,957	360,928	19,088	56.2	119.1	18.9	3.4
Total commercial banking system	462,519	356,390						
Percentage of total system	81.8	82.5						
Total (10) excluding three riskiest banks	268,690	201,437	255,456	15,081	55.2	119.1	16.9	2.9
Percentage of total system	58.1	56.5						

Note: The table shows bank-specific data for listed banks in the Republic of Korea as of year-end 1999. Values are in millions of U.S. dollars, unless otherwise noted. Equity volatility is annualized volatility, based on weekly equity returns (i.e., weekly equity volatility times the square root of 52). Italics indicate the three riskiest banks according to equity volatility. Individual bank data come from Bankscope and Datastream. Total commercial banking system data from the Korean Central Bank. Column (1) presents total banks assets. Column (2) presents bank deposits. Column (3) presents total bank debt. Column (4) presents the market value of equity. Column (5) presents the volatility of equity. Column (6) shows the dividend paid. Column (7) presents the debt-to-equity ratio. Column (8) presents the ratio of deposits to (equity plus nondeposit debt), also equal to the ratio of deposits to (assets minus deposits).

Table 3.9
Correlation matrix of weekly equity returns in U.S. dollars for the year 1999

							Korea						
	Chohung	Daegu	Hana	Hanvit	H & C	Kookmin	Koram	First	Kwangju	Kyongnam	Pusan	Seoul	Shinhan
Chohung	1.00												
Daegu	0.53	1.00											
Hana	0.46	0.59	1.00										
Hanvit	0.39	0.42	0.58	1.00									
H & C	0.26	0.48	0.50	0.41	1.00								
Kookmin	0.46	0.63	0.61	0.59	0.63	1.00							
Koram	0.41	0.65	0.76	0.56	0.60	0.71	1.00						
Korea First	0.45	0.33	0.18	0.17	−0.02	0.23	0.32	1.00					
Kwangju	0.56	0.78	0.52	0.47	0.46	0.69	0.57	0.31	1.00				
Kyongnam	0.45	0.75	0.39	0.33	0.45	0.61	0.50	0.08	0.80	1.00			
Pusan	0.46	0.81	0.46	0.39	0.25	0.53	0.53	0.29	0.81	0.74	1.00		
Seoul	0.56	0.42	0.20	0.31	0.18	0.35	0.39	0.80	0.42	0.32	0.35	1.00	
Shinhan	0.46	0.58	0.67	0.42	0.51	0.68	0.72	0.28	0.55	0.49	0.39	0.30	1.00

Note: This table presents the correlation matrix of equity returns for listed banks in the Republic of Korea. Correlations are based on weekly stock returns in U.S. dollars for the year 1999.

Next, we investigate the potential for risk reduction achieved by excluding the three riskiest banks in terms of equity volatility from the insurance contract. These three banks are highlighted in italics in table 3.8 and include Hanvit Bank (with an equity return volatility of 90 percent), Korea First Bank (with an equity return volatility of 120 percent), and Seoul Bank (with an equity return volatility of 124 percent). The share of the remaining ten banks in the assets of the total Korean commercial banking system drops to 58 percent. Note that one of these banks, Korea First Bank, is a bank with large risk diversification potential, as reflected by the low correlation of its equity returns with some of the other Korean banks. Nevertheless, we find that exclusion of these banks of above-average risk further reduces the risk of the portfolio and therefore the actuarially fair deposit insurance premium. The estimate of the actuarially fair deposit insurance premium for the portfolio of ten remaining banks is 1.28 percent of deposits.

The previously mentioned actuarially fair deposit insurance premiums have been estimated under the assumption that all debt is insured. Next, we carry out an extreme debt structure experiment where we assume that all nondeposit debt is subordinated to deposits.[23] Although in reality it is quite likely that all bank creditors in Korea were implicitly guaranteed by the government during the year 1999, so that insured bank debt equals total bank debt, this experiment highlights the potential reduction in costs if insurance and bailouts were to be strictly limited to bank deposits, and nondeposit creditors hold junior debt.

With nondeposit debt subordinated, the estimated actuarially fair deposit insurance premiums reduce further. Under this setup, insuring the deposits of the thirteen banks carries a price of only 0.39 percent of deposits (see column [4] in table 3.10). When the three "risky" banks are excluded, the estimated actuarially fair premium further reduces to 0.33 percent of deposits. The latter is dramatically lower than the original weighted average of 2.81 percent of deposits.

This section has shown that the potential for risk diversification should be taken into account when considering an appropriate level for the deposit insurance premium of a country. Countries with little diversification of risk should charge higher deposit insurance premiums. We have also shown that premiums can be set substantially lower if countries (have the option to) exclude risky banks from the deposit insurance system.

Table 3.10
Effect of risk diversification and exclusion of risky banks on deposit insurance premiums

Bank name	(1) Deposits (million USD)	(2) All bank debt is insured		(4) Nondeposit bank debt is subordinated	
		Insurance premium (in percent of deposits) (2)	Value of deposit insurance (million USD) (3)	Insurance premium (in percent of deposits) (4)	Value of deposit insurance (million USD) (5)
Chohung Bank	29,910	1.52	455	1.01	303
Daegu Bank	8,190	2.07	170	0.98	80
H&C Bank	31,418	1.86	585	1.07	338
Hana Bank	25,251	6.84	1,726	2.89	729
Hanvit Bank	55,371	2.71	1,503		
Kookmin Bank	46,692	1.52	712	1.28	599
Koram Bank	15,454	2.11	326	1.34	206
Korea First Bank	18,972	5.10	967		
Kwangju Bank	4,966	2.84	141	1.72	85
Kyongnam Bank	5,393	2.93	158	1.99	107
Pusan Bank	7,564	2.98	226	1.78	135
Seoul Bank	18,178	5.01	910		
Shinhan Bank	26,598	1.46	388	1.22	324

	(1)	(2)	(3)	(4)	(5)
Panel A: All banks					
Weighted average		2.81	8,265	2.73	8,221
Total (13 banks)	293,957	1.44	4,228	0.39	1,146
Panel B: Excluding risky banks					
Weighted average		2.43	4,886	1.43	2,906
Total (10 banks)	201,437	1.28	2,570	0.33	671

Note: This table presents Ronn and Verma estimates (1986) of actuarially fair deposit insurance premiums for Korean banks. These values of the deposit insurance guarantee are expressed in U.S. dollars and as a percentage of deposits. We assume a forbearance parameter of $\rho = 0.95$, and a constant annual dividend yield. Individual bank data from Bankscope and Datastream. Data are as of year-end 1999. The implied premiums in columns (2) and (3) assume that all bank debt is insured. The implied premiums in columns (4) and (5) assume that nondeposit bank debt is subordinated and set equal to equity, as in Hovakimian and Kane 2000. Panel A presents the weighted average premium for all banks (weighted by bank deposits) and the implied premium for the portfolio of all banks. Panel B excludes the three most risky banks according to their equity volatility, that is, Hanvit Bank, Korea First Bank, and Seoul Bank. Panel B presents for this subsample of banks the weighted average premium (weighted by bank deposits) and the implied premium for the portfolio of these banks.

3.4   Is Deposit Insurance Underpriced around the World?

The ultimate question on the pricing of deposit insurance in a particular country is whether deposit insurance is priced correctly. We employ some of the methods presented in section 3.2 to address this question. More specifically, we focus on the option pricing method and the expected loss pricing method. Since the outcome of over- or underpricing is highly sensitive to the model specifications, we choose the model parameters such that these alternative models give "conservative" estimates, namely, estimates that are likely to underestimate the true cost of deposit insurance.

In the case of option pricing models, we generate conservative estimates of the price of deposit insurance by not allowing for regulatory forbearance. As mentioned in section 3.2, there exist several reasons why Merton's (1977) option pricing model of deposit insurance gives downward biased estimates of the benefits bank stockholders derive from the safety net. One possible reason is that the level of regulatory forbearance is underestimated. Although Ronn and Verma (1986) incorporate capital forbearance by the bank regulators by permitting asset values to deteriorate to 97 percent of the value of bank debt before the bank is closed, the level of regulatory control is unknown ex ante. It is quite plausible that the level of regulatory forbearance is much higher in certain countries, notably developing countries, than suggested by the setup in the Ronn and Verma (1986) model, where a forbearance parameter of 0.97 is assumed. Other reasons why the option pricing model is likely to give downward biased estimates of the price of deposit insurance are the assumption of prompt option settlement and the assumption that no agency conflicts arise from the enforcement of regulatory requirements. For these reasons, we argue that the Ronn and Verma (1986) model without capital forbearance generates conservative estimates of the actuarially fair price of deposit insurance. For comparison purposes, we also use the Ronn and Verma (1986) model with a forbearance parameter of 0.97 to get less conservative estimates of the actuarially fair price of deposit insurance.

In the case of expected loss pricing methods, we generate conservative estimates of the price of deposit insurance by assuming low loss rates on bank assets. More specifically, we set the loss rate on bank assets equal to the U.S. historical average of 8 percent, which is likely to be a too low figure for most countries, in particular for countries with a weak insolvency framework such as many developing coun-

Table 3.11
Expected loss pricing using credit ratings

Moody's credit rating	(1) Average cumulative default rate for five years (1920–1999)	(2) Deposits/ assets	(3) Expected loss: 8 percent loss rate on assets (percent of deposits)	(4) Expected loss: 50 percent loss rate on assets (percent of deposits)
Aaa	0.20%	75%	0.00	0.03
Aa1–Aa3	0.36%	75%	0.01	0.05
A1–A3	0.55%	75%	0.01	0.07
Baa1–Baa3	1.97%	75%	0.04	0.26
Ba1–Ba3	12.88%	75%	0.27	1.72
B1–B3	30.16%	75%	0.64	4.02
Caa1–C3	43.37%	75%	0.93	5.78

Note: Column 3 reports expected loss rates by credit rating under the assumption of an 8 percent loss rate on assets and a deposit to assets ratio of 75 percent. Column (3) reports expected loss rates by credit rating under the assumption of a 50 percent loss rate on assets and a deposit to assets ratio of 75 percent. The average cumulative default rate for five years (1920–1999) is taken from exhibit 31, Moody's Historical Default Rates of Corporate Bond Issuers, 1920–1999, January 2000. The 8 percent loss rate on assets equals the historical loss rate on assets for U.S. banks with assets larger than US$5 billion, and is taken from FDIC 2000.

tries. We use country and bank credit ratings to generate estimates for the expected loss rates. The basic setup is identical to the one presented in panel A of table 3.4.

A consistent comparison of cross-country premiums should be based on deposit insurance premiums expressed as a percentage of insured deposits, because this figure does not depend on the deposit coverage, but only on the amount of total debt. Depending on the percentage of the value of total deposit covered by the deposit insurance fund, the premium expressed per insured deposits can differ substantially from the premium expressed per total deposits. We use the official premiums restated as a percentage of insured deposits and reported in table 3.6.

The procedure for transforming credit ratings into expected loss rates has already been explained in great detail in section 3.2. Table 3.11 presents estimates of the expected loss rates for different categories of Moody's credit ratings using loss rates on assets of 8 percent or 50 percent. The 8 percent loss rate represents the U.S. historical average.

Table 3.12
Assessment rate schedule of FDIC–insured institutions, 2001

		Supervisory group		
		A	B	C
Capital group	Well-capitalized	0.00	0.03	0.17
	Adequately capitalized	0.03	0.10	0.24
	Undercapitalized	0.10	0.24	0.27

Note: This table presents the assessment rate schedule of the U.S. FDIC risk–based assessment system as of year-end 2001. Assessment rates are by supervisory group and capital group. Rates are annual and are expressed in percentage points per insured deposits.

The expected loss rates presented in table 3.11 are generated using the same framework and under the same assumptions as those presented earlier in panel A of table 3.4. Column (3) in table 3.11 presents the expected loss rates under the assumption of loss rates on assets of 8 percent, while column (4) presents the expected loss rates under the assumption of loss rates on assets of 50 percent. The estimates in column (3) serve as a conservative estimate of the actuarially fair premium of deposit insurance. The estimates in column (4) are less conservative. The estimates in columns (3) and (4) differ only in the assumed loss rate on assets. Since expected loss rates are proportional to the loss rates on assets (other things equal), the expected loss rates calculated under the assumption of 50 percent loss rates on assets are 50/8 times higher than the expected losses calculated under the assumption of 8 percent loss rates on assets.

The expected loss rates per deposit derived under the assumption of the U.S. historical average loss rate on assets of 8 percent and presented in table 3.11 show a similar range of values as the actual assessment rates of FDIC insured deposit taking institutions in the United States. Table 3.12 presents the assessment rates for such institutions for the year 2001 by supervisory group and capital group. Supervisory group A denotes better quality than supervisory group B, and group B denotes better quality than group C.[24]

While the FDIC premiums range from 0.0 to 0.27 percent of insured deposits, the Moody's ratings implied premiums (under the assumption of 8 percent loss rates) range from 0.0 to 0.93 percent of insured deposits. Considering that the Moody's ratings of large banks in the United States range from Aa to Ba, the Moody's ratings implied premiums for a significant part of the U.S. banking system range from 0.1–

0.27 percent of insured deposits, very similar to the actual FDIC pricing schedule of 0.0–0.27 percent of insured deposits. These results do not indicate that deposit insurance is priced correctly in the United States, but merely seem to suggest that the expected loss pricing method gives reasonable estimates of the price of deposit insurance.

Next, we compare the conservative estimates of the actuarially fair price of deposit insurance with the actually charged premiums in countries around the world. If the conservative estimate of the true cost of deposit insurance is higher than the officially charged premium, we argue that deposit insurance is underpriced. Table 3.13 presents both the official premiums and the conservative estimates of actuarially fair premiums based on credit ratings and option prices. We use both country and bank credit ratings from Moody's to estimate expected loss rates. The country credit rating acts as a ceiling of the rating for (most) banks in the country. In several countries, country risk is so dominant that bank ratings equal the country rating. Since we focus on expected loss rates on bank deposits we use the Moody's ratings for long-term bank deposits. For countries, we use Moody's ratings on foreign currency denominated long-term bank deposits. For individual banks, we use Moody's ratings on long-term bank deposits (including both local currency and foreign currency denominated deposits).[25]

Column (1) in table 3.13 presents the country rating on foreign currency denominated, long-term bank deposits. Column (2) presents the median of the ratings on long-term bank deposits for individual banks. The median is taken across Moody's universe of rated banks in the country (see Moody's Investors Service 2001). Column (3) reports the actually charged deposit insurance premiums in the country. These official premiums are expressed as a percentage of insured deposits, and are taken from table 3.6.

The next four columns in table 3.13 present the credit rating implied estimates of the price of deposit insurance. Column (4) presents the country credit rating implied premium under the assumption of a 8 percent loss rate on assets. The country credit rating is also expressed as a percentage of insured deposits. For consistency with the actual premiums, all implied premiums are expressed as a percentage of insured deposits. The country rating implied premiums in column (4) are our most conservative estimates of the actuarially fair price of deposit insurance, because they assume a low loss rate on assets of 8 percent and because they use the credit rating of the country which is at least as good as the (median) credit rating of banks in the country.

Table 3.13
Official premiums and conservative estimates of fair premiums based on credit ratings and option prices

	(1)	(2)	(3)	Credit rating implied premium				Option pricing implied premium	
				(4)	(5)	(6)	(7)	(8)	(9)
Country	Country rating	Bank rating	Actual premium	Country rating implied premium: 8 percent loss rate	Bank rating implied premium: 8 percent loss rate	Country rating implied premium: 50 percent loss rate	Bank rating implied premium: 50 percent loss rate	RV implied premium: no forbearance	RV implied premium: with forbearance
Argentina	Caa3	Caa3	0.66–1.02	0.93	0.93	5.78	5.78	0.36	0.58
Bahamas	A3	n.a.	0.05	0.01	n.a.	0.07	n.a.	n.a.	n.a.
Bangladesh	n.a.	n.a.	0.02	n.a.	n.a.	n.a.	n.a.	0.07	0.77
Belgium	Aaa	Aa3	0.02	0.00	0.01	0.03	0.05	n.a.	n.a.
Brazil	B2	B2	0.70	0.64	0.64	4.02	4.02	0.92	1.70
Bulgaria	B3	n.a.	0.50	0.64	n.a.	4.02	n.a.	n.a.	n.a.
Canada	Aa1	Aa3	0.04–0.33	0.01	0.01	0.05	0.05	0.01	0.14
Croatia	Ba1	Ba1	0.80	0.27	0.27	1.72	1.72	n.a.	n.a.
Czech Republic	Baa1	Baa1	0.50	0.04	0.04	0.26	0.26	0.06	0.32
Denmark	Aaa	Aa3	Max. 0.20	0.00	0.01	0.03	0.06	0.09	0.18
Finland	Aaa	Aa3	0.05–0.30	0.00	0.01	0.03	0.06	0.01	0.11
Germany	Aaa	Aa3	0.01–0.11	0.00	0.01	0.03	0.05	0.00	0.15
Guatemala	Ba3	n.a.	1.00	0.27	n.a.	1.72	n.a.	n.a.	n.a.
Hungary	A3	A3	0.16–0.19	0.01	0.02	0.07	0.11	0.08	0.42

Country									
Iceland	Aa3	A3	0.15	0.01	0.01	0.05	0.05	n.a.	n.a.
India	Ba3	Ba3	0.07	0.27	0.27	1.72	1.72	0.19	0.60
Ireland	Aaa	A2	0.20	0.00	0.01	0.03	0.07	0.00	0.02
Jamaica	B1	n.a.	0.10	0.64	n.a.	4.02	n.a.	n.a.	n.a.
Japan	Aa1	A3	0.08	0.01	0.03	0.05	0.16	0.09	0.42
Kazakhstan	Ba3	Ba3	0.13–0.38	0.27	0.27	1.72	1.72	n.a.	n.a.
Kenya	n.a.	n.a.	0.94	n.a.	n.a.	n.a.	n.a.	0.71	1.02
Korea	Baa3	Ba1	0.05	0.04	0.20	0.26	1.27	0.28	0.85
Latvia	Baa3	Ba1	0.30	0.04	0.16	0.26	0.99	n.a.	n.a.
Lithuania	Ba2	n.a.	1.00	0.27	n.a.	1.72	n.a.	n.a.	n.a.
Macedonia	n.a.	n.a.	0.01–0.03	n.a.	n.a.	n.a.	n.a.	n.a.	n.a.
Mexico	Ba1	Ba1	0.40–0.80	0.27	0.27	1.72	1.72	n.a.	n.a.
Nigeria	n.a.	n.a.	4.46	n.a.	n.a.	n.a.	n.a.	n.a.	n.a.
Peru	B1	B1	>0.65	0.64	0.64	4.02	4.02	0.35	0.67
Portugal	Aaa	A1	0.08–0.12	0.00	0.01	0.03	0.10	0.01	0.06
Romania	Caa1	Caa1	0.30–0.60	0.93	0.93	5.78	5.78	n.a.	n.a.
Slovak Republic	Ba1	Ba1	0.10–0.30	0.27	0.27	1.72	1.72	n.a.	n.a.
Spain	Aaa	A1	0.10	0.00	0.01	0.03	0.07	0.05	0.07
Sweden	Aa1	Aa3	Max. 0.50	0.01	0.01	0.05	0.05	0.02	0.21
Taiwan	Aa3	A3	0.05–0.06	0.01	0.02	0.05	0.14	0.02	0.06
Tanzania	n.a.	n.a.	0.83	n.a.	n.a.	n.a.	n.a.	n.a.	n.a.
Trinidad and Tobago	Ba1	Ba1	0.59	0.27	n.a.	1.72	n.a.	n.a.	n.a.
Turkey	B3	B3	1.00–1.20	0.64	0.64	4.02	4.02	n.a.	n.a.
Uganda	n.a.	n.a.	0.77	n.a.	n.a.	n.a.	n.a.	n.a.	n.a.

Table 3.13
(continued)

Country	(1) Country rating	(2) Bank rating	(3) Actual premium	Credit rating implied premium				Option pricing implied premium	
				(4) Country rating implied premium: 8 percent loss rate	(5) Bank rating implied premium: 8 percent loss rate	(6) Country rating implied premium: 50 percent loss rate	(7) Bank rating implied premium: 50 percent loss rate	(8) RV implied premium: no forbearance	(9) RV implied premium: with forbearance
Ukraine	Caa1	Caa1	2.63	0.93	0.93	5.78	5.78	n.a.	n.a.
United Kingdom	Aaa	A1	<0.30	0.00	0.01	0.03	0.11	0.01	0.09
United States	Aaa	Aa3	0.00–0.27	0.00	0.01	0.03	0.20	0.00	0.01
Venezuela	B3	B3	2.00	0.64	0.64	4.02	4.02	n.a.	n.a.

Note: Column (1) presents the country rating on foreign currency denominated, long-term bank deposits as of year-end 2001. Column (2) presents the median of the ratings on long-term bank deposits for individual banks as of year-end 2001. The source of the credit ratings is Moody's Investors Service 2001. Column (3) reports the actually charged deposit insurance premiums in the country as a percentage of insured deposits. The source of these figures is table 3.6. Column (4) presents the country credit rating implied premium as a percentage of insured deposits under the assumption of a 8 percent loss rate on assets. Column (5) presents the bank credit rating implied premium as a percentage of the actuarially fair deposit insurance premium as a percentage of insured deposits under the assumption of a 8 percent loss rate on assets. Column (6) presents the premium implied by the country credit rating as a percentage of insured deposits under the assumption of a 50 percent loss rate on assets. Column (7) presents the bank credit rating implied estimates of the actuarially fair deposit insurance premium as a percentage of insured deposits under the assumption of a 50 percent loss rate on assets. Column (8) presents the Ronn and Verma (1986) implied estimates of deposit insurance premiums as a percentage of insured deposits under the assumption of no forbearance. Column (9) presents the Ronn and Verma implied estimates of deposit insurance premiums as a percentage of insured deposits under the assumption of substantial forbearance (equivalent to a forbearance parameter of $\rho = 0.97$). The source of Ronn and Verma (1986) implied deposit insurance premiums is Hovakimian, Kane, and Laeven 2003. These are averages for the period 1991–1999.

Column (5) presents the bank credit rating implied estimates of the actuarially fair deposit insurance premium under the assumption of a 8 percent loss rate on assets. This country-level estimate is a weighted average of the bank credit rating implied estimates for individual banks in Moody's universe of rated banks in the country. These estimates correspond therefore to the default probabilities implied by the median bank credit ratings presented in column (2). Column (6) presents the country credit rating implied premium under the assumption of a 50 percent loss rate on assets. These estimates differ from the estimates in column (4) only in the assumed loss rate, and are therefore a factor 50/8 larger than the implied premiums in column (4). Column (7) presents the bank credit rating implied estimates of the actuarially fair deposit insurance premium under the assumption of a 50 percent loss rate on assets. Similarly, these estimates are a factor 50/8 larger than the premiums in column (5). The implied premiums in columns (6) and (7) use higher loss rates on assets and are therefore less conservative than the estimates in columns (4) and (5), but possibly more realistic in the case of some countries.

The last two columns in table 3.13 present the option pricing implied estimates of actuarially fair deposit insurance premiums. Column (8) presents the Ronn and Verma (1986) estimates under the assumption of no forbearance (i.e., using a forbearance parameter of $\rho = 1.00$). Column (9) presents the Ronn and Verma (1986) estimates under the assumption of substantial forbearance (equivalent to a forbearance parameter of $\rho = 0.97$ in their model). The Ronn and Verma (1986) implied deposit insurance premiums are from Hovakimian, Kane, and Laeven (2003). These estimates are based on stock market and balance sheet data on a sample of listed banks in each of the reported countries, and are averages for the period 1991–1999. We do not have estimates for a number of countries due to lack of data.

Despite the fact that we calculate rather conservative estimates of the price of deposit insurance, we find that these estimates are still higher than the officially charged premiums in a number of countries. In the case of Bulgaria, India, and Jamaica, the actually charged premiums are even lower than the country credit rating implied premiums reported in column (4)—our most conservative estimates of the cost of deposit insurance. In Korea and Romania, the actual premiums levied are lower than the premiums implied by median bank credit in the country reported in column (5).[26] Based on less conservative estimates of the cost of deposit insurance that assume a loss rate on assets of 50 percent (reported in columns [6] and [7]), one would conclude that deposit insurance is underpriced in a large number of countries, most of which are developing countries.

The actuarially fair deposit insurance premiums implied by the Ronn and Verma (1986) option pricing model also suggest underpricing in several countries. When allowing for forbearance (to the equivalent $\rho = 0.97$ in the Ronn and Verma model), the implied premiums are higher than the actual premiums in the following countries: Bangladesh, Brazil, Germany, Hungary, India, Japan, Kenya, and Korea. More conservative estimates based on the assumption of no forbearance still suggest underpricing of deposit insurance in Bangladesh, Brazil, India, Japan, and Korea.

In sum, we find using two different methods of pricing deposit insurance that the actual premiums levied on banks are lower than the premiums implied by these theoretical models in many countries. Given that we have used different models and have set model parameters such that these models produce conservative estimates of the true cost of deposit insurance (in many countries, forbearance may well exceed the level implied by $\rho = 0.97$, and loss rates on assets may well exceed 50 percent), one could argue that deposit insurance is underpriced in many countries around the world. In particular in most developing countries, where the ability to control bank risk tends to be weak, underpricing of deposit insurance is likely to be greater than estimated here.

For many countries, we find such high levels of actuarially fair premiums as 5 percent or more of deposits. Few banks would be able to afford such high deposit insurance premiums. Our estimates thus suggest that many of these countries cannot afford deposit insurance, in particular countries with weak banks and institutions. This is another way of saying that countries with weak institutions should not adopt explicit deposit insurance.

3.5 Summary and Concluding Remarks

In section 3.2, we described alternative methods to price the value of deposit insurance. Each of these methods builds on one of two theoretical frameworks: Merton's (1977) option pricing model or the expected loss pricing approach. The first approach relies on market information on equity values of banks and its application is therefore limited to listed banks and to countries with well-developed capital markets. The second approach can also be applied if market-based information is not available, for instance, by using accounting-based information or credit ratings. Of course, when applying the second approach to market-based information, such as yields on debentures issued by banks, its application is also limited by the availability and quality of information on such securities. For these reasons, practical models of pricing deposit insurance typically embed both market- and accounting-based information. Nevertheless, the application of such market-based models is deemed to be important. Not only are these models to be preferred to models that do not use market information from a theoretical point of view, but they can also be used to create estimates of actuarially fair deposit insurance premiums for the banks in a particular country that could serve as a benchmark for the contributions of banks required to cover the expected losses from bank failures, even though such estimates are restricted to a limited subsample of all banks in the country. Given different values for the models input parameters, the tables in section 3.2 report estimates of such actuarially fair premiums. These tables can easily be used as ready reckoners by policymakers to assess the adequateness of existing deposit insurance premiums for different banks.

The actuarially fair price of deposit insurance is affected by several structure and design features of a deposit insurance system. In section 3.3, we presented several examples and studied several cases to document how different design features of deposit insurance affect its pricing structure. In particular, we focused on the relation between deposit insurance coverage and the price of deposit insurance, and how risk diversification and risk differentiation within a deposit insurance system can reduce the price of deposit insurance.

The potential to diversify nonsystemic risk among a pool of insured deposits of different banks has not drawn much attention in the literature. Because of such risk diversification, the cost of insuring the deposits of a banking system is lower than the sum of the cost of insuring each bank separately. Our case study of Korean banks in section 3.3 shows that the cost of insuring the pool of deposits of the entire Korean banking system is about half the cost of insuring the deposits of each bank separately. The potential for such risk diversification tends to be larger in countries with large economies with more diversified banking systems (such as banking systems with a large number of diverse banks). As a consequence, deposit insurance can be priced lower in a country like the United States, which has a large, diversified banking system with about ten thousand diverse banks, than in a country like Namibia, which has a small number of similar, medium-sized commercial banks, ceteris paribus.

Risk differentiation or the exclusion of risky banks from deposit insurance can also reduce the cost of deposit insurance, unless the excluded banks have great risk diversification potential. The case study of Korean banks in section 3.3 shows that by excluding the three riskiest banks in the system, as measured in terms of the volatility of their equity, would reduce the cost of deposit insurance of the Korean banking system by about 12 percent. Rather than excluding banks from coverage, countries may opt to differentiate premiums to reflect different risk profiles of banks, as is done in the United States. However, as discussed in section 3.3, introducing an equitable system of risk-adjusted premiums is difficult in practice.

The discussions and findings in section 3.3 indicate which design features could help avoid the excessive costs arising from informational asymmetries and principal-agent problems that are associated with deposit insurance. However, the objective of governments that implement deposit insurance is generally not to minimize such costs, but rather to achieve social goals such as protecting small depositors or enhancing public confidence and stability of the financial system. Most of these objectives, however, can also be reached with limited cost of deposit insurance. Clearly, the design and implementation of a deposit insurance scheme should fit country-specific circumstances, but certain "good practices" arise that can substantially limit the cost of deposit insurance. To avoid adverse selection, membership of the deposit insurance scheme should be compulsory. To avoid moral hazard, deposit insurance premiums should be risk-adjusted, the insurance coverage should be low, prompt corrective actions should be taken against banks, and early intervention should take place in weak banks. The insurance coverage should aim at insuring the deposits of small depositors, and should exclude part of large deposits, interbank deposits, government deposits, and possibly foreign currency deposits. Low coverage may be complemented with coinsurance for deposits larger than the smallest tranche of deposits.

By far the easiest and most effective way to contain the cost of deposit insurance is to limit insurance coverage. A lower coverage reduces proportionally the cost of deposit insurance, and to the extent that a lower coverage reduces moral hazard and reduces the asset risk of the bank, the reduction in the cost of insurance could be even larger. While this may seem obvious, in practice most governments seem pressed to ignore this and set coverage levels above what would seem to be the social optimum level, and such that most deposits in the system are covered in full rather than only those of small depositors. Improving the quality of the legal system to ensure speedy resolution of distressed bank assets and improving bank supervision to compensate for the depositor discipline displaced by the introduction of explicit deposit insurance, are two other necessary ingredients for a well-functioning safety net.

In section 3.3, we also argued that the assessment base for charging insurance premiums should be total insured deposits, otherwise there could be unequal treatment of banks. Total deposits may differ from insured deposits if there are coverage limits or if certain types of deposits are excluded from insurance. If premiums were to be levied over total deposits rather than total insured deposits, coverage limits would penalize banks with mostly large deposits and the exclusion of certain deposits from insurance would penalize banks with a large share of such deposits.

The ultimate question on the pricing of deposit insurance in a particular country is whether deposit insurance is priced correctly. In section 3.4, we investigated whether deposit insurance is underpriced in countries around the world using the different methodologies presented and discussed in section 3.2. We find that the actual premiums levied on banks are lower than the premiums implied by these theoretical models in many countries, and argue that deposit insurance is underpriced in many countries around the world, notably in several developing countries.[27] The implied premiums also suggest that many countries cannot afford deposit insurance, in particular countries with weak banks and institutions, as the estimated fair premiums imply contributions by the banks in these countries that would be unreasonably high. It follows that countries with weak institutions should not adopt explicit deposit insurance.

The pricing methods presented in this chapter can not only serve countries that have adopted deposit insurance when reassessing and revising their premium levels, but also be used by countries that are currently considering the adoption of deposit insurance when deciding on an adequate level of deposit insurance premiums. Since each of these methods has its own drawbacks, we would suggest that countries use a combination of methods to set premium rates. The actual premiums and historical losses in other yet comparable countries can also provide a useful benchmark for the pricing of deposit insurance. The challenge in practice is to estimate an appropriate premium markup and to adjust the premiums on the basis of the design features of the proposed scheme.[28]

Deposit insurance may not be a good recipe for each country, but for countries that do decide to adopt deposit insurance, pricing it as efficiently as possible is important. This means that prices should be set such that they reflect the risk shifted to the deposit insurer. In order to facilitate the efficient pricing of risk, banks should be given the incentives to reveal the necessary information to assess their risk. In an effort to price deposit insurance more fairly and to give better incentives to banks, many countries are considering the introduction of risk-based insurance premiums. We have argued that when banks have private information concerning the quality of the bank's assets, it may be difficult to achieve such an incentive-compatible outcome.

The success of a deposit insurance will depend critically on the well functioning of other components of the safety net of a country, such as lender-of-last-resort facilities, regulatory norms, supervisory policies and practices, intervention rules, loss sharing rules, and insolvency resolution policies and mechanisms. The well functioning of these components is interdependent. Therefore, each of these components should not be designed separately, but should be looked upon in conjunction.

Appendix

Table 3A.1 reports pricing information on existing deposit insurance schemes.

Acknowledgments

The author would like to thank Thorsten Beck, Jerry Caprio, Asli Demirgüç-Kunt, Oliver Fratzscher, Tom Glaessner, George Hanc, Jim Hanson, Patrick Honohan, Yongbeom Kim, Daniela Klingebiel, Giovanni Majnoni, Soledad Martinez Peria, Art Murton, Larry Promisel, Haluk Unal, and seminar participants at the 2003 American Finance Association Meetings in Washington D.C., the U.S. Federal Deposit Insurance Corporation, and the World Bank for helpful discussions and comments, and Ying Lin for research assistance.

Table 3A.1
Pricing of Deposit Insurance Schemes at Year-end 2000

Country	Assessment base	Annual premiums Percent of assessment base	Risk-adjusted yes = 1; no = 0	Basis for adjusting premiums
Argentina	Insured deposits	0.3 plus 0.36–0.72	1	CAMEL-like ratios and risk assets
Austria	Insured deposits	Pro rata, ex post	0	Not applicable
Bahamas	Insured deposits	0.05	0	Not applicable
Bahrain	Deposits	Ex post	0	Not applicable
Bangladesh	Deposits	0.005	0	Not applicable
Belgium	Insured deposits	0.02 plus 0.04 if necessary	0	Not applicable
Brazil	Deposits	0.3 plus 0.15 extraordinary contribution	0	Not applicable
Bulgaria	Insured deposits	0.5	0	Not applicable
Cameroon	Deposits plus NPLs	0.15 percent of deposits + 0.5 percent of NPLs	1	Nonperforming loans
Canada	Insured deposits	0.04–0.33	1	CAMEL-like ratios, asset concentration, regulatory rating and adherence to standards
Central African Republic	Deposits plus NPLs	0.15 percent of deposits + 0.5 percent of NPLs	1	Nonperforming loans
Chad	Deposits plus NPLs	0.15 percent of deposits + 0.5 percent of NPLs	1	Nonperforming loans
Chile	Not applicable	Not applicable	0	Not applicable
Colombia	Insured deposits	Risk-adjusted	1	Independent rating (is pending)

Table 3A.1
(continued)

Country	Assessment base	Annual premiums Percent of assessment base	Risk-adjusted yes = 1; no = 0	Basis for adjusting premiums
Congo, Republic of	Deposits plus NPLs	0.15 percent of deposits + 0.5 percent of NPLs	1	Nonperforming loans
Croatia	Insured deposits	0.8	0	Determined by central bank
Czech Republic	Insured deposits	0.5 (savings banks 0.1)	0	Not applicable
Denmark	Insured deposits	0.2 (maximum)	0	Not applicable
Dominican Republic	Deposits	0.1875	0	Not applicable
Ecuador	Deposits	0.65 + risk adjustment	1	Risk rating
El Salvador	Deposits	0.1 (can be raised to 0.3) + risk-based mark-up	1	Substandard securities
Equatorial Guinea	Deposits plus NPLs	0.15 percent of deposits + 0.5 percent of NPLs	1	Nonperforming loans
Estonia	Deposits	0.5 (maximum)	0	Not applicable
Finland	Insured deposits	0.05–0.3	1	Solvency ratio
France	Deposits plus one-third loans	Risk-adjusted	1	CAMEL-like ratios
Gabon	Deposits plus NPLs	0.15 percent of deposits + 0.5 percent of NPLs	1	Nonperforming loans
Germany	Insured deposits	0.008 (statutory scheme): 0–0.1 (private sector)	1	Risk category and length of membership
Gibraltar	Insured deposits	Administrative expenses and ex post	0	Not applicable
Greece	Deposits	Decreasing by size: 0.0025–0.125	0	Not applicable

Country				
Guatemala	Insured deposits	1.0 + 0.5 when the fund falls below its target	0	Not applicable
Honduras	Deposits	Not more than 0.25	0	Not applicable
Hungary	Insured deposits	0.16–0.19 (decreasing by size) + risk adjustment	1	Capital adequacy
Iceland	Insured deposits	0.15	0	Not applicable
India	Deposits	0.05	0	Not applicable
Indonesia	Not applicable	Not applicable	Not applicable	Not applicable
Ireland	Insured deposits	0.2	0	Not applicable
Italy	Insured funds	Ex post, adjusted for size and risk	1	CAMEL and maturity transformation
Jamaica	Insured deposits	0.1	0	Not applicable
Japan	Insured deposits	0.048 + 0.036	0	Not applicable
Kazakhstan	Insured deposits	0.125–0.375	1	CAMEL-like ratios
Kenya	Deposits	0.15	0	Not applicable
Korea	Deposits	0.05	0	Not applicable
Latvia	Insured deposits	0.3	0	Not applicable
Lebanon	Credit accounts	0.05	0	Not applicable
Lithuania	Insured deposits	1.0	0	Not applicable
Luxembourg	Insured deposits	Ex post to a maximum of 5 percent of capital	0	Not applicable
Macedonia	Insured deposits	0.01–0.025	1	CAMEL-like ratios
Mexico	Deposits and other liabilities	0.4–0.8	1	Determined by Ministry of Finance
Morocco	Deposits	0.2	0	Not applicable

Table 3A.1
(continued)

Country	Assessment base	Annual premiums Percent of assessment base	Risk-adjusted yes = 1; no = 0	Basis for adjusting premiums
Netherlands	Insured deposits	Ex post to a maximum of 10 percent of capital	0	Not applicable
Nigeria	Deposits	0.9375	0	Not applicable
Norway	Risk weighted assets and deposits	0.5 of risk weighted assets and 0.15 of deposits	1	Risk-weighted assets
Oman	Deposits	0.02, not to exceed 0.3	0	Not applicable
Peru	Insured deposits	0.65 plus risk adjustment	1	Determined by supervisor
Philippines	Deposits	0.2	0	Not applicable
Poland	Risk-weighted assets and deposits	Up–0.4	1	Risk-weighted assets
Portugal	Insured deposits	0.08–0.12	1	CAMEL-like ratios
Romania	Insured deposits	0.3–0.6	1	CAMEL-like ratios
Slovak Republic	Insured deposits	0.1–0.3	0	Not applicable
Spain	Insured deposits	0.1 (maximum of 0.2)	0	Not applicable
Sri Lanka	Deposits	0.15	0	Not applicable
Sweden	Insured deposits	0.5 (maximum)	1	Capital adequacy
Switzerland	Gross earnings and balance sheet items	Ex post, on demand, varies	1	Earnings and some discretion
Taiwan	Insured deposits	0.05–0.06	1	CAR and early warning system
Tanzania	Deposits	0.1	0	Not applicable

Thailand	Not applicable	Not applicable	Not applicable	Not applicable
Trinidad and Tobago	Deposits	0.2	0	Not applicable
Turkey	Insured savings deposits	1.0–1.2	1	Capital adequacy
Uganda	Deposits	0.2	0	Not applicable
Ukraine	Total deposits	0.5 plus special charges	0	Not applicable
United Kingdom	Insured deposits	On demand, not to exceed 0.3	0	Not applicable
United States	Domestic deposits	0.00–0.27	1	CAMEL-like ratios
Venezuela	Insured deposits	2.0	0	Not applicable

Note: This table presents several design features for all existing explicit deposit insurance schemes as of year-end 2000. Panel A presents information regarding membership, administration, and funding of deposit insurance by country. Panel B presents information regarding the coverage of the scheme. Panel C presents information regarding the pricing of deposit insurance. Since 2000, the introduction of deposit insurance has been planned or is under consideration in the following countries: Albania, Bolivia, China, Costa Rica, Hong Kong, Kuwait, Russia, and Zambia. n.a. indicates not available.

Notes

1. Bhattacharya and Thakor (1993) model the incentives by which deposit insurance invites insured banks to seek excessive portfolio risk and keep lower liquid reserves relative to the social optimum. An overview of the economics of deposit insurance is provided by Bhattacharya, Boot, and Thakor (1998).

2. Duan and Yu (1994) find that Taiwanese deposit-taking institutions were heavily subsidized by the deposit insurance fund of Taiwan during the period 1985 to 1992. Fries, Mason, and Perraudin (1993) find that Japanese institutions were heavily subsidized by the deposit insurer during the period 1975 to 1992. Hovakimian and Kane (2000) find that U.S. banks shifted risk onto the safety net during the period 1985 to 1994, despite regulatory efforts to use capital requirements to control risk shifting. Kaplan (2002) finds that Thai banks received implicit deposit insurance subsidies from the government during the years prior to the financial crisis in 1997. Laeven (2002a) interprets the estimate of the opportunity cost value of deposit insurance services as a proxy for bank risk and shows that this proxy has predictive power in forecasting bank distress. He also finds that this measure of bank risk is higher for banks with concentrated ownership and high credit growth, and for small banks.

3. While there has been some variation among EU accession countries in the degree and speed to which they intended to comply with these EU standards—with countries like Bulgaria and Poland increasing their coverage levels only gradually over time in line with the country's economic development and countries like Croatia shooting for a high level of coverage early on in the reform process—as of year-end 2004, all new member countries from Central and Eastern Europe have coverage levels of at least (sometimes exceeding) €20,000, except for the three Baltic states, which are expected to reach this level in the year 2008 (cf. chapter 8).

4. For example, Poland's coverage per depositor was about 4 times per capita GDP in 2003, significantly above the EU average of about 1.4 or the world average of about 2 times per capita GDP.

5. The IMF view culminated in the issuance of a set of guidelines on the development of deposit insurance in 1999 (Garcia 2000).

6. A precondition for efficient markets is that information is widely and cheaply available.

7. For private banks without traded equity, traded debt instruments, interest rates on uninsured debt, or credit ratings, pricing options are more limited. One option is to estimate a hazard model of default based on historical default probabilities of other banks in the country. Another option, proposed by Falkenheim and Pennacchi (2003) and known as the market-comparable approach, is to apply relations between equity model parameters and bank-specific data for listed banks to private banks. More generally, any of the previous methods can be used to estimate such relations for one set of banks for which data is available and apply these to extrapolate premiums for other banks for which underlying data is not available.

8. If deposit insurance is subsidized by the government, as is the case is most countries (see section 3.3), deposit insurance will generate a positive net present value I for each bank equal to the difference between the market value of the bank's liabilities D and equity E minus the bank's assets and franchise value V.

9. When estimating annual equity volatility from a sample of daily equity returns, it is recommended to follow Fama (1965), who suggests to ignore days when the exchange is closed.

10. When comparing premiums across countries, the value of deposit insurance per unit of deposits has to be normalized on a single currency unit by using the same currency for each country.

11. Hovakimian and Kane (2000) suggest assigning forbearance benefits only to economically insolvent banks.

12. Pennacchi (1987a) extends the model to endogenize mispriced deposit insurance. Allen and Saunders (1993) model deposit insurance as a callable put, namely, a compound option consisting of an infinite maturity put option held by the banks and a valuable call provision regarding timing of bank closure retained by the deposit insurer. Cooperstein, Pennacchi, and Redburn (1995) separate the cost of deposit insurance on a period-by-period basis, generalizing the Merton model that only gives an estimate of the current present value of deposit insurance. Saunders and Wilson (1995) incorporate interim dividend payments by allowing shareholders to receive dividends until the next audit occurs, even if the bank becomes insolvent in the interim.

13. To put this number in perspective, the historical default probability on Moody's A-rated corporate bonds for the period 1920–1999 is 0.11 percent and the current market yield spreads on A-rated U.S. bank bonds is about 0.3–0.5 percent.

14. For large banks the historical loss rate is 8 percent of bank assets.

15. For example, Brazil has been plagued by low asset recovery and high real interest rates. Improvements in both would significantly reduce the cost of deposit insurance.

16. The existence of a deposit rate premium has been documented in the banking literature. For example, using data on insured certificates of deposit (CDs) rates of U.S. banks, Hannan and Hanweck (1988) find statistically significant relationships between CD rates and institution risk as measured by such variables as leverage, variability of earnings, and risk assets. Using data on CD rates of U.S. thrifts, Cook and Spellman (1994) provide evidence that there is risk pricing of guaranteed deposits, implying expected loss from incomplete deposit insurance coverage. Cook and Spellman (1996) develop a framework that allows one to decompose observed CD premiums into firm and guarantor risk. They show that the premiums on guaranteed deposits are multiplicatively related to bank risk and guarantor risk. When bank risk is constant, the premiums as well as interest rate spreads are proportional to guarantor risk. Bartholdy, Boyle, and Stover (2003) find that the deposit premium is higher on average in countries without explicit deposit insurance than in countries with explicit deposit insurance.

17. For example, Martinez Peria and Schmukler (2001) find that depositors in Argentina, Chile, and Mexico discipline banks by withdrawing deposits and by requiring higher interest rates on deposits. Flannery and Sorescu (1996) find evidence of bank market discipline in the U.S. subordinated debt market.

18. While expected losses of banks are additive in the sense that the expected loss for a portfolio (system) of banks is the sum of expected losses for individual banks, the unexpected loss for a portfolio of banks is a function of unexpected losses of individual banks and of the correlation between individual losses. For the banking system of a particular country, the cumulative loss distribution thus reflects the expected loss of individual banks, the size of individual exposure, and the correlation of losses in the portfolio.

19. When setting initial contributions in countries where the deposit insurer also has regulatory functions, it should be decided who pays for such regulatory expenses (Buser, Chen, and Kane 1981).

20. Chan, Greenbaum, and Thakor (1992) show that, when banks hold nontraded private information assets, it is impossible to implement a risk-sensitive deposit insurance pricing scheme that is incentive compatible unless banks earn rents or are subsidized by the regulator. Giammarino, Lewis, and Sappington (1993) show that banks' asset quality is below the first-best level under a socially optimal deposit insurance scheme. Kanatas (1986) suggests to overcome such informational asymmetry problems by using a banks' access to discount window credit to reveal their asset quality, and proposes to integrate risk-based deposit insurance pricing with discount window policy. On the other hand, Craine (1995) shows that, if there exist intermediaries that hold traded public information securities and that are allowed to issue insured deposits, an efficient separating equilibrium can be reached by separating the market for insured deposits from private information financial intermediation.

21. For example, the correlation between the equity returns of Korea First Bank and Kyongnam Bank is only 0.08, and the correlation between the equity returns of Korea First Bank and Housing and Commercial Bank is even slightly negative at −0.02.

22. As the equity return correlations are unlikely to be stable over time, our quantitative results are sensitive to the sampled time period. However, our qualitative result does not alter.

23. In other words, we assume that nondeposit debt is junior to the deposit insurance agency claim and we classify such debt as equity. In effect, the bank's debt is made coterminous with deposits, and therefore the price of deposit insurance is reduced. See also Hovakimian and Kane 2000.

24. As defined by the FDIC, Supervisory group A consists of financially sound institutions with a few minor weaknesses and generally corresponds to the primary federal regulator's composite rating of 1 or 2 (1 being the higher rating). Supervisory group B consists of institutions that demonstrate weaknesses, which, if not corrected, could results in significant deterioration of the institutions. This group generally corresponds to the primary federal regulator's composite rating of 3. Supervisory group C consists of institutions that pose a substantial probability loss to the deposit insurer unless effective corrective action is taken. This group generally corresponds to the primary federal regulator's composite rating of 4 or 5.

25. Moody's deposit obligations ratings are issuer (rather than issue) ratings. For U.S. banks, this rating applies only to domestic deposit obligations. For non-U.S. banks, the deposit obligation rating applies to all deposit obligations.

26. These implied figures are likely to be underestimates of the true cost of deposit insurance in many countries, not only because we assume a low loss rate on assets of 8 percent, but also because rated banks tend to be the "better quality" banks in the country, so that the median rating would overestimate the average quality of bank assets.

27. The equity price experience model with limited capital forbearance of 3 percent suggests underpricing in about 50 percent of countries, and the credit risk model that uses credit ratings and historical default experience and assumes a loss rate of 50 percent suggests underpricing in about two-thirds of countries.

28. In Laeven 2001, we have applied the discussed methods to estimate an actuarially fair premium for Russia, at a time that the government was considering the adoption of

deposit insurance. Based on the proposed scheme stipulated in the deposit insurance law drafted in the 2001, the discussed methods would suggest a premium rate of about 2–4 percent, depending on the method used, much higher than the 0.6 percent per annum proposed by the draft legislation (Russian Federation 2001). Since then, the Russian parliament has passed the legislation and deposit insurance entered into force in 2003.

References

Allen, Linda, and Anthony Saunders. 1993. Forbearance and Valuation of Deposit Insurance as a Callable Put. *Journal of Banking and Finance* 17: 629–643.

Barth, James R., Gerard Caprio, and Ross Levine. 2004. Bank Regulation and Supervision: What Works Best? *Journal of Financial Intermediation* 13 (2): 205–248.

Bartholdy, Jan, Glenn Boyle, and Roger Stover. 2003. Deposit Insurance and the Risk Premium in Bank Deposit Rates. *Journal of Banking and Finance* 27 (4): 699–717.

Beck, Thorsten. 2001. Brazil: Deposit Insurance and Bank Failure Resolution—Recent Developments and Issues. Mimeo., The World Bank, Washington D.C.

Berliner, Baruch. 1982. *Limits of Insurability of Risks*. New York: Prentice-Hall.

Bhattacharya, Sudipto, Arnoud Boot, and Anjan Thakor. 1998. The Economics of Bank Regulation. *Journal of Money, Credit, and Banking* 30: 745–770.

Bhattacharya, Sudipto, and Anjan Thakor. 1993. Contemporary Banking Theory. *Journal of Financial Intermediation* 3: 2–50.

Black, Fisher, and Myron Scholes. 1973. The Pricing of Options and Corporate Liabilities. *Journal of Political Economy* 81: 637–653.

Buser, Stephen, Andrew Chen, and Edward Kane. 1981. Federal Deposit Insurance, Regulatory Policy, and Optimal Bank Capital. *Journal of Finance* 36 (1): 51–60.

Chan, Yuk-Shee, Stuart Greenbaum, and Anjan Thakor. 1992. Is Fairly Priced Deposit Insurance Possible? *Journal of Finance* 47: 227–246.

Cook, David, and Lewis Spellman. 1994. Repudiation Risk and Restitution Costs: Toward Understanding Premiums on Insured Deposits. *Journal of Money, Credit, and Banking* 26 (3): 439–459.

Cook, David, and Lewis Spellman. 1996. Firm and Guarantor Risk, Risk Contagion, and the Interfirm Spread among Insured Deposits. *Journal of Financial and Quantitative Analysis* 31 (2): 265–281.

Cooperstein, Richard, George Pennacchi, and F. Stevens Redburn. 1995. The Aggregate Cost of Deposit Insurance: A Multiperiod Analysis. *Journal of Financial Intermediation* 4: 242–271.

Craine, Roger. 1995. Fairly Priced Deposit Insurance and Bank Charter Policy. *Journal of Finance* 50 (5): 1735–1746.

Demirgüç-Kunt, Aslı, and Enrica Detragiache. 2002. Does Deposit Insurance Increase Banking System Stability? An Empirical Investigation. *Journal of Monetary Economics* 49 (7): 1373–1406.

Demirgüç-Kunt, Aslı, and Harry Huizinga. 2004. Market Discipline and Deposit Insurance. *Journal of Monetary Economics* 51 (2): 375–399.

Demirgüç-Kunt, Aslı, and Edward Kane. 2002. Deposit Insurance around the World: Where Does It Work? *Journal of Economic Perspectives* 16 (2): 175–195.

Duan, Jin-Chuan. 1994. Maximum Likelihood Estimation Using Price Data of the Derivative Contract. *Mathematical Finance* 4: 155–167.

Duan, Jin-Chuan. 2000. Correction: Maximum Likelihood Estimation Using Price Data of the Derivative Contract. *Mathematical Finance* 10: 461–462.

Duan, Jin-Chuan, and Min-Teh Yu. 1994. Assessing the Cost of Taiwan's Deposit Insurance. *Pacific-Basin Finance Journal* 2: 73–90.

Duffie, Darrell, Robert Jarrow, Amiyatosh Purnanandam, and Wei Yang. 2003. Market Pricing of Deposit Insurance. *Journal of Financial Services Research* 24: 93–119.

Falkenheim, Michael, and George Pennacchi. 2003. The Cost of Deposit Insurance for Privately Held Banks: A Market Comparable Approach. *Journal of Financial Services Research* 24: 121–148.

Fama, Eugene E. 1965. The Behavior of Stock-Market Prices. *Journal of Business* 38: 34–105.

Federal Deposit Insurance Corporation. 2000. Options Paper. Federal Deposit Insurance Corporation, Washington, D.C.

Financial Stability Forum. 2001. *Guidance for Developing Effective Deposit Insurance Systems*. Working Group on Deposit Insurance, Financial Stability Forum, Basel, Switzerland (September).

Flannery, Mark, and Sorin Sorescu. 1996. Evidence of Bank Market Discipline in Subordinated Debenture Yields: 1983–1991. *Journal of Finance* 51 (4): 1347–1377.

Fries, Steven, Robin Mason, and William Perraudin. 1993. Evaluating Deposit Insurance for Japanese Banks. *Journal of the Japanese and International Economy* 7: 356–386.

Garcia, Gillian G. 2000. Deposit Insurance: Actual and Good Practices. IMF Occasional Paper no. 197, International Monetary Fund, Washington, D.C.

Giammarino, Ronald, Tracy Lewis, and David Sappington. 1993. An Incentive Approach to Bank Regulation. *Journal of Finance* 48 (4): 1523–1542.

Hannan, Timothy, and Gerald Hanweck. 1988. Bank Insolvency Risk and the Market for Large Certificates of Deposit. *Journal of Money, Credit, and Banking* 20: 203–211.

Hovakimian, Armen, and Edward Kane. 2000. Effectiveness of Capital Regulation at U.S. Commercial Banks, 1985 to 1994. *Journal of Finance* 55: 451–468.

Hovakimian, Armen, Edward Kane, and Luc Laeven. 2003. How Country and Safety-Net Characteristics Affect Bank Risk-Shifting. *Journal of Financial Services Research* 23 (3): 177–204.

Iben, Thomas, and Robert Litterman. 1991. Corporate Bond Valuation and the Term Structure of Credit Spreads. *Journal of Portfolio Management* 17 (3): 52–64.

Kanatas, George. 1986. Deposit Insurance and the Discount Window: Pricing under Asymmetric Information. *Journal of Finance* 41 (2): 437–450.

Kane, Edward. 1995. Three Paradigms for the Role of Capitalization Requirements in Insured Financial Institutions. *Journal of Banking and Finance* 19: 431–454.

Kane, Edward. 2000. Designing Financial Safety Nets to Fit Country Circumstances. Mimeo., Boston College.

Kaplan, Idanna. 2002. Estimating the Value of Implicit Government Guarantees to Thai Banks. *Review of International Economics* 10 (1): 26–35.

Kroszner, Randall. 1998. The Political Economy of Banking and Financial Regulatory Reform in Emerging Markets. *Research in Financial Services* 10: 33–51.

Kroszner, Randall, and Thomas Stratmann. 1998. Interest Group Competition and the Organization of Congress: Theory and Evidence from Financial Services' Political Action Committees. *American Economic Review* 88: 1163–1187.

Kuester King, Kathleen, and James O'Brien. 1991. Market-Based, Risk-Adjusted Examination Schedules for Depository Institutions. *Journal of Banking and Finance* 15: 955–974.

Kuritzkes, Andrew, Til Schuermann, and Scott Weiner. 2002. Deposit Insurance and Risk Management of the U.S. Banking System: How Much? How Safe? Who Pays? Wharton Financial Institutions Working Paper no. 02-02, Wharton School of Business.

Laeven, Luc. 2001. Pricing the Adoption of Deposit Insurance: The Case of Russia. Mimeo., The World Bank, Washington, D.C.

Laeven, Luc. 2002a. Bank Risk and Deposit Insurance. *World Bank Economic Review* 16 (1): 109–137.

Laeven, Luc. 2002b. International Evidence On the Cost of Deposit Insurance. *Quarterly Review of Economics and Finance* 42 (4): 721–732.

Laeven, Luc. 2004. The Political Economy of Deposit Insurance. *Journal of Financial Services Research* 26 (3): 201–224.

Marcus, Alan, and Israel Shaked. 1984. The Valuation of FDIC Deposit Insurance Using Option-Pricing Estimates. *Journal of Money, Credit, and Banking* 16: 446–460.

Markowitz, Harry. 1952. Portfolio Selection. *Journal of Finance* 7: 77–91.

Martinez Peria, Maria Soledad, and Sergio Schmukler. 2001. Do Depositors Punish Banks for Bad Behavior? Market Discipline, Deposit Insurance and Banking Crises. *Journal of Finance* 56 (3): 1029–1051.

Merton, Robert. 1974. On the Pricing of Corporate Debt: The Risk Structure of Interest Rates. *Journal of Finance* 29: 449–470.

Merton, Robert. 1977. An Analytical Derivation of the Cost of Deposit Insurance and Loan Guarantees. *Journal of Banking and Finance* 1: 3–11.

Merton, Robert. 1978. On the Cost of Deposit Insurance When There Are Surveillance Costs. *Journal of Business* 51: 439–452.

Moody's Investors Service. 2000. *Historical Default Rates of Corporate Bond Issuers, 1920–1999*, Moody's Investors Service (January).

Moody's Investors Service. 2001. *Bank Credit Research: Monthly Ratings Lists*, Moody's Investors Service (December).

Pennacchi, George. 1987a. A Reexamination of the Over- (or Under-) Pricing of Deposit Insurance. *Journal of Money, Credit, and Banking* 19: 340–360.

Pennacchi, George. 1987b. Alternative Forms of Deposit Insurance: Pricing and Bank Incentive Issues. *Journal of Banking and Finance* 11: 291–312.

Ronn, Ehud, and Avinash Verma. 1986. Pricing Risk-Adjusted Deposit Insurance: An Option-Based Model. *Journal of Finance* 41: 871–895.

Russian Federation. 2001. *Proposed Russian Federation Federal Law on Deposit Insurance.* Moscow: Russian Federation.

Saunders, Anthony, and Berry K. Wilson. 1995. If History Could Be Rerun: The Provision and Pricing of Deposit Insurance in 1933. *Journal of Financial Intermediation* 4: 396–413.

4 Deposit Insurance and Bank Failure Resolution: Cross-Country Evidence

Thorsten Beck and Luc Laeven

4.1 Introduction

There is a broad variation in countries' framework and practice to resolve failing banks. Some countries rely on the court system to declare
banks insolvent and to resolve them. Other countries have delegated
the power to resolve failing banks almost completely to bank supervisors with little if any judicial recourse (see Hüpkes 2004; Beck 2004, for
a discussion of differences in bank failure resolution schemes across
countries). There is also variation in the degree to which bank failure
resolution interacts with deposit insurance, which is another increasingly popular component of the financial safety net. In some countries,
such as Brazil, the deposit insurer is set up as a paybox with the function to pay out depositors of failed banks, while in other countries,
such as the United States, the deposit insurer not only has important
supervisory functions, but has the lead role in resolving failing banks.

Resolving weak banks efficiently can have important repercussions
for financial and economic development. Honohan and Klingebiel
(2003) estimate the average fiscal cost of banking crisis resolution at 13
percent of GDP, while Claessens, Klingebiel, and Laeven (2003) show
that different approaches to resolving banking crises have led to very
different outcomes in terms of recovery of economic growth after the
crisis. But even the failure of individual banks can imply large financial
and economic costs for depositors, borrowers, and taxpayers, as the
failure of institutions such as the Bank of Credit and Commerce International (BCCI) has shown (see Bartholomew and Gup 1997 for an
overview of bank failures across non-U.S. G10 countries).

While there is a large theoretical and empirical literature on the insolvency and resolution of nonfinancial corporations, the literature on
financial corporation distress has focused mostly on systemic banking

crises, namely, the determinants and resolution strategies for wide-spread bank failures, rather than on the efficient resolution of idiosyn-cratic bank failures.[1] Similarly, while there is a large theoretical and empirical literature on the relationship between deposit insurance and bank fragility, its link with bank failure resolution has not been empiri-cally explored.[2] While policymakers' attention has recently shifted to the nonsystemic resolution of idiosyncratic bank failures, up to date there is no cross-country evidence on its optimal design.[3] In this chap-ter we assess empirically the relationship between the design of bank failure resolution arrangements and bank fragility. Specifically, this chapter addresses two questions: first, is a bank failure resolution sys-tem that relies more on the deposit insurer more conducive to market discipline? Second, which institutional structure of a deposit insurer involved in bank failure resolution is most conducive to bank stability?

There is little disagreement that banks need special insolvency rules compared to nonfinancial corporations (Hüpkes 2004). Their role in transforming maturity, namely, transforming short-term deposits into medium to long-term loans, makes banks more sensitive to short-term liquidity shortages that ultimately could result in bank runs (Dia-mond and Dybvig 1983). Specifically, an interruption of the access to their savings in the failed bank can cause depositors to panic and run on other, fundamentally sound, banks. Furthermore, the informa-tion value of an ongoing credit relationship, which serves as the basis for debtor discipline and access to credit, decreases substantially in the case of failing banks. Finally, banks' critical role in market-based economies—providing payment services and intermediating society's savings—and their role in the transmission of monetary policy may justify special insolvency rules for banks (Benston and Kaufman 1996).

While the special nature of banking and its importance for market economies justifies a special regulatory, supervisory, and insolvency regime, the rules for this regime have to be structured in an incentive-compatible way. Given the option character of bank equity, bankers face strong incentives to lend aggressively and take on excessive risks, ignoring prudent risk management (Merton 1977). The lower their capital base, the less they have to lose and the more they can gain through aggressive lending. Both discipline by creditors and deposi-tors and the regulatory and supervisory framework have an important role to play in checking these incentives. Similarly, the effective and timely intervention and resolution of failing banks is important to min-imize aggressive risk taking by banks and thus reduce bank fragility. If bankers know that they face immediate exit combined with the complete loss of all equity in the case of insolvency, they are less willing to take aggressive and imprudent risks. If depositors and creditors know that they will suffer losses in the case of bank failure, they will be more willing to exert market discipline. Effective and timely intervention and resolution of failing banks is thus crucial to maintain market discipline and reduce bank fragility. In practice, however, bank authorities are often slow to close banks, allowing for regulatory capital forbearance, particularly in the case of explicit deposit insurance and systemically important banks (see Ronn and Verma 1986 for a model of deposit insurance that incorporates regulatory forbearance). Empirical research shows that in particular during episodes of systemic financial crisis, bank authorities are often reluctant to close banks, resulting in large fiscal costs and a deeper crisis in terms of corporate sector slowdown (Honohan and Klingebiel 2003; Claessens, Klingebiel, and Laeven 2003; Brown and Dinc 2006).

Theory, however, does not provide an unambiguous answer to the question of who should resolve failing banks. In countries with explicit deposit insurance schemes, deposit insurers might be more likely to monitor banks carefully and intervene rapidly into failing banks as they have to carry the costs in terms of higher payout to indemnified depositors. On the other hand, the deposit insurer might intervene too soon to protect her funds, while other agencies might take into account the effects of regulatory action on financial intermediation. This would call for the Central Bank or another agency to be in charge of liquidity support and failure resolution in the case of small shocks, and for the deposit insurer to be in charge in the case of large shocks (Repullo 2000).[4] The deposit insurers might face other perverse incentives and conflicts of interest. First, if the deposit insurance agency is run by the banking industry itself, it might face a conflict of interest in dealing with failing banks. Second, similar as bank supervisors, deposit insurers might have incentives to postpone realization of bank losses to avoid that bank failure "happens on their watch." Third, if the deposit insurer is placed with uninsured depositors in the creditor preference during bankruptcy and ahead of other nondeposit creditors, they might face incentives to intervene too late (Bliss and Kaufman 2006).

The discussion on the role of the deposit insurance agency in bank failure resolution is also intimately linked to the design and structure of the deposit insurance scheme. On the one hand, the incentive compatible structure of deposit insurance can be enhanced by a proper alignment of interests. Funding and administration of the deposit insurance scheme by the banking industry can increase the incentives of the deposit insurer to minimize insurance losses Demirgüç-Kunt and Kane 2002). On the other hand, a deposit insurance scheme can only maintain market discipline and minimize moral hazard risks if problem banks are efficiently and timely intervened and resolved (Beck 2004). Theory suggests that the possibilities of the deposit insurer to minimize insurance losses can be further enhanced by aligning interests such as by yielding supervisory power to the deposit insurer. This can be taken even further by giving the deposit insurer the authority and responsibility to intervene into problem banks and resolve failing banks.

In this chapter we study empirically the link between the involvement of deposit insurers in bank failure resolution and bank risk. In section 4.2, we present cross-country indicators of the responsibility of deposit insurers to intervene into banks across fifty-seven countries. We also consider a second indicator, the power of deposit insurer to cancel or revoke the deposit insurance for one of their members. Further, we consider to which extent deposit insurers are independent from political pressure and have access to supervisory information and the interaction of these two institutional features with the role of deposit insurers in bank failure resolution. We enrich the data analysis with a discussion of some specific country cases to illustrate to which extent the institutional variation of deposit insurance and bank failure resolution varies across countries. In section 4.3, we turn to formal hypothesis testing. Specifically, we regress a measure of bank risk on the indicators introduced in section 4.2, controlling for other bank and country traits. Our results indicate the importance of the deposit insurer's role in maintaining bank stability. Banks are more stable, namely, farther away from insolvency in countries where deposit insurers have a greater role in bank failure resolution. This empirical finding is robust to controlling for other bank and country characteristics, most importantly to controlling for the generosity of deposit insurance and the independence and intervention powers of bank supervisors, but also to the incidence of systemic banking crises. However, we also find that this positive effect only takes place if the deposit insurer is politically independent and if it has sufficient access to supervisory information. Finally, we find that the importance of deposit insurers' involvement in failure resolution increases in the size of banks, which underlines the importance of this institutional feature to reduce too-big-to-fail moral hazard risks.

The analysis in this chapter is related to a large theoretical and empirical literature on the effect of deposit insurance on banks' risk-taking behavior, market discipline and systemic fragility (see Demirgüç-Kunt and Kane 2002 for an overview). Demirgüç-Kunt and Huizinga (2004) find that higher explicit coverage and having a funded scheme reduce market discipline, namely, the sensitivity of the deposit interest rate the bank has to pay to changes in profits and liquidity ratios. Demirgüç-Kunt and Detragiache (2002) likewise find that the probability of having a banking crisis increases in the coverage limit and in having a funded scheme. Hovakimian, Kane, and Laeven (2003) show that risk shifting to the government or subsidization of risk taking is stronger in poor institutional environments but can be reduced with an incentive compatible design.

Our analysis also falls within the broader literature on the optimal design of financial systems and financial sector regulation. Jayaratne and Strahan (1995) show that economic growth in U.S. states increased substantially following bank branch deregulation. Barth, Caprio, and Levine (2004) collect cross-country data on an array of regulatory and supervisory practices, including regulations on bank entry, activity restrictions, capital adequacy, loan classification, and provisioning, as well as information about the official power, independence, and resources of bank supervisors and the regulations fostering information disclosure and private-sector monitoring of banks. They find that banking systems with excessive supervision and regulation of banks are less developed and stable than banking systems where markets play an important role in monitoring banks. Similarly, Beck, Demirgüç-Kunt, and Levine (2006) find that firms face higher obstacles due to corruption in lending in countries with more powerful bank supervisors and less private sector monitoring. Often political economy factors affect the design of financial systems. Kroszner and Strahan (1999) show that lobbying by interest groups affected the decision to relax bank branching restrictions in the United States, while Kroszner and Stratmann (1998), Kane and Wilson (1998), and Laeven (2002) show that political interest groups affect the design of deposit insurance.

4.2 Deposit Insurance and Bank Failure Resolution across Countries

This section introduces several indicators of deposit insurers' involvement in bank failure resolution and the financial safety net in a broader sense. These indicators are constructed from raw data in Barth, Caprio, and Levine 2004 and Demirgüç-Kunt, Kane, Karacaovali, and Laeven (chapter 11). Table 4.1 presents the variables for the fifty-seven countries in our sample, all countries with explicit deposit insurance schemes, and the appendix describes the exact definition and source of all variables. We discuss cross-country differences in the institutional set up of bank failure resolution schemes, especially with respect to deposit insurers' involvement and illustrate with a short discussion of some specific countries.

4.2.1 Indicators of Deposit Insurance and Bank Failure Resolution

One of the most important institutional questions in bank failure resolution is the responsibility for intervening failing banks. Here we focus on the question whether in countries with explicit deposit insurance the deposit insurer has the authority and responsibility to intervene in a bank (*DI intervention*). In ten out of the fifty-seven countries, the deposit insurer has such responsibility; this is the case in such diverse countries as Algeria, Hungary, and the United States.

Almost as significant as the authority to intervene banks is the possibility to revoke membership of banks in the deposit insurance scheme. Does the deposit insurance authority have the legal power to cancel or revoke deposit insurance for any participating bank (*DI power to revoke*)? While revoking membership is certainly not the same as intervening and potentially withdrawing a banking license, the practical effect can be the same, especially if the deposit insurer and/or the bank have to inform the public. In twenty-three countries, the deposit insurer has the right to cancel or revoke membership, including in seven of the ten countries where the deposit insurer has the authority to intervene. Unfortunately, we do not have cross-country information, whether deposit insurers in these twenty-three countries have actually exercised the right to cancel or revoke deposit insurance before a bank is intervened or the bank license is canceled; evidence from the few countries for which we do have such information, however, suggests that this is a very rare event. Therefore, it must be the threat of revoking rather than the actual action that provides the necessary discipline.

The impact of the power to intervene banks and/or to revoke deposit insurance certainly differs with the degree of independence that deposit insurer enjoys. Deposit insurers that are not politically independent might see abuse of the authority to intervene and revoke membership. We therefore control for the independence of the deposit insurer from political pressure with a dummy variable called *DI independence* that takes the value one if the deposit insurance agency is

Table 4.1
Bank stability and bank failure resolution across countries

Country name	z-score	DI inter-vention	DI power to revoke	DI indepen-dence	DI in supervision
Albania	11.64	0	1	0	1
Algeria	60.22	1	0	0	1
Argentina	6.47	0	0	1	0
Austria	35.27	0	1	1	0
Bahrain	56.46	0	1	0	1
Belarus	9.09	1	1	0	1
Belgium	23.27	0	0	0	0
Bosnia and Herzegovina	24.33	0	1	0	0
Brazil	13.52	0	0	1	0
Bulgaria	10.62	0	0	0	0
Canada	32.39	1	1	1	0
Chile	18.56	0	0	1	0
Colombia	10.29	0	0	0	0
Croatia	29.40	0	0	0	0
Czech Republic	17.70	0	0	0	0
Denmark	33.20	0	1	1	0
El Salvador	36.88	0	0	0	0
France	31.74	0	1	1	0
Germany	47.99	0	0	1	1
Guatemala	23.27	0	0	0	0
Honduras	20.12	0	0	1	0
Hungary	13.27	1	1	0	0
India	18.35	0	1	0	1
Ireland	37.56	0	1	0	1
Italy	39.47	1	1	1	0
Japan	46.92	0	0	0	0
Jordan	37.48	0	0	0	0
Kazakhstan	10.87	0	1	0	1
Kenya	27.21	0	1	0	1
Korea, Republic	1.53	0	0	0	0
Latvia	8.54	0	0	0	0
Lebanon	23.38	0	0	0	0
Luxembourg	28.38	0	1	1	0
Macedonia, FYR	16.50	0	0	0	0
Mexico	11.68	0	0	1	0
Netherlands	40.25	0	0	0	1

Table 4.1
(continued)

Country name	z-score	DI intervention	DI power to revoke	DI independence	DI in supervision
Nicaragua	10.84	0	0	0	0
Nigeria	11.98	0	1	0	0
Norway	10.11	0	0	1	0
Oman	19.86	1	1	0	1
Peru	17.95	0	0	1	0
Philippines	37.44	0	1	1	0
Poland	13.99	0	0	0	0
Portugal	37.20	0	0	0	1
Romania	8.67	0	0	0	0
Slovak Republic	16.06	1	0	0	0
Slovenia	41.36	1	0	0	1
Spain	38.63	0	0	0	1
Sri Lanka	5.14	0	1	0	1
Sweden	32.60	0	1	0	1
Switzerland	51.14	0	1	1	0
Taiwan, China	17.69	0	0	0	1
Trinidad and Tobago	23.80	0	0	0	1
Ukraine	9.18	1	1	0	1
United Kingdom	36.19	0	0	1	1
United States	48.84	1	1	1	1
Venezuela, RB	13.30	0	0	0	0

either privately administered or in an independent public agency, and zero otherwise. In eighteen countries, the deposit insurer is either privately managed or politically independent, namely, housed in an institution such as a politically independent central bank or bank regulatory authority. Only three of the deposit insurers who have the authority to intervene are also independent. *DI independence* is not significantly correlated with either *DI intervention* or *DI power to revoke*.

The proper use of the power to intervene and revoke deposit insurance certainly depends on sufficient information about the member banks. We therefore control for the access of the deposit insurer to supervisory information with *DI in supervision*, a dummy variable that takes a value of one if the deposit insurance agency is housed inside the bank supervisory agency, and zero otherwise. We note, however, that this is a proxy variable for access to supervisory information; as we will discuss, not all countries where the deposit insurer is housed in the supervisory authority, use this institutional link adequately, while other deposit insurers have access to supervisory information without being housed in the corresponding authority. In twenty-one countries, the deposit insurer is housed inside the supervisory agency, including in six of the ten countries, where the deposit insurer has the authority to intervene. There is a positive correlation of *DI in supervision* with *DI intervention* and *DI power to revoke*, but a negative correlation with *DI independence* suggesting that deposit insurers are more likely to be housed in the supervisory authority, if the latter is not politically independent.

4.2.2 Deposit Insurance and Bank Failure Resolution: Country Examples

While the four variables introduced in the previous section give a first overview of the variation in deposit insurer's role in bank failure resolution across countries, they are not able to capture the institutional richness of safety net arrangements. We therefore now turn to a brief discussion of some specific countries to illustrate to which extent deposit insurance and bank failure resolution are linked with each other or not. We discuss the following countries for which we have information on safety net arrangements, including bank failure resolution: the United States, Germany, Brazil, Kenya, Uganda, and Bangladesh.

Take first the United States, perhaps the banking system where the link between deposit insurance, bank supervision, and bank failure resolution is institutionally strongest.[5] The Federal Deposit Insurance Corporation (FDIC), a politically independent entity, does not only insure its members' deposits, it is also a bank supervisor and has complete control over the bank failure resolution process, with only ex post judicial review. The FDIC is either the primary supervisor or the backup supervisor of all banks insured by its fund and has the obligation to intervene in any bank for which it is the primary supervisor and that is "critically undercapitalized," currently defined as a capital to weighted asset ratio of less than 2 percent.[6] The bank resolution process is completely administrative, without court involvement, and only some decisions subject to ex post judicial review and with damages the only available remedy. The FDIC is completely in charge of the process and has to resolve the bank according to the least cost criterion, namely, the method that results in the least cost for the deposit insurer. The FDIC's role in bank failure resolution was strengthened to its current form after the banking crisis of the 1990s. While certainly too early to draw any conclusion, its incentive compatible setup might have contributed to a more stable banking system over the past decade and a half.

Let us now turn to Germany, where there is also a close link between deposit insurance and bank failure resolution, but on an informal and private level (Beck 2002, 2004). While the data in table 4.1 refer to the European Union (EU) mandated limited deposit insurance for all banks, there are several privately run deposit insurance schemes, among them one for private commercial banks. The deposit insurance fund is managed by the German Bankers Association, which has the right to cancel membership for weak banks, an option it has, however, never exercised. The deposit insurer demands regular audit reports about all its members, can impose corrective actions on basis of these reports, and even impose penalties. While the resolution of failing institutions is the task of the Federal Financial Supervisory Authority as successor of the Federal Bank Supervisory Authority, the resolution has been traditionally undertaken in close informal cooperation with the banking association and creditor banks of the troubled bank. In most cases, a market-based solution, where creditor banks take over the troubled banks or the failed bank is sold to a third party with the deposit insurer filling the gap, has been achieved. In at least one case, the initiative for the resolution of a troubled bank was actually initiated by the Banking Association rather than the supervisory authority, testimony to the strong supervisory and monitoring role that the private deposit insurer takes. The private nature of deposit insurance and bank failure resolution has developed over the years out of the clublike nature of the banking system with institutional arrangements designed to enforce mutual monitoring, peer discipline and peer assistance.[7] While the incentive compatible structure of the German financial safety net might have contributed to banking system stability, there are also concerns of lacking competitiveness stemming from the strong role for incumbent banks in the current system.

Take next Brazil. As in Germany, the deposit insurance agency (FGC) of Brazil is independent and privately managed.[8] Unlike in Germany, however, the deposit insurance agency FGC is limited to a pay box function and does not have any involvement in the supervision of its member banks and no role in the resolution of failed banks. The resolution of troubled banks in Brazil is an extrajudicial process, led by interveners and liquidators appointed by the central bank. The central bank has the power to intervene in problem banks and has different options, including conservatorship and liquidation at its disposal; conservators and liquidators are appointed by the central bank. Brazil is thus an example of a banking system where deposit insurance, on the one side, and supervision and failure resolution, on the other side, are institutionally completely separated (Beck 2004).

Kenya is an example where the deposit insurer seems in a very good position to have a significant role in bank failure resolution. The Deposit Protection Fund (DPF) is housed inside the Central Bank of Kenya, which has also bank supervisory authority, and is in charge of liquidating closed banks. In reality, however, its role is limited. While it shares staff with the central bank, it does not have direct access to supervisory information and is not involved at all in supervisory decisions, especially with respect to problem banks. The decision to intervene failing banks is taken by the central bank, with approval of the Minister of Finance, a feature that also sheds doubts on the political independence of the central bank. The character of deposit insurance as pay box is even stronger in neighboring Uganda, where the deposit insurance fund is administered by the central bank without any separate institutional structure. While the Bank of Uganda (BOU) is also the bank supervisor, the housing of the deposit insurance fund inside the supervisory authority does not seem to provide any incentives for loss minimization.

Bangladesh illustrates how even the absence of bank failure resolution can have an important impact on the efficiency and fragility of banks (Beck and Rahman 2006). While there is an explicit deposit insurance scheme, housed inside the central bank, Bangladesh Bank, which is also responsible for banking supervision, it has never been used as Bangladesh Bank has never allowed a domestic bank to fail. Rather, weak banks are being referred to the Problem Bank Monitoring Department within Bangladesh Bank where they are subject to special supervisory oversight and certain regulatory restrictions and enjoy regulatory forbearance. There is thus an implicit blanket guarantee for depositors, creditors and even owners of all banks. The lack of exit of failed banks, together with a politicized licensing process, which also shows the lack of political independence of the bank supervisory entity, and the still high share of government-owned banks in the financial system, explain the lack of market discipline in the Bangladeshi banking system. This has resulted in several weak and undercapitalized

banks—both government-owned and privately owned—and inefficient intermediation, as the continuous operation of failed banks provides unhealthy competition on the depositor side and distorted
incentives for bank-borrower relationships. High spreads and a lack of
market-based lending (as opposed to connected or relationship lending) have been explained with these deficiencies.

Is deposit insurance necessary for an effective bank failure resolution
scheme? Recent efforts in Latin America have tried to link deposit insurance with a more effective bank failure resolution through the purchase and assumption technique. This technique implies that insured
deposits and good assets are carved out and sold to another, performing, bank while impaired assets and noninsured claims on the banks
are resolved through liquidation procedures.[9] Such schemes have been
introduced in Argentina, Bolivia, Guatemala, and the Dominican Republic. This close link between deposit insurance and bank failure
resolution through the technique of purchase and assumption seems
to imply the necessity of an explicit deposit insurance scheme for effective bank failure resolution.

Are there examples where effective failure resolution has happened
without deposit insurance? Consider first Brazil, where the current
deposit insurance scheme was introduced as a consequence of the financial crisis of the mid-1990s, when the central bank had to resolve
several large and medium-sized privately owned banks. As the constitution prohibits the use of any public funds for depositor compensation, the authorities had to rely on special lines of credit, tax
incentives, and regulatory forbearance to resolve the failing banks
through intervention and purchase and assumption techniques.[10] The
central bank took the leading role in this process, identifying purchas-
ers for troubled banks and providing liquidity support to fill the balance sheet gap. Only in one case was the deposit insurance scheme ex
post involved, while in all other cases, the central bank resolved the
banks without assistance from deposit insurance. Similarly, in South
Africa and Mauritius, two other middle-income countries, the authorities have resolved several small banks in recent years without a deposit insurance fund. In some cases, however, public funds were used
to facilitate the resolution and compensate depositors. While these
cases suggest that authorities can resolve failed banks without an explicit deposit insurance scheme, it also underlines that the institutional
structure of the financial safety net cannot be treated out of the context
of the overall institutional framework in a country including the moral

hazard risk arising from implicit or explicit guarantees provided by the government.

4.3 Deposit Insurance and Bank Failure Resolution: Cross-Country Regressions

After having discussed cross-country variation in deposit insurer's involvement in bank failure resolution, we now turn to empirically testing the relationship between the structure of bank failure resolution scheme and bank fragility. This section first introduces our indicator of bank fragility, presents control variables and methodology, and finally discusses regression results.

4.3.1 Indicator of Bank Stability

The z-score is a measure of bank stability and indicates the distance from insolvency. It combines accounting measures of profitability, leverage, and volatility. Specifically, if we define insolvency as a state where losses surmount equity $(E < -\pi)$ (where E is equity and π is profits), A as total assets, $ROA = \pi/A$ as return on assets, and $CAR = E/A$ as capital-asset ratio, the probability of insolvency can be expressed as $\text{prob}(-ROA < CAR)$. If profits are assumed to follow a normal distribution, it can be shown that $z = (ROA + CAR)/SD(ROA)$ is the inverse of the probability of insolvency. Specifically, z indicates the number of standard deviation that a bank's return on assets has to drop below its expected value before equity is depleted and the bank is insolvent (see Roy 1952; Hannan and Henwick 1988; Boyd, Graham, and Hewitt 1993; De Nicolo 2000). Thus, a higher z-score indicates that the bank is more stable.

While the z-score has been used widely in the financial and nonfinancial literature, it is subject to several caveats.[11] Specifically, it might underestimate banking risk for several reasons. First, it measures risk in a single period of time and does not capture the probability of a sequence of negative profits. Second, it considers only the first and second moment of the distribution of profits and ignores the potential skewness of the distribution (De Nicolo 2000). On the other hand, this measurement bias is less of a concern if it is uniformly distributed across banks and countries. A third concern is the reliance of the z-score on accounting data whose quality might vary across countries. Specifically, several papers have shown the tendency of firms to smooth reported earnings over time and that the degree of earning smoothing varies with the degree of institutional development (see, e.g., Leuz, Nanda, and Wysocki 2003). This, however, should bias our results against finding a significant relationship between measures of deposit insurance and bank failure resolution and bank fragility. As an alternative method, other authors have relied on stock market data to compute bank risk as a put option on the value of the bank's assets (Laeven 2002; Hovakimian, Kane, and Laeven 2003). Relying on stock market data, however, reduces our sample to a small set of large, listed banks in countries with stock markets, and we therefore decide to use z-scores that can be calculated for all banks instead.

We calculate the z-score for a sample of 1,752 banks across fifty-seven countries, with the number of banks included in our sample varying from a high of 315 in the United States and a low of 3 in the Republic of Korea, Oman, Sri Lanka, Sweden, and Trinidad and Tobago.[12] We calculate the return on assets, its standard deviation, and the capital-asset ratio over the period 1997–2003. In the regression analysis, we include the log of the z-score to control for nonlinear effects and outliers.[13] Since z-scores might vary with the time period over which they are measured, we will test the sensitivity of our results to the time period over which z-scores are computed. All bank data are from Bankscope, a commercial database of financial statements of financial institutions around the world. While it does not provide a perfect coverage of banks, it usually covers around 90 percent of countries' banking systems in terms of assets.

Table 4.1 shows a wide variation in bank fragility across countries. Here we present the unweighted average of z-scores across all banks for each country in the sample. The z-scores indicate that for banks' losses to deplete equity, profits have to fall more than sixty times below the average level of profits in Algeria, but only less than two standard deviations in Korea. The average bank in the average countries has a z-score of 24.

4.3.2 Control Variables

We include several bank level variables to control for bank characteristics that might influence the fragility of individual banks. Specifically, we include the log of total assets in U.S. dollars for the first available year. Larger banks might be better able to diversify risk and thus have more stable earnings, reducing their risk of insolvency. On the other hand, larger banks might take larger risks, especially if they consider themselves too large to fail. Next, we control for the extent to which the bank earns noninterest income using the ratio of other operating income to total revenues. Noninterest income, which includes income from fees, commissions and trading activities, tends to be more volatile than interest income, so we would expect that banks with a larger share of other operating income are less stable and have lower z-scores. We also control for the liquidity of banks by including the ratio of liquid assets to short-term debt, thus controlling for the ability of banks to match debt withdrawable on a short notice with liquid assets (or with assets that can easily be made liquid).

We include several country-level variables in our regressions analysis. Most importantly, we include a measure of the coverage of deposit insurance scheme in terms of average income. Specifically, we relate the coverage limit of deposit insurance to average GDP per capita (Demirgüç-Kunt and Huizinga 2004) and refer to this variable as *DI coverage*. Demirgüç-Kunt and Detragiache (2002) have shown that countries with higher deposit insurance coverage limits are more likely to suffer systemic banking crises. While some countries have low explicit coverage limit, coverage is often extended in the case of systemic failure or even failure of individual banks. Expanding coverage beyond the explicitly insured depositors, however, can negatively impact market discipline and thus increase the moral hazard risk of deposit insurance. In robustness tests, we therefore control for *Implicit coverage*, a dummy variable that takes value one if deposit insurance coverage was extended beyond the explicit coverage limit in recent bank failures.

We also include several other country level variables in order to separate the effect of the financial safety net design from other country characteristics that might influence bank fragility. First, we control for the log of GDP per capita in constant U.S. dollars in 1997 as countries at different income levels might be subject to different economic shocks and sources of volatility, which would affect the level and volatility of bank earnings. Second, we control for the growth rate of real GDP per capita and its standard deviation. While faster growing economies might be less subject to bank fragility, higher volatility in economic growth might subject banks to higher fragility. Finally, we control for an indicator of institutional development, constructed by Kaufman, Kraay, and Mastruzzi (2003), which is the average of six indicators measuring rule of law, control of corruption, government effectiveness, regulatory quality, political stability, and voice and accountability. Controlling for such an encompassing indicator of the institutional framework helps us ensure that our indicators of the financial safety net do not capture the impact of overall institutional quality on bank stability.

4.3.3 Methodology

In order to assess the effect of financial safety net traits on bank stability, we regress the z-score, computed for individual banks over the period 1997–2003, on bank and country characteristics. Our main regression specification is as follows:

$$Z_{i,k} = \alpha X_{i,k} + \beta Z_k + \gamma D_k + \varepsilon_{i,k}, \tag{1}$$

where Z is the z-score of bank i in country k, X is a vector of bank characteristics, Z is a vector of country characteristics, and D is a vector of variables capturing the institutional characteristics of deposit insurance. Although we control for an array of country characteristics, the stability of individual banks within a country might be driven by an omitted factor or might be otherwise correlated with each other. We therefore allow for clustering, namely, we relax the restrictions that the error terms of banks within a country are independent of each other.

In the discussion of the results, we will focus on the significance and sign of the coefficients in the vector γ. A negative coefficient on *DI coverage*, the ratio of explicit deposit insurance coverage to GDP per capita, would confirm previous results that more extensive explicit deposit insurance increases the incentives for banks to take aggressive risks. A positive coefficient on *DI intervention* and *DI power to revoke* would suggest a positive role for deposit insurers in bank failure resolution to the extent that they help dampen risk taking by banks, while a negative coefficient would indicate a damaging role of deposit insurers in bank failure resolution.

4.3.4 Results

The results in table 4.2 suggest that banks are more stable in countries with a more prominent role of the deposit insurer in bank failure resolution. We regress the z-scores of individual banks on *DI coverage*, *DI intervention*, bank level control variables and country level control variables. *DI intervention* enters positively and significantly in all regressions, even after controlling for a variety of bank and country characteristics and the coverage limit for deposit insurance. When we evaluate the economic effect at the mean z-score of 24, we find that banks in countries where the deposit insurer has the authority to intervene are on average better able to withstand a fall in profits that is at

Table 4.2
Bank stability and the design of bank failure resolution

	(1)	(2)	(3)	(4)	(5)
Log total assets	−0.010	0.000	−0.007	0.004	0.006
	(0.020)	(0.021)	(0.021)	(0.022)	(0.021)
Liquidity	−0.004	−0.003	−0.004*	−0.004	−0.004
	(0.002)	(0.003)	(0.002)	(0.002)	(0.002)
Noninterest income	−0.135*	−0.144*	−0.110	−0.134	−0.115
	(0.079)	(0.084)	(0.075)	(0.085)	(0.077)
Log GDP per capita	0.000	0.087	−0.009	−0.043	−0.004
	(0.094)	(0.086)	(0.097)	(0.093)	(0.102)
Growth	0.266	−0.359	−2.782	−4.279	−6.026
	(4.402)	(3.799)	(3.713)	(3.906)	(4.083)
Volatility	−14.386**	−16.295***	−18.763***	−20.368***	−20.207***
	(6.311)	(5.479)	(4.502)	(5.235)	(5.238)
DI coverage	−0.001**	−0.001**	−0.000	−0.000	−0.001**
	(0.000)	(0.000)	(0.000)	(0.000)	(0.000)
KK index	0.339*	0.176	0.264	0.399**	0.381**
	(0.173)	(0.152)	(0.173)	(0.172)	(0.181)
DI intervention	0.314***		0.231**	0.291***	0.355***
	(0.112)		(0.102)	(0.096)	(0.116)
DI power to revoke		0.330***			
		(0.102)			
Supervisory independence			0.131***		
			(0.041)		
Supervisory power				0.096***	
				(0.034)	
Private monitoring					−0.129
					(0.085)
Number of observations	1752	1752	1610	1623	1623
Number of countries	57	57	45	46	46
R-squared	0.21	0.22	0.22	0.22	0.22

Notes: Dependent variable is the z-score. We report OLS regressions with clustered standard errors between parentheses. * significant at 10 percent; ** significant at 5 percent; *** significant at 1 percent. For definitions and sources, see the appendix to chapter 4.

least six standard deviations higher than banks in countries with no role for the deposit insurer before becoming insolvent. This compares to a sample standard deviation in z-scores of 14. When we consider the deposit insurer's right to cancel or revoke a bank's deposit insurance, we get the same result (column [2]).

Consistent with previous research by Demirgüç-Kunt and Detragiache (2002), we also find that banks are more fragile in countries with more generous deposit insurance. DI coverage enters negatively and

significantly in all but one regression. On the other hand, banks are
more stable in countries with more independent and more powerful
bank supervisors (columns [3] and [4]). Controlling for the generosity
of deposit insurance and the role of the deposit insurer in bank failure
resolution, we cannot find a significant relationship between the importance of private monitoring in supervision and bank z-scores (column [5]). Our measures of the independence and power of bank
supervisors and on the degree of private monitoring of banks are from
Barth, Caprio, and Levine (2004). See table 4A.1 for a more detailed
definition of these variables.

Turning to the bank- and country-level control variables, we find
that banks are more fragile in countries with more volatile GDP per
capita growth rates. The other bank- and country-level variables do
not enter significantly and robustly the regressions.

Overall, these results confirm the hypothesis that a greater role for
the deposit insurer in bank failure resolution can strengthen bank stability by aligning incentives within the financial safety net properly.
Deposit insurers have most at stake when banks fail; therefore, giving
them higher responsibility within the financial safety net can reduce
the negative moral hazard effects of deposit insurance. We next investigate whether this positive impact differs across different institutional
settings.

Table 4.3 shows that the role of deposit insurance in bank failure resolution interacts critically with other elements of the financial safety
net. The results in columns 1 and 2 indicate that the positive impact of
the intervention power of deposit insurers is strengthened if the deposit insurer is politically independent. While DI Independence enters
negatively, but insignificantly, its interaction with DI Intervention
enters positively. It is more, as the DI Intervention does not enter significantly anymore, this suggests that the power to intervene only has
a positive impact on bank stability if exercised by politically independent deposit insurers. Columns 3 and 4 suggest that the positive role
of the deposit insurer in bank failure resolution can only be found in
countries where the deposit insurance is located in the supervisory
agency and thus has direct access to supervisory information. While
none of the three variables (*DI intervention*, *DI in supervision*, and their
interaction) enter significantly by themselves, DI Intervention is positive and significant if the interaction term is nonzero, namely, the
deposit insurer can intervene and is located in the supervisory authority.[14] This suggests that (1) the role of the deposit insurer in bank failure resolution has only a positive impact on banks' stability if the

Table 4.3
Bank stability and the design of bank failure resolution: Interaction with other features of the financial safety net

	(1)	(2)	(3)	(4)	(5)	(6)
Log total assets	−0.010	−0.017	−0.016	−0.015	−0.012	−0.012
	(0.021)	(0.022)	(0.021)	(0.021)	(0.020)	(0.020)
Liquidity	−0.004*	−0.004*	−0.004**	−0.004*	−0.004*	−0.004*
	(0.002)	(0.002)	(0.002)	(0.002)	(0.002)	(0.002)
Noninterest income	−0.134	−0.130	−0.122	−0.124	−0.141*	−0.141*
	(0.081)	(0.080)	(0.076)	(0.077)	(0.083)	(0.083)
Log GDP per capita	0.003	−0.017	0.056	0.035	0.017	0.012
	(0.093)	(0.090)	(0.099)	(0.102)	(0.092)	(0.091)
Growth	−0.201	0.656	−0.177	−0.099	−0.295	−0.253
	(4.356)	(4.361)	(4.388)	(4.395)	(4.567)	(4.567)
Volatility	−14.248**	−13.865**	−14.486**	−14.894**	−14.362**	−14.045**
	(6.084)	(5.768)	(6.262)	(6.256)	(5.880)	(5.850)
DI coverage	−0.001	−0.001	−0.001**	−0.001**	−0.001***	−0.001***
	(0.000)	(0.000)	(0.000)	(0.000)	(0.000)	(0.000)
KK index	0.359**	0.372**	0.239	0.270	0.317*	0.328*
	(0.174)	(0.172)	(0.188)	(0.189)	(0.171)	(0.168)
DI intervention	0.325***	−0.154	0.222**	0.082	0.285***	0.265**
	(0.118)	(0.238)	(0.089)	(0.174)	(0.106)	(0.127)
DI independence	−0.063	−0.118				
	(0.145)	(0.138)				
DI intervention*		0.597**				
DI independence		(0.261)				
DI in supervision			0.222**	0.151		
			(0.090)	(0.107)		
DI intervention*				0.232		
DI in supervision				(0.198)		
Implicit coverage					−0.148	−0.168
					(0.093)	(0.101)
DI intervention*						0.110
Implicit coverage						(0.132)
Number of observations	1752	1752	1752	1752	1730	1730
Number of countries	57	57	57	57	54	54
R-squared	0.21	0.22	0.22	0.22	0.21	0.21

Notes: Dependent variable is the z-score. We report OLS regressions with clustered standard errors between parentheses. * significant at 10 percent; ** significant at 5 percent; *** significant at 1 percent. For definitions and sources, see the appendix.

deposit insurer is located inside the bank supervisory agency, and (2) housing the deposit insurance inside bank supervision has only positive repercussions for bank stability if the deposit insurer is given sufficient tools to discipline its members. The results in columns (5) and (6) suggest that the positive impact of involving deposit insurer in bank failure resolution can be significantly undermined if deposit insurance is extended beyond insured deposits in the case of bank failure. *Implicit coverage* enters negatively, but insignificantly in columns (5) and (6), while its interaction with *DI intervention* enters positively, but insignificantly, in column 6. More important, evaluating the effect of *DI intervention* if *Implicit coverage* equals one yields an insignificant coefficient. Given that *DI intervention* enters positively and significantly in columns (5) and (6), this suggests that the positive role of deposit insurers in bank failure resolution only holds if deposit insurance is not extended beyond its explicit limit.

Table 4.4 offers further robustness tests on the role of deposit insurers in bank failure resolution. We are concerned that our results may be driven by the effect of banking crises. Specifically, countries might have implemented certain reforms to their bank failure resolution system in times of systemic distress. We therefore control for banking crisis episodes by including a dummy variable *Banking crisis* that takes a value of one if the country experienced a systemic banking crisis during the sample period, and zero otherwise, based on data on the timing of banking crises from Caprio et al. (2005) who define banking crisis to be systemic if bank losses have eroded total bank capital in the system. We find that controlling for banking crises over our sample period does not change our results, and the relationship between *DI intervention* and bank stability does not vary across countries that have or have not experienced systemic banking crises (columns [1] and [2]). Controlling for banking crises in the three decades before our sample period, we again confirm our findings, but also find that *DI intervention* is more effective in fostering bank stability in countries that have suffered from a systemic banking crisis before our sample period (columns [3] and [4]).

Finally, we find that the involvement of deposit insurers in failure resolution is more effective for larger banks. Specifically, we interact *DI intervention* and *DI power to revoke* with the log of total assets. Both interaction terms enter positively and significantly (columns [5] and [6]).[15] This suggests that the role of deposit insurer in reducing aggressive and imprudent risk taking by being involved in failure resolution increases in the size of the bank. These results underline the importance

Table 4.4
Bank stability and the design of bank failure resolution: Robustness tests

	(1)	(2)	(3)	(4)	(5)	(6)
Log total assets	0	−0.002	−0.008	−0.003	−0.038	−0.037
	(0.018)	(0.019)	(0.020)	(0.020)	(0.025)	(0.030)
Liquidity	−0.004	−0.004	−0.004	−0.004	−0.004*	−0.004
	(0.002)	(0.002)	(0.002)	(0.003)	(0.002)	(0.003)
Noninterest income	−0.119	−0.118	−0.136*	−0.138*	−0.137	−0.143
	(0.077)	(0.077)	(0.080)	(0.081)	(0.083)	(0.088)
Log GDP per capita	0.012	−0.001	−0.006	−0.034	0	0.072
	(0.093)	(0.097)	(0.098)	(0.100)	(0.093)	(0.086)
Growth	0.511	0.646	−0.084	−0.216	0.801	−0.303
	(3.509)	(3.546)	(4.356)	(4.202)	(4.431)	(3.911)
Volatility	−8.958*	−8.910*	−14.008**	−13.197**	−14.505**	−16.108***
	(5.108)	(5.151)	(6.208)	(6.084)	(6.143)	(5.563)
DI coverage	0	0	−0.001**	−0.001	−0.001**	−0.001***
	(0.000)	(0.000)	(0.000)	(0.000)	(0.000)	(0.000)
KK index	0.270*	0.284*	0.317*	0.324*	0.341**	0.199
	(0.158)	(0.163)	(0.172)	(0.168)	(0.169)	(0.153)
DI intervention	0.288***	0.315***	0.374**	−0.091	−0.838	
	(0.097)	(0.106)	(0.142)	(0.088)	(0.559)	
DI revoke						−0.489
						(0.460)
Banking crisis, 1997–2003	−0.535***	−0.507***				
	(0.122)	(0.130)				
Banking crisis 1997–2003* DI intervention		−0.229				
		(0.327)				
Banking crisis, 1970–1997			−0.101	−0.214*		
			(0.111)	(0.117)		
Banking crisis 1970–1997* DI intervention				0.592***		
				(0.173)		
Log total assets* DI intervention					0.085**	
					(0.038)	
Log total assets* DI revoke						0.064*
						(0.035)
Number of observations	1752	1752	1752	1752	1752	1752
Number of countries	57	57	57	57	54	54
R-squared	0.23	0.23	0.21	0.21	0.21	0.22

Notes: Dependent variable is the z-score. We report OLS regressions with clustered standard errors between parentheses. * significant at 10 percent; ** significant at 5 percent; *** significant at 1 percent. For definitions and sources, see the appendix to chapter 4.

of a proper design of financial safety nets to reduce the moral hazard risk of too-large-to-fail banks.

4.4   Conclusions

We study the link between the involvement of deposit insurers in bank failure resolution and bank risk. Using different indicators and discussion of specific countries, we show that there is a wide variation in deposit insurer's role in bank failure resolution. Regression analysis confirms the importance of the deposit insurer's role in maintaining bank stability. We find that banks are more stable in countries where deposit insurers can intervene in banks and/or revoke membership in deposit insurance. This empirical finding is robust to controlling for other bank and country characteristics, including the generosity of deposit insurance, the independence and intervention powers of bank supervisors, and the incidence of banking crises. We also find important interactions between the powers of deposit insurers and their access to supervisory information; deposit insurers' involvement in bank failure resolution is only beneficial in terms of lower fragility if combined with supervisory oversight. Similarly, housing deposit insurance in bank supervision is only beneficial if it comes with corresponding powers vis-à-vis its members. Deposit insurers are only effective in resolving failed banks and fostering bank stability if they are politically independent. Finally, we find that the role of deposit insurers in the failure resolution scheme is more important for larger banks, underlying the importance of an incentive-compatible design of safety nets for reducing the moral hazard risks of too-large-to-fail banks.

While our results reinforce previous findings that high explicit deposit insurance coverage increases bank fragility, an incentive compatible design can help dampen this negative effect by giving the necessary tools and powers to the deposit insurer to discipline its members and thus minimize insurance losses and bank fragility. Our findings send a strong policy message to countries with existing explicit deposit insurance schemes: strengthening the supervisory capacity and powers of the deposit insurer vis-à-vis its members can have positive implications for bank stability.

Appendix

Table 4A.1 provides the definitions and sources of all variables used in the empirical analysis in this chapter.

Table 4A.1
Variable definitions and sources

Variable name	Description	Source
Dependent variable		
Z	Average $Z = (roa + ear)/sdroa$ over time for each bank between 1997 and 2003. roa is return on average assets of a bank calculated as net income divided by the average total assets during the year; ear is equity adequacy ratio of a bank calculated as the ratio of equity-to-total assets; $sdroa$ is the standard deviation of roa over the sample period of a bank.	Bankscope and authors' calculations
Bank-level variables		
Log total assets	Natural logarithm of total assets for each bank, the first available year (1997, if not 1998)	Bankscope and authors' calculations
Liquidity	Liquid assets to short-term debt ratio for each bank, (short-term debt is deposits and short-term funding) first available year (1997, if not 1998)	Bankscope and authors' calculations
Noninterest income	Noninterest income/total operating income for each bank; first available year (1997, if not 1998)	Bankscope and authors' calculations
Country-level variables		
Log GDP per capita	Natural logarithm of GDP per capita constant US$2000, 1997; if not available 1998	World Development Indicators
Growth	Average yearly GDP per capita constant local currency growth, 1997–2003, namely, the average of the yearly differences between the logarithm of GDP per capita in constant local currency	World Development Indicators and authors' calculations
Volatility	Standard deviation of yearly GDP per capita constant local currency growth, 1997–2003	World Development Indicators and authors' calculations
DI coverage	Ratio of coverage limit of deposit insurance to GDP per capita	Demirguc-Kunt et al. 2005
KK index	The average of six governance indicators (voice and accountability, political stability, government effectiveness, regulatory quality, rule of law, and control of corruption) in 1998 (higher is better)	Kaufmann, Kraay, and Mastruzzi 2003

Table 4A.1
(continued)

Variable name	Description	Source
DI intervention	A dummy variable that is equal to 1 if the deposit insurance authority can make the decision to intervene a bank.	Barth, Caprio, and Levine 2004
DI power to revoke	A dummy variable that is equal to 1 if the deposit insurance authority has the legal power to cancel or revoke deposit insurance for any participating bank.	Barth, Caprio, and Levine 2004
Supervisory independence	Supervisor independence from political (government) pressure and supervisor independence from pressure by bank managers (indicator ranges between 1 and 4)	Barth, Caprio, and Levine 2004
Supervisory power	Principal component indicator of fourteen dummy variables: 1. Does the supervisory agency have the right to meet with external auditors to discuss their report without the approval of the bank? 2. Are auditors required by law to communicate directly to the supervisory agency any presumed involvement of bank directors or senior managers in elicit activities, fraud, or insider abuse? 3. Can supervisors take legal action against external auditors for negligence? 4. Can the supervisory authority force a bank to change its internal organizational structure? 5. Are off-balance sheet items disclosed to supervisors? 6. Can the supervisory agency order the bank's directors or management to constitute provisions to cover actual or potential losses? 7. Can the supervisory agency suspend the directors' decision to distribute: (a) dividends? (b) bonuses? (c) management fees? 8. Can the supervisory agency legally declare—such that this declaration supersedes the rights of bank shareholders—that a bank is insolvent? 9. Does the Banking Law give authority to the supervisory agency to intervene, that is, suspend some or all ownership rights, in a problem bank? 10. Regarding bank restructuring and reorganization, can the supervisory agency or any other government agency do the following: (a) supersede shareholder rights? (b) remove and replace management? (c) remove and replace directors?	Barth, Caprio, and Levine 2004

Private monitoring	Principal component indicator of nine dummy variables that measure whether 1. bank directors and officials are legally liable for the accuracy of information disclosed to the public, 2. whether banks must publish consolidated accounts, 3. whether banks must be audited by certified international auditors, 4. whether 100 percent of the largest ten banks are rated by international rating agencies, 5. whether off-balance sheet items are disclosed to the public, 6. whether banks must disclose their risk management procedures to the public, 7. whether accrued, though unpaid interest/principal enter the income statement while the loan is still nonperforming, 8. whether subordinated debt is allowable as part of capital, and 9. whether there is no explicit deposit insurance system and no insurance was paid the last time a bank failed.	Barth, Caprio, and Levine 2004
DI in supervision	A dummy variable that is equal to zero if the deposit insurance agency is separate from the bank supervisory institution and one if it is within the bank supervisory institution.	Demirguc-Kunt et al. 2005
DI independence	A dummy variable that is equal to 1 if the deposit insurance agency is *Private monitoring* or independent, and zero otherwise.	Demirguc-Kunt et al. 2005
Implicit coverage	A dummy variable that takes the value 1 if the answer is "Yes" to the following question: "Were any deposits not explicitly covered by deposit insurance at the time of the failure compensated when the bank failed (excluding funds later paid out in liquidation procedures)?" and zero otherwise.	Barth, Caprio, and Levine 2004
Banking crisis	Dummy variable that takes the value of one if the country experienced a systemic banking crisis during the period 1997–2003, and zero otherwise.	Caprio et al. 2005

Acknowledgments

We would like to thank Aslı Demirgüç-Kunt and Ross Levine for very useful comments and Baybars Karacaovali for excellent research assistance.

Notes

1. For a discussion of the resolution of bankruptcy of nonfinancial corporations, see Gilson, Hotchkiss, and Ruback 2000, Hart 2000, Wihlborg, Gangopadhyay, and Hussain 2001, and Claessens and Klapper 2005. For resolution strategies of systemic banking crises, we refer to Claessens, Djankov, and Klapper 2003 and Honohan and Laeven 2005, among others.

2. See, for example, Demirgüç-Kunt and Detragiache 2002 on the link between deposit insurance and the stability of banking systems.

3. Bank for International Settlement 2002 and World Bank 2005 compile best-practice principles for resolving weak financial institutions. Mayes and Liuksila (2004) discuss institutions and policies referring to resolving both systemic and idiosyncratic bank failure.

4. Similarly, Kahn and Santos (2005) argue that it is best to separate lender of last resort and deposit insurance mandates, as the deposit insurer might face perverse incentives of regulatory forbearance if she also assumes lender of last resort responsibilities.

5. See Bliss and Kaufman 2006 for a discussion of the U.S. bank resolution system, in comparison with the corporate insolvency system in the United States.

6. Other supervisory agencies include the Office of the Comptroller of the Currency, the Thrift Supervisor and state supervisory agencies.

7. The German deposit insurance scheme resembles the successful insurance schemes in several U.S. states during the nineteenth and twentieth centuries that also relied on peer monitoring and liquidity support during times of distress.

8. FGC, however, is subject to guidance from the National Monetary Council, a body including the central bank governor and the Minister of Finance.

9. The actual technical details can vary significantly, depending on the legal framework in the respective country. See De la Torre 2000 for a discussion.

10. See Maia 1999 for a detailed discussion.

11. Note that this z-score differs from z-score developed by Altman (1968). The Altman z-score is a predictor of corporate financial distress based on financial ratios. The score is derived from a predictive model of a company's probability of default that uses five financial ratios. Altman applied multiple discriminant analysis to determine which financial ratios to include in the predictive model.

12. We imposed a requirement of at least three banks per country. Our results, however, are not affected if we use a broader cross-country sample including countries with data on less than three banks. In order to have a sufficient number of observations to calculate

the standard deviation of return on assets over time, we also require at least four years of data for each bank.

13. All our results are confirmed when we use the level of the z-score.

14. We assess the significance of the sum of the coefficient on *DI intervention* and of the coefficient on its interaction with *DI in supervision*. The insignificance of the individual terms can be explained by the high correlation between the two (74 percent).

15. We also tested for the significance of interaction terms with other bank characteristics but did not find any significance.

References

Altman, Edward I. 1968. Financial Ratios, Discriminant Analysis and the Prediction of Corporate Bankruptcy. *Journal of Finance* 23: 589–609.

Bank for International Settlements. 2002. Supervisory Guidance on Dealing with Weak Banks. Basel, Switzerland.

Barth, James, Gerard Caprio, and Ross Levine. 2004. Bank Supervision and Regulation: What Works Best? *Journal of Financial Intermediation* 13: 205–248.

Bartholomew, Philip F., and Benton E. Gup. 1997. A Survey of Bank Failures in the Non-U.S. G-10 Countries since 1980. Unpublished manuscript.

Beck, Thorsten. 2002. Deposit Insurance as Private Club: Is Germany a Model? *Quarterly Review of Economics and Finance* 42: 701–719.

Beck, Thorsten. 2004. The Incentive Compatible Design of Deposit Insurance and Bank Failure Resolution—Concepts and Country Studies. In *Who Pays for Bank Insolvency?* ed. David G. Mayes and Aarno Liuksila, 118–141. Basingstoke: Palgrave–McMillan.

Beck, Thorsten, Asli Demirgüç-Kunt, and Ross Levine. 2006. Bank Supervision and Corruption in Lending. *Journal of Monetary Economics* 53 (8): 2131–2163.

Beck, Thorsten, and Habibur Rahman. 2006. Creating a More Efficient Financial System: Challenges for Bangladesh. World Bank Policy Research Working Paper no. 3938, The World Bank, Washington, D.C.

Benston, George, and George Kaufman. 1996. The Appropriate Role of Bank Regulation. *Economic Journal* 106: 688–697.

Bliss, Robert R., and George G. Kaufman. 2006. U.S. Corporate and Bank Insolvency Regimes: An Economic Comparison and Evaluation. Working paper no. 2006-01, Federal Reserve Bank of Chicago.

Boyd, John H., Stanley L. Graham, and R. Shawn Hewitt. 1993. Bank Holding Company Mergers with Nonbank Finical Firms: Effects on the Risk of Failure. *Journal of Banking and Finance* 17: 43–63.

Brown, Craig O., and Serdar Dinc. 2006. Too Many To Fail? Evidence of Regulatory Reluctance in Bank Failures When the Banking Sector Is Weak. Mimeo., Northwestern University.

Caprio, Gerard, Daniela Klingebiel, Luc Laeven, and Guillermo Noguera. 2005. Banking Crisis Database. In *Systemic Financial Crises: Containment and Resolution*, ed. Patrick Honohan and Luc Laeven, 307–340. New York: Cambridge University Press.

Claessens, Stijn, Simeon Djankov, and Leora Klapper. 2003. Resolution of Financial Distress: Evidence from East Asia's Financial Crisis. *Journal of Empirical Finance* 10 (1–2): 199–216.

Claessens, Stijn, and Leora Klapper. 2005. Bankruptcy around the World: Explanations of Its Relative Use. *American Law and Economics Review* 7: 253–283.

Claessens, Stijn, Daniela Klingebiel, and Luc Laeven. 2003. Financial Restructuring in Banking and Corporate Sector Crises: What Policies to Pursue? In *Managing Currency Crises in Merging Markets*, ed. Michael Dooley and Jeffrey Frankel, 147–186. Chicago: University of Chicago Press.

De la Torre, Augusto. 2000. Resolving Bank Failures in Argentina: Recent Developments and Issues. Policy Research Working Paper no. 2295, The World Bank, Washington, D.C.

Demirgüç-Kunt, Aslı, and Enrica Detragiache. 2002. Does Deposit Insurance Increase Banking System Stability? An Empirical Investigation. *Journal of Monetary Economics* 49: 1373–1406.

Demirgüç-Kunt, Aslı, and Harry Huizinga. 2004. Market Discipline and Deposit Insurance. *Journal of Monetary Economics* 51: 375–399.

Demirgüç-Kunt, Aslı, and Edward Kane. 2002. Deposit Insurance around the World: Where Does it Work? *Journal of Economic Perspectives* 16: 175–195.

De Nicolo, Gianni. 2000. Size, Charter Value and Risk in Banking: An International Perspective. International Finance Discussion Papers no. 689, Board of Governors of the Federal Reserve System, Washington, D.C.

Diamond, Diamond, and Philip Dybvig. 1983. Bank Runs, Deposit Insurance and Liquidity. *Journal of Political Economy* 91: 401–419.

Gilson, Stuart C., Edith S. Hotchkiss, and Richard S. Ruback. 2000. Valuation of Bankrupt Firms. *Review of Financial Studies* 13: 43–74.

Hannan, Timothy H., and Gerald A. Hanweck. 1988. Bank Insolvency Risk and the Market for Large Certificates of Deposit. *Journal of Money, Credit and Banking* 20: 203–211.

Hart, Oliver. 2000. Different Approaches to Bankruptcy. NBER Working Paper no. 7921, National Bureau of Economic Research, Cambridge, Mass.

Honohan, Patrick, and Daniela Klingebiel. 2003. The Fiscal Cost Implications of an Accommodating Approach to Banking Crises. *Journal of Banking and Finance* 27: 1539–1560.

Honohan, Patrick, and Luc Laeven, eds. 2005. *Systemic Financial Crises: Containment and Resolution.* New York: Cambridge University Press.

Hovakimian, Armen, Edward Kane, and Luc Laeven. 2003. How Country and Safety Net Characteristics Affect Bank Risk-Shifting. *Journal of Financial Services Research* 23: 177–204.

Hüpkes, Eva. 2004. Insolvency—Why a Special Regime for Banks? Mimeo., Swiss National Bank.

Jayaratne, Jith, and Philip E. Strahan. 1995. The Finance–Growth Nexus: Evidence from Bank Branch Deregulation. *Quarterly Journal of Economics* 111: 639–670.

Kahn, Charles M., and João A. C. Santos. 2005. Allocating Bank Regulatory Powers: Lender of Last Resort, Deposit Insurance and Supervision. *European Economic Review* 49: 2107–2136.

Kane, Edward, and Barry K. Wilson. 1998. A Contracting-Theory Interpretation of the Origins of Federal Deposit Insurance. *Journal of Money, Credit, and Banking* 30: 573–595.

Kaufmann, Daniel, Aart Kraay, and Massimo Mastruzzi. 2003. Governance Matters III: Governance Indicators for 1996–2002. Policy Research Working Paper no. 3106, The World Bank, Washington, D.C.

Kroszner, Randall, and Philip Strahan. 1999. What Drives Deregulation? Economics and Politics of the Relaxation of Bank Branching Restrictions. *Quarterly Journal of Economics* 114: 1437–1467.

Kroszner, Randall, and Thomas Stratmann. 1998. Interest Group Competition and the Organization of Congress: Theory and Evidence from Financial Services' Political Action Committees. *American Economic Review* 88: 1163–1187.

Laeven, Luc. 2002. Bank Risk and Deposit Insurance. *World Bank Economic Review* 16: 109–137.

Leuz, Christian, D. J. Nanda, and Peter Wysocki. 2003. Investor Protection and Earnings Management: An International Comparison. *Journal of Financial Economics* 69: 505–527.

Maia, Geraldo. 1999. Restructuring the Banking System—The Case of Brazil. In *Bank Restructuring in Practice*. BIS Policy Papers no. 6, 106–123, Bank for International Settlement.

Mayes, David G., and Aarno Luiksila. 2004. *Who Pays for Bank Insolvency?* Basingstoke, UK: Palgrave-McMillan.

Merton, Robert. 1977. An Analytical Derivation of the Cost of Deposit Insurance and Loan Guarantees. *Journal of Banking and Finance* 1: 3–11.

Repullo, Rafael. 2000. Who Should Act as Lender of Last Resort? An Incomplete Contracts Model. *Journal of Money, Credit, and Banking* 32: 580–605.

Ronn, Ehud I., and Avinash K. Verma. 1986. Pricing Risk–Adjusted Deposit Insurance: An Option-Based Model. *Journal of Finance* 41: 871–895.

Roy, Andrew D. 1952. Safety First and the Holding of Assets. *Econometrica* 20: 431–449.

Wihlborg, Clas, Shubhashis Gangopadhyay, and Qaizar Hussain. 2001. Infrastructure Requirements in the Area of Bankruptcy Law. Working Paper no. 01-09, Wharton Financial Institutions Center.

World Bank. 2005. Global Bank Insolvency Initiative: Legal, Institutional, and Regulatory Framework to Deal with Insolvent Banks. The World Bank, Washington, D.C.

III Deposit Insurance: Country Experiences

5 Lessons from the U.S. Experience with Deposit Insurance

Randall S. Kroszner and William R. Melick

5.1 Introduction

The literature on deposit insurance is voluminous. Annotated bibliographies prepared by the Federal Deposit Insurance Corporation (FDIC) covering only publications appearing between 1989 and 2003 run to almost 350 pages! As both the first country to adopt national deposit insurance, and one with a history of many nonnational deposit insurance schemes, the United States is the focus of much of this literature. Not surprisingly, this research usually analyzes a single episode in the U.S. experience, for example the state insurance plans of the early twentieth century or the savings and loan (S&L) crisis of the 1980s. Few studies have covered the entire U.S. history, and those that have are largely descriptive exercises that do not draw out the lessons taught by that history.[1]

This chapter offers a succinct summary of the U.S. experience and uses that summary to highlight the rationale for, and performance of, the varied deposit insurance plans put in place in the United States over the past century. Throughout, we emphasize three main points. First, the inherent fragility of a fractional reserve depository institution is magnified enormously by restrictions on branching and lines of service that impede the diversification of an institution's portfolio. This amplified fragility greatly increases the likelihood of an individual institution failing and thereby serves to also increase the likelihood of a panic. Second, the latest historical evidence accumulated from painstaking examinations of bank failures and panics suggests that contagion from unhealthy to healthy banks usually was not present during bank panics and failures. Rather, this evidence suggests that panics were usually associated with depositors moving from unhealthy banks

(and banks associated with unhealthy banks) to healthy banks, what
we term a separating equilibrium. Indiscriminate runs on all banks,
what we term a pooling equilibrium, were relatively rare and in one instance triggered by official recourse to statewide bank holidays. This
distinction between a separation and a pooling equilibrium provides a
new prism through which to view the function of deposit insurance. If
failures and panics are best viewed as separation equilibria, then using
deposit insurance to protect the medium of exchange may preserve
and encourage the expansion of unhealthy banks, potentially generating undesirable credit expansions that in the end prove quite costly.
Third, and as is well known, attempts to use deposit insurance to limit
self-fulfilling bank failures and associated contagion puts depository
institutions in a position of severe moral hazard that can only be mitigated by careful design of the deposit insurance plan and watchful supervision and regulation once the plan is in place.

   After discussing the rationales for deposit insurance and the U.S. history of banking panics and crises, the bulk of the chapter examines the
post–Civil War history of deposit insurance in the United States. We
conclude by using our history to shed some light on current reforms of
deposit insurance. At the outset, we acknowledge our heavy debt to
earlier research—we aim to synthesize the literature into a readable
narrative that offers a useful introduction to, and draws lessons from,
the history of deposit insurance in the United States.

5.2   What Makes Financial Intermediaries Prone to Panics and Failures?

Deposit insurance is almost always justified as both a way to safeguard
the medium of exchange by containing banking panics and crises as
well as a means to protect small, financially naïve depositors.[2] Therefore, any discussion of deposit insurance requires an understanding of
what makes financial intermediaries, in particular commercial banks
and S&Ls, prone to panics and failures.

   Liabilities of commercial banks are payable on demand according to
a first-come, first-served rule whereby the first in line at a bank is the
first to withdraw. At the same time, commercial bank assets do not
lend themselves to ready liquidation because banks develop longstanding and close ties to their loan customers making it difficult for
third parties to value a bank's loan portfolio. In this environment, all
depositors have an incentive to withdraw funds immediately from a
bank under the suspicion of an impairment of the bank's assets.

Unlike banks, the deposit liabilities of S&Ls, in the main, are not payable upon demand, leaving them less vulnerable to panics. However, waves of failures might still be possible as a result of the maturity mismatch between the S&L's assets and liabilities. By funding longer term mortgage lending with shorter maturity deposits, S&Ls are exposed to considerable interest rate risk. A sharp rise in interest rates will lower the value of the S&L's assets more than its liabilities, leading to insolvency. A large enough increase in interest rates will generate a wave of failures.

This inherent fragility of banks and S&Ls can be offset or compounded by the institutional and regulatory environment in which they operate. Cooperation among banks during a panic can allay depositor fears and prevent a panic or stop a panic that has already begun. This cooperation can be informal and arise as the result of a panic or be formalized, for example, through a clearinghouse arrangement. In normal times, the clearinghouse nets interbank claims, while during the crisis the clearinghouse can coordinate bank action by issuing scrip (a clearinghouse loan certificate) that is the joint liability of all banks. Individual bank members of the clearinghouse would then pay off withdrawing depositors with the scrip.[3]

Other institutional arrangements can compound the fragility of financial intermediaries. Populist concerns over the concentration of power in "money trusts" led to widespread prohibitions on branching by financial intermediaries in the United States. The resulting proliferation of single or unit intermediaries meant that bank portfolios were heavily concentrated in relatively small geographic areas. This lack of diversification left intermediaries open to substantial risk, particularly in rural areas where lending was concentrated on one or just a few crops. Inadequate rainfall in a single county could be enough of a shock to bring down the unit banks in that county.

Restrictions on the assets that financial intermediaries can hold as well as restrictions on their product lines can also heighten fragility. Requirements that S&Ls engage only in mortgage lending left them exposed in the event of a shock to the housing sector. The post-1933 separation of commercial and investment banking left bank assets less diversified than would have otherwise been the case.

Finding ways to minimize the frequency of panics and failures requires a theory that explains the behavior underlying these events. Calomiris and Gorton (2000) argue that there are two main models of bank panics, the random withdrawal theory and the asymmetric information theory. The random withdrawal theory builds on the work of Diamond and Dybvig (1983) and emphasizes the first-in-line, first-to-withdraw constraint. If depositors believe that other depositors are convinced that bank assets have fallen in value, then depositors will withdraw their funds to avoid the losses associated with being at the end of the withdrawal line. Random events (perhaps even a sunspot) cause depositors to form expectations of what turns out to be a self-fulfilling panic. Refinements to the random withdrawal model add detail by incorporating the structure of the U.S. banking system. In a correspondent network, rural banks that are geographically isolated hold reserves in reserve city banks that themselves hold reserves in the central reserve city (New York or Chicago). This pyramiding of reserves leaves the central reserve city vulnerable to a panic. A shock in the countryside leads to a heightened demand for reserves that eventually causes a panicked scramble for reserves in the central reserve city. The shock to the countryside might involve a seasonal demand for cash resulting from the harvest cycle.

In the asymmetric information model, depositors must expend resources to monitor their bank, a job that might be made more difficult if banks are small and geographically separated. If depositors are heterogeneous, the first-in-line, first-to-withdraw constraint arises as a way to reward those depositors who choose to pay the monitoring costs, since the informed depositors will never be at the end of the withdrawal line. Uninformed depositors do not know whether their bank (or any other bank) is solvent and choose to withdraw from all banks, generating the panic. Panics arise when information about deterioration in bank assets arrives, perhaps the onset of a recession or news of weakness in a sector that is dependent on bank financing. Eventually, the panic forces banks to suspend the conversion of deposits to cash. During the suspension, banks collectively sort out the solvent from the insolvent. Thus, the panic is an optimal response to the information asymmetry.

5.3   The Rationale for Deposit Insurance

In both models of banking panics, the panics and closures are costly, even though the contract between depositors and the bank that generates the panic may be optimal. These costs give rise to consideration of arrangements that might prevent panics without imposing additional costs on the financial system. In either model, a guaranty of deposits can remove the incentive for depositors to indiscriminately withdraw funds from banks and thereby short circuit the panic.[4] The guaranty can come from a third party such as the government or privately, perhaps through bank cooperation.

However, the benefits of deposit insurance may not outweigh its costs, especially if panics are actually separating equilibria. Although both the random withdrawal and asymmetric information models can provide a theoretical justification for deposit insurance, historical episodes have most often been used to argue in favor of deposit insurance. Thus, advocates of deposit insurance invariably pointed to the relatively large number of panics in the United States when making their case.

As figures 5.1 and 5.2 make clear, financial services has been a relatively tumultuous industry in the United States over the past 110 or so

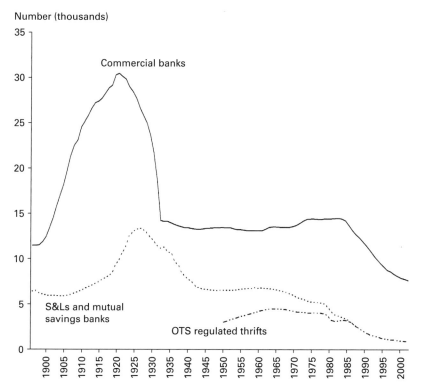

Figure 5.1
U.S. depository institutions

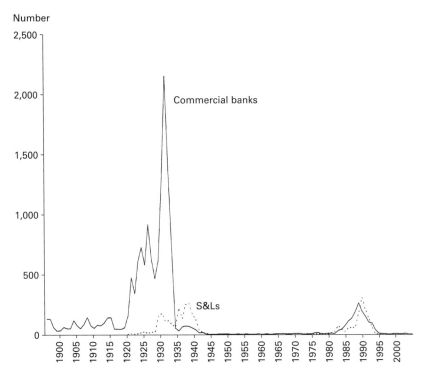

Figure 5.2
Bank and saving and loans failures

years. Taking an even longer view, historians count on the order of six-teen banking panics in the United States in the 160 years prior to 1934, the year in which national deposit insurance took effect.[5] Advocates of deposit insurance argue that these panics and waves of failures disrupt economic activity, often regionally, and on occasion nationally, and impose a cost to society of foregone economic activity and business for-mation and expansion. These costs can be large, both in the short run as transactions drop with a loss of confidence in the medium of ex-change, and in the long run as financial intermediation is key to eco-nomic growth.[6]

When assessing the validity of these historical arguments for deposit insurance, it is important to keep in mind our nomenclature of separa-tion and pooling equilibria. As mentioned earlier, a separation equilib-rium involves depositors shifting funds from insolvent or "bad" banks to solvent or "good" banks. A pooling equilibrium involves mass, in-discriminate withdrawals from all banks. Under this classification scheme, deposit insurance serves a useful function only by preventing a pooling equilibrium in which panicked depositors engage in indiscriminate systemwide withdrawals. However, if bank panics are really separation equilibria that serve to discriminate between healthy and ailing banks, then deposit insurance is not necessary and will likely be counterproductive.[7] Moreover, as we shall see, it is possible for the actions taken by regulators and political officials to inadvertently move the economy from a separation equilibrium to a pooling equilibrium. Misinterpreting the causal relationship between the official action and the pooling equilibrium mistakenly boosts the case for deposit insurance.

An examination of some pre-1934 banking panics illustrates this distinction between separation and pooling. As an example, consider the Panic of 1907, in which runs began in mid-October against a number of national banks in New York City controlled by individuals attempting to manipulate the copper market.[8] The New York Clearing House Association reorganized these banks and initially the runs did not spread to other banks. During the week of October 21, however, runs began to develop against major trust companies in New York City, particularly Knickerbocker Trust. These trusts were not clearinghouse members. During the last week of October 1907, a number of governors proclaimed legal holidays in their states (Andrew 1908). The demand for cash began to rise rapidly not only in New York but throughout the country. Banks then began to limit cash withdrawals, and the clearinghouses began to authorize the issuance of "clearinghouse certificates" that appear to have increased the money supply by roughly 5 percent (see Kroszner 2000, for details.)

Moen and Tallman (1992, 611) emphasize that the panic was largely directed at trust companies, "Our research indicates that in 1907 national banks were not stricken with widespread runs as in previous panics. Rather, the trust companies were the institution subject to severe depositor withdrawals." According to Calomiris and Gorton (2000), only six of more than 6,000 national banks failed during the panic. Moen and Tallman (1992) document that while loans at New York City trusts fell by roughly $250 million, they actually increased at national banks in the city by $60 million.[9] This evidence is consistent with a separation equilibrium, in which depositors were shifting away from trusts to cash and less risky national banks. Moen and Tallman (1992, 628) conclude, "The risk of trust portfolios, the lack of direct access to the clearinghouse, and lower reserves against deposits must be the main reasons why the Panic of 1907 was concentrated in the trust companies."

Recent research on panics during the Great Depression also provides examples of separation equilibria. Although banking was declining throughout the 1920s, the panics during the early 1930s were almost always associated with regionally concentrated withdrawals from particular types of banks or banks known to be insolvent. Wicker (1996) dates four major panics between 1930 and 1933. The first panic lasted from November 1930 until January 1931 with withdrawals concentrated in the South among banks associated with the investment banking firm of Caldwell and Company in Nashville Tennessee. Wicker, like Temin (1990) and White (1984) and unlike Friedman and Schwartz (1962), does not place central importance on the December 1930 failure of the Bank of United States: "There was no panic in New York City if by that term we mean the spread of uncertainty indiscriminately engulfing sound and unsound banks alike" (1996, 37). In short, the first panic of the Depression looks very much like a separation equilibrium in which depositors attempted to withdraw from struggling banks. "Managerial ineptness encompassing both poor loans and investments in the twenties and questionable legal practices deserve a fair share of the blame for the demise of both Caldwell and Company and the Bank of United States" (Wicker 1996, 51).

Richardson (2006a), exploiting newly discovered data on bank failures from the archives of the Federal Reserve (Richardson 2006b), also emphasizes the importance of correspondent relationships with Caldwell and Company in understanding the first banking panic. His argument that weaknesses inherent in correspondent networks help explain the banking panics during the Great Depression fit well with a separation equilibrium in which depositors were trying to move from impaired members of a correspondent network into healthy banks. He concludes, "For the entire contraction, banks that relied upon correspondents to clear checks failed at much higher rates than banks which cleared via clearing houses or the Federal Reserve" (Richardson 2006a, 29).

The second panic of the Depression lasted from April to August 1931 and was concentrated in Chicago and Toledo.[10] Wicker (1996, 62) states, "We conclude, unlike Friedman and Schwartz, that the second crisis was region specific without perceptible nationwide effects." The Chicago failures were heavily concentrated among newly created, small banks in the outskirts of Chicago that were chartered to provide funding for real estate developers. Here again, separation appears to be the central characteristic of the panic. Richardson (2006a) notes that the failures in Chicago were concentrated among correspondent banks affiliated with the John Bain Group and the Foreman Group.

With regard to the third panic, September to October 1931, the case for a separation equilibrium is even stronger, with failures heavily concentrated among savings banks and trust companies. Wicker concludes: "Our analysis would tend to suggest that the waves of bank suspensions in September–October do not appear to have conformed fully to the conventional view of a banking panic; that is, there was no *indiscriminate* run on banks by depositors whose confidence in banking institutions in a given area had been shattered. Bank runs, especially among urban banks, appear to have been directed against particular banks that were known to be weak" (1996, 99). Once again, there is little evidence of a pooling equilibrium with depositors blindly withdrawing from all banks.

The fourth panic of February and March 1933 does fit the characteristics of a pooling equilibrium, but only because of the precipitating action of state bank officials declaring a rolling wave of bank holidays. The panic had its origins in Detroit with the impending collapse of the Guardian Group of banks resulting from their large exposure to real estate. Following a breakdown in negotiations between the Reconstruction Finance Corporation and the Ford family interests (the major stockholders in the Guardian Group), the Governor of Michigan declared a bank holiday on February 14, 1933, at the request of the Detroit Clearing House Association. The holiday was declared despite the fact that there were no runs on any Detroit banks. According to Wicker, "The declaration of the Michigan holiday spread fear and uncertainty quickly to the contiguous states of Ohio, Indiana, and Illinois who promptly placed restrictions on deposit withdrawals" (1996, 121).

Thus, a series of governmental actions created a pooling equilibrium. "The panic that was sweeping the country during the last week of February and the first three days of March was a panic generated by officials in the several states who either declared bank holidays or limited deposit withdrawals. It was not depositor runs on the banks in the classic sense that prompted such drastic measures. Rather it was an unwillingness on the part of state officials to stand idly by while depositors attempted to transfer funds to surrounding states where deposit restrictions were not in effect" (Wicker 1996, 127–128). What was likely to be another separation equilibrium that would involve the failure of some Detroit banks was transformed into a nationwide panic that ended with President Roosevelt's declaration of a national holiday on March 6, 1933. The national holiday only affirmed what had already been brought about by holidays or deposit restrictions declared in each of the then forty-eight states.

This view that bank panics during the Great Depression are best thought of as separation phenomenon that do not jeopardize the medium of exchange is also consistent with the work of Calomiris and Mason (1997, 2003). In their study (1997, 881) of the Chicago minipanic of June 1932, they state: "We conclude that failures during the panic reflected the relative weakness of failing banks in the face of a common asset value shock rather than contagion. . . . While asymmetric information between depositors and banks precipitated a general run on banks, our evidence suggests that this asymmetric-information prob lem did not produce failures of solvent banks." Their findings are echoed by Richardson (2006c) using newly available Federal Reserve data. "In other words, during this event, most banks which experienced runs were wither insolvent or teetering on the edge of bankruptcy. Illiquidity and runds did not destroy solvent institutions" (Richardson 2006c, 16).

In brief, a panic generated by asymmetric information does necessarily result in a pooling equilibrium that requires a governmental solution. As Calomiris and Mason (1997, 881) note: "Deposit insurance and government assistance to banks since the Depression have been motivated in part by the perception that bank failures during the Depression were a consequence of contagion, rather than the insolvency of individual banks. If private interbank cooperation, buttressed by liquidity assistance from the monetary authority (like the assistance provided by the RFC to the Chicago clearinghouse), are adequate to preserve systemic stability, then a far less ambitious federal safety net might be desirable." Calomiris and Mason (2003) use detailed call report data on slightly more than 10,000 Federal Reserve member banks from 1929 to 1935 to analyze bank failures during the Great Depression. Again, their analysis is consistent with a separation equilibrium view of bank failures, with the exception of the 1933 panic. "We find no evidence that bank failures were induced by a national banking panic in the first three episodes Friedman and Schwartz identify as panics (late 1930, mid-1931, and late 1931). We do find, however, that in January and February 1933 there is a significant increase in bank failure hazard that is not explained by our model of fundamentals. . . .

Our findings suggest that disaggregated analysis of bank failures and deposit shrinkage leads to a much smaller role for contagion in understanding bank distress during the Great Depression" (Calomiris and Mason 2003, 1638–1639). Given the forgoing discussion, the exceptional case of the 1933 panic comes as no surprise. Banks closed not from confused depositors blindly withdrawing funds but rather from depositors fearing that their state would be the next to declare a bank holiday.

In sum, the historical evidence suggests that during the early 1930s healthy banks were not failing in contagion–induced waves. Healthy banks might temporarily suspend operations, but there is a clear difference between banks that failed and those that survived. Richardson (2006c, 14) finds that "more than eight in ten of the banks which went out of business, in other words, were judged to have problematic assets." All of this evidence calls into question the need for deposit insurance to calm panicky depositors in order to protect the medium of exchange. The fear of panic-induced contagion cannot by itself provide a complete rationale for deposit insurance.

The prevalence of unit banking in the United States provides an additional rationale for deposit insurance. Golembe (1960) emphasizes this view in his discussion of the forces leading to the adoption of deposit insurance. As figure 5.2 makes clear, bank failures were commonplace in the United States, both in good times and bad. The desire by state legislatures, expressed via restrictions on branch banking, for an industry comprised of small, independent banks left a very fragile banking system. This regulatory approach predictably led to many bank failures brought about by an almost complete lack of diversification. Deposit insurance was seen as a way to reduce bank failures without having to sacrifice the "democratic" ideals of unit banking. On this point, Golembe (1960) provides many supporting citations, including Joshua Forman, the architect of the earliest bank obligation insurance scheme, writing on the plan adopted by New York in 1829, which "is on the whole a more ample security to the public than that of a general bank with branches." Representative Steagall, the main force behind the 1933 adoption of national deposit insurance is quoted as saying, "This bill will preserve independent, dual banking in the United States.... This is what this bill is intended to do" (Golembe 1960, 198). Perhaps most telling, opponents of national deposit insurance clearly pointed out the link, as evidenced by Golembe's (1960, 197) quote from John W. Pole Comptroller of the Currency in 1932:

"A general guaranty of bank deposits is the very antithesis of branch banking."

Golembe's evidence from the historical record is bolstered by the empirical work of White (1983) and Calomiris and White (1994). White shows that states with branch banking provisions were much less likely to adopt deposit insurance schemes. Calomiris and White find that congressional representatives from unit banking states were more likely to put forward bills to establish a national deposit insurance scheme and that these representatives were also more likely to vote in favor of such schemes. They state, "Unit banking, small average bank size, and high rates of bank failure all were associated with support for legislation" (Calomiris and White 1994, 163). Dehejia and Lleras-Muney (2007) also find that bank failures and a larger fraction of state banks help to explain the adoption of deposit insurance. However, they find that larger bank size increases the probability of the adoption of deposit insurance.

Of course, the use of deposit insurance to preserve the unit banking structure will not come without costs. Dehejia and Lleras-Muney (2007) provide empirical evidence on this issue using the experience of states from 1900 to 1940 to document a negative relationship between the adoption of deposit insurance and economic growth. Even after controlling for the possibility of reverse causality whereby bad growth outcomes lead to the adoption of deposit insurance, they find that both farm and manufacturing output were subsequently depressed in states that adopted deposit insurance, the result of "indiscriminate expansions of credit, such as the one that resulted from deposit insurance laws" (Dehejia and Lleras-Muney 2007, 20). The next section provides several anecdotal accounts that support their empirical finding.

5.4 A Selected Survey of the Post–Civil War U.S. Experience with Deposit Insurance

Whether or not justified by theory or history, the pooling equilibrium view of bank failures and panics often has won the day in the United States. That is to say, there is a long U.S. history of deposit insurance schemes. Over that history, the moral hazard costs of deposit insurance have become clear while the benefits are harder to quantify, given that the counterfactual of the same institutions at the same time and place operating without deposit insurance is never observed.

The insurance of financial intermediary obligations (either deposits or notes) began in 1829 with the New York Safety Fund. In one form or another, five other states followed the lead of New York over the next thirty years. Some of the states guaranteed all bank debts while other plans were limited to bank notes (see Calomiris 1989 and Federal Deposit Insurance Corporation 1953 for details). Regardless, circulating bank notes comprised the bulk of bank liabilities, so these pre–Civil War plans can largely be viewed as guaranteeing bank notes. All of these plans ended by 1866, largely due to both the free banking movement that provided for an alternative guarantee of notes through the posting of securities with state officials and the establishment of a national banking system in 1865 that placed a 10 percent tax on the notes circulated by state banks.[11]

After the introduction of the national banking system, deposit banking grew rapidly and claims on deposits (checks) began to account for an increasing fraction of the money supply (Federal Deposit Insurance Corporation 1956; Golembe 1960). Within twenty years, plans for explicit deposit insurance began to be put forward. The first bill for a national deposit insurance plan was introduced in Congress in 1886 and Oklahoma passed legislation for a deposit insurance plan on December 17, 1907, in the midst of the Panic of 1907 and only one month after Oklahoma was admitted to the Union. Shortly after Oklahoma's program was created, Kansas, Nebraska, and Texas followed suit. By 1917, deposit insurance programs were also in place in Mississippi, South Dakota, North Dakota, and Washington. Table 5.1 presents some details on the eight state plans.

5.4.1 Early-Twentieth-Century State Plans

It is with these state plans that we begin our selected narrative of the U.S. experience with *deposit* insurance, focusing on the Oklahoma experience.[12] Participation in the Oklahoma plan was compulsory for state banks and trust companies. Although given the right to participate by the Oklahoma legislation, nationally chartered banks in Oklahoma were prohibited from participating by a 1908 ruling of the Comptroller of the Currency on the basis of advice from the U.S. Attorney General. At first, the fund was to amount to only 1 percent of deposits; subsequent amendments increased the fund to 5 percent of deposits and then reduced it to 2 percent of deposits. The fund was administered by the State Banking Board, originally composed of the

Table 5.1
State deposit insurance plans of the early 1900s

	Oklahoma	Kansas	South Dakota	Nebraska	Texas	Mississippi	North Dakota	Washington
Legislation	Dec. 17, 1907	March 6, 1909	March 1915[a]	March 25, 1909	August 9, 1909	March 9, 1914	March 10, 1917	March 10, 1917
Period of operation	1908–1923	1909–1929	1916–1927	1911–1930	1910–1927	1914–1930	1917–1929	1917–1921
Supervision	State banking board	Commissioner of banking	Fund commission	State banking board	State banking board	Three district examiners	Fund commission	Fund board
Participation	Compulsory	Voluntary	Voluntary	Compulsory	Compulsory	Compulsory	Compulsory	Voluntary
Enforcement	Possession, liquidate	Possession, receiver	Possession, liquidate	Possession, receiver	Possession, liquidate	Possession, liquidate	Possession, receiver	Possession, receiver
Initial assessment on deposits	1.0%	0.5%	0.1%	1.0%	1.0%	0.5%	0.05%	1.0%
Required capital ratio	None	Deposits <10*(capital and surplus)	Deposits <15*(capital and surplus)	Investments <8*(capital and surplus)	Deposits limited by size of capital	Deposits <10*(capital and surplus)	Set by board	Deposits <20*capital
Deposit coverage	All	All	All	All	Noninterest-bearing	All	All	All
Interest rate ceiling	3%	3%	5%	None	None	4%	Set by board	Set by board
Advertising	Permitted	Permitted, penalty for state protection	No provision	Permitted	Permitted, penalty for state protection	No provision	Permitted	Permitted, penalty for state protection
Average annual failures per 100 banks	1.6	1.2	4.2	2.0	1.1	1.4	5.0	0.3

Source: Cooke 1909, Robb 1921, Federal Deposit Insurance Corporation 1956, White 1983, Calomiris 1989.
[a] Earlier legislation of March 9, 1909, never resulted in a system as it imposed a substantial membership fee and required a minimum of one hundred banks.

governor, lieutenant governor, president of the Board of Agriculture, state treasurer, and state auditor. In 1913 the board membership was changed to the state bank commissioner, the assistant state bank commissioner, and three members selected by the governor from a list prepared by the State Bankers' Association. Depositors in the failed banks were to be paid immediately.

From the beginning, the Oklahoma plan was controversial. Analysts supported the separation equilibrium view of panics in wondering whether deposit insurance was even necessary, and raised questions regarding moral hazard and the appropriate size of the fund. According to Professor W. C. Webster of the University of Nebraska, an early critic,

> The guaranty of deposits, by removing or weakening the motive for honesty and conservatism, tends to turn, by gradual, easy and almost unconscious stages, a great deal of potential dishonesty into a positive force capable of doing the utmost harm. . . . Experience shows that lack of confidence in banks is usually the result or culmination of a panic rather than the cause. Even then "runs" are usually confined to banks whose management warrants special suspicion; sound banks are rarely closed by runs. Furthermore, the growth of reckless banking stimulated by this law and the undermining of the underlying security of all the "guaranteed" banks in the state, which we shall presently show is likely to result from it, will ultimately increase bank failures to an alarming extent. It may be predicted that, if this law is left on the statute books of the state, Oklahoma will soon give the world some startling examples of "high finance" and eventually experience such a panic as few states of like wealth have ever witnessed. And when that panic comes, of what avail will be the present paltry guaranty fund? (1909)

As evidence for his claims, Webster remarked on the rapid increase in the number of state banks chartered in Oklahoma and the thin capitalization required of these new banks. Cooke (1910), president of the Columbia National Bank of Kansas City, Missouri, notes that from February 1908 to June 1909 the number of state banks in Oklahoma increased from 470 to 631 while over the same period the number of national banks fell from 312 to 230.[13] There were also allegations of state bankers making illegal side payments to large depositors to circumvent the state-mandated deposit rate ceiling. This behavior is consistent with the Dehejia and Lleras-Muney (2007) finding of indiscriminate expansions of bank credit that were triggered by deposit insurance.

Webster was a prescient observer. There is little doubt that the deposit guarantee encouraged risky behavior among the state banks.

Calomiris (1989) calculates the failure rate for state banks to be 35.6 percent compared with 7.6 percent for the national banks and also notes that the state banks paid much higher dividends (presumably to compensate for risk) to their shareholders. Despite numerous amendments to the insurance plan, the fund was repealed in 1923 with $7.5 million owed to depositors.

The Oklahoma plan began operation on February 14, 1908, and faced its first test with the failure on September 28, 1909, of the Columbia Bank and Trust Company in Oklahoma City, at the time the largest bank in Oklahoma. The bank was organized in 1905 and in late 1908 control was taken over by W. L. Norton, an oil and real estate speculator, H. H. Smock, former State Bank Commissioner, and J. A. Menefee, Oklahoma state treasurer. Under their leadership, deposits grew rapidly from $365,000 to $2,800,000 in less than a year. Of the $2.8 million in deposits, $1.3 million belonged to individuals, $1.3 million to other banks, and $0.2 million to the state of Oklahoma. James K. Ilsley, a member of a Wisconsin committee sent to study the Oklahoma plan that happened to arrive on the day of Columbia's failure, remarked on the rapid growth in deposits:

How was this accomplished? Well, in about every way that can be imagined, legitimate and illegitimate. Norton, the president, had been engaged in oil speculation in eastern Oklahoma and gathered in a considerable line of deposits from his friends by promising loans on easy terms; Smock, the vice-president, had been state bank commissioner and had used his acquaintance with country bankers to obtain deposits; Menefee, a stockholder, also state treasurer, deposited large amounts of public funds directly with the Columbia Bank, and in addition distributed deposits among the country banks with a recommendation of the Columbia as a reserve agent and a strong hint that the opening of an account with this bank would be appreciated. Under the law four per cent had been named as the highest rate that state banks could pay on time deposits, but the managers of the Columbia apparently paid any rate up to six per cent and, in some instances, a commission besides. Now all these and other reckless methods were employed to get business, but at all times the guaranty law was worked for all it was worth and one cannot avoid the conclusion that this was directly responsible for most of the mushroom growth. (qtd. in Robb 1921, 44)

Cooke (1910) noted that while vacationing on Lake Ontario he saw advertisements in the Rochester, New York, paper by the Columbia bank soliciting deposits. The ads noted that the law of Oklahoma guaranteed the deposits. Norton also contracted with large banks outside of Oklahoma to process all of their checks drawn on residents of Oklahoma. He would remit to these large banks at par within a week, despite the fact that clearing the checks would involve charges from Oklahoma country banks and likely take much longer than a week. Without a doubt, the guarantee law allowed the Columbia bank to finance Norton's oil and real estate deals

At the time of Columbia's failure, the Oklahoma fund had about $400,000 in cash and easily liquidated assets of Columbia amounted to roughly $1.1 million. Thus, it was not possible to pay off immediately all $2.8 million of Columbia's deposits and an emergency assessment of three-quarters of a percent was levied against the state banks.

The Columbia failure is perhaps the perfect example of an incentive incompatible insurance scheme.[14] Moral hazard led to excessive risk taking on the part of Norris that was not reined in by regulators. Depositors of Columbia, including many banks, were lulled into complacency by the guaranty law. The prospects for the Oklahoma fund only got worse following the failure, as banks began to switch charters to avoid the assessments. This adverse selection is emphasized and documented by Calomiris (1989).

Although the seven other state insurance funds of the 1910s and 1920s avoided such egregious examples of moral hazard, adverse selection, and incentive incompatibility, they each eventually met the same fate as the Oklahoma fund. Although a large decline in the relative price of agricultural commodities played an important role in the dissolution of all the funds, there can be little doubt that deposit insurance only served to compound the problem. Wheelock and Kuhmbhakar (1994), Wheelock and Kuhmbhakar (1995), and Wheelock and Wilson (1995) present overwhelming empirical evidence of moral hazard and adverse selection in the Kansas deposit insurance scheme. Hooks and Robinson (2002), buttressed by Richardson (2006d), find the same results for banks in Texas.

In a wide-ranging comparison of national banks and state banks for states affected by the agricultural shock, Calomiris (1992, 289–290) extends the work of Calomiris (1990) and concludes:

The evidence on overall growth, average size, and membership patterns of banks during the 1920s indicates that the states can be grouped into three categories according to the banking systems in use at the time: states where deposit insurance made the system more fragile, magnified the expansion in response to the agricultural boom, and worsened the contraction during the bust; other unit banking states with less extensive swings in aggregate growth; and states with branch banking systems (restricted or statewide) that managed to respond most successfully to the challenges brought by the declining terms of trade in agriculture.

This result is seconded by Chung and Richardson (2006, 14), "These findings reinforce the cautionary conclusions drawn from the state deposit insurance experiments. Deposit insurance did not address the principal problems of the United States banking system during the first third of the twentieth century." By the late 1920s, the initial U.S. experience with deposit insurance was widely judged to have been a failure.

5.4.2 National Deposit Insurance

Nonetheless, with President Roosevelt's signing of the Banking (Glass-Steagall) Act of 1933 on June 16, 1933, the United States adopted national deposit insurance. Deposit insurance was championed by Representative Henry Steagall (D-AL), Chairman of the House Committee on Banking and Currency, but opposed by Senator Carter Glass (D-VA). Passage of the bill was seen as a compromise satisfying Glass' desire to separate commercial and investment banking while allowing Steagall to protect unit banking. Flood (1992) and Calomiris and White (1994) argue that despite important special interest opposition such as the American Bankers Association and the absence of administration support, deposit insurance became a public interest concern as a result of the public's distrust of banking fueled by the many failures and holidays of the early 1930s as well as hearings by the House Committee on Banking and Currency run by Ferdinand Pecora, the Committee's counsel.[15] This public interest married with the desire of small and rural banks to use deposit insurance as one way to reduce competitive pressure from large banks. The initial legislation created a temporary plan that began operation on January 1, 1934, and was to be replaced by a permanent plan later that year. This timetable proved unrealistic, and a permanent plan was not put in place until passage of the Banking Act of 1935.[16]

The debate surrounding, and legislation proposing, national deposit insurance was well informed by the experience of the state insurance schemes.[17] As Flood (1992) emphasizes, the legislation sought to address many of the problems faced by the state plans. With regard to moral hazard, insurance was initially limited to $2,500 per depositor although raised to $5,000 per depositor within seven months (see figure 5.3.) In addition, banks were prohibited from paying interest on demand deposits, limits were imposed on interest paid on time deposits, and bank regulation was systematized. Federal Reserve member banks were required to participate, reducing but not eliminating the problem of adverse selection. Importantly, however, no attempt was

Thousands of 2005 dollars

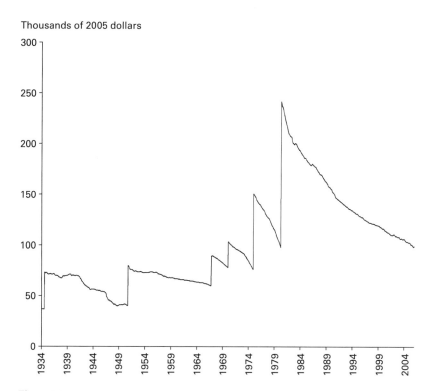

Figure 5.3
Inflation adjusted value of deposit insurance coverage

made to adjust insurance premiums according to risk. Premiums for all banks were set at one-twelfth of one percent of deposits. The plan proved popular with banks. In 1935, 91 percent of commercial banks joined the system.

In parallel with the treatment of banks, the Federal Savings and Loan Insurance Corporation (FSLIC) was created by the passage of the National Housing Act in 1934.[18] Failure rates for S&Ls were well below those for banks in the early 1930s (figure 5.2) as S&Ls had the right to refuse withdrawal requests. Thus there was no great outcry for S&L deposit insurance, and their take-up rate was much lower than that of the banks. By 1940, only 30 percent of S&Ls had obtained FSLIC insurance. This also resulted from the higher premium charged to S&Ls, one-eighth of a percent of total deposits compared to the bank charge of one-twelfth of a percent, see figure 5.4.

Relative to the crisis years of the early 1930s, the first few years of national deposit insurance were very favorable, judged both in terms

Percent of insured deposits

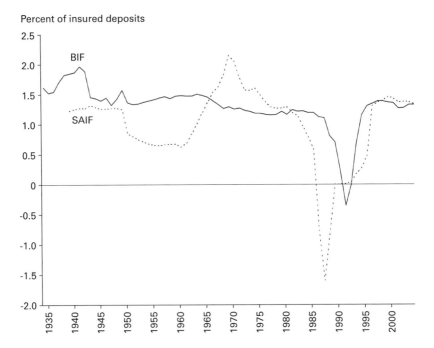

Figure 5.4
Insurance fund reserve ratios

of minimizing the effect of bank failures and the preservation of the dual banking system. "The FDIC handled 370 bank failures from 1934 through 1943, an average of more than 50 per year. Most of these were small banks. Without the presence of federal deposit insurance, the number of bank failures undoubtedly would have been greater and the bank population would have been reduced. The presence of deposit insurance also may have limited the necessity for some banks to merge, and may have indirectly encouraged retention of restrictive state branching laws" (Federal Deposit Insurance Corporation 1998, 39). However, the lessons learned from the experiences of the state plans gradually faded from the minds of regulators and politicians. This can be seen clearly in figure 5.3, which plots the inflation-adjusted value of deposit insurance coverage. After declining in the first fifteen years of operation, the real value of insurance was restored to initial levels in 1950. However, in 1966 the real value began to be ratcheted upward, reaching its peak in 1980. As will be shown, this increase exacerbated problems of moral hazard, compounding the difficulties facing the financial intermediaries during the 1970s and 1980s.

5.4.3   Mid-Twentieth-Century State Guarantee Plans

S&Ls insured under state guaranty plans first signaled the problems confronting depository institutions brought about by the great inflation of the 1960s and 1970s. Crises developed in Mississippi (1976), Nebraska (1983), Ohio (1985), Maryland (1985), and Rhode Island (1991). Table 5.2 provides details on these plans. We focus on the failure of the Ohio Deposit Guarantee Fund, drawing on the work of Kane (1987, 1992), McCulloch (1987), and English (1993).

Chartered in 1956 under Ohio law, the Ohio Deposit Guarantee Fund (ODGF) provided for the insurance of deposits at state-chartered Ohio S&Ls that were not members of the FSLIC. The insurance fund was financed by an assessment of 2 percent of deposits and, unlike FSLIC, member institutions reported this assessment as an asset in their statements of financial condition. By 1985, the ODGF had seventy members with roughly $4.3 billion in deposits insured by a fund of roughly $130 million.[19] Deposit coverage was unlimited and no ceilings were placed on interest rates paid on deposits. The largest S&L in the fund was Home State Savings Bank, owned by Cincinnati-based real estate mogul Marvin L. Warner. Warner was a contributor to both major political parties, but especially known for his Democratic ties—President Carter named him ambassador to Switzerland from 1977 to 1981 and Democrat Richard F. Celeste, Ohio's governor at the time of the crisis, named him chairman of the Ohio Building Authority in 1983.

On March 4, 1985, Florida-based E.S.M. Government Securities Inc. closed when it was discovered that ESM was short $300 to $350 million worth of securities that were to be held as a party to reverse repurchase agreements. Home State had close business dealings with ESM, and increasingly was using transactions with ESM to mask fundamental and longstanding insolvency associated with the sharp increase in interest rates in the early 1980s.[20] Within the next days it is determined that Home State's losses due to the failure of ESM will total $145 million, an amount that would essentially exhaust Home State's capital of $20 million and the $130 million available in the ODGF.[21] During March 6–8, 1985, depositor withdrawals from Home State total $150 million, and on Sunday March 10, 1985, Governor Celeste closes Home State.[22]

The next week, other members of the ODGF face runs, as it becomes clear that ODGF assets are insufficient to cover all of Home State's losses. Runs are concentrated in the Cincinnati area, with six institutions now technically insolvent as a result of the loss of the 2 percent

Table 5.2
Failed state deposit insurance plans of the late 1900s

	Mississippi	Nebraska	Ohio	Maryland	Rhode Island
Members	S&Ls	Industrial banks, cooperative credit cor- porations	S&Ls	S&Ls	Industrial banks, credit unions, banks and trust companies
First year of operation	1970	1978	1956	1962	1969
Year of failure	1976	1983	1985	1985	1991
Year problem known	1974	1982	1980	1978	1985
Problem members	Bankers Trust	Common- wealth	Home State	Old Court Community Merritt	Heritage RI Central
Problem members as a percent of insured deposits	45	20	19	28	16
Number closed	34	3	70	102	45
Losses ($ millions)	35	33	150	350	290
Convictions or guilty pleas	Yes	Yes	Yes	Yes	Yes

Note: Updated version of English 1993 (table 2) using information from Credit Union Journal 2002 and Kostrzewa 2005.

of deposits paid into the ODGF.[23] As both Kane (1987, 1989) and McCulloch (1987) emphasize, the run on the other ODGF members is rational—a separation equilibrium in our terminology.[24] After an attempt by the Ohio legislature to create a new guarantee fund of $90 million ($50 million loaned from the state and $40 million from an emergency assessment on ODGF members) fails to calm depositors, on Friday March 15, 1985, Governor Celeste declares a "holiday," closing the remaining ODGF members and thereby creating a pooling equilibrium. "This run on the remaining thrifts would have been a useful acid test to determine which ones were sound—i.e. able to meet their obligations as promised—and which ones were not, had the Governor not panicked and closed them all indiscriminately. A few of the closed thrifts were relieved to be released from their duties to their depositors, but many of the others were irate that they were not even allowed to fulfill their obligations. Two actually opened on March 15 in defiance of the Governor's order" (McCulloch 1987, 233). On Wednesday March 20, 1985, a bill passed by the Ohio legislature allowed ODGF members to reopen if they joined the FSLIC. The legislation also indemnifies the FSLIC for any losses incurred by ODGF members through July 1, 1987. After several attempts, the Ohio legislature on May 21 passes a $120 million Home State depositor bail out bill. On May 29, 1985, American Financial Corporation subsidiary Hunter S&L takes over Home State with a $21 million dollar bid, and Home State offices reopen under a new name on June 14, 1985. On September 26, 2000, Ohio announces that it has recovered $146 million (including interest charges) to offset the $120 million worth of payments in 1985 to Home State depositors.[25] Of this amount, $4.5 million came from the bankruptcy settlement of Marvin L. Warner. Warner served two and one-half years in prison during 1991 through 1993 and died in April 2002.

The failure of the ODGF is, like Oklahoma, a classic example of the demise of an incentive-incompatible scheme. Premiums were not risk-based, no limits were placed on the amount of insurance per deposit, and no limits were placed on the rates paid on deposits. This enabled Warner to pursue his increasingly risky and illegal dealings with ESM, funding them by paying interest rates on deposits that averaged 125 basis points more than deposit rates at FSLIC institutions.[26] Home State continued to attract deposits, including Governor Celeste's campaign funds, and fellow members of the ODGF registered no complaints. This lack of complaints may seem puzzling until it is recognized that Home State was by far the largest member of the ODGF and was quite active in the administration of the fund. The chairman of Home State, David J. Schiebel, was secretary of the ODGF board. Of the eleven ODGF board members, five were officers of institutions that failed in the crisis. Thus, Home State and like-minded institutions were able to hijack the insurance fund. Robert W. McAlister, interim S&L superintendent during the crisis, commented: "The division has been in a very weak position to deal with the persons it regulates. I think it has been subject to undue influence by the Marvin Warners of the world. It has been subject to undue influence by the Ohio Savings and Loan League. It is a classic example of regulators being subject to undue influence by the regulated" (Adams 1985, 24).

Regulators and politicians also followed their incentives, doing their best to push the resolution of the Home State situation onto successors. The Securities and Exchange Commission first detected the unsound business practices of ESM in 1976, with examiners from the Ohio Division of Savings and Loan (ODSL, the ODGF regulator) becoming aware of ESM's poor standing with the Federal Home Loan Bank Board in 1981. In 1982, an examiner with the ODSL characterized the Home State situation as a "veritable time-bomb" (Joint Select Committee on Savings and Loans 1986, 21). However, politically appointed heads of the ODSL never took action, preferring to negotiate agreements with Home State to reduce its exposure to ESM, agreements which were never honored. Despite the failure of politically appointed regulators and politicians to act in interest of Ohio taxpayers, twenty years after the fact the crisis is remembered in Ohio, at least by politicians involved in its resolution, as "democracy at its zenith."[27]

5.4.4 National Crises of the 1980s and Early 1990s

The same forces that led to the demise of the state private insurance schemes were also felt with the national FDIC and FSLIC plans. The national plans were generally better capitalized than the state plans, which helped to delay the resolution of the problems that developed relative to the experiences of Mississippi, Nebraska, Ohio, and Maryland. The difficulties encountered by the two federal systems during the 1980s and early 1990s have received enormous scrutiny. We present here only a brief account of the events, drawing on the excellent descriptions and analysis of Kane (1989), Barth (1991), National Commission on Financial Institution Reform, Recovery, and Enforcement (National Commission on Financial Institution Reform 1993), and Federal Deposit Insurance Corporation (1997).

Through the mid-1960s, S&Ls flourished as Congress's agents for promoting home ownership. Paying no taxes and operating with no deposit rate ceilings, unlike banks, the S&L strategy of using short-term deposits to fund long-term fixed rate mortgage lending was a winner. However, the increase in interest rates that began in the mid-1960s, signaling the beginning of the great inflation, eroded both S&L profits and net worth. Profits fell as the difference between the interest rates earned on the existing portfolio of mortgages and the interest rate paid on new deposits narrowed. The increase in interest rates also reduced the value of existing fixed rate mortgages on the asset side of the S&L balance sheet, leading to a decline in net worth. The Interest

Rate Adjustment Act of 1966, in an attempt to prevent S&Ls from competing with each other, imposed ceilings on deposit interest rates. These ceilings served only to drive depositors away from S&Ls in search of higher yields, leading to the "disintermediation" that gave rise to direct finance vehicles such as money market mutual funds.

The struggles of the S&Ls continued in the 1970s as nominal interest rates remained high and volatile. The struggle reached epic proportions in the 1979 when short-term interest rates jumped sharply when the appointment of Paul Volcker as chairman gave the Federal Reserve new resolve to fight inflation. In 1980, S&Ls recorded losses of $4.6 billion and by 1982 13 percent of S&Ls were insolvent.

The early regulatory and statutory responses to the thrift crisis attempted to buy time, hoping that as interest rates returned to more normal levels that the industry would regain its health. This response is not surprising—both regulators and politicians have a strong incentive to push resolution into the future to avoid damaging their reputations. Moreover, the FSLIC fund was poorly capitalized, severely constraining any serious effort that regulators might have made to address the mounting thrift insolvencies.

The Depository Institutions Deregulation and Monetary Control Act (DIDMCA) passed in 1980 was the first major statutory response to the crisis. The legislation expanded the powers granted to S&Ls, allowing them to hold consumer paper, commercial loans and corporate debt and letting them, as well as banks, offer interest bearing checking accounts. S&Ls were also allowed to increase their holdings of acquisition, development and construction (ADC) loans. The act called for the phaseout of deposit interest rate ceilings by 1986. Perhaps most importantly, the capital requirement of 5 percent of deposits was replaced with a requirement to be set by the Federal Home Loan Bank Board (FHLBB) that had to fall in the range of 3–6 percent. By 1981, the FHLBB had lowered the capital requirement to 3 percent. In addition, the limit on deposit insurance coverage was raised from $40,000 to $100,000 per account (see figure 5.4.) All of these changes were designed to improve the competitive position of S&Ls. However, the actual effect was to increase leverage, allow for riskier activities, make S&Ls easier to fund, and open the door to an expansion in the industry at a time when market forces called for a contraction.

The encouragement of thrift risk taking was heightened with passage of the Garn-St Germain Depository Institution Act of 1982, which effectively eliminated deposit rate ceilings, increased the allowable shares for nonresidential lending in S&L assets, eliminated limits on loan-to-value ratios, and gave both the FDIC and FSLIC the ability to issue net worth certificates to paper over insolvencies.

At the same time, the FHLBB was following a policy of regulatory forbearance, allowing institutions to meet the capital requirement under the more liberal regulatory accounting principles (RAP) rather than the more stringent generally accepted accounting principles (GAAP). The deposit base for the capital requirement was calculated on a five-year moving average, meaning that a fast growing institution would face a lower capital requirement. Moreover, S&Ls less than twenty years old faced yet a lower requirement. All of these changes created a dangerous situation:

> It is difficult to overstate the destructive effect of the regulatory actions that weakened net worth standards in an environment in which S&Ls could expand their insured deposit liabilities at will. Of course, in the absence of deposit insurance, S&Ls would not have been able to attract deposits so readily. Thus, it was the provision of deposit insurance to institutions pursuing risky activities that was, and indeed still is, the root cause of the problem. There was virtually no cushion to protect the FSLIC against losses, and for many S&Ls there was strong incentive to take on risky ventures because they had little or nothing to lose and a lot potentially to gain. (NCFIRRE 1993, 36)

Other regulatory changes only added fuel to the fire. Ownership requirements for S&Ls were also loosened, allowing for a single shareholder instead of the previous limit of at least four hundred shareholders. Troubled institutions could sell "income capital certificates" to the FSLIC to bolster their assets under RAP accounting. "Goodwill mergers" were encouraged, under which an acquiring institution could carry as an asset the difference between the market value of the acquired firm's assets and that firm's liabilities. Under this policy, two troubled thrifts could merge and appear to have formed a healthy institution when nothing fundamental had changed. In order to attract new capital to the industry and avoid FSLIC payouts, the FHLBB encouraged thrifts organized as mutuals to convert to stockholding corporations.[28] Finally, the FHLBB eliminated the restriction on brokered deposits, making it easier for S&Ls to fund themselves. All of these changes moved S&Ls into new activities that had the potential for large profits. For example, a real estate developer could now purchase an existing S&L, or charter a new S&L, to fund acquisition of undeveloped real estate and construction of new homes and offices. If the developer were corrupt, new deposits could be used to increase the dividends paid to the shareholders (possible a single shareholder) and raise the salaries of the S&Ls management: "Though aware of the likely consequences, the Bank Board allowed members of an essentially bankrupt industry to grow rapidly, and to enter potentially risky areas in which they had little or no experience, and in which there was unusual potential for abuse and fraud" (NCFIRRE 1993, 42).

Rather than closing insolvent thrifts, a policy of regulatory forbearance was put in place. Insolvent institutions were kept on life support, creating a class of "zombie" firms that had every incentive to take on high-risk, high-return strategies in an attempt to restore their health. These zombies pressured the healthy intermediaries by bidding up deposit rates and lowering returns in commercial ventures, a point emphasized by Kane (1989).

In the manner of a perfect storm, the problems of the thrift industry eventually also hit banks, and not just through zombie pressures on bank competitors. The passage of the Economic Recovery Tax Act of 1981 substantially reduced the depreciation life of real property and allowed passive investors to use real estate losses to offset income in other areas. These two changes dramatically increased the after-tax return on real estate investment. Real estate development boomed, attracting lending from both banks and thrifts.[29] Much of this lending was concentrated in the Southwest, which was then hit by the decline in the real price of oil that began in 1982 and intensified in 1986. Moreover, the Tax Reform Act of 1986 eliminated the accelerated depreciation schedule and the loss provisions for passive real estate investors, creating a commercial real estate bust. Bank and thrift insolvencies and failures increased sharply. Pressure was greatest on the FSLIC, which was officially declared bankrupt by the General Accounting Office in 1987, but the solvency of the FDIC was also open to question.[30]

By late 1983 it became clear that, despite a reduction in interest rates, new statutory and regulatory practices were called for to handle the looming crisis. In December 1983 the FHLBB raised the capital requirement to seven percent and in April 1984 the FHLBB and FDIC attempted to remove deposit insurance for brokered deposits although the courts struck down this action. Serious efforts to recapitalize FSLIC began in 1985, but the Competitive Equality Banking Act did not become law until August 1987 and allowed for only a $10.8 billion recapitalization, limited to no more than $3.8 billion in any twelve-month period. At this time, conservative, official estimates of the funds needed for recapitalization were around $25 billion.[31] Resolutions of failed thrifts picked up, but estimated resolution costs continued to mount. Final estimates from the GAO put the cost of resolving the S&L crisis at roughly $130 billion. To provide some perspective on this figure, that amount could be financed by a onetime $10 charge on every worker in the United States.

Full legislative resolution of the crisis began in February 1989, with the enactment of the Financial Institutions Reform Recovery and Enforcement Act (FIRREA). The act abolished the FHLBB and the FSLIC, creating the Office of Thrift Supervision in the Treasury to regulate thrifts and giving the FDIC responsibility for deposit insurance through the Bank Insurance Fund (BIF) and Savings Association Insurance Fund (SAIF). The Resolution Trust Corporation (RTC) was created to handle failed thrifts. Finally, borrowing authority for the FDIC was increased to $50 billion and the BIF and SAIF were mandated to eventually reach 1.25 percent of insured deposits.

Regulatory discretion was limited with the Federal Deposit Insurance Corporation Improvement Act (FDICIA) of 1991 that both laid out a series of prompt corrective actions that were to be taken by regulators as capital ratios of depository institutions declined and directed the FDIC to resolve failed banks in the least costly way to the deposit insurance fund. The motivation behind the least-cost resolution provisions was the failure of large banks such as Continental Illinois and Bank of New England during the 1980s in which all creditors had been bailed out to avoid "systemic" disruptions.[32] With regard to deposit insurance, the act mandated that risk-based premiums were to be put in place by 1994. The Omnibus Budget Reconciliation Act of 1993 established a national depositor preference system under which depositors and the FDIC have priority over nondepositor claims in the resolution of a failed financial intermediary.

The Depositors Insurance Funds Act of 1996 brought an official end to the crisis of the 1980s and early 1990s. It mandated a onetime assessment to bring the SAIF up to 1.25 percent of insured deposits and required that by the beginning of 1999 SAIF assessment rates be no lower than BIF rates. The Act also stipulated that banks judged to be well managed and capitalized would pay no insurance premiums so long as the funds reserves remained above 1.25 percent of insured deposits. Both the BIF and the SAIF reached the 1.25 percent threshold in 1996 bringing about a sharp reduction in insurance premiums as shown in figure 5.5. In 2005, only 6 percent of banks were not judged to be well managed and capitalized, thus 94 percent of banks paid no insurance premiums.

Basis points

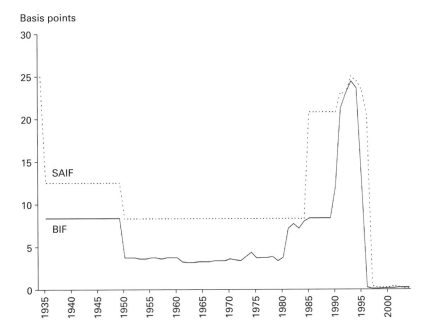

Figure 5.5
Insurance fund effective premium rates

5.5   Current State of Reform and Outlook for Deposit Insurance

The U.S. experience with deposit insurance demonstrates the fragility of any scheme applied to undiversified financial intermediaries. Much of this fragility has been removed over the past decade or so, starting in 1994 with the Riegle-Neal Interstate Banking and Branching Efficiency Act. Riegle-Neal ended branching restrictions, allowing banks geographic diversification. The Gramm-Leach-Bliley Financial Services Modernization Act of 1999 repealed the Glass-Steagall separation of commercial and investment banking, allowing banks to diversify their product lines. These last two pieces of legislation encouraged continued consolidation in financial services. Regulator discretion has also been curtailed—most important, in 1991 with the prompt corrective action regulations contained in FDICIA. The legislative changes combined with a very favorable economic environment left deposit insurance out of the headlines for at least a decade.

Most recently, rapid growth in bank deposits pushed the BIF below the 1.25 percent reserve threshold, potentially triggering assessments for even highly rated institutions.[33] The prospect of assessments and a desire on the part of smaller banks to increase deposit insurance coverage, led to legislative action culminating in passage of the Federal Deposit Insurance Reform Act of 2005.[34] The Act merged the BIF and SAIF into a new Deposit Insurance Fund (DIF), increased deposit insurance for retirement accounts to $250,000, provided for the adjustment of deposit insurance limits for inflation beginning in April 2010, and, perhaps most important, increased the FDIC's flexibility in setting risk-based premiums.

New rules for risk-based assessments were issued in November 2006, with a distinction made between small banks and large banks where a large bank has more than $10 billion in assets. All banks are placed in one of four risk categories based on their capitalization and supervisory ratings. For small banks, supervisory CAMELS ratings are combined with financial ratios to determine the assessment levied against insured deposits.[35] For large banks, CAMELS ratings are combined, if available, with long-term debt ratings to determine assessment rates. The highest-rated risk category, Category I, includes 95 percent of all insured institutions. Assessment rates set for January 2007 range from a minimum of 5 basis points for Risk Category I institutions to 43 basis points for Risk Category IV institutions. Currently, the DIF stands at 1.22 percent of insured deposits. Aggregate constraints on FDIC assessments remain, as the fund is capped and dividends must be paid to member institutions when the reserve ratio is above 1.35 percent.

Although the journey has been slow, and at times quite painful, bank regulation has come more than full circle since 1933. With no limits on branching and no wall separating commercial and investment banking, banking in the United States may enter a new era of stability similar to that enjoyed by Canada over the past century. In such an environment, and complemented by risk-rated premiums and prompt corrective action, deposit insurance is unlikely to be needed to protect the medium of exchange. It will continue to assuage the fears of small savers and as a result the intermediaries that serve this constituency will continue to support extensions of deposit insurance. This is evidenced by the advocacy of the Independent Community Bankers of America for increases in deposit insurance coverage. Constraints on regulatory forbearance make it unlikely that the moral hazard associated with deposit insurance will again manifest itself in a large crisis as in the 1980s.

The historical narrative in this chapter highlights several important points. First, lack of diversification puts depository institutions at risk, and well-intentioned regulation can inadvertently heighten that risk. Second, the most recent historical research suggests that failures and panics brought about by the lack of diversification were most often separation equilibria that involved transfers from unhealthy to healthy banks rather than pooling equilibria that involved indiscriminate withdrawals from all banks. In one important case, a separating equilibrium was transformed into a pooling equilibrium when state regulators began to impose a rolling wave of bank holidays. Both of these points suggest that the adoption of deposit insurance is a second-best response that imposes costs of its own. The first-best response would be to directly address the lack of diversification. Third, and finally, the costs of deposit insurance come through two main channels: increased risk taking brought about by the moral hazard implicit in any insurance scheme, and excessive credit creation on the part of the insured institutions. All of these points are illustrated by the U.S. experience that provides an important lesson for policymakers in other countries who are weighing the costs and benefits of deposit insurance. Looking forward, the United States over the past decade has largely moved to the first-best response of addressing the lack of diversification, leaving a deposit insurance apparatus that probably does little to curtail banking panics but does provide important competitive benefits to small depository institutions.

Acknowledgments

This chapter was written prior to Kroszner joining the Federal Reserve Board. The views expressed in this paper are those of the authors and not necessarily those of the Board of Governors, members of its staff, the Federal Reserve Bank of Cleveland, or the Federal Reserve System. We would like to thank Bin Li for helpful research assistance and Patrick Van Horn for historical information on central reserve cities.

Notes

1. See FDIC 1998.

2. See Golembe 1960. Like many others, Golembe downplays the motive of protecting small depositors, especially given the generous coverage limits of most U.S. plans.

3. Discussions of both the theory and evidence on clearinghouses can be found in Gorton 1985, Gorton and Mullineaux 1987, Kroszner 2000, and Moen and Tallman 2000. Richardson 2006a provides evidence of the superiority of clearing house arrangements over correspondent networks in the 1930s.

4. Stopping panics requires more than an active lender of last resort, a point emphasized by Calomiris (1989). The lender of last resort can safeguard the medium of exchange but does not change depositor incentives with regard to individual banks under the first-in-line, first-to-withdraw constraint.

5. See Calomiris and Gorton 2000, Bordo 1992, and Wicker 1996.

6. See Demirgüç-Kunt and Levine 2001 and Levine 2005.

7. See Dehejia and Lleras-Muney 2007 for empirical evidence on the potential negative relationship between deposit insurance and growth, a point we return to later in the chapter.

8. See Friedman and Schwartz 1962 for a fuller discussion of the panic.

9. Although figures are not provided, their charts show a similar movement for deposits.

10. Wicker's dating differs slightly from Friedman and Schwartz who have the panic starting in March.

11. Notes of the national banks were secured by the posting of U.S. government bonds and backed by the credit of the federal government.

12. Detailed discussions of the Oklahoma plan can be found in Cooke 1909, 1910, and Robb 1921. Our discussion of Oklahoma draws heavily on these sources. Summaries of the eight state plans can be found in FDIC 1953, Golembe 1960, White 1983, and Calomiris 1989.

13. This is one example of the excessive credit expansion that explains the Dehejia and Lleras-Muney (2007) finding of a negative relationship between deposit insurance and growth.

14. Kane (1989) constructs a political economy description of deposit insurance in the tradition of Stigler (1971) and Peltzman (1976).

15. Subsequent research by White (1986), Benston (1990), Kroszner and Rajan (1994), Kroszner and Rajan (1997), and Kroszner and Strahan (2006) has largely contravened the Pecora hearing's charges of bank misbehavior in the late 1920s and 1930s.

16. See Federal Deposit Insurance Corporation 1998 for details of the transition from the temporary to permanent plan.

17. See Association of Reserve City Bankers 1933 for an example and Flood 1992.

18. The adoption and early experience of S&L insurance is discussed in White 1998.

19. Federal Reserve Bank of Cleveland 1986.

20. Kane 1989, 131. Maggin 1989 describes in detail the transactions between Home State and ESM.

21. Warner's son-in-law was general counsel for ESM.

22. The second author of this paper was a depositor with Home State at the time of the crisis. He withdrew his funds a day or two before Home State's last day of business on March 8, 1985.

23. Federal Reserve Bank of Cleveland 1986, 5.

24. Cooperman, Wilson, and Wolfe (1992) find that less solvent, federally insured, banks and S&Ls in Ohio had to pay higher rates on CDs for the seven weeks following the

ODGF crisis, also consistent with a separation equilibrium. Interestingly, DeGennaro and Thomson (1995) find that nationwide, shares of firms insured by the relatively weaker FSLIC outperformed shares of firms insured by the relatively stronger FDIC. This result is consistent with the hypothesis that the resolution of the Ohio crisis led market participants to believe that regulatory forbearance would be continued for the FSLIC fund and/or that implicit guarantees to depositors in weak insurance funds were more likely to be honored.

25. Columbus Dispatch 2000.

26. Kane 1992.

27. Hallett 2005.

28. See Kroszner and Strahan (1996) who stress, along with Peltzman (1970), that firms near insolvency will also have an incentive to increase capital distributions to shareholders.

29. See Federal Deposit Insurance Corporation 1997, chap. 3.

30. See Kane 1985.

31. Barth 1991.

32. The Comptroller of the Currency announced publicly after Continental Illinois that some large banks were too big to fail. This public announcement was quickly seen as unwise, and the 1991 law attempted to correct market perceptions that some banks were too big to fail and thereby rein in excessive risk taking incentives.

33. Absent any congressional action, the FDIC would have begun charging BIF assessments in 2006.

34. The Act is part of the Deficit Reduction Act of 2005 (S 1932) that was signed into law on February 8, 2006. Details on the legislation and the process leading to its adoption can be found in Dalton 2006 and Paletta and Blackwell 2006.

35. CAMELS is an acronym for Capital adequacy, Asset quality, Management, Earnings, Liquidity, and Sensitivity to market risk.

References

Andrew, A. Piatt. 1908. Substitutes for Cash in the Panic of 1907. *Quarterly Journal of Economics* 22 (4): 497–516.

Association of Reserve City Bankers. 1933. *The Guaranty of Bank Deposits A Report of the Commission on Banking Law and Practice*. Bulletin no. 3, Chicago.

Barth, James R. 1991. *The Great Savings and Loan Debacle*. Washington, D.C.: American Enterprise Institute Press.

Benston, George J. 1990. *The Separation of Commercial and Investment Banking: The Glass–Steagall Act Revisited and Reconsidered*. New York: Oxford University Press.

Bordo, Michael D. 1992. The Lender of Last Resort: Some Insights from History. *Research in Financial Services Public and Private Policy* 4: 1–19.

Calomiris, Charles W. 1989. Deposit Insurance: Lessons from the Record. *Economic Perspectives* (May): 10–30. Federal Reserve Bank of Chicago.

Calomiris, Charles W. 1990. Is Deposit Insurance Necessary? A Historical Perspective. *Journal of Economic History* 50 (2): 283–295.

Calomiris, Charles W. 1992. Do "Vulnerable" Economies Need Deposit Insurance? Lessons from U.S. Agriculture in the 1920s. In *If Texas Were Chile: A Primer on Banking Reform*, ed. Philip L. Brock. San Francisco: Institute for Contemporary Studies Press.

Calomiris, Charles W., and Gary Gorton. 2000. The Origins of Banking Panics: Models, Facts, and Bank Regulation. In *U.S. Bank Deregulation in Historical Perspective*, ed. Charles Calomiris. New York: Cambridge University Press.

Calomiris, Charles W., and Joseph R. Mason. 1997. Contagion and Bank Failures During the Great Depression: The June 1932 Chicago Banking Panic. *American Economic Review* 87 (5): 863–883.

Calomiris, Charles W., and Joseph R. Mason. 2003. Fundamentals, Panics, and Bank Distress during the Depression. *American Economic Review* 93 (5): 1615–1647.

Calomiris, Charles W., and Eugene N. White. 1994. The Origins of Federal Deposit Insurance. In *The Regulated Economy: A Historical Approach to Political Economy*, ed. Claudia Goldin and Gary D. Libecap. Chicago: University of Chicago Press.

Chung, Ching-Yi, and Gary Richardson. 2006. Deposit Insurance and the Composition of Bank Suspensions in Developing Economies: Lessons from the State Deposit Insurance Experiments of the 1920s. NBER Working Paper no. 12594, National Bureau of Economic Research, Cambridge, Mass.

Columbus Dispatch. 2000. Ohio Ready to Close Book on Home State Savings Bank. *Columbus Dispatch*, September 26, 2E.

Cooke, Thorton. 1909. The Insurance of Bank Deposits in the West. *The Quarterly Journal of Economics* 24 (1): 85–108.

Cooke, Thorton. 1910. The Insurance of Bank Deposits in the West: II. *The Quarterly Journal of Economics* 24 (2): 85–108.

Cooperman, Elizabeth S., Winson B. Lee, and Glenn A. Wolfe. 1992. The 1985 Ohio Thrift Crisis, the FSLIC's Solvency, and Rate Contagion for Retail CDs. *Journal of Finance* 47 (3): 919–941.

Credit Union Journal. 2002. Key Figure in RISDIC Is Paroled after Ten Years. *Credit Union Journal* 6 (27): 2.

Dalton, Patrick. 2006. FDIC Insurance Reform. *ABA Bankers News* 14 (1): 1–2.

DeGennaro, Ramon P., and James B. Thomson. 1995. Anticipating Bailouts: The Incentive-Conflict Model and the Collapse of the Ohio Deposit Guarantee Fund. *Journal of Banking and Finance* 19 (8): 1401–1418.

Dehejia, Rajeev, and Adriana Lleras-Muney. 2007. Financial Development and Pathways of Growth: State Branching and Deposit Insurance Laws in the United States, 1900–1940. *Journal of Law and Economics* 50 (2): 239–272.

Demirgüç-Kunt, Aslı, and Ross Levine. 2001. *Financial Structure and Economic Growth: A Cross-Country Comparison of Banks, Markets, and Development*. Cambridge, Mass.: The MIT Press.

Diamond, Douglas, and Phillip Dybvig. 1983. Bank Runs, Liquidity and Deposit Insurance. *Journal of Political Economy* 91: 401–419.

English, William B. 1993. The Decline of Private Deposit Insurance in the United States. *Carnegie-Rochester Conference Series on Public Policy* 38: 57–128.

Federal Deposit Insurance Corporation. 1953, 1956. *Annual Report*. Washington, D.C.: Federal Deposit Insurance Corporation.

Federal Deposit Insurance Corporation. 1997. *History of the Eighties Lessons for the Future, Volume 1: An Examination of the Banking Crises of the 1980s and Early 1990s*. Washington, D.C.: Federal Deposit Insurance Corporation.

Federal Deposit Insurance Corporation. 1998. A Brief History of Deposit Insurance in the United States. Paper prepared for the International Conference on Deposit Insurance, Washington, D.C., September.

Federal Reserve Bank of Cleveland. 1986. Unfoldings in Ohio: 1985. In *Annual Report 1985*, 5–24. Cleveland: Federal Reserve Bank of Cleveland.

Flood, Mark D. 1992. The Great Deposit Insurance Debate. *Federal Reserve Bank of St. Louis Review* 74 (4): 51–77.

Friedman, Milton, and Anna J. Schwartz. 1962. *A Monetary History of the United States, 1867–1960*. Princeton: Princeton University Press and NBER.

Golembe, Carter H. 1960. The Deposit Insurance Legislation of 1933: An Examination of Its Antecedents and Its Purposes. *Political Science Quarterly* 75 (2): 181–200.

Gorton, Gary. 1985. Clearinghouses and the Origin of Central Banking in the U.S. *Journal of Economic History* 45 (2): 277–283.

Gorton, Gary, and Donald Mullineaux. 1987. The Joint Production of Confidence: Endogenous Regulation and 19th Century Commercial Bank Clearinghouses. *Journal of Money, Credit, and Banking* 19 (4): 458–468.

Hallett, Joe. 2005. S&L Crisis Brought Out Statesmanship; 20 Years Later, Handling of Home State Failure Stands the Test of Time. *Columbus Dispatch*, March 7, 1A.

Hooks, Linda, and Kenneth Robinson. 2002. Deposit Insurance and Moral Hazard: Evidence from Texas Banking During the 1920s. *The Journal of Economic History* 62 (3): 833–853.

Joint Select Committee on Savings and Loans. 1986. Protecting the Depositor: Report and Recommendations. 116th Ohio General Assembly, February 1.

Kane, Edward J. 1985. *The Gathering Crisis in Federal Deposit Insurance*. Cambridge, Mass.: The MIT Press.

Kane, Edward J. 1987. Who Should Learn What from the Failure and Delayed Bailout of the ODGF. In *Proceedings, A Conference on Bank Structure and Competition, Merging Commercial and Investment Banking: Risks Benefits Challenges*, 306–326. Chicago: Federal Reserve Bank of Chicago.

Kane, Edward J. 1989. *The S&L Insurance Mess: How Did It Happen?* Washington, D.C.: The Urban Institute Press.

Kane, Edward J. 1992. How Incentive-Incompatible Deposit-Insurance Funds Fail. *Research in Financial Services Public and Private Policy* 4: 51–91.

Kostrzewa, John. 2005. John Kostrzewa Column. *The Providence Journal*, January 16.

Kroszner, Randall S. 2000. Lessons from Financial Crises: The Role of Clearinghouses. *Journal of Financial Services Research* 18 (2–3): 157–171.

Kroszner, Randall S., and Raghuram Rajan. 1994. Is the Glass-Steagall Act Justified? A Study of the U.S. Experience with Universal Banking before 1933. *American Economic Review* 84 (4): 810–832.

Kroszner, Randall S., and Raghuram Rajan. 1997. Organization Structure and Credibility: Evidence from Commercial Bank Securities Activities before the Glass-Steagall Act. *Journal of Monetary Economics* 39 (3): 475–516.

Kroszner, Randall S., and Philip E. Strahan. 1996. Regulatory Incentives and the Thrift Crisis: Dividends, Mutual-to-Stock Conversions, and Financial Distress. *Journal of Finance* 51 (4): 1285–1319.

Kroszner, Randall S., and Philip E. Strahan. 2006. Regulation and Deregulation of the U.S. Banking Industry: Causes, Consequences and Implications for the Future. In *NBER Conference Volume on Economic Regulation and Its Reform: What Have We Learned?* Chicago: National Bureau of Economic Research.

Levine, Ross. 2005. Finance and Growth: Theory and Evidence. In *Handbook of Economic Growth*, ed. Philippe Aghion and Steven Durlauf, 865–923. Amsterdam: Elsevier.

Maggin, Donald L. 1989. *Bankers, Builders, Knaves, and Thieves: The $300 Scam at ESM.* Chicago: Contemporary Books.

McCulloch, J. Huston. 1987. The Ohio S&L Crisis in Retrospect: Implications for the Current Federal Deposit Insurance Crisis. In *Proceedings, A Conference on Bank Structure and Competition, Merging Commercial and Investment Banking: Risks Benefits Challenges,* 230–251. Chicago: Federal Reserve Bank of Chicago.

Moen, Jon, and Ellis Tallman. 1992. The Bank Panic of 1907: The Role of Trust Companies. *Journal of Economic History* 52 (3): 611–630.

Moen, Jon, and Ellis Tallman. 2000. Clearinghouse Membership and Deposit Contraction during the Panic of 1907. *Journal of Economic History* 60 (2): 145–163.

National Commission on Financial Institution Reform, Recovery, and Enforcement. 1993. *Origins and Causes of the S&L Debacle: A Blueprint for Reform.* Washington, D.C.: U.S. Government Printing Office.

Paletta, Damian, and Rob Blackwell. 2006. FDIC on Verge of Much Freer Hand on Policy. *American Banker* 171 (2): 1.

Peltzman, Sam. 1970. Capital Investment in Commercial Banking and its Relationship to Portfolio Regulation. *Journal of Political Economy* 78 (1): 1–26.

Peltzman, Sam. 1976. Towards a More General Theory of Regulation. *Journal of Law and Economics* 19 (2): 211–240.

Richardson, Gary. 2006a. Correspondent Clearing and the Banking Panics of the Great Depression. NBER Working Paper no. 12716. National Bureau of Economic Research, Cambridge, Mass.

Richardson, Gary. 2006b. Records of the Federal Reserve Board of Governors in Record Group 82 at the National Archives of the United States. *Financial History Review* 13 (1): 123–134.

Richardson, Gary. 2006c. Bank Distress during the Great Depression: The Illiquidity-Insolvency Debate Revisited. NBER Working Paper no. 12717, National Bureau of Economic Research, Cambridge, Mass.

Richardson, Gary. 2006d. A Comment Concerning Deposit Insurance and Moral Hazard. NBER Working Paper no. 12719, National Bureau of Economic Research, Cambridge, Mass.

Robb, Thomas Bruce. 1921. *The Guaranty of Bank Deposits*. Boston: Houghton Mifflin.

Stigler, George J. 1971. The Theory of Economic Regulation. *Bell Journal of Economics and Management Science* 2 (1): 3–21.

Temin, Peter. 1990. *Lessons from the Great Depression*. Cambridge, Mass.: The MIT Press.

Webster, W. C. 1909. The Depositors' Guaranty Law of Oklahoma. *Journal of Political Economy* 17 (2): 65–81.

Wheelock, David C., and Subal C. Kumbhakar. 1994. 'The Slack Banker Dances' Deposit Insurance and Risk-Taking in the Banking Collapse of the 1920s. *Explorations in Economic History* 31 (3): 357–375.

Wheelock, David C., and Subal C. Kumbhakar. 1995. Which Banks Choose Deposit Insurance? Evidence of Adverse Selectiona and Moral Hazard in a Voluntary Insurance System. *Journal of Money, Credit, and Banking* 27 (1): 186–201.

Wheelock, David C., and Paul W. Wilson. 1995. Explaining Bank Failures: Deposit Insurance, Regulation, and Efficiency. *The Review of Economics and Statistics* 77 (4): 689–700.

White, Eugene N. 1983. *The Regulation and Reform of the American Banking System, 1900–1929*. Princeton: Princeton University Press.

White, Eugene N. 1984. A Reinterpretation of the Banking Crisis of 1930. *Journal of Economic History* 44 (1): 119–138.

White, Eugene N. 1998. The Legacy of Deposit Insurance: The Growth, Spread, and Cost of Insuring Financial Intermediaries. In *The Defining Moment: The Great Depression and the American Economy in the Twentieth Century*, ed. Michael D. Bordo, Claudia Goldin, and Eugene N. White, 87–121. Chicago: University of Chicago Press.

Wicker, Elmus. 1996. *The Banking Panics of the Great Depression*. New York: Cambridge University Press.

6 Banking with and without Deposit Insurance: Mexico's Banking Experiments, 1884–2004

Stephen Haber

6.1 Introduction

The creation of a banking system requires the resolution of a fundamental problem. Unless individuals and business enterprises deposit their wealth in banks, the banking system will be small and its ability to finance consumption and investment will be reduced. Once individuals and business enterprises deposit their wealth, however, they relinquish control over it to bank insiders (managers and directors) who can lose it by lending it in an imprudent manner. Depositors will therefore not deploy their wealth unless they can be convinced that insiders will behave prudently or unless they can be assured that their wealth is not at risk, regardless of the actions of the insiders.

There are three groups that police imprudent lending by insiders and by extension protect the wealth of depositors. The first are depositors themselves, who can move their funds out of imprudently run banks. The second are shareholders, whose wealth is also at stake, and who can remove imprudent directors and managers. The third are government regulators, who mitigate the risk of imprudent behavior by limiting competition among banks, by enforcing minimum capital and reserve requirements, and by restricting the scope of contracts that banks may create.

The incentives of these three groups are not perfectly aligned. From the point of view of depositors, the solution that provides them with the most protection is deposit insurance. The greater the extent of deposit insurance, however, the weaker are the incentives of depositors to monitor insiders, shifting more of the burden of monitoring to shareholders and regulators. Indeed, deposit insurance creates well-known problems of adverse selection and moral hazard. Thus, banking systems with deposit insurance require strong institutions of corporate governance and close supervision of banks by regulators. Shareholders do not always have strong mechanisms, however, to police insiders: the institutions of corporate governance vary widely across countries. Moreover, deposit insurance tends to reduce the incentives of shareholders to monitor insiders, because attempts by governments to protect depositors through bank rescues have the effect of preserving shareholder equity.

As a consequence, banking systems with deposit insurance tend to shift most of the responsibility of monitoring onto regulators. Regulators do not, however, always have strong incentives to carry out their supervisory functions so as to maximize social welfare. Indeed, there is a high degree of variance across countries in terms of the independence of regulators from political pressures, the quality of the tools that regulators have at their disposal, the proclivity of public officials to corruption, and the political institutions that align the incentives of public officials with the taxpayers who ultimately fund the deposit insurance system.

Precisely because there is such a high degree of variance in the network of institutions that work to mitigate imprudent behavior by bank insiders, there does not appear to be any single set of arrangements that is optimal for all countries. Understanding which sets of institutions work best in particular political and economic environments is not, however, an area that has been fully researched.

One approach to furthering our understanding is to use the historical record as a natural laboratory, focusing on a single case over an extended period of time. This chapter therefore examines Mexico's various experiments with bank regulation over a period of 120 years, from 1884 to 2004.

Mexico is an ideal case in which to carry out such an analysis for three reasons. First, Mexico created a private banking system de novo on three separate occasions: 1884–1911, 1924–1982, and 1991–2004. Significantly, the first two episodes ended not because of the failure of the institutions that protected depositors, but because the government expropriated the banking system for fiscal reasons and then held onto the banks for a period of years. This means that each of Mexico's experiments was as independent of the others as one is likely to find in any single country. Second, Mexico's underlying political institutions did not vary dramatically over the three experiments. From 1876 to 2000, the country was ruled by authoritarian governments that had high degrees of authority and discretion. Third, Mexico's property and contract rights environment was weak over the three experiments. While there have been improvements in credit reporting and bankruptcy procedures in the last five years, these reforms took place after the banking system collapsed in 1995–1996 because of inadequate institutions to mitigate imprudent lending. This means that what varied from experiment to experiment were the institutions that protected depositors. Mexico's other institutions, while by no means immutable, were as stable as one is likely to find in any single case study.

Mexico's first experiment, 1884–1911, did not involve deposit insurance. The problem of imprudent behavior by insiders was mitigated by institutions that promoted good corporate governance and by limiting competition among banks through regulated entry. The resulting banking system was stable and profitable, but it attracted extremely low levels of deposits.

Mexico's second experiment, 1924–1982, also did not involve deposit insurance. The problem of imprudent behavior by insiders was again mitigated by the institutions that promoted good corporate governance: bank insiders monitored each other through a complex network of interlocking directorates. Reckless lending was also checked by the government's practice of requiring banks to hold a significant portion of their deposits as reserves, which is to say that much bank lending was forced lending to the government. But, good governance and high reserve requirements appear to have been only part of the story. Mexico's banking system was also characterized by government development banks, which made long term loans to private enterprises. The evidence suggests, but is by no means conclusive, that entrepreneurs (many of whom were bankers) funded their riskiest ventures through the development banks, thereby shifting risk from the private banking system to the taxpayers who ultimately funded the government banks. As a consequence, the private banking system was profitable and stable, but government development banks wound up owning a large number of inefficient enterprises.

Mexico's third experiment, 1991–2004, involved deposit insurance. In fact, during the first phase of this experiment, 1991–1996, deposit insurance was unlimited. At the same time, however, the ability of the government to regulate Mexico's banks was minimal and the institutions that promoted good corporate governance were weak. The combination was disastrous: reckless lending, high default rates, and a taxpayer financed bailout of depositors, borrowers, and some stockholders. Many of these institutions were then reformed in 1997—

particularly as regards the unlimited nature of deposit insurance and the ability of regulators to monitor banks. The result of these reforms has been extremely prudent lending practices.

6.2   Experiment One: Banking without Insurance in Porfirian Mexico, 1884–1911

In the late 1870s Mexico's banking system was so small as to be practically nonexistent. Only two chartered banks existed in the entire country. One was a branch of a British bank that operated in Mexico City and focused primarily on financing foreign trade. The other was a small American-founded operation chartered by the government of the border state of Chihuahua. The reason for the absence of a banking system is not hard to divine: Mexico's nineteenth-century governments, fighting for their survival against numerous rebellions, coups, secessions, and foreign invasions, preyed-upon private wealth. Bankers feared that as soon as they made their capital visible, by obtaining a charter, the government would confiscate it via forced lending.

Within a few years, however, Porfirio Díaz (Mexico's dictator from 1876 to 1911) enacted legislation that engendered the rapid expansion of the banking system. The key to Díaz's banking policies was that he provided bankers with a series of segmented monopolies and oligopolies that raised rates of return high enough to compensate them for the risk of expropriation (Maurer and Gomberg 2004).

The banking system was divided into three sectors: banks of issue, which issued bank notes, discounted bills, and made commercial loans; mortgage banks, which lent long term on agricultural and urban properties; and investment banks (bancos refaccionarios), which were supposed to make long-term loans to agricultural and industrial enterprises. Only one of these sectors, the banks of issue, prospered. As Riguzzi (2002) has shown, limitations on the number of charters the government was willing to grant to mortgage banks, along with difficulties in enforcing contract rights on real property, meant that there were never more than three mortgage banks in the entire country. From 1897 to 1911, total mortgage bank assets averaged only 6 percent of total banking system assets. The investment banks also faltered. They were at a distinct disadvantage against banks of issue, because they could not issue bank notes. They had to compete, however, in the same markets as banks of issue, because the latter were able to skirt the laws that restricted the term of their loans (to six months) by continually renewing credits as they expired (Maurer 2002). As a consequence, there were never more than six chartered investment banks, and the combined assets of these banks, on average, accounted for only 10 percent of total banking system assets. Moreover, the largest bank of this type (the Banco Central Mexicano) did not actually make any long term loans at all. Instead, it operated a clearinghouse for the notes emitted by smaller banks of issue. The investment banking charter was simply a way to get around regulatory restrictions on creating a clearinghouse.

The banks of issue, which accounted, on average, for 84 percent of all bank assets, operated a series of segmented oligopolies. Only two banks of issue—the Banco de Londres y México (which had a charter dating from the 1860s, granted during the period when France occupied Mexico) and the Banco Nacional de México (which received a charter from the Díaz government in 1884 that made it the treasury's fiscal agent)—were permitted to branch across state lines. All other banks of issue were prohibited from branching outside their concession territories, which were generally contiguous with state lines.

A series of regulatory barriers to entry then insured that only one bank of issue would receive a charter for that concession territory. First, banks without a federal charter were prohibited from issuing notes, meaning that they could not effectively compete against chartered banks. Second, the government levied a 2 percent tax on bank capital and a 5 percent tax on banknotes—but exempted the first bank of issue in each state to receive a federal charter. Third, the government established a minimum capital requirement for a bank of issue equivalent to $250,000—five times the minimum capital needed to found a national bank in the United States. Finally, the law specified that new issues of bank stock had to receive the approval of the finance minister. The effect of these laws, as Maurer (2002) has shown, was that there were usually only three banks in any state: a branch of the Banco Nacional de México, a branch of the Banco de Londres y México, and the bank of issue that held the territorial concession.

The high barriers to entry erected by Díaz produced a rapid expansion of the banking system. In 1897, when Díaz's regulatory system was finally in place, the entire banking system, including mortgage banks, investment banks, and banks of issue, was comprised of just ten banks with total assets equal to only 12 percent of GDP (see table 6.1). By 1910 (Díaz's last full year in office before he was overthrown), there were thirty-two banks with total assets equal to 32 percent of

Table 6.1
The Mexican banking industry, 1897–1913

Year	Number of banks[a]	Average equity ratio[b] (percent)	Total assets (millions of nominal pesos)	Deposits as percent of assets	Deposits as percent of GDP	Assets as percent of GDP	Bank of issue: Assets as percent of total assets	Bank of issue: Rate of return on book equity	
								Weighted average[c] (percent)	Unweighted average (percent)
1897	10	32	147	2	0	12	93		
1898	16	32	175	3	0	15	94		
1899	18	31	211	2	0	18	90		
1900	20	31	259	5	1	20	90		
1901	24	35	264	4	1	15	87	10	10
1902	25	31	317	5	1	19	88	14	13
1903	31	31	380	4	1	20	86	1	0
1904	32	30	435	3	1	24	88	4	7
1905	32	28	535	6	2	24	87	40	29
1906	32	32	629	9	3	28	88	23	13
1907	34	30	724	9	3	31	83	4	6
1908	34	31	757	9	3	31	81	0	4
1909	32	26	917	16	6	35	80	14	9
1910	32	24	1,005	16	5	32	80	4	3
1911	33	22	1,119	13			81	20	14
1912	34	23	1,086	15			78	11	10
1913	28	21	1,105	15			77		

Source: Number of banks, book equity, assets, and deposits calculated from Secretaria del Estado y del Despacho de Hacienda y Credito Publico y Comercio 1914. Bank of issue rates of return from Maurer and Haber 2007. GDP from Instituto Nacional de Estadistica Geografia e Informática 1994, 401.

[a] Includes banks of issue, mortgage banks, and investment banks (bancos refaccionarios). The 1913 figure does not include six banks that did not report because of the revolution.

[b] Weighted by assets.

[c] Weighted by market capitalization.

GDP. Not only was this a sizable banking system by the standards of developing countries at the turn of the century, it was large by Mexico's current standards: the ratio of commercial bank assets to GDP in Mexico in 2004 was 33 percent.

Obtaining a concession for a bank of issue was a highly politicized affair. The founders of these banks tended to be wealthy merchants who had been engaged in private banking prior to seeking a charter from the Díaz government. In order to obtain and protect their charters, these merchants and private bankers recruited powerful public officials onto their boards of directors, including federal senators and deputies, state governors, cabinet ministers, the brother of the treasury secretary, and Porfirio Díaz's son (Haber, Razo, and Maurer 2003, chap. 4).

One might imagine that Mexico's institutional environment—a dictatorship in which the dictator's cronies were among the bank insiders—would have given rise to reckless lending, if not outright looting. One might especially imagine this to be the case, considering that most bank loans went to bank directors themselves, or to firms controlled by them (Maurer and Haber 2007). In fact, in Mexico's largest bank, the Banco Nacional de México, 100 percent of all nongovernment lending from 1888 to 1901 went to insiders. For other firms, Maurer and Haber's (lower bound) estimates indicate that insider loans, as a percentage of all loans, varied from a low of 29 percent (the Banco de Nuevo León) to a high of 86 percent (the Banco Mercantil de Veracruz).

The evidence indicates, however, that banks practiced insider lending because, given the high costs of assessing default risk, it was the prudent thing to do. We know this to be the case for three reasons.

First, a reading the minutes of boards of directors meetings makes it clear that board members viewed insider loans as less risky than arms' length loans. In one particularly informative debate that took place among the board members of the Banco Nacional de México, some members objected to a loan being made to another bank (the Banco Oriental), until it was pointed out that the recipient bank was a good credit risk because it only made loans to its own board members. The reason why they viewed arms' length loans as risky was because experience had taught them that they lacked good mechanisms to assess the quality of borrowers. Unable to tell good credit risks from bad, they had responded by placing onerous requirements on borrowers, but these had worked to create adverse selection (Maurer and Haber 2007).

Second, had insider loans been a mechanism for insiders to loot the banks at the expense of depositors, we would not expect the banking system to have been stable or profitable. As table 6.1 demonstrates, however, the annual real return on the book value of equity from 1901–1912 averaged 12 percent (these returns were not driven by the profits earned by a few large banks: the unweighted average was 10 percent). Moreover, there were no years in which the average rate of return was negative, and only one year (1908), when the average rate of return was zero. Mexico's banking system was also remarkably stable: as table 6.1 demonstrates, the number of reporting banks and total bank assets increased steadily. The only downturn was in 1909, when, as a result of an externally generated crisis in 1908, seven small banks of issue failed (two were later rechartered as investment banks, while the others were purchased by larger, more solvent banks).

Third, as a result of the 1908 crisis, the government quickly organized a rescue by chartering a bank (the equity coming from four of Mexico's largest banks, and debt financing coming from European bond holders), the *Caja de Préstamos para Obras de Irrigación y Fomento de la Agricultura*, whose purpose was to purchase bank loans and bank-issued mortgage bonds in order to inject liquidity into the banking system (Maurer 2002). One of the striking aspects of the *Caja* was that it only repurchased high quality, performing loans from banks, and it turns out that these high quality performing loans were exactly those loans that the banks had made to their own board members. Lest readers remain skeptical about the quality of these insider loans, I hasten to point out that the *Caja de Préstamos* may be the only banking rescue in history to actually make money: the *Caja de Préstamos* generated a real return to all claimants of its assets (bondholders and shareholders) of 4.9 percent in 1909, 6.0 percent in 1910, and 5.7 percent in 1911. As a consequence, neither the crisis of 1908, nor any previous bank failures, produced a single centavo in losses for depositors (Maurer and Haber 2007).

Why were Mexico's bankers so prudent? Why didn't they use insider lending, especially in the midst of a financial crisis to loot their own banks at the expense of depositors and minority shareholders? The answer is good corporate governance: bank directors had strong incentives to monitor each other, and minority shareholders could monitor bank insiders. As a result, loans, even those made to directors, were often structured as secured lines of credit.

One of the most striking characteristics of Mexico's banks during this period was that they had amazingly high capital adequacy ratios, which is to say that their stockholders had significant amounts of capital at risk. From 1897 to 1910, the ratio of equity to assets never fell below 24 percent—three times Basel II standards (see table 6.1). Even the banks of issue, which had lower capital asset ratios because of their ability to create bank notes, had extremely high capital-asset ratios: from 1897 to 1910, the ratio of equity to assets never fell below 21 percent. In part, these capital ratios were driven by the legal requirement that note issues not exceed two (sometimes three) times a bank's cash on hand, or three times its paid-in capital (Maurer 2002). In equal part, however, these capital ratios were driven by risk aversion on the parts of both bankers and noteholders. Banks usually did not, in fact, issue notes up to their legal maximum.

In addition, a sizable proportion of stockholder capital was owned by the insiders, and what was not owned by them was represented by independent directors. As of the 1884 Commercial Code, receiving a bank charter required the founding group (who became the directors) to subscribe to the first tranche of the bank's capital. Banks could later sell additional tranches of capital to outsiders. In addition, bank directors could (and often did) sell parts of their original stakes. These outside shareholders (who owned a majority of bank stock) then insisted on the appointment of independent directors (typically other bankers) who monitored the founding board members. As Razo (2003) and Musacchio (2005) have shown, the prevalence of independent directors, who were recruited from other bank boards, meant that there was a dense network of interlocking directorates which produced cross-monitoring of bankers by one another. In short, outside shareholders had a mechanism to monitor the insiders. There is direct historical evidence that this mechanism was employed by outside shareholders. In March 1908, the outside shareholders of the Banco de Jalisco, displeased with the discovery of "severe irregularities" in the bank's books, replaced the entire board of directors except the vice president (Maurer and Haber 2007). Moreover, the fact that they owned much of the capital, and that there was cross-monitoring of boards through interlocking directorates gave insiders very strong incentives to monitor each other: both their capital and their reputations in the broader business community were at stake.

Precisely because bank insiders had much at stake, the lending policies of Mexico's banks tended to be quite conservative. Typically, banks extended lines of credit to businessmen as individuals, not to the firms that they owned, and required that the lines of credit be secured by liquid assets, such as cash, government securities, or corporate securities, which were physically held by the bank. When lines of credit were secured by a cash deposit, they were obviously not 100 percent secured. Nevertheless, the existence of a security deposit substantially raised the cost of defaulting and lowered the cost of collateral repossession: the bank simply kept the security that it already held in its vault (Maurer 2002).

Even though this banking system was stable, it attracted a low level of deposits—other than those held by banks to secure lines of credit. The data presented in table 6.1 indicates that it took some time before savers were willing to trust their wealth to the banks. In 1897, deposits (exclusive of those securing credit lines) accounted for only 2 percent of total bank assets (and less than one percent of GDP). The deposit base then grew gradually, but even at its peak in 1910, deposits only equaled 16 percent of bank assets and 5 percent of GDP.

The banking experiment of Porfirian Mexico came to an end in 1911, when Díaz was overthrown, beginning a ten year period of coups, countercoups, and civil wars that are collectively referred to as the Mexican Revolution. All sides in this conflict preyed on the banking system, but the coup de grâce for the private banks came in 1916 when one faction, led by Venustiano Carranza, intervened the banks, expropriating all of their liquid assets and leaving them in a state of suspended animation until the early 1920s. That is, the ultimate threat to bank deposits came not from imprudent bankers, but from a predatory government (Haber, Razo, and Maurer 2003, chap. 4).

6.3 Experiment Two: Development Banks as Implicit Deposit Insurance, 1924–1982

The lack of a functioning financial system jeopardized the survival of the governments that came to power immediately after the end of the Mexican Revolution in 1920. The two presidents who succeeded Carranza—the mechanism of succession being a bullet in Carranza's head—(General Alvaro Obregón, 1920–1924; and General Plutarco Elias Calles, 1924–1928) were threatened by two civil wars and three attempted military coups. They therefore had strong incentives to create a banking system from which they could borrow in order to repel these attempts to overthrow them. Obregón and Calles therefore reconstituted the banking system by calling a special convention at the end of 1924 of government officials and bankers, some of whom had been major figures in the prerevolutionary banking system.

The laws that were crafted at the 1924–1925 convention recreated two crucial elements of the Díaz era banking system. First, the law did not provide for deposit insurance. Second, it grandfathered in all pre-existing banks and then gave the central government the right to regulate new entrants. The new laws also contained an added twist to the Porfirian banking system: it created a commercial bank that was owned by the government, the Banco de México. The purpose of the Banco de México was threefold: it served as the treasury's fiscal agent; it rediscounted notes and made loans to private banks; and it lent money to business enterprises owned by prominent public officials (Haber, Razo, and Maurer 2003, chap. 4).

These arrangements succeeded in coaxing capital bank into the banking system. As table 6.2 demonstrates, the ratio of bank assets to GDP doubled from 1925 to 1926, and then continued growing to 1929. Nevertheless, this banking system was quite small compared to that which had existed at the end of the Díaz period. The ratio of bank assets to GDP was only 12 percent in 1929, compared to 32 percent in 1910 (see tables 6.1 and 6.2).

Table 6.2
The Mexican banking industry during the 1920s

Year	Total assets (millions of nominal pesos)	Ratio of assets to GDP (percent)	Average equity ratio (percent)
1921	285	5	35
1922	149	3	34
1923	141	3	64
1924	206	4	63
1925	225	4	51
1926	417	8	52
1927	515	10	52
1928	521	10	38
1929	577	12	36

Source: Assets and equity from Haber, Razo, and Maurer 2003 (chap. 4). GDP from Instituto Nacional de Estadistica Geografia e Informática.

Indirect evidence indicates that this banking system mobilized very little in the way of deposits. In 1924, the year before the new laws went into effect, the average equity ratio was 63 percent, implying a very small deposit base (see table 6.2). As the banking system grew in later years, there is some evidence that deposits grew as well: the equity ratio in 1929 had fallen to 36 percent. A large portion of the decline in the equity ratio, however, was almost certainly the product of note issues by the Banco de México. Indeed, there is reason to believe that wealthy individuals and business enterprises deposited much of their wealth in U.S. banks, because even Mexico's commercial banks did so. On average, from 1926 to 1929, 7.5 percent of Mexican commercial bank assets were deposited abroad (Haber, Razo, and Maurer 2003, chap. 4).

In 1929, Mexico's remaining military leaders who had survived the civil wars and coups of the 1920s, were convened by President Calles with the purpose being to create a political party that would arbitrate disputes peacefully, as well as divide up spoils. This political party, the Partido Nacional Revolucionario, would, after several reforms, eventually become Mexico's modern Partido Revolucionario Institucional (PRI), which ran Mexico until the 2000 presidential elections. The creation of a stable political system allowed the government to then undertake a series of reforms to the banking laws that gave the government greater regulatory authority. In 1932, the Banco de México was converted into a central bank, giving it the ability to regulate the rest of the banking system by establishing reserve requirements. A reform of the law in 1936 increased the authority of the Banco de México by requiring commercial banks to maintain reserves in cash at the central bank. It also moved many bank supervisory functions from the National Banking Commission to the Banco de México. A further set of reforms occurred in 1941, when, mimicking Glass-Steagal, commercial banks were forced to divest their investment banking operations into separate corporations (Del Ángel Mobarak 2002).

As a legal matter, Mexico possessed at least three different types of banks from 1941 to 1982. There were commercial banks, which handled most retail banking operations as well as made short-term loans to business enterprises. There were investment banks (financieras), which made long term loans to businesses, as well as held equity positions in those firms. Finally, there were government-run development banks, the first of which had been founded in the 1930s, which make long-term loans to business enterprises, collateralized by shares in those firms. As table 6.3 demonstrates, as early as the 1940s, the development banks were as an important a source of credit as the commercial banks, with other private financial entities (of which investment banks were the most important) accounting for but a small fraction of total credit. By the 1950s, the commercial banks began to stagnate, with other private banks and development banks providing progressively larger amounts of credit. By the early 1970s, the investment banks were the most important source of credit, followed by development banks, with commercial banks a distant third.

As a practical matter, however, all three types of banks worked together to finance Mexico's largest industrial and commercial enterprises. Indeed, as Del Ángel Mobarak (2002) has shown, Mexico's industrial conglomerates typically owned both a commercial bank and an investment bank, and the portfolios of these banks tended to be composed of shares held in the enterprises that were part of the conglomerates. The commercial and investment banks were, in essence, the treasury divisions of the conglomerates: they had little relationship to the impersonal credit intermediaries of economic theory. As a result, in 1974 the Mexican government gave up the legal fiction that the commercial and investment banks were independent of one another, and allowed them to merge into enterprises that were called multibanks.

In theory, government development banks existed in order to make up for an inadequate private banking system. For example, Nacional Financiera, SA (National Credit Bank, NAFINSA, founded in 1934) was supposed to provide credit to small and midsized manufacturers. As a practical matter, however, NAFINSA (along with other government development banks) tended to allocate most of its credit to the very same industrial conglomerates that received financing from private banks. The political pressure to lend to large firms, which tended to have large, unionized, and politically influential labor forces, simply outweighed whatever original mandate the banks may have had (Cárdenas 2000).

This system of government and private banks coaxed a significant amount of deposits into the banking system. Table 6.4 presents data on total deposits and credits, as enumerated by Mexico's central bank to the International Monetary Fund. In 1948, deposits amounted to 16 percent of GDP (roughly three times their 1910 level). Deposits then climbed throughout the 1950s and 1960s, hitting 40 percent of GDP by 1969. In the late 1970s the size of Mexico's deposit base contracted, falling back to 27 percent of GDP in 1980.

Table 6.3
The extension of credit, as percent of GDP, by source, 1940–1978

Year	Commercial banks	Other private banks	Total private banks	Government banks	System total
1940	4	1	5	3	8
1941	5	1	6	4	10
1942	6	1	7	4	11
1943	6	2	8	4	12
1944	5	2	7	4	10
1945	5	2	8	4	12
1946	4	2	6	4	11
1947	4	3	7	5	12
1948	5	3	7	6	13
1949	5	2	7	6	13
1950	5	2	7	6	14
1951	5	2	7	7	14
1952	5	2	7	6	14
1953	5	2	8	8	16
1954	5	2	8	9	16
1955	5	2	8	7	14
1956	5	3	8	6	14
1957	5	3	8	6	14
1958	5	3	7	7	14
1959	5	4	9	8	17
1960	5	4	9	10	19
1961	5	5	10	12	21
1962	5	5	10	13	23
1963	5	5	11	13	23
1964	5	6	11	12	23
1965	6	7	12	11	23
1966	5	8	13	11	24
1967	6	9	14	12	26
1968	6	10	15	11	27
1969	6	11	17	12	29
1970	6	13	19	12	31
1971	6	13	19	13	32
1972	6	13	19	2	21
1973	5	12	17	12	29
1974	5	10	15	12	27
1975	5	10	15	12	27
1976	5	9	14	16	30
1977	5	8	13	17	30
1978	7	7	13	15	28

Source: Del Ángel Mobarak 2002, 45.

Table 6.4
Deposits, credit, and financial represssion, 1948–1982

Year	Banking system deposits as percent of GDP[a]	Total bank claims on private sector as percent of GDP	Deposits minus credits as percent of GDP	Reserve ratio (deposits divided by reserves)
1948	16	15	1	26
1949	17	16	0	24
1950	16	16	0	35
1951	17	16	2	25
1952	17	15	2	23
1953	19	17	2	22
1954	20	19	1	18
1955	19	16	3	18
1956	18	16	1	18
1957	18	16	2	15
1958	18	16	2	15
1959	20	19	1	15
1960	22	22	0	12
1961	24	24	0	10
1962	26	26	0	11
1963	28	26	2	12
1964	30	27	2	10
1965	30	26	4	9
1966	32	27	5	10
1967	36	29	6	10
1968	38	30	7	11
1969	40	33	7	11
1970	40	33	7	10
1971	42	34	7	11
1972	41	34	8	22
1973	40	32	8	24
1974	37	29	8	30
1975	38	29	9	33
1976	42	32	10	14
1977	25	17	8	48
1978	27	19	8	43
1979	28	20	8	44
1980	27	19	8	45
1981	30	19	10	44
1982	30	15	14	58

Source: International Monetary Fund, International Financial Statistics.
[a] Demand deposits, time deposits, money market instruments, and government deposits.

Table 6.5
Commercial bank nonperforming loans and returns on equity, 1940–1980

Year	Nonperforming loans (as percent of total loans)	Return on equity
1940	13	3
1943	4	10
1945	6	15
1947	8	17
1950	4	20
1952	4	19
1955	4	16
1957	5	18
1960	5	23
1962	5	19
1965	3	30
1968	4	24
1970	4	20
1972	6	19
1975	5	25
1977	5	30
1980	2	55

Source: Del Ángel Mobarak 2002, 57.

The evidence amassed by Del Ángel Mobarak (2002), reproduced in table 6.5, does not indicate that this decline in the deposit base was caused by reckless lending by bankers. The ratio of nonperforming loans in the commercial banks was more or less constant from 1943 to 1977 at 4–6 percent (the ratio dropped considerably in 1980 to 2 percent). Data on the rate of return on equity is also not consistent with reckless lending. Indeed, rates of return in the late 1970s were astronomically high: 25 percent in 1975, 30 percent in 1977, and 55 percent in 1980. Indeed, all of the evidence points to a stable banking system. Rather, the evidence indicates that what drove down deposit rates in the late 1970s was financial repression.[1]

What kept bank insiders from making imprudent loans to their own enterprises? There are two answers that one might advance. First a combination of government regulation and cross-monitoring by bank directors discouraged reckless behavior. As table 6.4 demonstrates, Mexico's central bank appears to have forced banks to retain very high proportions of their deposit base as reserves. (In effect, much bank lending was forced lending to the government). In addition, as Del

Ángel Mobarak (2002) has demonstrated, Mexico's commercial and investment banks were governed by a complex network of interlocking directors. Information about imprudent behavior would have been transmitted quickly throughout the entrepreneurial community, tarnishing the reputation of directors and managers.

A second explanation would focus on the impact of government-run development banks on the allocation of risk in the banking industry. In the first place, the development banks served as second tier lenders, repurchasing loans made by commercial banks through special programs designed to channel credit to sectors the government deemed crucial. In fact, the credit law of 1941 actually required private banks to allocate 60 percent of their loans to such directed credit programs (Del Ángel Mobarak 2002). These directed credit programs represented a guarantee by the government to the private banks: all of the default risk was born by the development bank, but the private bank earned income from originating and servicing the loan.

In the second place, the lending practices of the development banks allowed industrial and commercial conglomerates to fund risky enterprises from government-owned banks, rather than from the private banks that were under their control. Nacional Financiera, the largest development bank, typically took a minority shareholder position in companies to which it extended credit. If the firm performed well, Nacional Financiera's stake would, over time, become purely nominal. If the firm performed badly, however, Nacional Financiera typically bought out the other shareholders. This policy of bailouts encouraged moral hazard: knowing that they would be bailed out, manufacturers undertook enterprises of doubtful profitability (Cárdenas 2000). Ultimately, the Mexican government came to own a wide range of commercial and industrial enterprises, including sugar refiners, steel mills, airlines, and hotels. This meant that the group that bore the downside risk of imprudent lending were not depositors in the private banks, but taxpayers who came to own enterprises of dubious value.

This banking experiment came to an end in much the same way as that of Porfirian Mexico: the banks were expropriated by the government. In the late 1970s the Mexican government began to fund expenditures by borrowing from foreign banks, rather than by increasing taxation. It rationalized this strategy by assuming that the price of oil would continue to rise indefinitely and that interest rates in the United States would remain constant. In early 1982, both assumptions were undermined: the price of oil dropped and the U.S. Federal Reserve raised interest rates. By the summer of that year the situation had become desperate: the government therefore expropriated the dollar accounts held by Mexicans and foreigners in the country's banks (converting them into pesos at an exchange rate about one-third below the market rate), and it instituted capital controls. Both actions only increased capital flight, further reducing the stock of dollars that could be used to meet debt payments. On August 20, the government suspended payment of its international debts. The moratorium on the foreign debt made it clear that a major devaluation was inevitable, and thus individuals and business enterprises converted their liquid assets into dollars and moved them to U.S. banks. Thinking that control of the banking system was the key to stanching the flow of dollars out of Mexico, the government expropriated the banks on September 1, 1982.

6.4   Experiment Three: Unlimited Deposit Insurance, 1991–1996

During the 1980s, Mexico's banks were essentially run as vehicles to finance government budget deficits. As table 6.6 demonstrates, from 1983 to 1987, bank deposits were typically twice the level of private sector lending, which averaged only 13 percent of GDP. The other half of the deposit base was invested in government bonds. In order to encourage deposits, which could then be invested in Treasury bonds, the Mexican government instituted deposit insurance in 1986, creating the Fund for the Protection of Bank Savings, known by its Spanish acronym, FOBAPROA. FOBAPROA was a trust fund, funded by premiums paid by banks, and was supposed to cover deposits only up to the amount of FOBAPROA's reserves. As we shall see, however, in the process of the privatization of Mexico's banks in 1991, the FOBAPROA trust fund was converted into a central bank program to provide unlimited deposit insurance. Ultimately, it became a mechanism for the government to organize a costly bank rescue that not only protected depositors, but also protected debtors and some shareholders as well.

In 1991 the government of Carlos Salinas de Gortari (1988–1994) sought to privatize Mexico's moribund banking system (along with a broad range of other state-run enterprises). The purpose of this privatization program was largely fiscal. Fiscal success, however, also had crucial political implications. Salinas needed to balance the federal budget, and at the same time find revenue sources to fund social programs that would help the PRI win the 1994 presidential election. As had been the case for most of Mexico's history, raising tax rates was

Table 6.6
Bank deposits and credits, 1982–2004

Year	Banking system deposits as percent of GDP[a]	Total bank claims on private sector as percent of GDP	Deposits minus credits as percent of GDP
1983	27	13	14
1984	28	14	14
1985	25	13	12
1986	28	13	15
1987	27	13	14
1988	18	11	7
1989	19	16	4
1990	21	17	4
1991	24	21	3
1992	25	28	−3
1993	27	32	−4
1994	29	39	−9
1995	31	29	2
1996	29	19	10
1997	41	25	15
1998	38	23	16
1999	38	19	18
2000	30	17	13
2001	35	15	20
2002	34	17	17
2003	32	15	17
2004	32	14	17

Source: International Monetary Fund, International Financial Statistics.
[a] Demand deposits, time deposits, money market instruments, and government deposits.

both politically and practically difficult. The auction of state-owned firms was therefore an attractive option: their sale would not only reduce the drain that these (perennially unprofitable) firms put on the annual budget, but it would also provide a onetime windfall.

The fiscal incentives of the government, however, set off a chain of events that were not foreseen at the time that the banks were privatized. The government sought to maximize the prices at auction for the banks. In order to get Mexico's bankers to pay high prices, however, the government was compelled to make a series of decisions that reduced the incentives of bank directors, bank depositors, and bank regulators to enforce prudent behavior by the privatized banks. The end result were lending strategies that, at the very least, were reckless.

These institutions that undermined prudent behavior by bank insiders were not created in a single stroke. Rather, they emerged over time, out of the interaction of the government and the bankers during the process of privatization and afterwards: each discrete decision or agreement drove the next decision or agreement. The outcome of this game, however, was a banking system in which the group that had the most at risk—Mexico's taxpayers (who had to fund the deposit insurance system when the banks became insolvent)—had no active voice in the game as it was being played.

The first step in aligning the incentives of the bankers with the government was that the government signaled bidders that they would not have to operate in a competitive environment. The Mexican banking industry at the time of privatization in 1991 was composed of eighteen banks, four of which controlled 70 percent of total bank assets. The government did not break these up, but sold them as is. The government also signaled potential bidders that they would not have to compete against foreign banks. Foreign banks were not allowed to participate in the 1991–1992 bank auctions. Moreover, through limits on their capital investment and market share, the provisions governing banking in the 1994 NAFTA agreement severely limited the participation of foreign banks in Mexico.

At the same time that the government signaled bankers that they were purchasing secure oligopolies, it structured the auction process so as to maximize the prices on offer. The formal rules of the auction specified that bids would be sealed and that the managerial expertise of the bidding groups would be taken into account (Unal and Navarro 1999). The notion that the government would take the quality of management into account was, however, eviscerated by a decision to do so only if the second highest bid was within 3 percent of the first highest. Consistent with its goal of maximizing prices on offer, the government also did not bring Mexico's accounting standards in line with generally accepted accounting standards. In particular, a very lax definition of nonperforming assets led to overvaluations of many banks. The government then auctioned the banks sequentially, increasing competition for the banks in the later rounds of bidding. As Haber (2005) has demonstrated, the most important determinant of the price paid for a bank (in terms of its bid-to-book ratio) was the bidding round in which it was purchased: each additional round of bidding pushed up the bid-to-book ratio by 0.30.

This set of institutional arrangements produced an average (weighted) bid-to-book ratio of 3.04, and an income of \$12.4 billion for the Mexican government. Indeed, bid-to-book ratios of 3.04 suggest that the government received a substantial premium. In United States bank mergers during the 1980s, for example, the average bid-to-book ratio was 1.89 (Unal and Navarro 1999).

Readers may wonder why bankers were willing to pay a substantial premium for the banks at auction. The reason was that much of the money that they were putting at risk was not their own. The original payment plan devised by the government called for a 30 percent payment three days after the announcement of the auction winner, with the remaining 70 percent due in thirty days. The bankers, however, convinced the government to replace those rules with one that gave them time to finance their purchases with outside sources of funds. Under the new plan, the first payment was reduced to 20 percent, a second payment of 20 percent was to be paid thirty days later, and the remaining 60 percent was to be paid four months after that. The bankers used the five-month period between the auction and the final payment to raise the funds to purchase the banks from outside investors, sometimes with the help of loans from the very banks being purchased (Unal and Navarro 1999; Mackey 1999). This meant that bank insiders did not have strong incentives to monitor each other, because they actually had little capital at risk.

This set of arrangements implied that Mexico's regulators would have to be vigilant monitors of the banks. The problem was that Mexico's regulators were inexperienced, and the tools they had at their disposal were blunt in the extreme. It was, after all, the government itself that had designed Mexico's extremely permissive bank accounting standards. Moreover, prior to 1995, the National Banking Commission (known by its Spanish acronym, CNB) did not have sufficient information technologies on hand to actually gather information from the banks in a timely manner. It also lacked the authority and autonomy to properly supervise the banks (Mackey 1999).

The lack of effective monitoring by bank regulators and bank directors meant, of course, that Mexico's depositors faced considerable risk. Thus, the logic of the situation now required that they too be protected. As a technical matter, bank deposits in Mexico were only insured up to the available resources in FOBAPROA. As a practical matter, however, FOBAPROA had the ability to borrow from the central bank (Mackey 1999). The Banco de México's guarantee, moreover, was not just implicit, as a consequence of its fiduciary relationship to FOBAPROA. It was an explicit promise. The Banco de México was supposed to publish, in December of each year, the maximum amount of obligations that would be protected by FOBAPROA during the following year. Its 1993, 1994, 1995 statements did not, however, actually list amounts. Instead, the Banco de México stated that FOBAPROA would provide a blanket guarantee of virtually all bank liabilities (deposits, loans, and credits, including those from other banks), with the exception of subordinated debt. That is, deposit insurance was unlimited—and even included loans made by banks to one another (Mackey 1999). Precisely because there was unlimited deposit insurance, bank depositors did not police banks by withdrawing funds from banks with risky loan portfolios. Research by Martinez Peria and Schmukler (2001) that analyzes changes in time deposits and interest rates in Mexico from 1991 to 1996 finds that various measures of banks' riskiness did not influence deposit growth through September 1995.

Inadequate monitoring produced exactly the outcome that would be predicted by economic theory: bank credit in Mexico grew at a prodigious rate. As table 6.7 demonstrates, total real bank lending nearly doubled in the space of just three years (1991–1994). Housing loans grew at an even faster rate: from December 1991 to December 1994 real lending for housing and real estate nearly tripled. Moreover, this is a lower bound estimate of the growth of housing lending because it includes only performing loans. Much of the housing portfolio was nonperforming, and the principal value and past due interest of those loans were continually rolled over into an accounting category called "rediscounts" (see table 6.7, column [4]). Inasmuch as the value of rediscounts was nearly equal to the total value of housing loans in December 1994, the threefold increase in housing loans from December 1991 to December 1994 is a lower bound estimate. The actual rate of growth might have been nearly twice that. The rapid growth in lending was not matched by an equally rapid growth in deposits. As table 6.6 demonstrates, in 1992, 1993, and 1994, loans outstripped deposits by roughly 20 percent: the difference was funded through interbank lending, predominantly from foreign banks in foreign currency (Mackey 1999).

Even more rapid than the growth in lending, was the growth of nonperforming loans. Table 6.8 presents estimates of nonperforming loans based on different ways of treating the various rollovers and restructurings that were permitted under Mexican accounting rules. One way that banks handled past due principal was to "rediscount" them— essentially creating a category of rollovers that reflected the low

Table 6.7
Mexican bank lending, by category (balances at year-end, millions of real December 2000 pesos)

Year	Commercial[a]	Consumer	Housing	Renewed, restructured, or rediscounted[b]	SOFOL	Government[c]	Fobaproa and IPAB[d]	Total private lending[e]	Total lending
1991	776,386	91,312	114,805	112,256				1,094,759	1,094,759
1992	961,879	127,757	178,439	148,728				1,416,803	1,416,803
1993	1,181,744	118,880	248,808	187,766				1,737,197	1,737,197
1994	1,423,325	109,387	299,437	244,066				2,076,215	2,076,215
1995	801,937	51,617	192,304	339,796		957	156,237	1,385,654	1,542,849
1996	513,686	27,745	80,338	364,298		18,587	273,760	986,068	1,278,415
1997	405,675	39,415	173,251		12,297	88,181	340,212	630,637	1,059,030
1998	388,886	32,400	178,847		16,388	92,705	346,423	616,520	1,055,648
1999	312,687	35,238	147,583		17,899	91,707	377,561	513,407	982,675
2000	318,320	40,596	131,224		13,809	153,331	290,161	503,950	947,442
2001	288,685	54,548	119,868		16,542	147,977	258,939	479,643	886,559
2002	296,116	71,837	114,223		23,658	188,042	216,169	505,834	910,045
2003	275,532	99,609	100,128		22,056	179,940	179,538	497,324	856,802
2004	316,272	140,240	102,307		35,660	136,512	156,757	594,479	887,749

Source: Aggregates created by the author from the loan portfolios published in Comisión Nacional Bancaria, Banca Múltiple, 1982–1993; and Comisión Nacional Bancaria y de Valores, Boletín Estadístico de Banca Múltiple, 1993–2004. Deflated using wholesale price index from the Banco de Mexico.

[a] The commercial loan category did not exist before 1997, thus it was estimated as a residual of total loans minus consumer, housing, government, restructured and renewed, loans, and nonperforming loans.

[b] Rediscounted loans are nonperforming loans whose principal was rolled over. Restructured and renewed represent loans in danger of default. In 1997, new accounting standards required banks to either declare these as nonperforming or treat them as performing loans.

[c] Does not include government bonds, which are held in the securities portfolio.

[d] Value of Fobaproa and IPAB promissory notes held by banks. They are treated as loans because they represent loans transferred to Fobaproa and IPAB.

[e] Includes commercial, consumer, housing, and SOFOL loans.

Table 6.8
Nonperforming loans (at year-end)

Year	Declared nonper- forming loans (NPL) as percent of total loans	Declared NPL plus rediscounts as percent of total	Declared NPL plus rediscounts plus renewed and restruc- tured as percent of total	FOBAPROA or IPAB as percent of total	Declared NPL plus redis- counts, restruc- tured and FOBAPROA- IPAB as percent of total loans
1991	3.6	13.5	13.5	0.0	13.5
1992	4.7	14.7	14.7	0.0	14.7
1993	6.0	16.2	16.2	0.0	16.2
1994	6.1	17.1	17.1	0.0	17.1
1995	6.2	13.3	26.8	9.5	36.3
1996	5.7	10.8	32.5	20.1	52.6
1997	10.2	10.2	10.2	28.9	39.0
1998	10.2	10.2	10.2	29.5	39.7
1999	8.2	8.2	8.2	35.3	43.5
2000	5.5	5.5	5.5	28.9	34.4
2001	4.9	4.9	4.9	27.8	32.7
2002	4.4	4.4	4.4	22.7	27.1
2003	3.2	3.2	3.2	21.0	24.1

Source: Calculated from data in Comisión Nacional Bancaria, Banca Múltiple, 1982–1993; Comisión Nacional Bancaria y de Valores, Boletín Estadístico de Banca Múltiple, 1993–2004.

probability that the loans would be repaid. These rediscounts were not listed in the portfolio of performing loans, but they were not listed as being nonperforming either. If we add these rediscounts to declared nonperforming loans, then the default rate jumps dramatically. For example, instead of being 3.6 percent in December 1991 (the declared ratio of nonperforming to total loans), the ratio would have 13.5 percent. Instead of being 6.1 percent in December 1994 (the declared rate) it would have been 17.1 percent. The practice of "rediscounting" loans began to be phased out by banks in 1995. Instead, they began to renew or restructure unpaid principal, and treated these rollovers as perform- ing. In the third column of table 6.8 we include the value of these renewed or restructured loans along with rediscounts and declared nonperforming loans. Treating these rollovers as past due loans produ- ces even more striking results. Instead of a nonperforming ratio of 5.7 percent in December 1996, the ratio jumps to 32.5 percent.

The situation was even worse, however, than these figures demonstrate. Beginning in February 1995 banks were allowed to swap many of their loans for promissory notes from Mexico's deposit insurance system as part of a bailout (a subject to which we will return at length). If we add the value of these promissory notes to the value of declared nonperforming loans, rediscounts, and restructured or renewed loans, then the percentage of loans that were nonperforming actually exceeded the percentage of loans that were in good standing: in December 1996 the nonperformance ratio would have been 52.6 percent.

Even had there been no peso crisis of 1994–1995, the Mexican banking system would have collapsed (Gonzalez-Hermosillo, Pazarbasioglu, and Billings 1997). The government's mishandling of the exchange rate merely hastened the banking system's demise (Krueger and Tornell 1999). The crawling peg exchange rate policy of the Salinas government had been established to help fight inflation, and it had been largely successful in accomplishing that goal. Given the fact that Mexican interest rates were considerably higher than U.S. rates, and that the government was signaling an intention to maintain a stable (and overvalued) exchange rate, there were strong incentives for both Mexicans and foreigners to deposit funds in Mexican banks. There were also incentives for Mexican firms, including banks, to sign debt contracts denominated in dollars. By the end of 1994, however, it was becoming increasingly clear that the exchange rate was seriously overvalued. Once that happened, bank depositors had every incentive to withdraw their funds and convert them to dollars before the government allowed the currency to float freely. Firms with dollar denominated debts could not, however, act so quickly: as a result, the peso value of their debts nearly doubled in the space of a few days once the exchange rate was allowed to float.

The collapse of the exchange rate created two problems for the banking system. First, foreign currency loans represented roughly one-third of total loans made by Mexican banks. Many of these loans, however, had been made to firms without sources of foreign currency income (Krueger and Tornell 1999). Second, the collapse of the peso gave foreign portfolio investors strong incentives to pull their funds out of Mexico. Net foreign portfolio investment flows turned negative in the last quarter of 1994, and stayed there all through 1995 (Mishkin 1996). This required that the government pursue a tight monetary policy, raising central bank interest rates. The interbank loan rate, at its peak, hit 114 percent. Mortgage interest rates jumped to 74 percent by March

1995, from 22 percent just five months before (Gruben and McComb 1997). The rapid rise in interest rates pushed risky, but performing, loans into default. As the stock of nonperforming loans mounted, and as the size of the deposit base shrank because of the run on the peso, the banks became insolvent.

The government responded with a bailout of the banking system—the particulars of which warrant some discussion. First, Mexican banks had significant amounts of short-term, dollar-denominated debt. The government therefore opened a special dollar credit window at the Banco de México to provide them with foreign currency.

Second, the government sought to prop up the banks by lending them the capital necessary to maintain adequate reserves. A trust fund was created (known by its Spanish acronym, PROCAPTE) by the government's bank deposit insurance agency (FOBAPROA) with funds provided by the central bank. This trust fund lent the banks capital sufficient to maintain a 9 percent capital ratio in exchange for five-year subordinated debentures from the bank. In the event of nonpayment, the debentures were convertible to ordinary stock. Banks were enjoined, during the period that they participated in PROCAPTE, from issuing dividends or from issuing additional debt instruments to capitalize the bank (Mackey 1999).

Third, the government moved to protect borrowers. There were several debtor protection programs, and as time went on the extent and terms of these programs became gradually more lenient. As a first step, the government created an indexed accounting unit (known by its Spanish acronym, UDIS) and allowed loans to be redenominated in these units. Banks were then allowed to transfer loans to a government trust fund, which converted them to UDIS and which bore a real interest rate of four percent plus a margin to reflect the credit risk of the borrower. A series of additional programs soon followed, each of which was targeted at different groups of debtors (including consumers, the holders of home mortgages, small businesses, and agriculture) and each of which was reformed over time to offer debtors even larger discounts off of their payments (Mackey 1999).

Fourth, the government cleaned the bank's balance sheets of nonperforming loans through a loan repurchase program run by FOBAPROA. In exchange for their nonperforming assets, the banks received a nontradable, zero coupon ten-year FOBAPROA promissory note that carried an interest rate slightly below the government CETES (Treasury bond) rate. The bankers agreed that for each peso in FOBAPROA bonds they received, they would inject 50 centavos of new capital, so as to recapitalize the bank. Banks were charged with collecting the principal and interest on the loans transferred to FOBAPROA. As a practical matter, however, they did not do so (Krueger and Tornell 1999; Murillo 2002).

Banks that were in serious financial distress were intervened by the government's National Banking and Securities Commission (known by its Spanish acronym, CNBV). When a bank was intervened, the CNBV seized control of the bank and suspended shareholder rights. It then replaced the management of the banks and appointed a managing intervener. The CNBV intervener cleaned the nonperforming loans from the balance sheet through the FOBAPROA bond mechanism discussed above and injected new capital through the PROCAPTE program. The government, via FOBAPROA, also guaranteed all of the deposits of the bank. Finally, the CNBV arranged for the bank to be sold to another institution. In some cases, the CNBV carried out a de facto intervention, in which it removed the bank's management and then arranged for another financial institution to invest in or acquire control of the bank. In all, twelve banks were formally intervened, with another three undergoing de facto intervention.

Mexico's bankers may have anticipated the intervention and bailout. Indeed, given that Mexico had unlimited deposit insurance and that many of the banks were "too big to fail," it is hard to see how they would not have expected one to take place. The anticipated intervention and bailout, however, appears to have given some bankers the incentive to make large loans to themselves—and then default on the loans. As La Porta, Lopez-de-Silanes, and Zamarripa (2003) have shown, 20 percent of all large loans from 1995 to 1998 went to bank directors. These insider loans carried lower rates of interest than arm's length loans (by 4 percentage points), had a 33 percent higher probability of default, and had a 30 percent lower collateral recovery rate.

Not surprisingly, the FOBAPROA bailout was not (as originally anticipated in early 1995) a one-time event. Rather, it became an open-ended mechanism, with loans being transferred from the banks to FOBAPROA through 1999 (see table 6.7). Thus, the percentage of bank loan portfolios composed of FOBAPROA bonds grew from 9 percent in 1995, to 20 percent in 1996, 29 percent in 1997 and 1998, and finally topped out at 35 percent in 1999 (see table 6.8). For the same reason, bank interventions were also not a one time event, but were spread out from 1994 to 2001. As of June 1999, the total cost of the bail-out programs was 692 billion pesos ($65 billion) roughly 15 percent of Mexican GNP (Murillo 2002). This puts Mexico's bank bailout in the mid-range of LDC bank rescues (Keefer 2004).

The fact that the banking system bailout involved an implicit transfer from taxpayers to bank stockholders, who included some of Mexico's wealthiest men, produced a political firestorm in Mexico. It was one of the reasons why the PRI lost its control of the lower house of Congress in 1997. That opposition congress then held up the approval of the 1999 budget for nearly nine months while it carried out an investigation of the FOBAPROA bailout. Ultimately, Congress agreed to disband FOBAPROA and replace it with a new (more autonomous) deposit guarantee agency, the Bank Savings Protection Institute (known by its Mexican acronym, IPAB). Most (although not all) FOBAPROA bonds were swapped for IPAB bonds, and IPAB was given the task of recouping and liquidating the assets backed by those bonds. Congress also agreed that the annual cost of the banking sector rescue would be paid for by the government out of each year's budget (McQuerry 1999). This was a de facto admission that the new IPAB bonds had the status of sovereign debt.

6.5   Post-1996 Reforms

Saving the Mexican banking system not only required that the government bail out depositors (and some of the stockholders), it also required that the banks be put on a more sound footing. The government therefore engaged in a series of reforms to the institutions that encourage prudent behavior by bankers. These included changes in accounting standards, lending rules, deposit insurance, and foreign bank ownership.

First, insider lending has been made more difficult. Banks are required to publish consolidated accounts that include the operations of their subsidiaries. They are also precluded from making loans to bank officers and employees that are not part of their employee benefits. Related party loans are permitted, but they cannot exceed the net capital of the bank (Mackey 1999).

Second, banks are required to diversify risk. As of June 1998, bank loans to any individual cannot exceed 10 percent of the bank's net capital, or 0.5 percent of the total net capital of all banks. The same law also enjoins banks from granting loans to companies that exceed 30 percent of the bank's net capital, or 6 percent of the total net capital of all banks.

Third, capital requirements have been increased and regulations introduced that establish reserve minimums in accordance with the riskiness of a bank's portfolio. In particular, banks are required to access the credit record of borrowers (by using a credit bureau). Loans in which the credit record are not checked (or where it is checked and it is poor) must be provisioned at 100 percent (Mackey 1999).

Fourth, as of January 1, 1997, stricter accounting standards went into effect. For example, the accounting treatment of past due loans has been reformed to bring it into line with generally accepted standards. In addition, repurchase agreements are no longer treated as assets, and interbank loans must be separately grouped in financial statements. Mexican banks still do not, however, adhere to all features of generally accepted accounting standards. In particular, banks are still allowed to record deferred taxes as Tier I capital. This may overstate the quantity and quality of the capital available to the banks (Mackey 1999).

Fifth, the rules governing deposit insurance have been reformed. Unlike its predecessor (FOBAPROA), IPAB does not provide unlimited insurance. Deposit insurance, as of January 1, 2005, is limited to 400,000 UDIS (roughly $100,000 at the current rate of exchange) and covers bank deposits only.

The government also lifted the restrictions on foreign ownership of Mexican banks. Restrictions on foreign bank acquisitions of Mexican banks were eased in February 1995, when foreign banks were permitted to purchase Mexican banks with market shares of 6 percent or less. In 1996, all restrictions were removed on foreign bank ownership in Mexico (with the new regulations going into effect in 1997). As a result, foreign banks began to purchase controlling interests in Mexico's largest banks. As of December 2004, the share of Mexican bank assets under foreign control was 83 percent.

The net effect of these reforms, as Haber and Musacchio (2005) have demonstrated, is that Mexico's banks follow extremely prudent lending practices. Indeed, Mexico's bankers are so prudent that they have dramatically reduced the amount of credit that they provide to firms and households. As table 6.6 indicates, lending by the banking system has declined monotonically since 1997: the ratio of loans to GDP in 2004 was only 14 percent, about what it was when the Mexican government ran the banks. The banks invest the balance of their deposit base (equal to an additional 17 percent of GDP, above and beyond what they allocate to private credit) in government securities.

6.6   Lessons and Implications

Are there any general lessons that we may extract from the history of Mexico's various experiments in banking regulation?

The first is that unlimited deposit insurance requires strong corporate governance and strong regulation. When neither is present, the result is reckless behavior. In the Mexican case, this occasioned a banking bailout that still weighs heavily on the economy.

The second is that even if there is no formal deposit insurance system, the existence of government run development banks may create an implicit system. Mexico's experience from the 1940s to the 1980s suggests, but is by no means conclusive, that private banks were able to shift much of their riskiest loans onto the development banks. This protected depositors and shareholders, but it came at a cost to taxpayers, who wound up owning enterprises of dubious value.

The third is that there was at least one banking experiment in Mexico, that which took place between 1884 and 1911, in which there was no deposit insurance of any kind, and in which the resulting banking system was stable. The key to this system appears to have been twofold: strong institutions of corporate governance, and limits on competition among banks imposed by regulators. This banking system had a distinct disadvantage: it allowed banks to earn monopoly profits by limiting competition. Nevertheless, even when it was hit by a financial crisis it neither resulted in losses to depositors nor required a taxpayer financed bailout. Moreover, by the standards of Mexico today, this banking system was of remarkable size: the ratio of bank assets to GDP in Mexico in 1910 was 32 percent, compared to 33 percent in 2004.

The fourth is that researchers tend to assume that the only threat to depositors is imprudent lending by bank insiders. Mexican history suggests that this assumption may not be reasonable. In both of the cases in which depositors lost all or some of their wealth (1913–1916, and 1982), the cause was not imprudent bankers but imprudent governments. This highlights one of the findings of much recent research on bank regulation: the institutions required to create a stable banking system include the institutions that limit the authority and discretion of public officials. (Haber 2004; Barth, Caprio, and Levine 2005).

Acknowledgments

Research assistance for this project was provided by Latika Chaudhary. This chapter benefited from discussions with Noel Maurer and Gustavo Del Ángel Mobarak.

Note

1. The central bank established interest rate ceilings and raised bank reserve requirements. By the late 1970s, the ratio of bank reserves to private credit was on the order of 50 percent. As a result, private credit collapsed even more quickly than the deposit base, resulting in a substantial gap between deposits and private-sector credits in the late 1970s that was on the order of 10 percent of GDP (see table 6.4).

References

Barth, James, Gerald Caprio, and Ross Levine. 2005. *When Angels Rule*. Unpublished book manuscript.

Cárdenas, Enrique. 2000. The Process of Accelerated Industrialization in Mexico, 1929–1982. In *An Economic History of Twentieth Century Latin America, Volume III: Industrialization and the State in Latin America, The Postwar Years*, ed. Enrique Cárdenas, José Antonio Ocampo, and Rosemary Thorp. London: Palgrave.

Del Ángel Mobarak, Gustavo A. 2002. Paradoxes of Financial Development: The Construction of the Mexican Banking System, 1941–1982. Ph.D. diss., Stanford University.

Gonzalez-Hermosillo, Brenda, Ceyla Pazarbasioglu, and Robert Billings. 1997. Determinants of Banking System Fragility: A Case Study of Mexico. *IMF Staff Papers* 44 (September): 295–314.

Gruben, William C., and Robert McComb. 1997. Liberalization, Privatization, and Crash: Mexico's Banking System in the 1990s. *Federal Reserve Bank of Dallas Economic Review* (First Quarter): 21–30.

Haber, Stephen. 2004. Political Institutions and Financial Development: Evidence from the Economic Histories of the United States and Mexico. Working paper, Stanford Center for International Development, Stanford, Calif.

Haber, Stephen. 2005. Mexico's Experiments with Bank Privatization and Liberalization, 1991–2003. *Journal of Banking and Finance* 29 (8–9): 2325–2353.

Haber, Stephen, and Aldo Musacchio. 2005. Foreign Banks and the Mexican Economy. Mimeo., Stanford University.

Haber, Stephen, Armando Razo, and Noel Maurer. 2003. *The Politics of Property Rights: Political Instability, Credible Commitments, and Economic Growth in Mexico, 1876–1929*. New York: Cambridge University Press.

Keefer, Philip. 2004. Elections, Special Interests, and the Fiscal Cost of Financial Crises. Mimeo., The World Bank, Washington, D.C.

Krueger, Anne O., and Aaron Tornell. 1999. The Role of Bank Restructuring in Recovering from Crises: Mexico 1995–1998. NBER Working Paper no. 7042. National Bureau of Economic Research, Cambridge, Mass.

La Porta, Rafael, Florencio Lopez-de-Silanes, and Guillermo Zamarripa. 2003. Related Lending. *Quarterly Journal of Economics* 118: 231–268.

Mackey, Michael W. 1999. Report of Michael W. Mackey on the Comprehensive Evaluation of the Operations and Functions of the Fund for the Protection of Bank Savings "FOBAPROA" and the Quality of Supervision of the FOBAPROA Program 1995–1998. No publisher.

Martinez Peria, Maria Soledad, and Sergio L. Schmukler. 2001. Do Depositors Punish Banks for Bad Behavior? Market Discipline, Deposit Insurance, and Banking Crisis. *Journal of Finance* 56: 1029–1051.

Maurer, Noel. 2002. *The Power and the Money: The Mexican Financial System, 1876–1932.* Stanford: Stanford University Press.

Maurer, Noel, and Andrei Gomberg. 2004. When the State Is Untrustworthy: Public Finance and Private Banking in Porfirian Mexico. *Journal of Economic History* 64 (4): 1087–1107.

Maurer, Noel, and Stephen Haber. 2007. Related Lending and Economic Performance: Evidence from Mexico. *Journal of Economic History* 67 (3): 551–581.

McQuerry, Elizabeth. 1999. The Banking Sector Rescue in Mexico. *Federal Reserve Bank of Atlanta Economic Review* (Third Quarter): 14–29.

Mishkin, Frederic. 1996. Understanding Financial Crises: A Developing Country Perspective. Working Paper no. 5600, National Bureau of Economic Research, Cambridge, Mass.

Murillo, José Antonio. 2002. La banca en México: Privatización, crisis, y reordenamiento. Working paper, Banco de México.

Musacchio, Aldo. 2005. Can Civil Law Countries Get it Right? Institutions and Financial Market Development in Southeastern Brazil, 1890–1940. Ph.D. diss., Stanford University.

Razo, Armando. 2003. Social Networks and Credible Commitments in Dictatorships: Political Organization and Economic Growth in Porfirian Mexico, 1876–1991. Ph.D. diss., Stanford University.

Riguzzi, Paolo. 2002. The Legal System, Institutional Change, and Financial Regulation in Mexico, 1870–1910: Mortgage Contracts and Long Term Credit. In *The Mexican Economy, 1870–1930: Essays in the Economic History of Institutions, Revolution, and Growth*, ed. Jeffrey Bortz and Stephen Haber, 120–160. Stanford: Stanford University Press.

Secretaria de Estado y del Despacho de Hacienda y Credito Publico y Comercio. 1914. *Anuario de Estadistica Fiscal, 1912–1913.* Mexico: Tipografia de la Oficina Impresora de Estampillas.

Unal, Haluk, and Miguel Navarro. 1999. The Technical Process of Bank Privatization in Mexico. *Journal of Financial Services Research* 16 (September): 61–83.

7 The EU Deposit Insurance Directive: Does One Size Fit All?

Harry Huizinga

7.1 Introduction

Over time the number of countries that have adopted an explicit system of deposit insurance has steadily increased. To explain this, Demirgüç-Kunt, Kane, and Laeven (chapter 2, henceforth DKL) estimate a binary choice model of deposit insurance adoption. Rising income levels and an apparent desire to emulate best practice may have led many countries to opt for explicit deposit insurance. For EU member states, however, the adoption of explicit deposit insurance is an obligation of EU membership rather than a choice, following the EU Directive on Deposit Guarantee Schemes of 1994 (see European Commission 1994). Specifically, the ten countries that joined the EU in 2004 had had no choice in this area, and by the time of accession all adopted explicit deposit insurance schemes. A main feature of the directive is the minimum insured amount of 20,000 euros per depositor per financial institution. Per capita income levels in Eastern Europe are about a quarter of those in the EU-15, and hence the minimum insured amount of 20,000 euros is relatively high in these countries.

Following a slate of banking crises in Asia and elsewhere in the 1990s, deposit insurance policies have caught the attention of researchers and policymakers alike. Among other things, researchers have addressed the potential for explicit deposit insurance to contribute to financial fragility (see, e.g., Eichengreen and Arteta 2002 and Demirgüç-Kunt and Detragiache 2002) and to reduce the market discipline imposed on insured banks (see, e.g., Martinez-Peria and Schmukler 2001 and Demirgüç-Kunt and Huizinga 2004).[1] Policymakers, gathered in the Financial Stability Forum, have addressed the issue of deposit insurance adoption as well, resulting in a set of recommendations on what constitutes best practice in the area (see Financial

Stability Forum 2001 for a report). In all of this, deposit insurance adoption is primarily seen as a national responsibility. Against this background, the EU is unique in imposing far-reaching harmonization of deposit insurance policies on its member states through the directive of 1994.

In evaluating the EU Directive, a main question is whether it makes sense at all to harmonize deposit insurance policies internationally. Why, in fact, would national deposit insurance policies that are best for the adopting countries also not be best for other countries? If banking markets were characterized by full information and perfect competition, it would probably be difficult to argue in favor of such harmonization. Banking markets, however, are often opaque—at least to banking customers—and often far from competitive.[2] Lack of information could be a reason to adopt minimum deposit insurance coverage EU-wide—to offer adequate protection to ill-formed international depositors. Similarly, lack of bank competition could motivate common restrictions on deposit insurance policies—for instance in the form of a minimum deposit insurance premium—to dull international regulatory competition to favor national banking systems. At any rate, a necessary condition for the harmonization of international deposit insurance policies to make sense is that banking markets are internationally integrated. Banking market integration means that banks have international customers and perhaps that their ownership is international as well. Banking market integration thus implies that foreign residents are directly affected by national deposit insurance policies. In both the customer and ownership categories, banking markets in the Europe are already well integrated as shown in this paper.

Any benefits of deposit insurance policy harmonization have to be balanced against the costs of forcing the same policy on countries that differ widely in their states of overall and financial development. DKL find that richer countries are more likely to adopt explicit deposit insurance, and that richer countries tend to provide broader insurance coverage given deposit insurance adoption. The EU chose the 20,000 euros coverage minimum to fit the needs and circumstances of the relatively wealthy Western EU member states. This suggests that the 20,000 euros minimum may be considerably higher than the insurance that the Eastern member states would offer, if any, in the absence of the directive. If so, the directive could impose considerable costs on these countries. These costs can take several forms. The adoption of explicit deposit insurance with a relatively high insurance coverage can increase the likelihood of a banking crisis (see, e.g., Demirgüç-Kunt and Detragiache 2002). This reflects that generous insurance may cause moral hazard and increased risk taking on the part of some or all insured banks. Efficiency may be hampered if generous deposit insurance brings about the cross-subsidization of weak banks by the strong banks through the premium payments. In addition, generous deposit insurance can impose high fiscal costs if a crisis were to occur.

For costs of this kind to be relevant, the minimum coverage of 20,000 euros indeed has to be binding for some EU member states. To see whether this is the case, we need to know what coverage EU member states would have been likely to adopt in the absence of the EU Directive. For this purpose, we adopt the approach of DKL of estimating a two-stage Heckman (1979) selection model of deposit insurance adoption and minimum coverage determination. After estimating this model with data for non-EU countries, we can predict "out-of-sample" the probability of deposit insurance adoption of EU member states as well as their expected insurance coverage. On the basis of these estimates, we find that the EU Directive may not much constrain deposit insurance policies in the EU-15 (because the probabilities of deposit insurance selection are relatively high and the predicted coverage amounts are well above 20,000 euros). The EU Directive, however, deviates considerably from the estimated preferred policies in Eastern Europe (as predicted adoption probabilities are considerably less than one and expected coverage amounts in several instances less than 20,000 euros). This does not prove that the EU Directive is the wrong policy, precisely because there may be (positive) external effects of deposit insurance adoption and high coverage levels that would not be reflected in countries' own preferred (and predicted) policies. Nonetheless, the evidence of this chapter casts doubt on the wisdom of an across-the-board minimum coverage of 20,000 euros for the entire EU.

In the remainder, section 7.2 describes some main features of deposit insurance policies in the EU as in part determined by the directive. Section 7.3 turns to the international aspects of deposit insurance. First, it discusses conceptually under what circumstances international coordination or even harmonization of deposit insurance policies may be beneficial. Coordination of deposit insurance policies would limit or eliminate international regulatory competition in this area. To see whether national deposit insurance policies potentially have international ramifications, the section also (1) provides some evidence on the current level of international banking market integration in the EU, and (2) reviews some evidence on how national deposit insurance policies may affect international flows of bank deposits. Section 7.4 turns to the question of whether the EU Directive imposes binding constraints on policymaking in EU member states regarding insurance adoption and minimum coverage. Section 7.5 concludes.

7.2   Deposit Insurance Policies in the European Union

The EU deposit insurance directive of 1994 imposes minimum standards on national deposit insurance policies. As with all EU banking regulation, the principles of home country control and mutual recognition assign regulatory responsibilities in the case of internationally active banks. Foreign branches thus are affected by parent country deposit insurance, while foreign subsidiaries are subject to host country policies. The main objectives of the EU Directive appear to be to increase the stability of the banking system and to protect depositors. To further these objectives, the directive requires the adoption of an explicit system of deposit insurance with a minimum coverage of 20,000 euros.[3] Table 7.1 provides information on actual coverage levels for the EU-15 in panel A and for the ten accession countries in panel B. Seven of the fifteen countries in panel A, in fact, have a coverage limit exceeding 20,000 euros in 2002, with the highest coverage of 103,291 euros in Italy. The average coverage level of 33,656 euros is much higher than the minimum of 20,000 euros. The average per capita income in the EU-15 is 26,396 euros, while the average ratio of the coverage limit to per capita GDP is 1.414. In panel B, we see that the average coverage limit in the accession countries is 14,931 euros in 2002. Note that Malta only adopted explicit deposit insurance in 2003. The average per capita GDP in the accession countries is only 7,508 euros, while the mean coverage ratio (to per capita GDP) at 2.17 is much higher than in the EU-15.

In designing the directive, EU policymakers do not appear to have been concerned greatly with limiting potential regulatory competition in the area of deposit insurance. Perhaps this explains that the directive does not prescribe a minimum deposit insurance premium. This leaves countries free to determine the deposit insurance premium, if any, and in practice we see that deposit insurance premiums are rather low. As seen in the two panels of table 7.1, many EU member states charge a deposit insurance premium on an ex post or on demand basis, which means that effectively the deposit insurance premium is zero. The directive similarly is agnostic on several key deposit insurance design elements. For instance, there are no prescriptions as to whether a permanent fund should be established, and on the public/private mix of the funding and on scheme administration.[4]

The writers of the directive were not totally free of fear of international regulatory competition, however, as the directive contains three paragraphs that appear to aim to limit the scope for such competition. First, the directive includes an "advertising prohibition" that prohibits banks from using differences in their deposit insurance schemes in their commercial ads (article 9, paragraph 3). Second, there was the "export prohibition" provision that limited the coverage of the insurance of EU foreign branches to the level of the deposit insurance scheme of the host member state (article 4, paragraph 1). This provision was allowed to expire at the end of 1999 after review by the European Commission (1999) on the grounds that the export prohibition had only been necessary during a transitory period (with some countries imposing temporarily low coverage limits below 20,000 euros). Third, there still is the "topping up" clause that makes it possible for foreign EU branches to top up their insurance coverage to the level of the EU host member state by joining the host country deposit insurance scheme (article 4, paragraph 2). The operation of the topping up clause was also reviewed by the European Commission (2001). This report indicates that the practical importance of the topping up clause has been small, as only the Danish and British deposit insurance schemes have ever concluded topping up agreements with bank branches from European Economic Area (EEA) countries operating within their territories. All the same, the Commission recommended that the topping up provision is maintained to enable branches of banks in accession countries—with still relatively low coverage levels in 2001—to compete in the EU-15. Hence, it is fair to say that concerns about potential regulatory competition in the area of deposit insurance policies are reflected in the directive.

7.3 The International Repercussions of Deposit Insurance

7.3.1 Does It Make Sense to Harmonize Deposit Insurance Policies?
Several authors have started to analyze potential international competition among bank regulators and the scope for international policy

Table 7.1
Deposit insurance policies at year-end of 2002

Country	Date enacted	Coverage limit (euros)	GDP per capita (euros)	Coverage divided by per capita GDP	Annual premiums
Panel A: EU-15					
Austria	1979	20,000	26,635	0.75	Pro rata, ex post
Belgium	1974	20,000	25,266	0.79	0.02 + 0.04 of insured liabilities
Denmark	1988	40,377	34,196	1.18	0
Finland	1969	25,000	26,877	0.93	Risk-based: 0.05–0.3
France	1980	70,000	25,585	2.74	On demand but limited
Germany	1966	20,000	25,555	0.78	Official is 0.03 but can be doubled
Greece	1993	20,000	13,276	1.51	Decreasing from 0.125 to 0.0025 by size
Ireland	1989	20,000	33,280	0.6	0.2
Italy	1987	103,291	21,726	4.75	Risk-adjusted, ex post 0.4–0.8 of protected funds
Luxembourg	1989	20,000	50,373	0.4	Ex post
Netherlands	1979	20,000	27,506	0.73	Ex post
Portugal	1992	25,000	12,879	1.94	Risk-based: 0.1–0.2
Spain	1977	20,000	16,851	1.19	Maximum of 0.2
Sweden	1996	27,322	28,657	0.95	Risk-based: 0.5
United Kingdom	1982	53,846	27,271	1.97	On demand
Average		33,656	26,396	1.41	

Panel B: Accession countries

Cyprus	2000	35,088	14,132	2.48	Banks 0.1, building societies 0.05
Czech Republic	1994	25,023	7,058	3.55	0.5 (maximum)
Estonia	1998	2,556	5,083	0.5	Risk-based to 0.3
Hungary	1993	4,232	7,069	0.6	0.3
Latvia	1998	4,918	3,647	1.35	Banks and foreign branches 0.45, credit unions 0.2
Lithuania	1996	13,043	4,226	3.09	
Malta	2003				
Poland	1995	18,026	10,064	3.63	0.4
Slovak Republic	1996	13,242	4,783	2.77	0.1–0.3
Slovenia	2001	18,248	11,507	1.59	Ex post
Average		14,931	7,508	2.17	

Notes: Coverage data are for 2002. Averages are unweighted and in panel B exclude Malta.
Coverage information is from DKL. Annual premium are mostly for 1999 and are from Demirgüç-Kunt and Sobaci 2000. Premium data for the Czech Republic, Denmark, Finland, Greece, Lithuania, Poland, Portugal, and Slovenia are from the international deposit insurance survey conducted by the Canada Deposit Insurance Corporation in 2002.

coordination in this area. A rather general treatment of the problem is offered by Dell'Ariccia and Marquez (2006). These authors consider two countries with different (relative) preferences over banking profits and banking system stability. National bank regulation in one country—for instance, in the form of deposit insurance or capital requirements—lowers banking profits in that country, but it serves to increase banking system stability in both countries. Acting independently, national bank regulators fail to take into account that higher domestic regulation also leads to increased banking system stability in the other country. Hence, in the absence of policy coordination there will be "underregulation" in this two-country world. Coordination of bank regulation in this analysis is taken to imply the introduction of a common, harmonized regulation in both countries. The question is then whether both countries can benefit from the international coordination of bank regulatory policies. The answer depends on how different are regulators' preferences over banking profits and banking system stability. If these preferences are the same or very similar in the two countries, then the introduction of a common regulatory policy can be beneficial. If preferences are rather dissimilar, however, there may exist no harmonized regulatory policy that makes both countries better off. Along similar lines, Sinn (2003, chap. 7) analyzes international bank regulatory competition in the area of capital standards. Adding some realism, he argues that the foreign share in bank deposits and international bank ownership are key parameters in the transmission of national capital standards to foreign welfare. Equally important is whether international depositors can distinguish among different countries on the basis of capital adequacy requirements.[5]

International competition in the area of deposit insurance policies, if it exists, could provide a rationale for international coordination or harmonization of deposit insurance policies, as we see in the form of the EU Directive. Along the lines of Dell'Ariccia and Marquez (2006), EU member states can be expected to have different preferences over deposit insurance coverage. The introduction of a 20,000 euros common minimum coverage can be expected to impose some costs on some member states. The question is whether the introduction of explicit deposit insurance—along the lines of the directive—introduces sufficient offsetting benefits by limiting policy competition in this area.

What are the external international effects created by deposit insurance introduction? These importantly depend on how deposit insurance is priced and how banks respond to deposit insurance. In an idealized world, we could assume there are (1) sophisticated bank depositors that value deposit insurance appropriately, (2) fair deposit insurance premiums just sufficient to cover expected deposit insurance payouts, and (3) risk-based deposit insurance premiums so that the introduction of deposit insurance does not create moral hazard. Under these rarefied assumptions, the main effects of deposit insurance would be to eliminate the possibility of costly bank runs not based on fundamentals. Financial stability no doubt is a common good prized by all countries. Hence, international coordination of deposit insurance policies that mainly increased financial stability will be to the benefit of all countries.

Potential international conflicts of interest over deposit insurance policies, however, arise if we relax one (or more) of these three assumptions. To start, unsophisticated international depositors may not be able to distinguish sufficiently between countries with and without deposit insurance. In this instance, depositors will undervalue deposit insurance. This implies that they may not accept lower deposit interest rates in countries with deposit insurance, even if banks in these countries have to pay a deposit insurance premium. Deposit insurance then benefits international depositors at the expense of (mostly domestic) bank shareholders. This could make the introduction of deposit insurance undesirable from a national perspective. Hence, international coordination of deposit insurance policies could be called for to ensure its introduction in all concerned countries.

Alternatively, we can assume deposit insurance is not fairly priced, but instead implies a net subsidy to the banking system (because the premium payment is less than the expected deposit insurance payout).[6] Lowly priced deposit insurance can be interpreted as "strategic trade policy" along the lines of the analysis of export subsidies in Brander and Spencer 1985. Thus, domestic regulators could introduce cheap domestic deposit insurance to help domestic banks gain market share at the expense of foreign banks.[7] Needless to say, international regulatory competition on the basis of deposit insurance prices is harmful and policy coordination can play a useful role in limiting such competition. As indicated before, the EU deposit insurance directive currently does not regulate deposit insurance pricing.

Finally, we could assume that the pricing of deposit insurance is not risk-based and hence does not fully reflect the riskiness of banking assets. Deposit insurance then introduces or enhances the problem of moral hazard in that banks are induced to finance relatively risky projects with a high probability of default and a low expected return to the bank. For given deposit premium rates, this mechanism serves to transfer resources from the deposit insurance agency to bank shareholders. As long as we maintain that deposit insurance premiums are fair, however, these premiums would have to rise to make up for the higher probability of bank failure. In the end, banks' predilection for risky, low-return projects would therefore be self-defeating. If so, bank shareholders would stand to lose and perhaps depositors as well, if inefficiently operating banks can only pay lower deposit rates. The international external effects of mispriced deposit insurance in one country depend on the international ownership of bank deposits and bank stocks as well as on the way domestic banks and foreign banks compete. At any rate, mispriced deposit insurance is likely to have large net costs, which suggests that international cooperation so as to introduce "best practice" in this area should only be beneficial. The EU Directive, however, is silent on all aspects of the deposit insurance premium, and hence also on whether it should be risk-based.

To summarize, countries have a common interest in introducing deposit insurance with some minimum coverage insofar as this prevents unwarranted bank runs. Countries may have diverging interests regarding the level of the deposit insurance premium, as a low deposit insurance premium can benefit national banks at the expense of foreign banks. Finally, countries have a common interest in eliminating deposit insurance premiums that are not appropriately risk-based to prevent moral hazard on the part of banks. Reflecting concerns about financial stability, the EU Directive requires explicit deposit insurance. The deposit insurance premium, however, is not regulated, as regulatory competition in this area is apparently not a serious concern for policymakers.

7.3.2 The Internationalization of Banking in the European Union

This section reviews some evidence on two key measures of banking integration in the EU: the magnitude of external deposits and the foreign ownership share of the banks themselves. To start, table 7.2 provides figures on the external deposits of EU banking systems, defined as deposits owned by nonresidents, from the Bank of International Settlements in 2003. Unfortunately, BIS membership in Europe is limited

Table 7.2
External deposits of banks in the EU-15 in 2003

Country	Total external deposits		External deposits owned by nonbanks	
	Billions of euros	As percent of GDP	Billions of euros	As percent of total
Austria	75	33	14	19
Belgium	340	126	111	33
Denmark	87	46	11	13
Finland	22	16	2	9
France	620	40	70	11
Germany	897	42	307	34
Greece	28	18	10	34
Ireland	246	182	50	20
Italy	311	24	22	7
Luxembourg	354	1,479	129	36
Netherlands	391	86	90	23
Portugal	116	89	14	12
Spain	314	42	128	41
Sweden	88	33	8	10
United Kingdom	2,268	143	615	27
Average for EU-15	6,157	66	1,579	26
Japan	413	11	44	11
United States	1,375	14	321	23

Sources: BIS 2005 (tables 3A and 3B) and Eurostat.
Note: External deposits are deposits owned by nonresidents. Averages for the EU-15 are unweighted.

to the EU-15. Total external deposits in the EU-15 are 6.2 trillion euros. The United Kingdom has by far the largest external deposits at 2.3 trillion euros, followed by Germany with 0.9 trillion euros. As a percent of GDP, external deposits are largest in Luxembourg at 1,479 percent. External deposits exceed GDP as well in Belgium, Ireland, and the United Kingdom. External deposits as a share of GDP are higher in each EU-15 country than in either Japan or the United States, which shows that EU banking markets are relatively international. Total external deposits can be divided into nonbank external deposits and bank-owned external deposits. Nonbank external deposits are external deposits held by individuals, businesses and public authorities.[8] In the table, we see that nonbank external deposits amount to 1.6 trillion euros in the EU-15. As a share of total deposits, nonbank external deposits are

Table 7.3
Foreign banking in the EU-15 in 2002

| | Foreign share (in %) | Of which | | | |
| | | EEA | | Non-EEA | |
		Branches	Subs	Branches	Assets/GDP
Austria	21	1	20	0	2.56
Belgium	24	3	18	1	2.97
Denmark					
Finland	8	8	0	0	1.18
France	18	3	7	0	2.55
Germany	6	1	4	1	3.02
Greece	21	6	12	3	1.43
Ireland	50	13	25	0	3.7
Italy	4	4	0	1	1.61
Luxembourg	100	16	78	1	30.18
Netherlands	10	2	7	0	3.05
Portugal	25	5	20	0	2.72
Spain	10	5	4	1	1.94
Sweden					
United Kingdom					
Average	23	6	19	1	4.74

Source: ECB 2003, tables 5, 18, 20, 22 and 24.
Note: Foreign share is the percentage of assets of foreign banks. Averages are unweighted.

relatively high in Luxembourg and Spain at 36 and 41 percent, respectively. On average, the share of nonbank external deposits in total external deposits is 26 percent in the EU-15.

Next, we consider the international ownership of the banks themselves in the EU. Table 7.3 provides information on the importance of foreign banks in the EU-15 taken from European Central Bank (2003). At one extreme, all banks in Luxembourg appear to be foreign-owned. At the other end of the spectrum, foreign-owned banks hold less than 10 percent of banking assets in Finland, Germany, and Italy. The table makes a distinction between foreign-owned banks with parent companies in the EEA and elsewhere. This reveals that foreign banks in the EU in fact mostly originate from EEA countries (as measured by assets). The table provides a further breakdown into foreign branches and foreign subsidiaries. Here we see that foreign banks from EEA and non-EEA countries are mostly organized as subsidiaries. Finally,

Table 7.4
Foreign ownership in Eastern Europe in 1996–2000

	Number of banks	Foreign ownership
Czech Republic	24	81
Estonia	3	100
Hungary	30	86
Latvia	20	34
Lithuania	8	76
Poland	33	64
Slovenia	18	29
Slovak Republic	17	71
Average	19	68

Source: Bonin, Hasan, and Wachtel 2003, table 7.29.
Note: Foreign ownership is percentage of observations with majority foreign ownership. Average is unweighted.

the table provides some information on the overall importance of banking markets in the EU as measured by banking assets relative to GDP. On average, the ratio of banking assets to GDP amounts to 4.74 in the EU. This ratio is more than 30 for Luxembourg, while it is less than 2 for Finland, Greece, and Italy.

Table 7.4 provides some information on the foreign ownership of banks in Eastern Europe as calculated by Bonin, Hasan, and Wachtel (2003) from Bankscope data. The average foreign ownership share in eight EU member states in Eastern Europe over the 1996–2000 period is calculated as 68 percent. In Estonia, all banks are reported to be foreign-owned. Slovenia has the lowest foreign ownership rate of these eight countries at a still considerable 29 percent. Any international ramifications of EU deposit insurance policies are thus expected to be rather important in Eastern Europe.

7.3.3 The Impact of Insurance on International Deposit Flows and Banking Organization

Depositors potentially shop around internationally to obtain the best deposit insurance conditions. Similarly, internationally active banks may choose their international organizational structure, and in particular whether they operate foreign branches or subsidiaries, with a view to obtain the best possible deposit insurance conditions. The EU Directive in principle opens the door to the latter type of arbitrage by stipulating that foreign branches and subsidiaries are subject to home and host country deposit insurance regimes, respectively. Arbitrage by either bank customers or the banks themselves implies that international differences in deposit insurance regimes distort economic behavior. In this section, we discuss whether there is any evidence for either type of arbitrage.

Two papers have addressed whether capital flows are affected by deposit insurance policies.[9] First, Lane and Sarisoy (2000) examine the impact of deposit insurance on several measures of private capital inflows (gross and net private capital inflows and capital inflows in the form of syndicated loans and international bonds) for a cross-section of twenty-seven countries over the 1990–1995 period. The authors fail to find a significant impact of explicit deposit insurance, which perhaps is not surprising given that their capital inflow measures include many financial instruments other than the banks deposits that are covered by deposit insurance. Refining this work, Huizinga and Nicodème (2006) examine whether explicit deposit insurance affects bilateral stocks of external bank liabilities for a sample of sixteen BIS reporting countries during the 1983–1998 period. A distinction is made between external nonbank liabilities and external bank-owned liabilities. External nonbank deposits are generally covered by any deposit insurance, while bank-owned or interbank deposits are typically excluded. In line with this, Huizinga and Nicodème (2006) find that deposit insurance is relatively attractive to nonbank owners of external bank liabilities. The introduction of deposit insurance specifically is estimated to increase nonbank external deposits by 31 percent, while bank-owned external deposits increase by about a third of this. This evidence suggests that in principle countries can compete in the area of deposit insurance adoption. In the past, they may have indeed introduced deposit insurance with a view to attracting additional international deposits. In the EU, the directive has made a system of explicit deposit insurance compulsory, and hence competition regarding deposit insurance adoption can no longer exist in the EU. The EU Directive allows countries to set their own deposit insurance premium, and in principle counties can still compete in this area to attempt to attract international depositor customers. Huizinga and Nicodème (2006), however, fail to find any impact of the deposit insurance premium on the international location of nonbank or bank-owned external bank liabilities.

Ratio of assets of foreign
branches to subsidiaries

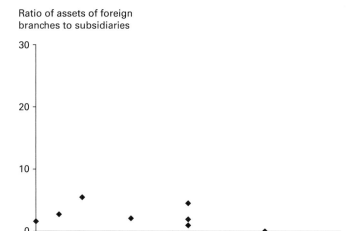

Figure 7.1
The ratio of assets of foreign subsidiaries to foreign branches from EEA countries in
EU-15 and the maximum premium
Note: Data available for eight countries among the EU-15. The maximum premium is the
maximum number mentioned in the last column of table 7.1, panel A. Source for assets of
foreign branches and subsidiaries of EEA countries is ECB (2003, tables 18 and 20) for
2002.

The EU Directive follows the principle of home country control in
assigning responsibilities for internationally active banks. This provides international banks with an incentive to operate foreign branches
if the home deposit insurance premium is lower than the host country
premium, and vice versa. Do banks in the EU respond to this incentive? To see this, we can relate the data on the assets of foreign
branches and subsidiaries in the EU-15 from the European Central
Bank (2003, tables 7.18 and 7.20) with information on the deposit insurance premium in panel A of table 7.1. Specifically, the ECB data is used
to construct the ratio of foreign subsidiary assets to foreign branch
assets of banks from EEA countries in individual EU member states.
From table 7.1, we take the highest explicitly stated deposit insurance
premium (hence excluding premiums that are determined ex post or
on demand). In figure 7.1, we plot the foreign subsidiary/branch assets
ratio against the maximum explicit premium.[10] There appears to be a
negative relationship indeed suggesting that foreign subsidiaries are

less important in high-premium countries. Notably, Greece, the country with the highest explicit deposit insurance premium of 0.3 percent per annum, has no foreign bank subsidiaries. The figure thus offers some evidence that bank organizational choices in the EU are distorted by the directive's provision deposit insurance is subject to home country control.

7.4 Does the EU Directive Lead to Overinsurance?

The EU deposit insurance directive forces member states to adopt a system of explicit deposit insurance with a minimum coverage of 20,000 euros. This section examines whether these two main features of the directive appear to constrain policymaking in EU member states. Specifically, we first ask whether EU member states would have been likely to adopt explicit deposit insurance without the directive. Second, we examine whether the minimum coverage of 20,000 euros exceeds the expected coverage in the absence of the Directive. To address these issues, we use the two-stage Heckman (1979) selection model of deposit insurance adoption and coverage determination of DKL.[11] In this approach, a first-stage regression explains deposit insurance adoption with a logistic probability model. A second-stage regression explains the ratio of the maximum coverage to per capita GDP in case explicit deposit insurance is adopted in the first stage. The Heckman two-stage model takes into account that some of the unobserved factors (or "errors") that affect the deposit insurance choice also affect the coverage ratio in case of adoption to ensure unbiased parameter estimates in the second-stage regression. The sample consists of a large set of developing and developed countries over the 1961–2002 period.

   Among the variables included in both regressions are three macro-variables: inflation, GDP growth, and GDP per capita. Next, there is the External Pressure variable which is a dummy variable that takes on a value of 1 for the years 1999 and onwards. This reflects that 1999 was the year in which the IMF starting expressed support of explicit deposit insurance as evidenced by a paper on best practice and guidelines regarding deposit insurance. Next, the Executive constraints variable is an index measuring the extent of institutionalized constraints on decision-making powers of chief executives. This variable is included to test whether countries with more democratic political systems are more likely to adopt deposit insurance. Finally, the crisis dummy variable equals one if a deposit insurance system was adopted between zero and three years following a systematic banking crisis. This variable is allows us to see whether deposit insurance systems tend to be adopted following a banking crisis.

In table 7.5, there are two pairs of regressions: pair 1 is based on a sample that excludes all twenty-five EU member states, while pair 2 only excludes the accession countries. Closely mirroring DKL, in the two first-stage regressions we see that deposit insurance adoption is more likely given (1) a low inflation, (2) a high per capita GDP, (3) the period from 1999 onward, (4) a more democratic political system (a high value for the executive constraints index), and (5) the occurrence of a financial crisis. The two second-stage regressions of the coverage ratio reveal that the same factors that make deposit insurance adoption more likely also work toward a higher coverage ratio.

The estimated parameters in table 7.5 can be used to estimate the probability of deposit insurance adoption and the expected coverage ratio. To construct the expected coverage ratio, the coverage ratio is taken to be zero in case deposit insurance is not adopted. Specifically, regression 1 in table 7.5 is used to estimate "out-of-sample" adoption probabilities and coverage ratios for all twenty-five EU countries for 2002. In addition, regression 2 in table 7.5 is used to produce out-of-sample adoption probabilities and expected coverage ratios for the accession countries only for 2002.

In table 7.6, panel A gives the results for the EU-15 based on regression pair 1 of table 7.5. The average probability of adoption is estimated to be 0.59, which suggests that by 2002 the majority of EU-15 countries would have adopted explicit deposit insurance even without the directive.[12] Relatively low probabilities of adoption are estimated for Greece and Portugal at 0.47 and 0.45, respectively. As seen in table 7.1, Greece and Portugal were rather late adopters of explicit deposit insurance in 1993 and 1992, respectively. Hence, it is likely that these two countries were forced into deposit insurance adoption by the prospect of the EU Directive taking effect in 1994. Next, the average predicted coverage ratio is 3.96. Interestingly, this is far higher than the average actual coverage ratio for the EU-15 that is seen to be 1.41 in table 7.1.[13] The model may overpredict EU-15 coverage ratios as the United States and Japan—countries with similar levels of economic development to the EU-15—have coverage ratios of 2.78 and 2.54 that are much higher than the EU-15 average.[14] In absolute numbers, the EU-15

Table 7.5
Heckman two-step selection model for the coverage ratio

	Dependent variable coverage ratio	
Second-stage	(1)	(2)
Inflation	−0.015***	−0.014***
	(0.004)	(0.004)
GDP growth	−0.0003	−0.033
	(0.052)	(0.040)
GDP per capita	0.160***	0.141***
	(0.027)	(0.018)
External pressure	3.724***	2.823***
	(0.607)	(0.428)
Executive constraints	1.166***	0.905***
	(0.122)	(0.092)
Crisis dummy	4.357***	3.702***
	(0.712)	(0.549)
Postcrisis adoption	3.201***	2.772***
	(0.647)	(0.481)
Heckman Lambda	8.123***	6.498***
	(0.307)	(0.197)
	Dependent variable deposit insurance	
First-stage	(1)	(2)
Inflation	−0.001**	−0.001**
	(0.000)	(0.000)
GDP growth	0.006	0.002
	(0.006)	(0.006)
GDP per capita	0.023***	0.029***
	(0.003)	(0.003)
External pressure	0.591***	0.560***
	(0.070)	(0.064)
Executive constraints	0.163***	0.162***
	(0.014)	(0.013)
Crisis dummy	0.510***	0.534***
	(0.085)	(0.082)
Postcrisis dummy	0.419***	0.471***
	(0.078)	(0.072)
Number of observations	3798	4336
Number of censored observations	3281	3564

Table 7.5
(continued)

Notes: The endogenous variable in the first stage is the explicit deposit insurance indicator, while the endogenous variable in the in second stage is the coverage ratio. Regressions are based on those in column (1) in table 2.12. However, regression 1 excludes observations for all EU member states, while regression 2 excludes observations for the accession countries. Sample period is 1961–2002. Inflation is based on GDP deflator and in percent. GDP growth is the real GDP growth rate in percent. GDP per capita is in constant 1995 thousands of U.S. dollars. External pressure is a dummy variable that takes on a value of one for the years 1999 and onward. Crisis dummy equals 1 if the country experiences a systematic crisis in that year and 0 otherwise from 1976. Postcrisis adoption equals 1 if a deposit insurance system was adopted between zero and three years following a crisis and 0 otherwise. Executive constraints is an index measuring the extent of institutionalized constraints on decision-making powers of chief executives. The index ranges from 1 to 7, where 1 represents unlimited authority and 7 executive parity or subordination. Estimates are efficient or maximum likelihood (ML) estimates. Data has been made available by DKL. See chapter 2 for data sources. *, **, and *** indicate significance at the 10 percent, 5 percent, and 1 percent level, respectively.

are expected to have an average coverage limit of about 100,000 euros as seen in the table. For each of the EU-15 countries, the expected coverage limit in fact exceeds the minimum coverage of 20,000 euros by a wide margin. Effectively taking the United States and Japan as comparator countries, the model thus suggests that the EU Directive does not bind choices as to the coverage limit in the EU-15. If this is true, however, it is surprising that eight countries among the EU-15 set their coverage limits to exactly 20,000 in 2002 (see table 7.1). This apparent contradiction just underscores that it may not be correct to take coverage levels in the United States and Japan—rather high among developed countries—to be the norm for the EU-15.

Given our model, we can next calculate the predicted adoption probabilities and coverage limits for the accession countries based on regression pair 1 in table 7.5. The average predicted adoption probability for these countries is seen to be relatively low at 0.48 (see panel B of table 7.6). In line with this, the predicted adoption probability is less than half in the Czech Republic, Estonia, the Slovak Republic, and Slovenia. Similar results are reported in panel C of table 7.6—on the basis of regressions that include the EU-15 in the sample.[15] By 2002, all accession countries apart from Malta had, in fact, adopted deposit insurance—with Malta falling in line in 2003. The EU Directive no doubt was a major catalyst in this development.

Panel B of table 7.6 indicates that the average predicted coverage ratio is 2.95 for the accession countries, while panel C reports an average

Table 7.6
Deposit insurance adoption probabilities and expected coverage limits

Panel A: EU-15

Country	Proba-bility of adoption	Coverage ratio	Coverage limit (euros)	Is pre-dicted coverage less than 20,000 euros?	In addition, is the actual coverage equal to 20,000 euros?
Austria	0.64	4.42	117,712	No	No
Belgium	0.62	4.21	106,430	No	No
Denmark	0.69	4.99	170,581	No	No
Finland	0.64	4.33	116,443	No	No
France	0.55	3.51	89,853	No	No
Germany	0.63	4.35	111,270	No	No
Greece	0.47	2.78	36,856	No	No
Ireland	0.62	4.05	134,934	No	No
Italy	0.53	3.33	72,286	No	No
Luxembourg					
Netherlands	0.62	4.18	115,061	No	No
Portugal	0.45	2.7	34,790	No	No
Spain	0.66	4.84	81,498	No	No
Sweden	0.63	4.29	122,883	No	No
United Kingdom	0.55	3.47	94,613	No	No
Average	0.59	3.96	100,372		

Panel B: Accession countries based on model 1 in table 7.5

Country	Proba-bility of adoption	Coverage ratio	Coverage limit (euros)	Is pre-dicted coverage less than 20,000 euros?	In addition, is the actual coverage equal to 20,000 euros?
Cyprus					
Czech Republic	0.39	2	15,657	Yes	No
Estonia	0.39	2.16	11,001	Yes	Yes
Hungary	0.56	3.64	25,747	No	No
Latvia	0.54	3.49	12,732	Yes	Yes
Lithuania	0.54	3.47	14,657	Yes	Yes
Malta					
Poland	0.54	3.55	17,643	Yes	Yes
Slovak Republic	0.39	2.14	10,248	Yes	Yes
Slovenia	0.45	2.62	30,139	No	No
Average	0.48	2.95	15,383		

Table 7.6
(continued)

Panel C: Accession countries based on model 2 in table 7.5

Country	Predicted values Probability of insurance	Coverage divided by GDP	Coverage limit (euros)	Is predicted coverage less than 20,000 euros?	In addition, is the actual coverage equal to 20,000 euros or less?
Cyprus					
Czech Republic	0.41		13,532	Yes	No
Estonia	0.4	1.92	9,237	Yes	Yes
Hungary	0.59	1.82	22,570	No	No
Latvia	0.57	3.19	10,967	Yes	Yes
Lithuania	0.57	3.01	12,574	Yes	Yes
Malta		2.98			
Poland	0.57	3.15	15,663	Yes	Yes
Slovak Republic	0.4	1.81	8,680	Yes	Yes
Slovenia	0.48	2.27	26,155	No	No
Average	0.50	2.52	14,922		

Note: Averages are unweighted.

predicted coverage ratio of 2.52.[16] These numbers are not too far from the average actual average coverage ratio of 2.17.[17] Hence, in 2002 the regression model does a reasonable job of predicting actual coverage ratios for the accession countries. As in 2002 predicted coverage ratios exceeded the actual ones in the accession countries, the deposit insurance directive apparently was not yet constraining coverage policies in the accession countries.[18] This, of course, is not surprising as accession only took place in 2004. All the same, it is interesting to check whether the 20,000 euros limit would have been binding, if it were already in effect in 2002. The table indicates that for six countries—of the eight for which we have data—the 20,000 euros minimum indeed exceeds the predicted coverage for 2002, which suggests that in these six countries the minimum of 20,000 euros would have been binding. For five of these six countries, actual coverage in 2002 was below the 20,000 euros minimum. For these five countries, the 20,000 euros minimum thus is likely to be binding after the directive takes full effect. The same conclusion is reached in panel C of table 7.6—based on regression 2 of table 7.5.

The accession treaty grants three countries with predicted 'over-insurance,' Estonia, Latvia, and Lithuania, temporary derogations from the requirement to institute a minimum coverage level of 20,000 euros. Specifically, Estonia is allowed to maintain a coverage limit of 6,391 euros until the end of 2005, to be followed by a coverage limit of 12,782 euros during 2006 and 2007. For Latvia, the allowed coverage limit is 10,000 until the end of 2005, and 15,000 during 2006 and 2007. Finally, Lithuania can maintain a coverage limit of 14,481 until the end of 2006, and of 17,377 during 2007. Thus by the end of 2007, the three Baltic states will also have to comply with the minimum coverage of 20,000 euros as stipulated by the directive.

Overall, the evidence suggests that the EU Directive appears to force deposit insurance on at least some of the accession countries and, in addition, is likely to lead to higher deposit insurance coverage than these countries would choose otherwise. This outcome may produce some benefits for the other EU countries if it reduces the likelihood of bank runs and protects depositors from these countries. This outcome, however, necessarily implies some costs for the accession countries (relative to their preferred outcome). A first cost of forced deposit in-surance adoption and 'overinsurance' may be a reduction in financial stability in these countries. This is suggested by Demirgüç-Kunt and Detragiache (2002, tables 7.2 and 7.3) who find that the likelihood of a financial crisis is positively related to the existence of explicit deposit insurance and to a higher explicit coverage limit. The reasoning is that explicit deposit insurance with high coverage limits may increase moral hazard and risk taking on the part of banks, thus contributing to financial fragility.[19] If so, explicit deposit insurance adoption in the accession countries could well imply negative external effects for the EU-15. Demirgüç-Kunt and Detragiache (2002) have found that the potential link between explicit deposit insurance adoption and the like-lihood of financial crises is stronger in countries with weaker institu-tional environments. This is relevant as the adoption of explicit deposit insurance in the accession countries is only part of the overall accession process. The accession countries in fact are led to adopt an entire *acquis communautaire* relating to financial markets. This presumably leads to improved overall bank regulation and supervision, even if the upgrad-ing of bank supervision in practice may take some time. Better bank regulation and supervision should reduce the scope for the adoption of explicit deposit insurance in developing countries to lead to a financial crisis. Finally, a second and related cost of high coverage deposit insurance in the accession countries is the potential for high fiscal outlays if a financial crisis were to occur.

7.5 Conclusion

The EU deposit insurance directive is unique in imposing minimum standards of deposit insurance policies on several countries. In essence, the Directive requires countries to adopt an explicit system of deposit insurance with a minimum coverage level of 20,000 euros. This reflects that the main objectives of the directive appear to be to increase banking system stability and to protect depositors. The directive certainly reduces the scope for bank runs and it protects small and unsophisticated savers. In an integrated financial area such as the EU, this is to the benefit of the entire EU. By its very nature, the directive eliminates the scope for international competition in the area of deposit insurance adoption. Hence, it may have eliminated competitive advantages on account of explicit deposit insurance in countries that were early adopters of deposit insurance. Beyond its main coverage provision, the directive leaves several key elements of deposit insurance design, and in particular the height of the deposit insurance premium, up to national policymakers. Hence, national policymakers in the EU in principle can compete in the area of deposit insurance design with a view to improving the competitive positions of their banking systems. The generally low levels of deposit insurance premiums in the EU may be an outcome of this.

The directive was designed to fit the needs of the EU as it existed in 1994. Specifically, the relatively high minimum coverage of 20,000 euros is appropriate for the rather wealthy countries that made up EU membership in the 1990s. For the new member states, adopting deposit insurance systems along lines of the Directive was a requirement of EU membership, even if the accession treaty provides the three Baltic states temporary reprieve from the minimum coverage requirement of 20,000 euros. Evidence presented in this chapter suggests that the accession countries as a group have relatively low probabilities of deposit insurance adopted and equally low expected coverage. Hence, as a group they adopt explicit deposit insurance with a coverage of 20,000 euros because the EU deposit insurance directive forces them to do so. The adoption of deposit insurance thus is a cost of EU membership that the accession countries have to bear. The high coverage of 20,000 euros may lead to moral hazard an increased risk taking on the part of banks and thus reduce financial stability. Also, the high coverage level may lead to rather high fiscal costs in case of a financial crisis. Perhaps the equally forced adoption of other aspects of the *acquis communautaire* related to banks—leading to an overall better regulatory and supervisory environment—could serve to mitigate the potential costs of high coverage deposit insurance in the new member states. Counterbalancing these costs would be any positive effects of explicit deposit insurance in the accession countries for the EU-15. On net, coverage levels in the accession countries as forced by the directive will probably be too high.

Notes

1. See Demirgüç-Kunt and Kane 2002 for a survey.

2. According to Morgan (2002), the pattern of disagreement among bond raters offers evidence that banks are inherently more opaque than other types of firms. Demirgüç-Kunt and Huizinga (1999) find that bank concentration is positively related to bank profitability as evidence of uncompetitive behavior. Claessens and Laeven (2004) construct a measure of bank competition that reflects the sensitivity of revenues to input prices. Banking systems with greater foreign bank entry and fewer entry and activity restrictions are found to be more competitive.

3. Until the end of 1999, maximum insured amounts less then 20,000 euros (but not less than 15,000 euros) were grandfathered. The directive allows, but does not prescribe, coinsurance with the depositor up to a share of 10 percent. At the same time, the directive explicitly excludes interbank deposits, but it provides member states with options regarding whether to insure the deposits of authorities, insurance companies, pension funds, and deposits in non-EU currencies.

4. In practice, we see some variation in the EU regarding these design elements. See Demirgüç-Kunt and Sobaci 2001.

5. A separate issue is how deposit insurance affects bank competition within a single banking market. See Cordella and Yeyati 2002.

6. Laeven (2002) calculates "fair" deposit insurance premiums for a large set of countries and compares these to actual premiums. In particular in Germany, deposit insurance premiums—both public and private—are calculated to be lower than the fair benchmark.

7. The domestic banks that benefit from low domestic deposit insurance include domestically located banks and the branches of domestic banks located abroad in the EU Directive. The impact on foreign welfare would depend on the market structure, the mode of competitive interaction and on the international ownership of deposits and banking firms.

8. These businesses include nonbank financial firms such as mutual funds, hedge funds and insurance companies.

9. Several studies have examined policy determinants of deposit location other than deposit insurance. Grilli (1989) finds some evidence of that aggregate nonbank deposits are affected by the nonresident interest withholding tax and by bank secrecy. Alworth and Andresen (1992) conclude that bilateral nonbank deposit outflows are positively related to the difference between the reserve ratios of the deposit and the bank countries. Huizinga and Nicodème (2003) provide some evidence that bilateral deposits are related to income taxes and to bank reporting of domestic interest payments to the tax authorities.

10. Data are plotted for Belgium, Denmark, France, Germany, Greece, Ireland, Portugal, and Spain.

11. Specifically, we start from regression 1 in panel A of table 7.12 in DKL.

12. Note that the predicted adoption probability for a country summarizes the impact of country-specific circumstances (such as whether the country has suffered a systematic banking crisis) on the likelihood of insurance adoption. It does not imply whether a country in fact should adopt deposit insurance, not least because deposit insurance can have international external effects as argued in section 3.1.

13. The average coverage ratio in panel A of table 7.1 rises to 1.49 if Luxembourg is excluded to make the numbers fully comparable.

14. In unreported regressions, a squared per capita GDP variable was included to yield an even higher average predicted coverage ratios for the EU-15 of 4.27.

15. Note that the first pair of regressions suggests that it is appropriate to include the EU-15 in the sample, as the EU Directive apparently does not constrain coverage levels for these countries. The EU Directive may similarly not be materially binding coverage levels in the EU-15 as these countries themselves supported the adoption of the directive.

16. Note that Slovenia has the highest predicted absolute coverage limit of 30,139 euros reflecting its relatively high per capita GDP.

17. Excluding Cyprus from panel B of table 7.1 would yield a very similar average actual coverage ratio of 2.13.

18. Nenovsky and Dimitrova (2003) assume that best practice implies an optimal coverage ratio of about one to two times GDP per capita. They note that the average coverage ratio in the accessions countries is higher than this best practice level and also higher than the average coverage ratio in the euro area of 1.44 in 2002. On the basis of this, they conclude that there is overinsurance in the accession countries.

19. Deposit insurance could reduce financial stability by weakening market discipline of banks. See Demirgüç-Kunt and Huizinga 2004. Gropp and Vesala (2001), however, argue that the EU Directive has improved market discipline in the EU by excluding interbank deposits from coverage.

References

Alworth, Julian S., and S. Andresen. 1992. The Determinants of Cross Border Non-Bank Deposits and the Competitiveness of Financial Market Centres. *Money Affairs* 5: 105–133.

Bank for International Settlements. 2005. *BIS Quarterly Review*. Basel, Switzerland: Bank for International Settlements.

Bonin, John P., Iftekhar Hasan, and Paul Wachtel. 2003. Bank Performance, Efficiency and Ownership in Transition Countries. Mimeo., New York University.

Brander, J., and B. Spencer. 1985. Export Subsidies and International Market Share Rivalry. *Journal of International Economics* 18: 82–100.

Claessens, Stijn, and Luc Laeven. 2004. What Drives Bank Competition? Some International Evidence. *Journal of Money, Credit, and Banking* 36: 563–584.

Cordella, Tito, and Eduardo Levy Yeyati. 2002. Financial Opening, Deposit Insurance and Risk in a Model of Banking Competition. *European Economic Review* 46: 471–485.

Dell'Ariccia, Giovanni, and Robert Marquez. 2006. Competition among Regulators and Financial Market Integration. *Journal of Financial Economics* 79: 401–430.

Demirgüç-Kunt, Aslı, and Enrica Detragiache. 2002. Does Deposit Insurance Increase Banking System Stability? An Empirical Investigation. *Journal of Monetary Economics* 49: 1373–1406.

Demirgüç-Kunt, Aslı, and Harry Huizinga. 1999. Determinants of Commercial Bank Interest Margins and Profitability: Some International Evidence. *World Bank Economic Review* 13: 379–408.

Demirgüç-Kunt, Aslı, and Harry Huizinga. 2004. Market Discipline and Deposit Insurance. *Journal of Monetary Economics* 51: 375–399.

Demirgüç-Kunt, Aslı, and Edward J. Kane. 2002. Deposit Insurance around the Globe: Where Does It Work? *Journal of Economic Perspectives* 16: 175–196.

Demirgüç-Kunt, Aslı, and Tolga Sobaci. 2001. Deposit Insurance around the World: A New Development Database. *World Bank Economic Review* 15: 481–190.

Eichengreen, Barry, and Carlos Arteta. 2002. Banking Crises in Emerging Markets: Presumptions and Evidence. In *Financial Policies in Emerging Markets,* ed. Mario I. Blejer and Marko Skreb, 48–94. Cambridge, Mass.: MIT Press.

European Central Bank. 2003. Structural Analysis of the EU Banking Sector.

European Commission. 1994. Directive 94/19/EC of the European Parliament and of the Council of 30 May 1994 on Deposit-Guarantee Schemes. *Official Journal of the European Commission* L135: 5–14.

European Commission. 1999. Report on the Application of the Export Prohibition Clause, Article 4(1) of the Directive on Deposit Guarantee Schemes. COM (1999) 722 final.

European Commission. 2001. Report on the Operation of the "Topping-up" Provision, Article 4, paragraphs 2–5 of the Directive on Deposit Guarantee Schemes (94/19/EC), COM(2001) 595 final.

Financial Stability Forum. 2001. Guidance for Developing Effective Deposit Insurance Systems. Available at http://www.fsforum.org/publications/Guidance_deposit01.pdf.

Grilli, Vittorio. 1989. Europe 1992: Issues and Prospects for the Financial Markets. *Economic Policy* 4 (9): 387–421.

Gropp, Reint, and Jukka Vesala. 2001. Deposit Insurance and Moral Hazard: Does the Counterfactual Matter? Working Paper no. 47, European Central Bank, Frankfurt, Germany.

Huizinga, Harry, and Gaëtan Nicodème. 2003. Are International Deposits Tax-Driven? *Journal of Public Economics* 88: 1093–1118.

Huizinga, Harry, and Gaëtan Nicodème. 2006. Deposit Insurance and International Bank Deposits. *Journal of Banking and Finance* 30: 956–987.

Laeven, Luc. 2002. Pricing of Deposit Insurance. Policy Research Working Paper no. 2871, The World Bank, Washington, D.C.

Lane, Philip R., and Selen Sarisoy. 2000. Does Deposit Insurance Stimulate Capital Inflows? *Economics Letters* 69: 193–200.

Martinez Peria, Maria Soledad, and Sergio L. Schmukler. 2001. Do Depositors Punish Banks for Bad Behaviour? Market Discipline, Deposit Insurance, and Banking Crises. *Journal of Finance* 56: 1029–1051.

Morgan, Donald P. 2002. Rating Banks: Risk and Uncertainty in an Opaque Industry. *American Economic Review* 92: 874–888.

Nenovsky, Nikolay, and Kalina Dimitrova. 2003. Deposit Insurance during EU Accession. Working Paper no. 617, William Davidson Institute, University of Michigan Business School.

Sinn, Hans-Werner. 2003. *The New Systems Competition*. London: Blackwell Publishing.

8   Deposit Overinsurance in EU Accession Countries

Nikolay Nenovsky and Kalina Dimitrova

8.1   Introduction

In the beginning of the 1990s the centrally planned economies in Central and Eastern Europe started a long process of transformation into becoming functioning market economies. This process was accompanied by the recovery of the banking intermediation, which also involved the establishment of the deposit insurance (DI) systems as a feature of the contemporary safety nets (including also lender of last resort and banking regulation characteristics). This was necessitated by the need for financial stability in these countries that experienced banking crises and panic that caused considerable loss of income and credibility in the banking system.[1] Those crises resulted from a complex set of causes, related to the difficulties of reconstructing the basic market economy institutions and establishing modern banking and financial systems. A major factor that contributed to the crises is the contradiction between the lax and discretional monetary and fiscal policies on the one hand, and the weak banking regulation on the other hand. The latter could not be compensated by the market discipline due to the weak credit culture in the formerly centrally planned economies.[2]

The crises forced the competent authorities to introduce explicit DI in order to avoid bank runs, calm down the population, and restore banking system credibility. Chronologically, almost at the same time (in the middle of the 1990s) it turned out that the former socialist countries would apply for EU membership, which automatically imposed overall harmonization requirements for financial legislation. Thus, the second major reason for the establishment of the new DI schemes was the EU integration and the requirement for harmonization (Directive 91/19 EC of 30 May 1994).

The common problems of DI (moral hazard, adverse selection, agency problems, incentive compatibility, and cost of intermediation)[3] gain a particular meaning in the transition countries. It is especially interesting to study the DI practices in the accession countries from the point of view of their potential impact on the euro after being integrated into the European Monetary Union (EMU).

In this study our goal is to provide a basic comparison of the DI systems in ten accession countries (Bulgaria, Czech Republic, Estonia, Hungary, Latvia, Lithuania, Poland, Romania, Slovakia, and Slovenia) looking for some common and specific features, assessing the current level of harmonization with the EU and future developments. At the same time, we try to address three questions: (1) Is there overinsurance of deposits in accession countries? (2) What are the basic factors behind this overinsurance? and (3) What are the consequences for the banking system stability and efficiency in the accession countries (taking into consideration the specific design of the safety nets) and the impact of overinsurance on the whole Euro Area?

This chapter argues that the dynamics of the DI goes through two major phases: (1) implicit and full DI inherited from our socialist past, and (2) explicit and high level of DI as a result of the banking crises and EU harmonization. Unfortunately, at the proper moment when it was possible to foster market discipline and banking system efficiency, a new high level of DI was enforced, which further increased moral hazard and weakened market discipline. Moreover, the process of mechanically carried out nominal harmonization of the DI systems which did not pay attention to the real condition of the economies and of the banking systems may impose great costs to the EU. The nominal and real overinsurance could lead to increased general risk level in the financial system, to lower efficiency of the banking intermediation, and to larger inequalities within the euro area as a whole.

In section 8.1 we briefly review the EU Directive on Deposit Guarantee Schemes of 1994 and present a detailed study of the features of the DI systems in the accession countries on the basis of their legislation. We argue that deposits in the accession countries are overinsured with supporting evidence in nominal and real terms as well as in the future development of DI in line with EU integration process. Moreover, we analyze the overinsurance in the context of banking system development and supervision, and the quality of institutions as well. In section 8.2, we analyze the reasons for the high level of overinsurance in the accession countries and its specific relation to moral hazard. In section

8.3, we describe some possible channels, through which this overinsurance could influence the financial system in the Euro Area.

8.2 The Design of DI in Accession Countries

The design of the DI systems in countries negotiating for EU accession is to a great extent predetermined by the Directive 94/19/EC of 30 May 1994, which intends to harmonize DI practice (European Commission 1994). As the EU Directive is a "soft law," accession countries differ in how they treat the individual versus corporate deposits, how they view coinsurance issues, risk adjusted premiums, coverage level, and institutional features (whether there is a special body managing the scheme, its legal status and scope of powers, the manner in which funds for deposit protection are raised and managed). All these features should be considered as country specific and closely related to the level of financial intermediation development. The process of EU integration leaves little space for free choice except for the level of contributions to the fund, which is more or less determined by the volume and characteristics of deposit creation process and banking stability. For the purpose of analyzing the DI as an element of the safety net, we present a short comparative analysis of selected institutional features that represent DI "best practices," based on most up-to-date survey data and information (see table 8.1).[4] Best practices in DI should contribute to the financial safety net by decreasing moral hazard and imposing market discipline that promotes bank development, efficiency, and stability (Garcia 1999; chapter 2, this volume).

As required by the directive, all DI systems in the EU should be mandatory for depository institutions in the member countries and branches of home credit institutions abroad. Voluntary membership is not considered good practice as it contributes to the problems of adverse selection, however it is argued to strengthen market discipline (Demirgüç-Kunt and Huizinga 2004). Hence, some of the EU-15 members (France, Germany, and Italy) have been forced to revise the design of their DI schemes to come into compliance with the directive. In addition to compulsory DI, some accession countries provide additional insurance. In the Czech Republic for instance, foreign bank branches may take out supplementary deposit insurance under a contract with the fund if the DI system to which they are members does not provide the same level and size of protection. In Poland there is a de jure contractual system that extends the guarantee coverage beyond the

Table 8.1
Basic characteristics of deposit insurance in accession countries

Country	Type: explicit = 1 implicit = 0	Date enacted	Foreign currencies: yes = 1 no = 0	Coverage limit (EUR)	Coinsurance: yes = 1 no = 0	Permanent fund: funded = 1 unfunded = 0	Premium or assessment base
Bulgaria	1	1995	1	7,670	0	1	Insured deposits
Czech Republic	1	1994	1	25,000	1	1	Insured deposits
Estonia	1	1998	1	6,391	1	1	Insured deposits
Hungary	1	1993	1	25,000	1	1	Insured deposits
Latvia	1	1998	1	8,535	0	1	Insured deposits

Annual premiums (percent of base)	Risk-adjusted premiums: yes = 1 no = 0	Source of funding: private = 1 joint = 2 official = 3	Administration: private = 1 joint = 2 official = 3	Membership: compulsory = 1 voluntary = 0
Entry contribution is equal to 1 percent of bank's registered capital but no less than 100,000 BGN (51,129 EUR); annual premium is 0.5 percent of the total amount of the deposit base for the preceding year.	0	2	2	1
Annual premium for banks is 0.1 percent of the average volume of insured deposits of the previous year, and 0.05 percent for building savings banks.	0	1	2	1
Entry fee equals 50,000 kroons (3,195 EUR); quarterly premiums of up to 0.125 percent (0.07 percent at present) of the insured deposits.	0	2	2	1
Entry fee is 0.5 percent of the registered amount of deposits; annual premium is up to 0.2 percent of the total amount of insured deposits (up to 0.3 percent for risky banks).	1	2	2	1
Entry fee is 50,000 LVL (81,994 EUR) for banks and 100 LVL (164 EUR) for credit unions; quarterly premiums equal 0.05 percent of the insured deposits.	0	2	3	1

Table 8.1
(continued)

Country	Type: explicit = 1 implicit = 0	Date enacted	Foreign currencies: yes = 1 no = 0	Coverage limit (EUR)	Coinsurance: yes = 1 no = 0	Permanent fund: funded = 1 unfunded = 0	Premium or assessment base
Lithuania	1	1996	1	14,481	1	1	Insured deposits
Poland	1	1995	1	22,500	1	1	Insured deposits
Romania	1	1996	1	3,157	0	1	Insured deposits
Slovakia	1	1996	1	20,000	1	1	Insured deposits

Annual premiums (percent of base)	Risk-adjusted premiums: yes = 1 no = 0	Source of funding: private = 1 joint = 2 official = 3	Adminis-tration: private = 1 joint = 2 official = 3	Membership: compulsory = 1 voluntary = 0
Annual premium of 0.45 percent of the insured deposits for banks and foreign banks departments, and 0.2 percent for credit unions.	0	1	2	1
Annual premium not exceeding 0.4 percent of the deposit base, which is used as the basis for the calculation of obligatory reserve.	0	2	2	1
Entry fee is 0.1 percent of the statutory capital of a bank; annual premium of 0.8 percent of total household deposits, and a special premium of 1.6 percent of total household deposits for banks conducting higher-risk transactions.	1	2	2	1
Entry fee of 1,000,000 SKK (24,874 EUR) for banks and 100,000,000 SKK (2,487,433 EUR) for the central bank, quarterly premiums from 0.1 percent to 0.75 percent of the amount of insured deposits from the preceding quarter, and an extraordinary premium ranging from 0.1 percent to 1.0 percent of the amount if insured deposits of the preceding quarter.	0	2	2	1

Table 8.1
(continued)

Country	Type: explicit = 1 implicit = 0	Date enacted	Foreign currencies: yes = 1 no = 0	Coverage limit (EUR)	Coinsurance: yes = 1 no = 0	Permanent fund: funded = 1 unfunded = 0	Premium or assessment base
Slovenia	1	2001	1	21,273	0	0	Insured deposits

Notes and source: All data is valid at the end of 2004. The maximum coverage and entry fees are calculated on the basis of the exchange rate at the end of 2004. Information from national legislation, surveys, and the Internet database of NDIF of Hungary (http://www.oba.hu/). The layout of the table and content of indicators follows the one developed by Demirgüç-Kunt and Sobaci 2001.

minimum specified in the mandatory scheme, which has not yet been put into practice. All subjects, rules, rights, and obligations are specified in the agreement on establishment of contractual guarantee fund. Also in Slovakia, banks may insure their deposits over and above the level of deposit protection required by the law by taking out insurance with a legal entity authorized by the ministry to carry on such business.

In terms of best practices, it is not clear which institutions shall be considered eligible for DI, although intuitively all deposit collecting institutions should be considered for inclusion. Depending on the depth of financial intermediation, we distinguish between bare-bones DI schemes providing deposit insurance guarantee only for deposit banks (Bulgaria, Poland, Slovenia, Romania, Slovakia, and the Czech Republic), while other more sophisticated systems extend their scope to credit unions, savings and loan association (Lithuania, Latvia, Hungary, and Estonia).[5] The nationally recognized DI system usually covers also foreign banks' branches on its territory in case the home

Annual premiums (percent of base)	Risk-adjusted premiums: yes = 1 no = 0	Source of funding: private = 1 joint = 2 official = 3	Adminis-tration: private = 1 joint = 2 official = 3	Membership: compulsory = 1 voluntary = 0
Annual liabilities of 3.2 percent of guaranteed deposits held with the individual bank, there is an obligation to invest in first-rate, short-term securities in the amount equal to 2.5 percent of the guaranteed deposits held with the individual bank.	0	1	3	1

country of the foreign bank does not provide adequate deposit protection in terms of scope and size. The bare-bones DI system common among accession countries is a result of "universal" rather than specialized banks playing the most important role in financial intermediation (representing 86 percent of the financial markets in the accession countries on average) and of the unavailability of alternative direct financing opportunities (the average stock market capitalization as a percent of GDP is 15.8 percent).

Concerning the different kinds of deposits covered by the guarantee schemes, there are two contrasting approaches as summarized by Garcia (1999) and Demirgüç-Kunt, Kane, and Laeven (chapter 2). One is to cover depositors of all types at a low level of protection, which is easy to administer, and the other is to keep coverage low and to exclude some sophisticated depositors like financial institutions, governments, and large corporations to provide market discipline. In this way, DI systems can protect small depositors while larger creditors will monitor the condition of the banks. Thus, most systems in the accession countries cover natural and legal entities' (residents and nonresidents) deposits in national and foreign currency except in Romania, where only deposits of natural persons are protected, and in Estonia,

Slovenia, and Poland, where there is a special treatment of different corporate depositors. In addition to those deposits excluded from protection in the directive (interbank deposits, government deposit and some others), almost all ten accession countries prefer to keep the scope of coverage limited, and further exclude deposits of insurers, pension and insurance funds, privatization funds and deposits at other nonbank financial institutions. Concerning foreign currency deposits, the EU excludes some non-EU currency deposits from coverage, while all accession countries that insure foreign currency deposits reimburse them in national currency in order to avoid foreign currency risk.

Credit institutions' liabilities per depositor are set in terms of coverage limit, which should be low enough to encourage large depositors and sophisticated creditors to discipline their banks. The logic of defining the amount of coverage is to encompass a relatively high percentage of the number of accounts, but a smaller percentage of the total volume of deposits in the system (Garcia 1999). Speaking in nominal terms, countries that are ahead in their negotiation process with the EU have higher coverage limits like the Czech Republic, Slovakia, Slovenia, Poland, and Hungary,[6] while Bulgaria and Romania should logically be on the low coverage side. It is interesting to note that Estonia, Lithuania, and Latvia are lagging behind their peers from the first accession wave in terms of the nominal DI insurance, which we interpret as a country specific feature justified in the process of negotiation taking into account the possibility of increased moral hazard in their banking system. However, according to the directive all accession countries should attain the EU minimum coverage limit in foreseeable future.

With respect to coinsurance issues, since the directive permits EU member countries to decide whether to choose or avoid coinsurance, equal number of accession countries will either maintain or eliminate their existing coinsurance systems by 2004. Coinsurance means that depositors are contractually required to share in their bank's losses (usually up to a maximum percentage of deposits—10 percent) regardless of deposit size, thus curbing moral hazard and introducing market discipline (Demirgüç-Kunt and Huizinga 2004). The EMU countries also try to strike a balance between discouraging moral hazard and avoiding systemic runs by adopting a system of coinsurance, so almost half include coinsurance, while the other half does not. Although the coinsurance might impose some transaction costs in practice, it is a good sign that the country is interested in controlling moral hazard as illustrated by Hungary's recent introduction of coinsurance into its DI.

The contributions collected for DI funds are diverse in type and size and there is no binding requirement in the EU Directive on that subject. According to the common practice, they should be set according to the explicitly announced Fund target of accumulated resources. There is no doubt that DI funds need to be privately funded to encourage bankers to keep their institutions sound. There are mandatory annual premiums paid by commercial banks, but apart from them usually there are entry premiums (Bulgaria, Estonia, Hungary, Latvia, Romania, and Slovakia[7]), and under special circumstances special premiums are collected as well (Slovakia and Romania). The size of the annual premiums (some of them collected on a quarterly basis) to maintain a healthy fund should depend on the current condition of the banking system and its future prospects. Most commonly, the assessment base includes only insured deposits; however, there is an ex ante assistance fund in Poland, where annual contributions are based on total balance sheet assets and guarantees and off-balance sheet liabilities. In Slovenia there is no permanent fund, and the maximum annual liabilities payable by an individual bank amounts to 3.2 percent of the guaranteed deposits, as the commercial banks have the obligation to invest their premium in first-rate, short-term securities in the amount equal to 2.5 percent of the guaranteed deposits.

Little attention was paid to enforce market disciple through risk adjusted premiums as there is no consensus on this issue at the EU level (Garcia and Prast 2002; chapter 3, this volume). The directive gives full freedom to member countries and accession countries to choose whether or not premiums will be risk-adjusted. In the euro area half of the countries have introduced risk-adjusted premiums (Belgium, Finland, France, Germany, Italy, Portugal, and Spain), while others do not impose risk-adjusted premiums as an alternative means to address adverse selection. Among all accession countries, in Hungary the system of increased premium payment is based on the capital adequacy ratio as the maximum premium is 0.3 percent of the premium payment base. The risk-adjusted contribution system in Romania provides a special premium of 1.6 percent of total household deposits for banks conducting higher risk transactions. The extraordinary premiums in Slovakia are not due to risk adjustment but are related to the funding target.

The DI fund usually assumes the existence of a special body established explicitly by law with its functions described in a statute. On the debate whether to introduce ex ante or ex post DI system, the directive gives no recommendations. Consistent with common practice, accession countries are generally characterized by an ex ante funded DI system. Slovenia is the only exception with an ex post DI scheme (probably due to the lack of banking crisis experience) and it is not the only one in the EU since one third of the Euro Area has established ex post schemes—as in Italy, Austria, Luxemburg, and the Netherlands. Although it is more costly to maintain a permanent DI fund, there is much ambiguity in ex post DI systems regarding the base on which the insurance obligation is to be calculated as well as information sharing problems (Garcia 1999).

Following common practice, most DI systems in accession countries have a permanent fund managed by a legal entity with either mixed (private and official) or official administration (Latvia, Slovenia[8]). The choice between the private, mixed or officially managed DI funds raises a number of issues. Serving both the private deposit institutions' interests and the public interest, mixed or joint administrations usually involve private or nongovernment agencies and they have limited authorities, namely, their decisions need to be approved by the central bank. Government members should not dominate the board and no bankers can be present due to conflict of interest issues. The management of the DI funds involves investment activities of the money raised by banks' contributions. Investments opportunities are limited by the law as a major part of the resources are most often invested in government securities.

The funding and management of the fund is closely related to the backup funding when the resources of the fund become insufficient for the payment of insured and inaccessible deposits. There are three DI systems among accession countries which are entirely funded by the private sector (Lithuania, Slovenia, and the Czech Republic). Apart from the credit institutions' contributions, in the Czech Republic additional resources can be raised on the market. In Lithuania, where there are sectoral insurance funds, when the DI fund is short of resources while the other has such resources, insurance compensations may be paid by the fund possessing the resources. There is no permanent fund in Slovenia; hence the central bank can temporarily finance it until the contributions of the banks are collected. In the other seven countries the additional resources are collected either from official or private sources. The lack of explicitly announced fund target for most of the accession countries could lead to insufficient resources in time of need.

The principal duties of all deposit guarantee institutions are to determine and collect the premiums, invest its assets and pay the guaranteed amount of deposits. Since deposit reimbursement is usually provoked by declaring a bank insolvent, most DI funds in accession countries have some additional functions and powers provided by the law on bank bankruptcy in the context of safety nets. The fund in Poland has a second explicit function apart from DI, which is bank failure avoidance. In fulfillment of its task, the fund may extend to the entities covered by the deposit guarantee system, loans, guarantees or endorsements on conditions that are better than generally offered by banks (although with limitations under certain conditions). This financial assistance is provided by the separate assistance fund. In order to increase the reliability and stability of the financial sector, the fund in Hungary also has other functions like granting credits, subordinate loans, acquisition of ownership participation in a credit institution, providing cover for the transfer of stock deposits against adequate collateral.

8.3   Overinsurance in Accession Countries

One conclusion of the brief comparative study of the different DI systems in accession countries is that some countries have already coverage limits close or above the level required by the EU Directive (e.g., Poland, the Czech Republic, Hungary, Slovenia). If we do not look at absolute but rather at relative coverage (coverage ratio) the picture of overinsurance is confirmed. Assuming best practice optimal coverage of deposits is about one to two times GDP per capita, and taking into account that the indicator for the Euro Area (1.3) is lower than the world average, it is obvious that the average coverage ratio of the accession countries (2.8) is above the optimal and much higher than the Euro Area-level (about two times the ratio for the euro area). In relative or real terms overprotection spreads among other countries as well, like Bulgaria (3.1) and Lithuania (2.9), which in nominal terms do not seem to be overprotected. Among the accession countries under study, countries with the lowest coverage ratio are Estonia (1.0), followed by Slovenia (1.6), Romania (1.6),[9] and Latvia (1.8).

Putting DI coverage limits of accession countries and individual EMU members together (figure 8.1), there is a clear inverse relationship

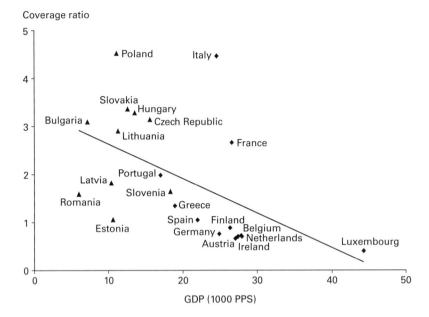

Figure 8.1
Coverage ratios in accession countries and the euro area
Sources: Data for 2004, PPS—purchasing power standard; Eurostat, national DI funds, national statistical institutes, European Commission.

between income per capita and coverage ratio for the whole group. If we may interpret the trend line as the average coverage ratio for the whole area, all countries that fall above the line are overinsured, including Italy and France. The high coverage ratios in these countries are a result of their banking sector instability during the 1990s. In 1994–1995 Credit Lyonnais experienced serious solvency problems in France, which is regarded as the largest bank failure up to that time in the country. Similarly, since 1990 there has been huge banking restructuring in Italy (Caprio and Klingebiel 2003).

At the same time, it is interesting to note that over time some of the accession countries plan to move beyond the minimum requirements of the EU Directive (see table 8.2). After 1999, the prohibition of high export coverage was eliminated and now there is no maximum guarantee limit, which allows for nominal and real overprotection although this could create moral hazard. It is important to notice that countries joining the EU at the same time have set different coverage development programs. For example, Hungary has joined the Czech Republic, Poland, Slovakia, and Slovenia, whereas the Baltic countries are slower

Table 8.2
Development of the coverage limit in some accession countries

Years	2004	2005	2006	2007	2008
Bulgaria	7,670 ⟶	12,782 ————————————⟶		20,042	
Estonia	6,391 ⟶	12,782 ——————————————————⟶			20,000
Lithuania	14,484 ——————————————⟶			17,380 ⟶	20,000
Latvia	8,535 ——————————⟶		12,802 ——————————⟶		18,492
Hungary	25,000				

Notes and sources: Coverage limit in EUR calculated on the base of the exchange rate at the end of 2004. Information provided by surveys, the Internet database of the NIDF of Hungary (http://www.oba.hu/) and national legislations.

in converging to the level required by the EU Directive. Setting coverage limits can be seen as a negotiation process and political will, suggesting that those countries have negotiated optimal coverage ratios, paying special attention to limiting moral hazard by increasing DI coverage limits slowly, and will reach the EU minimum at the very end of the financial integration process. The growth in coverage limit is part of the overall safety net and will be affected by the monetary regime practiced in the countries. Not surprisingly, the three of the Baltic states have fixed exchange rate regimes (currency boards), which limits the flexibility of the safety nets, putting constraints on the lender of last resort (LLR) function.

Another factor that is closely related to the development of the coverage limit in the accession countries is the dominant presence of foreign-owned banks that represent 76.4 percent of total banking system assets (table 8.3). The presence of foreign banks inevitably stimulates the introduction of similar DI systems like in their home countries. Hence we can identify a relationship between the share of foreign ownership in the banking system and the coverage limit among the accession countries. The hypothesis of overinsurance could also be supported by the banking supervision features and particularly capital adequacy requirement of commercial banks, since in the accession countries under study, solvency ratio is de jure and de facto considerably higher than the international standards.

As DI is an element of the overall safety net, this coverage has to be analyzed jointly with other characteristics of the banking systems. The accession countries have a low share of deposits to GDP ratio (42.8 percent) compared to the Euro Area average (81.9 percent) and there are great differences among the banking systems of different accession

Table 8.3

Some deposit insurance relevant indicators in accession countries

Country	Coverage ratio	Total capital adequacy ratio		Foreign ownership (percent of total assets)	Deposits/ GDP (percent)	GDP per capita (in 1000 PPS)
		Law provision	Practice			
Bulgaria	3.1	12	22.2	85.0	36.6	7.2
Czech Republic	3.1	8	14.5	96.0	56.3	15.6
Estonia	1.1	10	14.3	97.3	35.5	10.6
Hungary	3.3	8	11.9	83.3	38.4	13.5
Latvia	1.8	10	10.3	47.2	24.8	10.4
Lithuania	2.9	10	13.2	95.6	23.9	11.3
Poland	4.5	8	13.8	69.2	33.4	11.1
Romania	1.6	12	18.2	58.2	21.8	6.0
Slovakia	3.4	8	21.6	96.3	49.8	12.6
Slovenia	1.6	8	11.6	36.0	53.6	18.3
Accession countries	2.8		15	76.4	42.6	11.7
Euro area (average)	1.3	8	9.9	15	81.9	24.7

Notes and sources: Data for the coverage ratio and GDP per capita valid at year-end 2004, the rest valid at year-end 2003. Deposits in Euro Area include demand (overnight) deposits, deposits with agreed maturity and deposits redeemable at notice in other MFIs, and deposits in accession countries include demand, time, savings and foreign currency deposits. ECB, European Commission database, annual reports.

countries. This might support the logic of establishing a coverage limit, which covers a relatively high percentage of the number of accounts but a smaller percentage of the total value of deposits in the system. However, calculating the optimal coverage limit, the DIF staff should take into consideration the distribution of deposits. Although we do not have such data at our disposal, GDP per capita could be a good proxy to show that the distribution of deposits in accession countries is skewed towards small deposits much more than in developed countries and the Euro Area. This also suggests that the majority of the deposits in accession countries is likely to be fully covered, reducing the incentives of depositors to monitor and impose market discipline.

Taking all these factors together, we see that there is overinsurance of deposits in accession countries. Furthermore, coinsurance practices are weak and premiums are not risk-adjusted. By 2004 only half of the accession countries include coinsurance in their DI systems (Lithuania,

Figure 8.2
Prospective stages of DI development in accession countries

Poland, Hungary, the Czech Republic, and Estonia) while only two impose risk-adjusted premiums. Although they are likely to improve market discipline, these features are not explicitly encouraged by the EU Directive,[10] and hence they were neglected by most accession countries in the process of their legal harmonization.

8.4   The Reasons for Overinsurance in Accession Countries

Why is there overinsurance in accession countries? The answer to this question can be found only when DI is studied in the context of the systemic change which characterized all accession countries.[11] The accession economies and their financial systems were subjected to two exogenous events, political and global in nature. The collapse of the centrally planned economies was shortly followed (sometimes with a short period of time of not more than few years) by the prospective of EU enlargement and integration into the European financial arena. Almost all accession countries suffered from some form of financial crisis during the transition, and most often reforms in DI systems occurred either in the depth of a crisis or shortly after that. Before DI was established, all accession countries had implicit and full state guarantee, inherited from the socialist regime. The establishment of the explicit DI was also in line with the goal of harmonization with the EU Directives and integration with the developed financial systems of the EU. Hence, the different stages of the DI adoption and design in accession countries is associated with their process of EU integration (figure 8.2), which we analyze in the following sections.

8.4.1   The Legacy of the Centrally Planned Economy
The centrally planned economies were conceptually designed to be low risk, giving full protection to the savings and other deposits of the population.[12] The savings and other deposits were a part of the centralized monetary plan and the deposits were concentrated in the so-called

state saving funds.[13] In contrast to the enterprises, individuals had their deposits at their disposal and they could withdraw them at any time.[14] The administrative control of the financial system substituted for the market discipline which is vital in market economies. There was no need for developing a safety net because according to the system ideology, the public was the co-owner of the national wealth (national product).

The government took decisions on behalf of the economic agents and the population gradually lost its sensitivity toward risk.[15] After the collapse of the centrally planned economy and the start of the basic reforms (liberalization and privatization), in a short time a two-tier banking system was established by converting the ex-branches of the monobank into independent banks. The central bank started conducting active monetary policy. Large, loss-making, state-owned enterprises in different sectors of the economy were transferred to the banking sector and the budget. The active monetary policy was also combined with lack of banking expertise, weak bank regulation and supervision, and barriers against foreign entry.

In spite of the early signs of the banking problems in the 1990s, the implicit DI was still in place and the population believed that the state would take responsibility and reimburse the depositors in case of banking crises. Economic agents were willing to take a higher risk against relatively lower returns. This was true not only for the depositors who placed their money with more unstable banks in return for higher interest rates, but also for the banks as well, which invested their money in risky and potentially unprofitable investments. Among some accession countries different kinds of financial pyramids and schemes appeared that led to income and wealth redistribution (Bulgaria, Romania, and others). Although accession countries had different monetary and exchange rate regimes,[16] the overall dynamics of the transition was similar and can be described in the following pattern: the central banks monetized the losses as it was difficult to distinguish between their LLR function and monetary policy.[17] In the context of the safety nets there were discrepancies between its elements—the deposits were de jure implicitly fully insured, the LLR function was abused and the bank regulation was weak (leaving aside corruption and fraud).

Inflation and the depreciation of the national currency benefited the debtors at the expense of the creditors (particularly those who held deposits and treasury bonds).[18] The winners (including the banks) had no interest in changing the system of implicit DI since the inflation helped them to achieve their goals. Therefore, the roots of the banking crises can be found in the weak credit culture, lack of market discipline, which were exacerbated by the weak bank regulation, the underdeveloped institutional environment, and barriers against entry of foreign banks. The overinsurance and systemic moral hazard continued the exploitation by the winners of the systemic change.

8.4.2 Reforms

During the transition that led to financial crises, the implicit state protection came into conflict with the gradually developing market mechanisms. In order to calm down the population, to avoid further problems in the national financial systems and to restore the credibility in the banking sector and national currencies, the monetary authorities decided to replace the old DI system with a modern explicit one. Though accession countries introduced the explicit DI systems at different times, the common element between them is that these were times of financial difficulty (see table 8.4).[19] Among the ten CEEC, Hungary and the Czech Republic are the first to introduce the explicit DI (in 1993 and 1994, respectively) in line with the dynamics of their transition processes and in response to problems in their banking sector.[20]

Most of the other accession countries set up the new DI practice in 1995 and 1996 soon after the approval of the EU Directive with the view to provide explicit deposit protection in their fragile banking sectors. In 1995 Lithuania had problems with the credibility of its banking sector and had to close eighteen out of twenty-five banks. Poland in the early 1990s experienced huge bank insolvency problems which led to recapitalization costs equivalent to 2 percent of GDP in 1993, Bulgaria's banking and financial crisis started in 1995 when the explicit DI system was introduced and ended in hyperinflation in the beginning of 1997. In the same period, Romania suffered from a domestic currency crisis which imposed large-scale banking restructuring, and Slovakia took measures to boost banking intermediation and precautions against bank panics, as its financial system was very sensitive to the condition of the financial problems in the Czech Republic (due to their common economic development in the past as Czechoslovakia). Latvia and Estonia delayed the explicit DI introduction to 1998 as both of them experienced a strong impact of the Russian crisis.[21] Slovenia is the last to introduce the explicit deposit guarantee scheme in 2001 because it

Table 8.4
Financial and banking crises in accession countries

Country	Bulgaria	Czech Republic	Estonia	Hungary	Latvia	Lithuania	Poland	Romania	Slovak Republic	Slovenia
Banking crises*	1995–1997	1992–1995	1992–1995	1991–1995	1995–1999	1995–1996	1991–1996	1990–1998	1991–1997	1992–1994
Financial crises**	1996–1997	1997	Stock market crash in 1997 and Russian crisis impact in 1998	1994–1995	Russian crisis impact in 1998	1995–1996, and Russian crisis impact in 1998	High exchange rate volatility in 1998 and Brazilian crisis impact	1996–1997 banking crisis	1997–1998	no
Deposit insurance introduction	1995	1994	1998	1993	1998	1996	1995	1996	1996	2001
Exchange rate development**	Floating up to 1997, after that currency board	Fixed ER up to 1996, managed float since 1997	Currency board since 1992	Frequently adjusted peg, crawling peg in 1995, crawling band since 1998	Fixed ER	Floating rates up to 1994, then currency board	Adjustable peg, crawling peg in 1991, crawling bands in 1995, fully floating since 2000	Managed float	Fixed ER to a basket with a fluctuation band, since September 1998 managed float	Managed float

Notes and sources: Data valid until year-end 2003. * Information from Caprio and Kindgebiel 2003. ** Information from Árvai and Vincze 2000 and Blaszkievicz et al. 2004.

did not experience severe banking crisis, delayed the process of banking privatization and hence had a low level of foreign ownership in its banking system.

As discussed in chapter 2, crises are the worst times to introduce explicit DI. However, countries are often tempted to begin a limited explicit DI system when a crisis is imminent or in progress in the mistaken belief that it will avoid or cure the crisis. Have accession countries chosen the optimal DI system and coverage limit? As very low coverage levels will not prevent uninsured depositors from running, most accession countries considered setting higher coverage rates although at the beginning they were lower than required by the EU Directive. Another reason for setting higher coverage rates in times of crises is that it is difficult to determine whether the public is going to withdraw its deposits from the weak banks selectively and deposit in the safe ones, or whether all banks are perceived to be weak, leading to a systemic crisis (as in the case of the Czech Republic, Bulgaria, and Romania). Setting a high yet limited coverage does not solve the dilemma, as it may not prevent runs of those depositors who are above the limit, and it may prove to be politically very difficult to reduce the coverage limit afterwards in order to reduce moral hazard. Faced with a systemic crisis, Garcia (1999) recommends a country either to (1) retain its existing implicit (full) guarantee, or (2) set explicit, but full and temporary guarantee.[22]

Accession countries applied neither of the two prescriptions. The implicit insurance was not adequate as a feature of the old centrally planned economy in the process of transition on one hand, and in response to the worldwide development of new financial safety net, on the other hand. Any form of full DI was out of question because the authorities and the other groups of interest (private debtors) did not want to bear the accumulated losses due to their irresponsible actions that lead to mass outbreak of crises in the mid-1990s. During periods of major transformation, it is easy to give up the responsibilities designated by the old system and introduce new rules. The establishment of explicit DI at that time was justified and closely connected with countries' commitment to the EU integration process. Hence, accession countries set high limited real coverage levels as the nominal coverage levels were not very high at the beginning, however, aiming to achieve the target minimums of the EU Directive in a short time. Crises considerations and the need to ensure stability overshadowed the reductions in market discipline the explicit DI would entail. However, as a result of the financial crises, strict banking supervision was also enforced, some improvements in the bankruptcy law were introduced, the monetary policy became rule-based (such as the introduction of the currency board in Bulgaria), and hard budget constraints were imposed.

8.4.3   Regulations on Deposit Insurance

Soon after the collapse of the centrally planned economy, all accession countries decided to join the EU. The process of accession requires both nominal convergence and real integration. Apart from many other aspects, integration includes legislative harmonization as the regulations in the field of DI (EU Directive on DI, chapter 3 of the negotiation package), requiring the countries to establish DI with the minimum level of coverage regardless of the conditions in their banking systems. Therefore, the explicit DI was once again exogenously imposed under systemic change circumstances. As we saw in most accession countries it was an emergency measure in critical times, while we can envision Slovenia as the only exclusion to this rule since it introduced explicit DI in the late 2001 under normal circumstances. Although pressed by the turmoil in their financial sectors in the early 1990s, Estonia and Latvia not only delayed the introduction of the explicit DI (1998), but also negotiated the lowest starting coverage limits among the ten CEEC. According to their timetable they plan to reach the EU minimum level in 2008 at the earliest, trying to achieve a better synchronization with the functioning of the other elements of the safety net (currency boards, development of financial intermediation and supervision).[23]

The process of accession to the EU should imply that nominal and real integration go hand in hand, although the observations of the ten CEEC show that nominal harmonization not only is far ahead of the real synchronization but it does not contribute to the real integration as argued (Süppel 2003). Being new members or having just signed the accession contract, all countries have implemented the EU legislation, although the performance of the sectors is far behind the one in the euro area (table 8.5).[24] Above all, we want to focus on the fact that financial intermediation in accession countries is dominated by the commercial banks (96.4 percent) and there is a high concentration in the banking sector (66 percent), although there is no obvious positive correlation between the two. The former has implications for monetary policy and safety net issues in the enlarged EMU.

Despite the fact that the banking sector appears profitable (average ROA $= 1.3$ and average ROE $= 15$), this is not so when the rate of

Table 8.5
Banking systems indicators in accession countries and the Euro Area

Country/indicator	Bulgaria	Czech Republic	Estonia	Hungary	Latvia	Lithuania	Poland	Romania	Slovak Republic	Slovenia	Euro Area
Market share of commercial banks (percent)	100	99.9	100	85	100	100	94.7	91.9	94.2	98.7	
Concentration index (CR5) for CI (percent)	52.2	65.8	99	52.3	63.1	81.6	52.3	61.7	67.5	67.4	53
ROE	18.7	22.5	15.6	16.7	18.9	11.1	5.7	15.6	15.0	10.2	8.2
ROA	2.0	1.2	1.5	1.3	1.3	1.3	0.5	2.2	1.2	0.6	1.1
Interest margin	6.3	3.0	2.7	2.5	2.7	4.9	7.7	15.4	4.7	5.1	
Stock market capitalization (as percent of GDP)	7.9	16.5	37.4	18.7	9.6	17.2	17.2	6.4	3.5	23.3	68.0
Domestic credit to private sector (as percent of GDP)	25.8	17.9	33.7	42.3	38.8	19.9	17.8	9.5	25.0	43.3	117.0
Nonperforming loans (as percent of total loans)	4.4	5.0	0.5	3.8	1.5	2.6	25.1	1.6	9.1	9.4	3.4
EBRD Index of banking sector reform	3.3	3.7	3.7	4.0	3.7	3.0	3.3	2.7	3.3	3.3	
EBRD index of reform in non-bank financial institutions	2.3	3.0	3.3	3.7	3.0	3.0	3.7	2.0	2.7	2.7	

Sources: ECB (2004, 2005), EBRD 2004 and annual reports for national central banks.
Note: Data refer to the year 2003.

inflation is taken into account. The higher coverage ratios do not only increase the moral hazard in the national banking systems but also contribute to lower efficiency of banks in accession countries as expressed in high interest margins (5.5 percent) and credit growth rates (ECB 2005; EBRD 2004). This view is also reinforced by the fact that the quality of asset portfolios are very strong on average, with a share of nonperforming loans to total loans at 6.3 percent compared to 3.4 percent for the Euro Area. Although the EDBR index of banking reforms (3.3) illustrates that accession countries have achieved substantial progress in strengthening their prudential regulation and supervision framework, there is still room for more improvement. The moral hazard and low banking efficiency are particularly important issues in countries with fixed exchange rates or currency board (Estonia, Bulgaria, Lithuania, and Latvia) where the LLR function is limited,[25] causing concerns about exchange rate stability during ERM II.

Nominal harmonization and the real integration of the financial sectors depend on the whole institutional environment in the accession countries. Since they are natural buffers (or the compensating mechanisms) against the moral hazard imposed by the explicit DI, recent empirical studies show that the negative effects of DI on financial sector stability and efficiency can be significant in countries with weak regulatory and institutional settings.[26] Demirgüç-Kunt and Detragiache (2002) show that the poor institutional environment enforces the deteriorating effect of DI on bank fragility, Laeven (2002), and Demirgüç-Kunt and Huizinga (2002) argue that it reduces market discipline by lowering banks' interest rate costs and making it less sensitive to bank risk and liquidity. The vital institutional environment which might cushion the negative effects of the established practice of deposit overinsurance is not developed enough in accession countries in comparison to the EU (table 8.6). In terms of regulatory quality, rule of law, political stability, control of corruption, government effectiveness, and voice and accountability (WB database on government effectiveness indicators) accession countries lag quite a bit behind the euro zone average level (except in terms of political stability, where surprisingly Slovenia and Hungary are the leaders). Bulgaria and Romania rank last, as we might expect, since they have always been criticized by the European Commission for their poor regulatory quality, rule of law, and corruption practices. The picture presented by the economic freedom indicators is similar, with remarkable advances for Estonia, whose institutions have been developing, enforcing the excellent performance of its market economy.

Table 8.6
Indicators of institutional environment and performance

Indicators	Bulgaria	Czech Republic	Estonia	Hungary	Latvia	Lithuania	Poland	Romania	Slovak Republic	Slovenia	Eurozone
Governance indicators											
Voice and accountability	66.7	74.7	80.3	85.4	75.3	73.7	83.3	61.1	76.3	82.8	91.3
Political stability	64.3	84.9	82.7	88.6	77.8	80	69.7	58.4	84.3	90.8	87.2
Government effectiveness	56.2	73.7	74.7	74.2	72.2	70.6	71.1	46.4	67.5	76.8	91.6
Regulatory quality	69.6	82	86.6	84	75.8	79.4	71.1	55.7	73.2	75.3	91.6
Rule of law	55.7	73.2	74.7	78.9	67.5	68	70.6	54.1	65.5	83.5	91.6
Control of corruption	52.6	68.6	74.2	73.7	60.8	64.4	69.1	45.4	64.9	80.4	91.3
Economic freedom indicators											
Economic freedom	3.1	2.4	1.8	2.6	2.4	2.2	2.8	3.7	2.4	2.7	2.2
Trade policy	2	3	1	3	2	2	2	3	3	2	2.0
Fiscal burden	2.4	3.6	2	2	2.1	2.8	2.9	3.3	1.8	3.4	3.9
Government intervention	2.5	2.5	2	2	2.5	2	2	2.5	2	2.5	2.5
Monetary policy	2	1	1	2	1	1	1	5	3	3	1.3
Foreign investment	3	2	1	2	2	2	3	4	2	3	1.7
Banking and finance	2	1	1	2	2	1	2	3	1	3	2.1
Wages and prices	2	2	2	3	2	2	3	3	2	2	2.2
Property rights	4	2	2	2	3	3	3	4	3	3	1.5
Regulation	4	3	2	3	3	3	3	4	3	2	2.8
Informal market	3.5	3.5	2.5	3	3.5	3	3.5	4	3.5	2.5	1.7

Sources: 2002 World Bank database on Governance Indicators and 2005 Index of Economic Freedom, Heritage Foundation.

As far as insolvency law is concerned, the EBRD (2004) legal indicator survey finds that there is no common relationship between the extensiveness of the bankruptcy law and its effectiveness. For example, in spite of the high level of compliance with the international insolvency standards in some accession countries like Bulgaria and Slovak Republic, there is low speed, efficiency, and predictability in the resolution of insolvency cases. In Hungary and Slovenia, the opposite is true. Another observation is that the insolvency regimes tend to be more favorable to debtor initiated processes, which sheds light on the weaknesses in other areas of the institutional environment such as the protection of creditors' rights.

8.5   Possible Consequences of Overinsurance in Accession Countries: Discussion

Tracing DI back to the centrally planned economies, we can conclude that accession countries have kept the high levels of insurance throughout the whole transition process and this might have two consequences. First, from the point of view of the accession countries, the efficiency of the banking system may be undermined and hence probability of banking crisis may be increased. And second, from the prospective of the EMU enlargement, this could deteriorate the conditions of the banking system of the whole Euro Area and inevitably have an indirect impact on the common monetary policy and on its transmission mechanism.

First, the overly generous deposit insurance may reduce the efficiency of the banking systems in accession countries, and increase the risks through interest spreads. There is some support for this hypothesis since in econometric studies DI has been shown to increase lending interest rates rather than to decrease deposit rates (Carapella and Di Giorgio 2004). Furthermore, according to Demirgüç-Kunt and Detragiache (2004), DI deteriorates market discipline by decreasing deposit interest rates and lowering the risk elasticity of the interest rates. The results of these studies could partially explain the high lending deposit interest spreads observed in accession countries (5.5 percent) as well as the higher than the euro area growth rate of credit.

Second, DI as an element of safety net should contribute to bank sector stability. However, DI overinsurance might increase the level of asymmetric information and the likelihood of banking crisis (Demirgüç-Kunt and Detragiache 1997).[27] A quick look at the time dynamics of the introduction of the explicit DI and the occurrence of bank crises would lead us to argue that even if DI does not predict a bank crisis, it is not able to prevent them either. Therefore, we can presume that moral hazard in accession countries will not be decreased due to the existing explicit limited DI schemes but rather that it will increase.[28] This vulnerability to banking instability is likely to contradict the requirements of ERM II on interest rates and exchange rates, and EMU integration might turn out to be very costly for accession countries.

Third, from the EU point of view, the increase of bank crisis probability in accession countries, ceteris paribus, combined with the uneven development of the banking sectors, could be potentially translated into an increased probability of crisis in the whole European banking system. The dominant role of commercial banks in financial intermediation combined with high bank concentration in the accession countries may have important implications for monetary policy and safety net issues. The DI systems (and to a lesser degree the access to LLR refinancing) gives a unique advantage to commercial banks in offering loan commitments with fixed formula floating interest rates over investment banks which specialize in loans for corporate restructuring, and insurance companies that provide longer-term fixed interest rate spot loans (Booth and Booth 2004). Hence, DI may deter the expected enhancement of the financial services competition and the interest lending deposit margin will stay higher than in the Euro Area.

Furthermore, the banking sectors in the ten CEEC are dominated by foreign (mainly EU-15) banks and their parent banks have recently reported increasing dependence on earnings from the CEEC in their total operating profits, especially because of the high competition/low margins in their home markets. The strong ownership links between the EU and the ten CEEC may give rise to a risk transmission channel within the enlarged EU as adverse effects could be quite uneven with a stronger impact on the systemic risk in accession countries (ECB 2005). From the point of view of EMU integration, the exchange rate regimes in accession countries are more inclined to be fixed (ERM II or the currency boards), which constrains the flexibility of the functioning of the safety nets and eventually increases banking crisis likelihood. During the ERM II period, ECB has no liability to perform LLR function in the accession countries but only when they become full members. However, it is arguable whether the European Central Bank (ECB) will really take refinancing actions since on the one hand, these new members will not be significant for the whole Eurozone system, but on the other hand, big European banking groups might have a strategic presence in the accession countries. As a whole, in the case of potential problems, the costs of overcoming the crisis would be unevenly distributed—the richer countries in the EU would be burdened with greater expenses than the poorer new members.

Hence, meeting the requirements for nominal harmonization,[29] which are not in compliance with the real development of the financial sectors in accession countries, could have an adverse result—increasing the probability of financial crisis and decreasing the efficiency of the enlarged European banking system. The problems that will be encountered by the common fiscal and monetary policies will not be minor and could not be discarded (although we do not describe them here in detail).[30]

One of the purposes of the nominal harmonization of the European legislation in the field of DI is to avoid competition among national banking systems via DI. In fact, in the presence of different real deposit coverage levels (as a ratio to the GDP per capita), banks in accession countries are "punished" in terms of the higher expenses they bear (higher capital adequacy ratios, lower than the potential banking sector efficiency, etc.). However, it is not likely that the higher level of DI in accession countries will attract deposits from the EU countries and lead to economies of scale in fund-raising. The overinsurance of deposits in accession countries (combined with the higher capital adequacy requirements) would cause higher costs for banking intermediation not only in accession countries but also in the Euro Area as a whole.

Some practical solutions are possible. Probably, next to the best practice solutions like coinsurance and risk-weighted premiums, we can propose some more specific ones in accession countries. For example, despite the advancing nominal harmonization process, it would be better to link increases in DI coverage to GDP dynamics and indicators of banking system development. Such reconsideration of the DI convergence process would benefit not only the accession countries to avoid banking-sector instability and successful adherence to the ERM II, but also the EMU as a whole by achieving a better integrated banking system with lower likelihood of banking crisis and more efficient/symmetric monetary policy transmission mechanism. In order to enhance market discipline, it seems to be reasonable to allow for institutional competition in DI, similar to the model of fiscal competition. Whatever measures will be taken on behalf of the accession countries and EU depends not only on their economic justification but also the question of political realization and will.

Notes

1. See for a survey ECB 2004, Tang, Zoli, and Klytchnikova 2000, Enoch, Guide, and Hardy 2002, and Caprio and Klingebiel 2003.

2. In some sense, we can speak of genetically inherited systemic moral hazard or moral hazard path dependence.

3. See, for example, Demirgüç-Kunt and Detragiache 1997, Demirgüç-Kunt and Huzinga 2004, Carapella and Di Giorgio 2004. For theoretical aspects of DI and financial regulation as a whole, see the discussion in *Economic Journal*, particularly Dowd 1996, Benston and Kaufman 1996 and Dow 1996, as well as Garcia 1999, and Dale 2000. Concerning the role of DI in the system of financial regulation, see Llewellyn 2001, while on the specificities of deposit guaranty in the financial system of accession countries, see Hermes and Lensink 2000 and Scholtens 2000. For a detailed description of financial sector development in transition economies during the first decade, see Bonin and Wachtel 2002, Thimann 2002, EBRD 2004, and ECB 2005.

4. For an earlier and detailed comparison, see Nenovsky and Dimitrova 2003.

5. Among them the DI system in Estonia is the most developed one extending its coverage to funds deposited by clients of credit, investment institutions, and unit holders of mandatory pension funds. However, there are three sectoral funds raised by different institutions and used for different purposes.

6. The EU Directive provides for limiting the minimum guaranteed amount to a certain percentage of deposits that should not be less than 90 percent of the total deposited amount, and for the guarantee to be up to the amount of 20,000 euros.

7. It is interesting to note that in Slovakia the central bank participates in the DI system with an entry premium and in Latvia both the budget and the central bank.

8. The management of the Deposit Guarantee Fund in Latvia is ensured by the Financial and Capital Market Commission, while in Slovenia the fund is run by the central bank.

9. The real coverage ratio for Romania is higher as it is said that the nominal coverage limit should be adjusted to inflation twice a year.

10. During the negotiations leading to the directive, German views prevailed and the proposal for a mandatory ceiling on protection and for a requirement of coinsurance was rejected, on the grounds that the dangers of moral hazard had been overstated (Garcia and Prast 2002).

11. An analysis of the system change is offered by Kornai (2000). A review of the theoretical disputes about the character, the forms of centrally planned economies' transformation, as well as some summaries can be found in Roland 2002.

12. For more details on planed economy, see Atlas 1969, Sevic 2002, and Litviakov 2003.

13. Apart form the monetary plan, there was a credit plan as well (often divided into short-term and long-term part), which reflected the artificial separation of the money flows between cash and noncash corresponding to the two money functions: means of exchange and store of value. Deposits were included into the credit plan and were accounted as resources.

14. We have to remind that there was an artificial division between the consumer and investment goods (which is described in details in the theoretical models of Oscar Lange),

as the former allowed some market elements, the latter was totally centrally planned until the very end of the collapse of the regime. The dynamics of the deposits was closely related with the dynamics of the consumer goods' deficit (analyzed in the models of Janos Kornai; see Kornai 2000, which determined to a great extent the interest rates on deposits (Litviakov 2003).

15. The phenomenon of low-risk culture is a theoretical parallel to the role of DI in protecting naïve consumers of financial services in the theoretical framework if DI models.

16. It seems that countries which started the reforms with a fixed exchange rate and passive monetary policy were more successful.

17. Berlemann and Nenovsky (2004) analyze the evolution of the LLR function in Bulgaria.

18. For the political economy approach of the DI, see Laeven 2004. In Nenovsky and Rizopoulos 2003, the political economy approach is applied to the transition form discretionary central bank to the currency board regime in Bulgaria.

19. For details about financial crises, see Caprio and Klingebiel 2003.

20. The Czech Republic had a significant banking system under the socialist regime and suffered from a banking crisis in the period 1993–1995, while Hungary in particular is characterized by a strong corporate sector with extensive access to financing abroad due to the high share of multinationals (Caviglia, Kraus, and Thimann 2002) as in 1993 eight banks (25 percent of financial system assets) were deemed insolvent.

21. The banking system in Latvia was very fragile between 1994–1995 when thirty-five banks saw their licenses revoked, were closed, or ceased operation. In Estonia by 1995 the insolvent banks accounted for 41 percent of the GDP, and in 1997 there was a stock market crash.

22. Sweden and Finland offered temporary full coverage during the Nordic banking crises, which later on was replaced by a system of limited coverage. Note that others, such as Mexico, had a difficult time claiming back coverage, however (see chapter 2).

23. The negotiation about AC integration into the EU is a matter of politics and should be studied in the context of groups of interests and other approaches in the field of social sciences.

24. For a comprehensive comparison of the integration of the financial systems of the new EU members, see ECB 2005.

25. Under currency board, the foreign reserves are used not only to pay the foreign debt, to cover the money base, to maintain the pegged exchange rate, but also to guarantee the deposits.

26. For different aspects of the relationship between the institutional development and efficiency of the banking system, see Barth, Caprio, and Levine 2001.

27. According to Demirgüç-Kunt and Huizinga (2004, 396) "Overgenerous protection of banks may easily introduce risk enhancing moral hazard, and destabilize the very system it is meant to protect." Theoretical foundations of moral hazard development under banking regulation are discussed by Freixas and Rochet 1999; see also Calomiris 1999.

28. About the relation between DI and systemic risk, see Llewellyn 2001. On one hand, deposit guarantee protects against bank panic (in the model of Diamond and Dybvig

1983), namely, systemic risk decreases, while on the other hand, it triggers moral hazard thus increasing the systemic risk.

29. Referring to the harmonization of the deposit insurance in the EU see Garcia and Prast 2002, Huizinga and Nicodeme 2002, Gropp and Vesala 2001.

30. Undoubtedly, there would be certain macroeconomic consequences on the level of the common monetary policy conducted by ECB, and on the fiscal policy synchronization process since while the monetary policy is centralized, the banking supervision stays on a national level).

References

Árvai, Zsófia, and János Vincze. 2000. Financial Crises in Transition Countries: Models and Facts. NBH Working Paper no. 2000/6, National Bank of Hungary, Budapest Hungary.

Atlas, Zaharii. 1969. *Socialist Monetary System*. Moscow: Finance.

Barth, James, Gerard Caprio, and Ross Levine. 2001. Bank Regulation and Supervision: What Works Best?" Policy Research Working Paper no. 2725, The World Bank, Washington, D.C.

Benston, George, and George Kaufman. 1996. The Appropriate Role of Bank Regulation. *Economic Journal* 106 (May): 688–697.

Berglof, Erik, and Patrick Bolton. 2002. The Great Divide and Beyond: Financial Architecture in Transition. *Journal of Economic Perspectives* 16 (1): 77–100.

Berlemann, Michael, and Nikolay Nenovsky 2004. Lending of First versus Lending of Last Resort: The Bulgarian Financial Crisis of 1996/1997. *Comparative Economic Studies* 46 (2): 245–271.

Błaszkievicz, Monika, Przemysław Kowalski, Łukacz Rawdanowicz, and Przemysław Woźniak. 2004. Harrod–Balassa Samuelson Effect in Selected Countries in Central and Eastern Europe. CASE Reports no. 57.

Bonin, John, and Paul Wachtel. 2002. Financial Sector Development in Transition Economies: Lessons from the First Decade. BOFIT Discussion Paper no. 9.

Booth, James, and Lena Booth. 2004. Deposit Insurance and Specialization in Commercial Bank Lending. *Review of Financial Economics* 13: 165–177.

Calomiris, Charles. 1999. Building and Incentive-Compatible Safety Net. *Journal of Banking and Finance* 23: 1499–1519.

Caprio, Gerard, and Daniela Klingebiel. 2003. Episodes of Systemic and Borderline Financial Crises. World Bank Financial Crises Database. Available at http://econ.worldbank.org/WBSITE/EXTERNAL/EXTDEC/EXTRESEARCH/0,,contentMDK:20699588~pagePK:64214825~piPK:64214943~theSitePK:469382,00.html.

Carapella, Francesca, and Giorgio Di Giorgio. 2004. Deposit Insurance, Institutions, and Bank Interest Rates. *Transition Studies Review* 11 (3): 77–92.

Caviglia, Giacomo, Gerhard Krause, and Christain Thimann. 2002. Key Features of the Financial Sectors in EU Accession Countries. In *Financial Sectors in EU Accession Countries*, ed. Christian Thimann. Frankfurt am Main: ECB Publication.

Commission of the European Communities. 2001. Report from the Commission on the Operation of the "Topping up" Provision, Article 4, paragraphs 2–5 of the Directive on Deposit Guarantee Schemes (94/19/EC).

Dale, Richard. 2000. Deposit Insurance in Theory and Practice. In Strengthening Financial Infrastructure—Deposit Insurance and Lending of Last Resort, ed. Richard Dale, France Bruni, and Christian de Boissieu. Amsterdam: Société Universitaire Européenne de Recherches Financières.

Demirgüç-Kunt, Asli, and Enrica Detragiache. 1997. The Determinants of Banking Crisis in Developing and Developed Countries. Working Paper no. 97/106. International Monetary Fund, Washington, D.C.

Demirgüç-Kunt, Asli, and Tolga Sobaci. 2001. Deposit Insurance around the World: A Database. World Bank Economic Review 15: 481–490.

Demirgüç-Kunt, Asli, and Harry Huzinga. 2004. Market Discipline and Deposit Insurance. Journal of Monetary Economics 51: 375–399.

Diamond, Douglas, and Philip, Dybvig. 1983. Bank Runs, Deposit Insurance, and Liquidity. Journal of Political Economy 91 (3): 401–419.

Dow, Sheila. 1996. Why the Banking System Should Be Regulated. Economic Journal 106 (May): 698–707.

Dowd, Kevin. 1996. The Case for Financial Laissez–faire. Economic Journal 106 (May): 679–687.

EBRD. 2004. Transition Report 2004. London: European Bank for Reconstruction and Development.

ECB. 2004. Financial Stability Review. Frankfurt, Germany: European Central Bank.

ECB. 2005. Banking Structures in the New EU Member States. Frankfurt, Germany: European Central Bank.

Enoch, Charles, Anne-Marie Guide, and Daniel Hardy. 2002. Banking Crises and Bank Resolution Experiences in Some Transition Economies. Working Paper no. 02/56, International Monetary Fund, Washington, D.C.

European Commission. 1994. Directive 94/19/EC of the European Parliament and of the Council of 30 May 1994 on Deposit-Guarantee Schemes. Official Journal of the European Communities L135: 5–14.

Freixas, Xavier, and Jean-Charles Rochet. 1999. Microeconomics of Banking. 4th ed. Cambridge, Mass.: MIT Press.

Garcia, Gillian. 1999. Deposits Insurance: A Survey and Best Practices. Working Paper no. 99/54, International Monetary Fund, Washington, D.C.

Garcia, Gillian, and Henriëtte Prast. 2002. Deposit and Investor Protection in the EU and the Netherlands: A Brief History. DNB Research Series Supervision No. 54, De Nederlandsche Bank, Amsterdam, The Netherlands.

Gropp, Reint, and Jukka Vesala. 2001. Deposit Insurance and Moral Hazard: Does the Counterfactual Matter?" Working Paper no. 47. ECB (March).

Hermes, Niels, and Robert Lensink. 2000. Financial System Development in Transition Economies. Journal of Banking and Finance 24: 507–524.

Huizinga, Harry, and Gaëtan Nicodème. 2002. Deposit Insurance and International Bank Deposits. EC Economic Paper no. 164 (February).

Kornai, Janos. 2000. What the Change of System from Socialism to Capitalism Does and Does Not Mean. *Journal of Economic Perspectives* 14 (1): 27–42.

Kyei, Alexander. 1995. Deposit Protection Arrangements: A Survey. IMF Working Paper no. 95/134, International Monetary Fund, Washington, D.C.

Laeven, Luc. 2002. Bank Risk and Deposit Insurance. *World Bank Economic Review* 16: 109–137.

Laeven, Luc. 2004. The Political Economy of Deposit Insurance. *Journal of Financial Services Research* 26: 201–224.

Llewellyn, David. 2001. A Regulatory Regime for Financial Stability. OeNB Working Paper no. 48, Austrian National Bank, Vienna.

Litviakov, Micheal. 2003. Monnaie et économie de pénurie en USSR. L'Harmattan, Collection, Pays de l'Est, Paris.

Nenovsky, Nikolay, and Kalina Dimitrova. 2003. Deposit Insurance during EU Accession. WDI Working Paper no. 617, William Davidson Institute, Michigan.

Nenovsky, Nikolay, and Yorgos Rizopoulos. 2003. Extreme Monetary Regime Change: Evidence from Currency Board Introduction in Bulgaria. *Journal of Economic Issues* 37 (December): 909–941.

Roland, Gerard. 2002. The Political Economy of Transition. *Journal of Economic Perspectives* 16 (1): 29–50.

Scholtens, Bert. 2000. Financial Regulation and Financial System Architecture in Central Europe. *Journal of Banking and Finance* 24: 525–553.

Sevic, Zeljko, ed. 2002. *Banking Rreforms in South-East Europe*. London: Edward Elgar.

Süppel, Ralph. 2003 Comparing Economic Dynamics in the EU and CEE Accession Countries. ECB Working Paper no. 267.

Tang, Helena, Edda, Zoli, and Irina Klytchnikova. 2000. Banking Crises in Transition Countries: Fiscal Costs and Related Issues. Policy Research Working Paper no. 2484, The World Bank, Washington, D.C.

Thimann, Christian, ed. 2002. *Financial Sectors in EU Accession Countries*. Frankfurt, Germany: European Central Bank.

9 Deposit Insurance Reform in Russia

Modibo K. Camara and Fernando Montes-Negret

9.1 Introduction

The adoption by the Russian Federation of a deposit insurance system (DIS) in late 2003 represents a significant development for Russia's banking system. However, taking away such functions from the Central Bank of Russia (CBR)—which is also vested with the banking regulatory and supervisory powers—and making the DIS mandatory to cover all banks—including the large, retail, publicly owned Savings Bank (Sberbank)—was not an easy task. Moreover, the new DIS was seen as a golden opportunity to "filter" some "undesirable banks," by requiring all banks to be de facto relicensed by the CBR.

In this chapter we assess the progress made in restructuring the Russian banking system with this instrument and we flag the remaining traditional (moral hazard) and new emerging challenges (coordination problems with the CBR). A general review of the literature on the pros and cons of deposit insurance systems will not be undertaken here as it can be found in chapter 1.

The chapter starts with a brief review of the key features of the Russian banking market (section 9.2), followed by a description of the Russian DIS and market evolution since its adoption (section 9.3). Subsequently, we discuss the risks of adopting a DIS in the Russian context per se, critically looking at the scope and sequencing of the reforms adopted (section 9.4). The rest of the chapter offers a more normative discussion of reform steps considered to be prerequisites to an effective deposit insurance system in Russia (section 9.5), followed by some concluding remarks (section 9.6).

Table 9.1
Overview of recent financial-sector evolution in Russia

	2000	2001	2002	2003	2004	2005
Number of institutions	1,311	1,319	1,329	1,329	1,299	1,253
of which: Banks	1,274	1,271	1,276	1,277	1,249	1,205
of which: licensed to take deposits	1,239	1,223	1,202	1,190	1,165	1,045
Nonbank credit institutions	37	48	53	52	50	48
Total number of branches	3,793	3,433	3,326	3,219	3,238	3,295
of which: Sberbank	1,529	1,233	1,162	1,045	1,011	1,009
Number of branches outside Moscow	3,430	3,113	3,023	2,927	2,956	3,003
Branches per institution	2.9	2.6	2.5	2.4	2.5	2.6
Other indicators (in percent)						
M2/GDP	21.1	23.2	25.8	29.8	31.0	33.3
Banking sector assets/GDP	n.a.	35.3	38.3	42.3	42.0	45.0
Domestic credit/GDP	24.1	24.9	26.3	26.6	21.4	20.6
Credit to domestic real sector/GDP	11.6	14.8	16.6	20.3	22.9	25.2
Deposits/GDP	17.2	19.2	21.2	21.9	23.3	26.3
Household deposits/GDP	n.a.	7.6	9.5	11.5	11.7	12.7

Source: CBR, IMF.
Note: n.a. denotes not available.

9.2   Key Features of the Russian Banking Market

As shown in table 9.1, the Russian banking system is highly frag-
mented, while at the same time very concentrated at the top and
mainly centered in the wealthier Moscow-St. Petersburg corridor. The
five largest banks accounted for 45.1 percent of total bank assets as of
early 2005, whereas the top two hundred banking institutions represented jointly 89 percent of total assets. In spite of the large number of
banking institutions (1,205), only a small fraction of them can be considered "true" financial intermediaries with stable franchises. Many of
the country's banks are tiny with over 80 percent of Russian banks
operating with capital of less than $10 million.[1] Many smaller banks,
so called "pocket banks," are serving a single company or its controlling financial industrial group (FIG), often for tax avoidance or money
laundering purposes (Laeven 2001; OECD 2004). This market structure
is the legacy of the lax entry policies followed in the early 1990s by the
CBR in granting banking licenses, as well as CBR's reluctance or inabil-

ity to force exits or consolidations by using stricter regulatory standards and higher capital requirements.[2] Mergers and acquisitions are just beginning and they are likely to accelerate, reducing the number of deposit taking banks from 1,239 in 2001 to 1,045 by early 2006.

Although the majority of Russian banks are privately owned, the state–owned banks control more than 50 percent of banking assets. Sberbank is still by far the largest institution with about 60 percent of total retail deposits and about one-third of total loans outstanding. The remaining twenty state banks are much smaller and usually specialized on a particular market niche or region. The only exception is Vneshtorgbank, which accounts for about 6 percent of total bank assets. Nonetheless, the weight and preferences enjoyed by publicly owned banks are holding back the development of private sector banking in Russia (uneven playing field). In spite of this disadvantage, foreign controlled banks have been growing substantially in recent years, but they only represent 7.6 percent of total bank assets. Although the interest of the latter to enter the booming Russian economy has increased, they see as an impediment to their entry or further expansion the existing legal uncertainty and they claim to face significant "informal barriers" to their operation and growth.

Overall, the level of penetration of banking services is low and competition is insular. Banking institutions, in general, offer three kinds of services: depository, lending, and transfer services. In all three areas Russian banks have a long way to go. With a branch serving 43,642 persons on average, the level of development of Russian banks' branch network is far below that of its OECD peers (e.g., 1,555 persons for France; 2,763 persons for the United States; 9,992 persons for Brazil) and other transition economies (e.g., 8,718 persons for Hungary) (see Bank for International Settlements 2005; the European Central Bank 2005). In Moscow, the national average decreases to about 29,631 people per branch. As of year-end 2003, the average deposits amounts to R$6,827 for individual deposits, and total bank deposits represent less than 22 percent of GDP in contrast to 46.6 percent in Hungary and 79.9 percent in the Czech Republic. Only an average of 23 percent of the population has a bank account.

Such lack of development of the domestic financial sector is reflected in the credit-to-GDP ratio of only 20.6 percent, as well as significant borrowing abroad from large Russian companies (reported at $19 billion), while the share of domestic banks' funding in overall investment is estimated at a low of 7 percent (Moody's Investors Service 2005).

Total bank assets amount to only 45 percent of GDP as of year-end 2004, compared to an EU average of 280 percent. Yet, this number is the result of an impressive growth of the financial sector since the transition to a market economy began, with a major disruption resulting from the 1998 crisis and some turbulence in the summer of 2004. A result of this low penetration rate is that only a limited number of institutions are involved in head-to-head competition for client deposits. Most Russian banks have either a limited geographical focus or are specializing on a niche client base. The same is true for foreign-controlled banks, which have been mainly active in the securities market and a few "blue chip" companies, and are now only venturing into consumer lending which is growing lately at exponential rates (with growth rates of about 270 percent since 2004).

While public oversight is improving, a high percentage of Russian banks are also weak by international standards and potentially vulnerable. In a recent report, Fitch Ratings (2004) assessed most of Russia's thirty largest banks as weak. Another rating agency, Standard & Poor's, considers the Russian banking system "to be one of the world's riskiest from a credit perspective." Given the poor accounting practices and their relative lack of transparency, smaller institutions are believed to be in an even more precarious state. Poor governance, lack of business diversification, portfolio concentration (partly due to related party lending), volatile and concentrated deposits, and poor loan quality are considered to be the primary sources of risks. Such weaknesses are somewhat mitigated by strong economic growth, a reduction in the underground economy and rapid asset growth, particularly consumer lending. As shown in table 9.2, the rapid growth of the banks' real sector loan portfolio in recent years (e.g., 44 percent in 2004 and 37 percent in 2005) is to be monitored closely as it may expose systemic vulnerabilities in the years to come.

According to CBR statistics, the quality of the banks' loan portfolio is low, with loans classified as "standard" accounting for a mere 48.2 percent of the total outstanding loan portfolio, compared to 90.7 percent two years earlier (table 9.2).[3] Such figures combined with a share of large credit risks (defined as exposure to a single borrower or group in excess of 5 percent of the lender's capital) over 70 percent of the portfolio reflect the challenges currently faced by Russian regulators.

These figures must be taken with "a grain of salt" in view of the adoption in mid-2004 of a new loan classification system, which for the first time introduces "the principles of estimated recoverable amount

Table 9.2
Selected soundness indicators for Russian banks

	2002	2003	2004	2005
Large credit risks (bn. RUR)	1,328.9	1,964.4	2,298.2	2,978.1
in percent of outstanding portfolio to real	80.3	82.4	70.3	69.7
sector in percent of equity	272.7	241.1	242.8	239.8
Percent standard loans	n.a.	90.7	46.9	48.2
Loan loss provisions, as percent of outstanding portfolio	n.a.	5.90	5.3	5.0
Outstanding loans with real sector (bn. RUR)	1,654	2,385	3,268.7	4,274.8
Total equity of banking sector	581.3	814.9	946.6	1,241.8

Source: CBR Banking Supervision report 2005, 2004, and 2003.
Note: n.a. denotes not available.

on loans and qualitative judgments on borrowers' creditworthiness."[4] However, it is undeniable that reported nonperforming loans (NPLs), with doubtful and irrecoverable loans at only 1.2 percent of the aggregate loan portfolio at year-end 2005 and with loan loss reserves of 5 percent, are possibly seriously underestimated. Notice that NPLs—as a lagging indicator—are likely to fall even more as loans (the denominator of the ratio) grows exponentially.

9.3   The Russian Deposit Insurance System

9.3.1   Background
The adoption by the Russian Federation of a deposit insurance system in late 2003 was not without controversy. The discussion in Parliament and the adoption of the new DIS took quite some time (almost ten years) because it was not seen initially as a priority by the government and because there was strong opposition from a number of parties with vested interests. The Russian government feared assuming additional liabilities from weak and insolvent banks. Also, there were concerns about the potential difficulties associated with setting up a new agency and deposit insurance fund, which would take away functions initially assigned to the Central Bank of Russia. Opposition came also from the public banks—in particular Sberbank, which until a few years ago had almost a complete monopoly of retail deposits in Russia—as well as from some large commercial banks which feared the incremental operational costs associated with the proposed deposit insurance premium.[5]

Beyond the traditional arguments offered in defense of a DIS,[6] proponents of the system in Russia argued that it would provide an effective tool for strengthening the banking system, enhancing the country's financial and macroeconomic stability and dealing with the many small unviable banks in operation. The stated objective herein was to create a two-tiered banking system with a presumably safer insured segment and a segment of weaker uninsured banks. With the creation of such "dual" system, it was thought that competition would drive out the uninsured banks, resolving the problem of weak banks caused by lax licensing policies of earlier years.

The Russian deposit insurance agency (DIA) itself was set up in January 2004 as an independent entity headquartered in Moscow and governed by a thirteen-member board of directors, consisting of seven government representatives, five officials from the Central Bank of Russia, and a director general elected by the board at the request of the government. The primary responsibilities of the DIA include determining the deposit insurance premium, receiving the payments from registered banks, making payouts to depositors in case of bank failures and managing the DIF. Through the amendment of the Law on Insolvency (Bankruptcy) of Credit Institutions in late 2004, the Russian DIA is now also responsible for administering bankruptcy proceedings to liquidate insolvent banks. It is with this new role where the coordination problems with the CBR could be more acute.

9.3.2 Legal Framework and Structural Design

The Russian DIS was established by the Federal Law Nr. 177-FZ of December 23, 2003.[7] The stated objectives of the law are threefold: (1) the protection of the rights and legal interests of depositors, (2) the strengthening of public confidence in the banking system of the Russian Federation, and (3) the reintermediation of savings by the population into the domestic banking system. Another objective of the law, albeit not explicitly mentioned, is the need to enhance competition by creating a level playing field between state-owned banks (who enjoy implicit state guarantees on deposits) and private-sector credit institutions.

In many respects, the structural framework provided by the law reflects good practices from international experience. The system has clearly been designed to cover only healthy institutions, while encouraging weak ones to exit the market. The coverage is extensive, but low enough to minimize moral hazard problems with participating banks. Participation is compulsory for both private and public banks willing to take public deposits, which in turn should help prevent the adverse selection problems often affecting voluntary schemes. The insurance covers "automatically" (i.e., without the need of a legal formality) all "natural persons' deposits" up to R$100,000 (about US$3,500).[8] This refers to the net total liability of the bank with the depositor, namely, subtracting outstanding obligations of the depositor with the failed bank.

Corporate deposits, bearer deposits, trust deposits and offshore deposits in Russian banks are excluded from the system. Deposits placed with Sberbank before October 1, 2004, were also excluded from the DIS and continued to enjoy a full guarantee from the Russian State until January 1, 2007. Foreign currency–denominated deposits are covered (up to R$100,000 equivalent), payable in rubles, converted at the foreign exchange rate determined by the CBR. There is no coinsurance of the deposit insurance coverage.

Insurance premiums are uniform—not risk-based—for all banks, payable in rubles on a quarterly basis, assessed on daily averages of insured deposits. The insurance premium cannot exceed 0.15 percent of deposits per quarter in the last accounting period (Article 36 of the deposit insurance law), or 0.6 percent per annum.[9] The assets collected by the insurance fund can be invested in government paper, bonds and equities of Russian issuers, as well as securities of member states of the OECD. Claims of insured deposits are to be paid by the DIA within three days of the date of a depositor submitting all required documentation. Any delay in reimbursing depositors is penalized by accruing interest at the refinancing rate established by the CBR.

Financing of the DIS is both from public and private sources, with initial capital provided by the state. The DIA started its activities with an initial capital endowment of two billion rubles provided by the Russian government. This amount corresponds to about 0.09 percent of the deposit base as of July 2005. Additional one billion rubles was provided to cover the administrative expenses of the Agency in the startup phase until when premium income is insufficient. Further State support can be provided if required. The ex ante guarantee, combined with the commitment for ex post state support, were thought to be powerful confidence-building instruments in the volatile Russian environment.[10]

9.3.3   Implementation Status and Recent Market Trends

At the end of 2005, the Russian DIS covered about 98.5 percent of the *number* of deposit accounts held by insured banks and 39.1 percent of the nominal *value* of deposits (*Russian Business Monitor*, September 26, 2005). The latter figure reflects the high concentration of individual deposits as well as the exclusion of all corporate deposits. A total of 870 out of the 1,097 banks collecting private deposits participate in the DIS, covering about 99.2 percent of banking assets. Overall 1,150 banks filed for relicensing under the new law, out of which 824 banks were accepted to participate in the system in a first round of evaluations conducted by the CBR in its capacity of supervisory agency. Four banks withdrew their application and a few institutions lost their license to collect deposits. Using the appeal procedure provided by the law, 265 banks resubmitted their applications to the DIS. As of January 2006, 931 banks have been admitted to the DIS. The CBR was to complete the review of all applications in early 2006. Yet, it appears that those banks not accepted into the DIS are still being allowed to operate albeit without authorization to accept new depositors or extend the existing ones.

The size of the deposit insurance fund increased rapidly from 2 billion rubles in January 2004 to 16.6 billion rubles as of January 2006, of which 36.7 percent are government contributions. However, this amount is still small compared to the size of the banking system and represents only about 0.6 percent the deposit base. Private deposits grew strongly since the introduction of the DIS, particularly those of household deposits denominated in rubles, suggesting increased confidence in the domestic banking system, as well as growing household income. Total bank deposits of individuals (in rubles) doubled during the first two years following the introduction of the deposit insurance scheme in January 2004.

However, deposit growth varied widely across different types of banks. Individual retail deposits grew faster in the regions outside Moscow, especially in the Urals, Volga, and the Russian Far East. Most of this growth seems to be driven by deposits collected by branches of credit institutions headquartered in Moscow, but it also reflects the emergence of healthy and dynamic regional banks. Since the introduction of the DIS, ruble deposits grew faster than deposits in foreign currency, coinciding with the rapid appreciation of the rubble vis-à-vis foreign currencies. With the notable exception of foreign banks, most of the growth in deposits took place via term deposits with maturities between 181 days and three years. However, changes in the composition of deposits from sight to term deposits, for example, is less significant in Russia than in other countries in view of the fact that retail deposits can be withdrawn on demand regardless of their contractual maturity. The latter might create unexpected liquidity problems for banks and it brings a generalized uncertainty as to duration gaps, at a time when the demand for longer-term funding from consumers and enterprises is on the rise.

Sberbank's market share of retail deposits continued to slide down. Interestingly, the market share of some of the largest Russian banks (such as Alfa Bank) declined as well. This could reflect increased competition for retail deposits in the banking sector. Anecdotal evidence suggests that foreign banks in particular have stepped up their acquisition efforts, with positive repercussions on overall bank competition. Overall, all banks increased their reliance on deposits to finance their activities as witnessed by the increasing share of deposits among their liabilities in their consolidated balance sheets. Yet, real interest rates on deposits still remain negative for all maturities. Interest rates spreads have also not changed significantly since 2003.[11]

9.4 An Assessment

9.4.1 Market Structure Matters

As mentioned earlier, private deposits grew strongly since the introduction of the DIS suggesting increased confidence in the domestic banking system, growing household incomes, the rapid growth of the Russian economy and the increasing monetization accompanying the transition to a market economy. Russian financial sector assets have been growing since the transition began, despite the strong decrease in real interest rates observed since 2000, and the financial crisis of 1998 and the turbulence of mid-2004. While the increasing monetization process should be expected to continue, the rate of growth of deposits is likely to moderate as the deposit base grows. In fact, it has halved since the introduction of the DIS. This finding is even less surprising if one bears in mind that the overwhelming share of retail deposits are held by public banks (mainly Sberbank). Consequently, an implicit state-sponsored insurance guarantee was already in place creating a market advantage for Sberbank which took the form of a flight to "quality" by smaller depositors (i.e., a cheaper source of funds). None of these market fundamentals are significantly altered by the new DIS.

Given the current weakness of Russian banks, the provision of deposit insurance may instead be fuelling systemic instability. The high number of institutions (over 80 of total) accepted into the DIS can be seen as an evidence of the dilemma faced by Russian authorities. On the one hand, applying strict rules in terms of soundness requirements may have led to the selection of only a small set of banking institutions in the volatile Russian environment, including the exclusion of some larger institutions. Because of the signaling effect of such a decision, the result might have been a systemic run on deposits and even a payment system crisis. On the other hand, providing insurance to weak institutions with solvency problems and poor growth prospects—as authorities are likely to have done—creates moral hazard problems of its own. It can lead to an increased systemic exposure to these institutions as well as to "gambling for resurrection" which can also trigger a delayed financial sector crisis as international evidence suggests.[12]

While it is also true that Sberbank has been losing market share in the retail deposit market (about 13.5 percentage points between 2001 and 2006), this evolution may be more linked to the closing of more than a third of its branches since 2001, rather than to a weakening of its market position. In fact, Sberbank has been gaining market share on the lending side reaching almost one third of total bank assets. Moreover, Sberbank's sheer size in comparison to its private sector competitors would have led to a significant subsidy by the Russian state to private banks if its pre-DIS deposits had been immediately included under the new DIS. Their exclusion until January 1, 2007, is therefore understandable, although it is not clear whether the Russian banking market structure will have changed significantly by then, unless Sberbank is restructured or privatized. Even if these deposits had been included from the inception of the DIS, the perception of an implicit 100 percent insurance by the state would most likely remain with Sberbank's depositors. The new explicit DIS may help to level the playing field somewhat, but expectations in this regard should be guarded.[13]

9.4.2 Sequencing of the Reforms

Following the "near death" experience in 1998, Russia's banking system experienced new, milder volatility in 2004. This minicrisis temporarily called into question the tentative trust of the population in the local banking system. The turmoil started in May 2004 with the intervention by the CBR of Sodbiznesbank, a small bank, whose banking license was withdrawn on charges of money laundering in view of CBR's limited range of instruments to resolve banks. Shortly after, Novocherkassk City Bank, a small regional bank, also lost its license due to charges of money laundering and failure to comply with prudential regulations. Rumors of the existence of a "blacklist" of weak banks to be targeted by the CBR, including even larger institutions, was circulating in the "rumor mill," quickly leading to loss of confidence by contagion and acute liquidity shortages at a number of banking institutions. By June, the interbank market had almost entirely dried up. A number of banks started to have liquidity problems in honoring the increasing withdrawals of deposits. On July 6, Guta Bank, Russia's then twenty-second largest bank, collapsed. As Guta Bank depositors started to have problems withdrawing money at ATMs, rumors of an imminent crisis at Alfa Bank, Russia's largest private bank, spread quickly. Within just three days, panicking depositors withdrew some $160 million from Alfa Bank or about 12 percent of its retail deposits (*Business Week Online*, July 26, 2004).

To defuse the crisis, the CBR launched a package of measures that included: (1) slashing the minimum reserve requirement on deposits from 7 percent to 3.5 percent, thereby providing additional liquidity to the banking system; (2) acquiring by the government through a public bank (VTB) Guta Bank; and (3) communicating to bank clients the isolated nature of financial problems in a few banks, dispelling rumors of systemic problems. On July 10, the Russian Duma enacted new emergency legislation providing a state sponsored blanket guarantee to all private depositors up to 100,000 rubles. This guarantee covered deposits at all banks, including those not formally under the DIS. These two measures prevented a further deterioration of the situation, and the panic among depositors abated within days. Private deposits in the banking system started to grow again shortly after.

What can be learned from this episode? First, it is evident that there is a high level of wariness among depositors in Russia, many of whom lost their savings during the 1998 crisis. Although nobody lost their deposits in 2004, a recent survey by the polling agency VTsIOM indicated that 70 percent of Russians have not had a savings account in the past eight years, either because they had no money or simply because they did not trust the banks. Second, although the CBR responded with skill and in a coordinated way with other stakeholders in 2004, this episode revealed that the CBR's ability to resolve banks is limited (partly due to a lack of legal tools) and there are deficiencies in enforcing prudential regulations. Third, while a blanket guarantees is often provided by the state to avert systemic crisis (such as the one in Mexico in 1995), they should be temporary to avoid moral hazard. Although many countries have not been successful in dismantling blanket guarantees quickly, this was not the case in Russia. Fourth, ideally a DIS should only be adopted after the foundations of the banking system are considered to be solid and the supervisors are confident that they have a good handle of the risks in the system, as well as the legal and operational tools to take both preventive actions (i.e., cease and desist orders, mandate increased provisions or equity, replace managers, among other) as well as swift remedial measures (i.e., efficient, least cost, sale of assets and deposits, and liquidation of banks).

In Russia's case, it would have been advisable to first strengthen the CBR's monitoring and enforcement capabilities before introducing a DIS. In other words, proper sequencing is critical to the effectiveness of a DIS, although the "ideal sequencing" may not always be feasible politically. The strategy adopted to "recertify" banks willing to access the new DIS was most probably the correct one. The real challenge has been its execution in view of the ambitious timetable set for the process, BCR's limited capabilities and political clout, and the informational problems faced, but, above all, by the limited support offered to the CBR for a strict implementation of the strategy. Some market views have been very negative, suggesting that "due to some political pressure, the CBR by accepting an overwhelming majority of banks into the DIS, has missed an opportunity to create a dual system of banks comprising those acting as deposit taking banks and others more resembling nonbank financial companies (bearing in mind that non-accredited banks will lose their right to take deposits from the population). Thus the opportunity to begin to seriously tackle the extreme fragmentation of the banking system was missed" (Moody's Investors Service 2005). Only time will tell the extent to which the selection process of the CBR has been successful. However, it is likely that due to deficiencies in the selection process too many weak banks will be included into the DIS. These decisions are not necessarily irreversible, but if problems resurface with the banks accepted into the DIS not only the costs for the DIF are likely to be higher, but also there is the risk of discrediting the DIS and eroding the franchise value of being a good bank in the Russian financial system.

9.4.3   Political Economy Considerations

As Laeven (2004) notes, the introduction and design of DIS is usually the outcome of a complex interplay between various political constituencies with often conflicting interests. Politicians and lawmakers acting as "agents" on behalf of a large number of small and dispersed depositors must—even in perfect democracies—also consider in their decision–making the interests of other groups among their electorate. Conflicts of interest may arise, sometimes even within the same constituency, and trade-offs have to be made. A certain coverage level by the insurance scheme may, for instance, be perceived as optimal by a group of depositors and suboptimal by another depending on their wealth. Some taxpayers may be concerned about the costs of the scheme and lobby for an entirely private insurance scheme (like in Brazil), whereas bankers may be interested in some form of state subsidy. Small or weak banks that are perceived to be risky may be very much interested in a deposit insurance scheme, whereas large banks with a clear competitive edge and solid standing on the market may not.[14] Cross-subsidies is a clear source of concern for the stronger banks.

Reconciling the diverging interests of these various constituencies can, in some cases, unfortunately, lead to suboptimal outcomes from a public policy perspective. The fear of another traumatic banking crisis among policymakers seems to have led to such an outcome in the Russian case. Considering the potential weakness of the Russian banking system, it is surprising that over 80 percent of all Russian banks have been admitted to the DIS and that the number looks set to grow further.

International experience provides ample evidence that extending a DIS to weak institutions increases moral hazard risks and contingent fiscal liabilities by making institutional failures more likely.[15] One of the participating banks already had to be intervened recently.

Equally troubling are recent proposals to gradually increase the coverage ceiling from R$100,000 to R$300,000 until 2007, and up to R$600,000 in the medium term (Financial Izvestia 2005).[16] These proposals are being considered by the Duma. Interestingly, these efforts are spearheaded by the DIA itself with the objective of bringing the coverage levels of the Russian scheme up to "international levels" when compared to countries' GDP per capita. As of year-end 2005, according to the official figures from the DIA, 98 percent of Russian deposits are currently under R$100,000 limit and therefore fully insured. This covers by far all small, uninformed depositors in Russia, and a further increase of coverage therefore does not seem warranted.

As mentioned earlier, Russian depositors also already have the opportunity to place their funds in public banks, in particular Sberbank and Vneschtorgbank, where they de facto enjoy an implicit 100 percent guarantee. It is questionable whether public trust in private banks and therefore their attractiveness will improve with a higher coverage given their still unresolved institutional problems and the limited enforcement power and capabilities of the supervisors and limited public disclosure of information. By increasing the coverage, it seems that Russian policymakers will most likely increase the fiscal contingent liabilities without any major positive impact. Here again, the "political economy" factor appears to be leading to a suboptimal outcome.

9.5 Prerequisites to an Effective Deposit Insurance System in Russia

9.5.1 Strengthening Charter Values of Russian Banks
The weakness of some institutions in the Russian banking system is without doubt the most pressing reform issue for the DIS to be effective. The policy options to be considered should include the facilitation of mergers and acquisitions, as well as orderly exit of the weakest players.

Such a market and prudentially driven consolidation process may in fact be increasingly required for banks to meet capital adequacy requirements. The rapid growth in bank lending is making the capitalization model of the past—consisting basically in increasing bank capital via retained earnings—more difficult to sustain. Asset growth is now clearly outpacing the increase in banks' capacity to generate new capital internally. Without a new approach to strengthening their capital base, Russian private banks will face a growing challenge in their ability to compete with state-owned and foreign banks.

Additional reforms are required for the CBR to have an effective framework for a quick and orderly exit of nonviable banks. Currently, it is, for instance, very cumbersome to transfer deposits from the failed or distressed bank to another bank because prior consent from the depositor is required. This proved to be a problem during the management of the minicrisis of 2004. Moreover, the DIA is not allowed to assume losses directly or through the purchase of bad loans in the event of bank rescue operations (i.e., acquire NPLS with assessed values lower than the nominal value of the deposits). It also cannot provide open bank assistance to banks which might end up failing (i.e., banks that do have a solvency problem and are not eligible to access the liquidity window of the CBR). This is important since experience has shown that bank liquidations are often more costly than the cost incurred by using other support mechanisms. Further, the DIA cannot securitize loans in support of bank resolutions. Nor can it exclude on its own a bank from the DIS. It is only when the CBR withdraws the banking license that the bank is formally dealt with by the DIA. The DIA also cannot initiate on its own a bank inspection, or request a special audit of a bank or its controlling group. The latter are faculties of the CBR as supervisor. The issues discussed above point to the weaknesses the DIA might face in the case of liquidations, as well as the existence of nonnegligible coordination and access to information problems vis-à-vis the role of the CBR as lead supervisor.

Finally, there is the issue of the public banking system, in particular the role of Sberbank. There is no doubt that the market share and privileged position of these banks have a distorting effect on market dynamics, at least in those urban markets where they are competing with a significant number of private banks. Yet, at the same time, a big bang privatization of this sector may lead to a substantial level of financial disintermediation in the short to medium term and is likely to be politically not feasible under the current circumstances.[17] A gradual approach is required. In the short term, the focus should be on minimizing duplications and inefficiencies in the operation of these banks (e.g., Sberbank competing with Vneschtorgbank), limiting their growth in areas with strong influx of private banks, transparency on the explicit and implicit subsidies provided to them, improved governance and a more arm's-length relationship with the government and the CBR, as well as the introduction of a hard budget constraint to limit the fiscal impact of eventual losses and enhanced and more timely financial disclosure.

9.5.2 Reforming the Regulatory Environment and Property Rights

While acknowledging existing risks posed by current market structure, a vigorous enforcement of the CBR's prudential regulation and enhanced disclosure are critical for the effectiveness of the DIS and the stability of the Russian banking system. At the same time, there is a need to enhance the CBR's prudential standards. Consolidated and risk-based supervision and IT audits ought to be introduced, and solvency requirements (including minimum capital requirements) should be progressively increased. The current limit of 25 percent of capital established on large exposures is meaningless and needs to be adjusted as the structure and dealings of conglomerates controlling banks are identified. Similarly, the high loan concentrations and lending to related parties are major sources of risk for banks as well as, ultimately, for the DIF itself. We do not underestimate the difficulties of passing better regulations but above all the risks for an effective enforcement of prudential norms.

The issue of corporate governance in banks and corporations is also of paramount importance. Without clarity of ownership, responsibilities and accountabilities, basic requirements for the safe operation of banks, like effective internal control systems are not credible. Given the prevalence of financial industrial groups, further progress in the Russian banking system must also be accompanied by changes in the corporate sector toward better definition of intercompany structures, with well defined holding company structures, better corporate and bank governance, and increased transparency. In the meantime, the risks taken by the DIF could be largely unknown and quite likely higher than those that it would assume in an environment of more transparent legal and organizational arrangements.

Finally, reforms are also needed to reduce prevailing legal uncertainties for the safe and sound operation of financial intermediaries, including a revision of the secure lending legislation, the bankruptcy regime, the fairness and effectiveness of commercial courts. Similarly, it will be important to differentiate and enforce an adequate time structure of liabilities. Retail deposits can currently be withdrawn any time regardless of their actual contractual maturity, with little or no penalty. This implies significant liquidity risks for banks, as all their liabilities are de facto on demand. A system of penalties for early withdrawal seems important to reduce the liquidity risks faced by Russian banks today.

9.5.3 Ensuring Incentive Compatibility of the Deposit Insurance System

At the more micro level, Russian policymakers need to address some design aspects of the deposit insurance scheme itself to reduce moral hazard. First, the approach selected for setting the insurance premium ought to be reviewed. The deposit insurance premium by law must be uniform for all banks irrespective of their level of risk, which implies a subsidy of the stronger to the weakest banks with a "welfare loss" from an economic perspective. While fairly priced deposit insurance may not be feasible,[18] some form of risk-calibrated insurance pricing[19] would be highly recommended. Ideally, such a system would be based on actuarially estimated probabilities of defaults for individual banks. But given the quality and paucity of historical data on Russian banks, a probably more practical alternative in the Russian context could be to link premium levels to a CAMEL-type rating system for banks that the CBR could refine over time. To align incentives and prevent ex ante disclosure of financial weaknesses, banks could be charged the same fee as required by the law, but could receive an ex post rebate calibrated on the basis of the bank's compliance with, let say, CAMEL-type ratings.

A closely related issue to adequate pricing is the actuarial soundness of the DIF. Given the current uniform pricing system, the current size of the fund stands in no relation with default probabilities in the banking system or macrofinancial risks in Russia. Without an adequately capitalized insurance scheme, the likelihood of a future need for state bailout will remain substantial.[20] The current strength of Russian public finances may conceal the importance of this issue. But, this contingent fiscal liability will continue to grow as the financial system keeps expanding at a rapid pace as well as the coverage of the DIS.

Finally, Russian authorities may be well advised to complement the current deposit insurance scheme with an ambitious financial education and communication initiative. In a recent survey by the Russian news agency Izvestiia, only 30 percent of respondents were aware of the existence of the DIS.

9.6   Concluding Remarks

The Russian experience with the DIS suggests that, while such a system can have a positive impact on financial sector stability, stimulate savings, and help create a level playing field, it is not a "silver bullet" by itself. As suggested by the new industrial organization approach to banking theory, market structure matters for the effectiveness of the scheme, as well as how and in which regulatory environment deposit insurance is being introduced.[21] In other words, deposit insurance should not be considered in isolation of other key reforms that must be undertaken in particular to avoid the potentially negative effects resulting from the change in incentives related to its introduction.

Whereas some immediate and possibly temporary benefits can be attributed to the new DIS in Russia, it is so far largely irrelevant as an instrument to mitigate systemic risks. In fact, the extension of coverage to weak institutions and current political economy considerations may be leading to increased moral hazard, assuming significant new fiscal contingencies. A strengthening of the legal and institutional framework is called for to mitigate the potential costs and avoid future instability which could eventually discredit the DIS and bankrupt the DIF. Certainly the latter will never be a sufficient instrument to deal with systemic problems.

Policy reforms are required in particular in the following areas: (1) enforcement of prudential regulations; (2) contracting environment; (3) resolution of problem and insolvent banks; (4) banking sector consolidation; (5) restructuring and privatization of state-owned banks; (6) pricing of deposit insurance; (7) corporate governance and corporate sector reform; and (8) preparation of contingency plans among regulatory agencies to simulate eventual crisis and resolve coordination problems. While Russia has made some progress in delicensing weak banks, much more needs to be done to improve the health and stability of the banking system and to create conditions for a well-functioning financial safety net for small, uninformed depositors.

Acknowledgments

We would like to thank Joaquin Gutierrez, Edward Kane Luc Laeven, and Thorsten Beck for their comments and suggestions, the Russian Deposit Insurance Agency for valuable discussions and providing market information, Olga Vybornaia and Elena Kantarovich for their assistance in data analysis.

Notes

1. Standard & Poor's 2005.

2. Moody's Investors Service 2005.

3. Although the underlying trend may be clearly toward a deterioration of credit quality, this apparent surge in substandard loans may also reflect a tightening in loan classification rules by the Central Bank of Russia.

4. The new loan classification system increases the number of categories from four to five, setting a range for the loan loss provisions within each category (in parenthesis). The five new risk categories are standard (0 percent), watch (1–20 percent), substandard (21–50 percent), doubtful (51–100 percent) and loss (100 percent).

5. The proposed scheme was not met with much enthusiasm by the international community either, including the World Bank, as it was considered too risky to extend the DIS and out of sequence (i.e., "fix the banks first, adopt the DIS later").

6. These include (1) protecting small, uninformed depositors, (2) enhancing the reintermediation of deposits and the social equity of it, (3) ensuring a level playing field for competition between different classes of banks, and (4) fostering trust in financial institutions.

7. The law took more than a decade to be approved by the Duma. The law was enacted together with five other pieces of legislation, which amended the central bank law, the tax code, the banking law, and other existing laws affected by the new deposit insurance scheme (see OECD 2004).

8. This ceiling is a nominal amount, which is not indexed to inflation.

9. The law stipulates that this premium is due to fall to 0.05 percent once the fund has accumulated the equivalent of 5 percent of the deposit base.

10. See OECD 2004, for a detailed discussion of this issue

11. The interest rates shown in the following section are weighted averages based on the volume of deposits by type of instruments.

12. See Demirgüç-Kunt and Kane 2002.

13. Similarly, Vneshtorgbank, Russia's second-largest public bank, has been expanding rapidly its market share in deposits from 0.7 percent to 3.2 percent since the introduction of the new DIS and through the "forced" acquisition of Guta bank following the mini-crisis of mid–2004.

14. As Laffont and Tirole (1993) indicate, the multiple principal agent problem also extends to bureaucracies and can lead government agencies to seek undesirable outcomes.

15. See Demirgüç-Kunt and Kane 2002.

16. In fact, the coverage ceiling was increasing on August 8, 2006, to RUR 100,000 plus 90 percent of amount in excess of RUR 100,000, with the total guaranteed amount capped to RUR 190,000.

17. Russia is by no means unique in this situation. Western European countries, such as Germany and France, also display similar levels of public participation in their financial system.

18. See Freixas and Rochet 1997, 270–271. See also Bhattacharya and Thakor 1993, as well as Bhattacharya, Boot, and Thakor 1998.

19. See Bhattacharya, Boot, and Thakor 1998.

20. See Laeven 2004 for a more detailed discussion.

21. The application of the industrial organization approach to banking theory is fairly recent. Yet this new strand of research has proved to be a very useful complement to the more traditional financial intermediation theory in explaining the structure and different dynamics on financial markets. In particular, the industrial organization approach has shown that competition in banking is analytically more complex than on other markets

and not always desirable from a public policy perspective. Yanelle (1989) was one of the pioneers of this new approach. See also Freixas and Rochet 1997.

References

Bank for International Settlements. 2005. Statistics on Payment and Settlement Systems in Selected Countries—Figures for 2004. Bank for International Settlements, Basel.

Bhattacharya, Sudipto, Arnoud Boot, and Anjan V. Thakor. 1998. The Economics of Bank Regulation. *Journal of Money, Credit, and Banking* 30: 745–770.

Bhattacharya, Sudipto, and Anjan V. Thakor. 1993. Contemporary Banking Theory. *Journal of Financial Intermediation* 3: 2–50.

Demirgüç-Kunt, Asli, and Edward J. Kane. 2002. Deposit Insurance around the Globe: Where Does it Work? *Journal of Economic Perspectives* 16: 175–195.

European Central Bank. 2005. Banking Structure in the New EU Member States. European Central Bank, Frankfurt (January).

Financial Izvestia. 2005. People Are Bringing "Under Mattresses" Savings to Banks and This Is Only the Beginning. Interview with A. Tourbanov, General Director, State Corporation Deposit Insurance Agency, November 23.

Fitch Ratings. 2004. The Banking System: Russia's Achilles Heel. Special Report (July).

Freixas, Xavier, and Jean–Charles Rochet. 1997. *Microeconomics of Banking*. Cambridge, Mass.: MIT Press.

Laeven, Luc. 2001. Insider Lending and Bank Ownership: The Case of Russia. *Journal of Comparative Economics* 29 (2): 207–229.

Laeven, Luc. 2004. The Political Economy of Deposit Insurance. *Journal of Financial Services Research* 26 (3): 201–224.

Laffont, Jean-Jacques, and Jean Tirole. 1993. *A Theory of Incentives in Procurement and Regulation*. Cambridge, Mass.: MIT Press.

Moody's Investors Service. 2005. Russia Banking System Outlook. Moody's Investors Service (October).

OECD. 2004. OECD Economic Survey of the Russian Federation 2004: Russia's Deposit Insurance Law. Paris: OECD.

Standard & Poor's. 2005. The Russian Federation. Bank Industry Risk Analysis. Standard & Poor's (June 28).

Yanelle, Marie-Odile. 1989. The Strategic Analysis of Intermediation. *European Economic Review* 33: 294–301.

10   Protecting Depositors in China: Experience and Evolving Policy

Patrick Honohan

10.1   Introduction

Despite the absence of any formal deposit insurance or guarantee system, China has developed one of the deepest banking systems in the world. Indeed, in absolute terms only the United States and Japan have more bank deposits. Why then would the Chinese authorities feel the need to introduce such a scheme at this stage? Can it achieve the goals they might have for it? And what of the possible side effects?

The health and effectiveness of the Chinese financial system is a matter of global concern. Continued growth of China's economy increasingly depends on an effective financial system for channeling investable funds to productive uses, as the sources of Chinese growth increasingly come to depend not solely on factor accumulation in the modern sector, but also on the productivity of that sector. Furthermore, any destabilization of Chinese depositor and saving behavior (however unlikely it may seem now) has the potential to send ripples through the global financial system, given the current scale and importance of the Chinese money supply (over US$4 billion) and foreign exchange reserve accumulation (over US$1 billion—the highest in the world).

This chapter reviews some of the distinctive features of the Chinese banking environment, noting that, in addition to the very large and growing scale of bank deposits, there have been huge loan losses. Official entities have, in effect, recapitalized China's big four banks to the tune of almost US$350 billion so far, with more needed for the last of the four to be part privatized and additional funds also applied to other insolvencies in the banking system in recent years. Household depositors have, in fact, been protected, but enterprises have lost deposits in some instances.

China's low and deteriorating scores in cross-country indicators of governance quality suggest that the preconditions for deposit insurance to improve bank soundness are not present. Instead, there could be a worsening of moral hazard. Even the hoped-for clarification of the respective roles of different government agencies may not be achieved by the proposed insurance system, nor will the central bank be clearly insulated from pressures to contribute to bank rescues.

The introduction of deposit insurance has in many countries been motivated by the importance of protecting the functioning of the payments system against bank runs, and by governments' desire to protect small depositors who do not have the capacity to assess the soundness of individual banks. Legislators have sometimes also been motivated by a desire to reduce the market power of incumbents by facilitating the establishment of new banking entrants (effectively by subsidizing deposit mobilization by newer banks while they are still building public confidence). Advocates of formal deposit insurance systems claim that they might facilitate speedy compensation for the insured, that they could place a cap on the exposure of the public authorities to payouts in the case of a bank failure and perhaps that they could provide the focus of an effective and professional agency for intervening and resolving bank failures.

The potential moral hazard associated with deposit insurance, as with other types of insurance, is well known, but enthusiasts for deposit insurance have hoped that effective official prudential supervision and adequate capitalization of banks and other intermediaries might be adequate to limit this hazard. The disappointing experience of the first, and long the only, national bank deposit insurance system, that of the United States, has cast doubt on such optimism. Indeed, it became clear, during the protracted banking and near-banking crisis in that country, especially in the 1980s, that the deposit insurance systems were being gamed and that the moral hazard had not been contained.

Nor have all of the supposed advantages of deposit insurance been realized. For one thing, insuring small depositors has little effect on the likelihood of damaging bank runs as these mainly involve the withdrawal of wholesale funds. And the provision of insurance is not a prerequisite for the establishment of an effective bank intervention agency or for ensuring that it has the necessary advance information to preposition for intervention. Indeed, most European deposit insurance systems are of the "pay box" type, where the insurer has no function in supervising or intervening banks, but merely stands ready to pay out claims with accumulated funds.

Cross-country regression analysis covering the experience of both advanced and developing countries finds discouraging correlations between the existence of a formal deposit insurance system and the likelihood, frequency and scale of banking crises, in particular where underlying legal, information, and regulatory institutions are poorly developed (Demirgüç-Kunt, Kane, and Laeven 2006). In particular, the hope that fiscal liability would be capped is not given support by the data. And there is little indication that having a formal deposit insurance system helps to promote financial deepening.

Against this background, the proposed introduction of formal deposit insurance in China becomes a matter more for concern than for endorsement. For one thing, despite China's outstanding economic growth performance during this period, the overall institutional environment cannot be said to be well developed, and governance indicators have even been deteriorating. This suggests that the preconditions for a successful deposit insurance scheme are not yet coming into place.

The absence to date of a formal system of depositor protection does not imply that small depositors have been unprotected in China. Indeed, household depositors have been fully protected so far. The recapitalization of China's big banks has already entailed one of the largest fiscal or quasifiscal outlays for any banking system in history.

So far, these huge outlays have not raised any depositor concerns about the continued ability and commitment of the authorities to protect deposits at the big banks. On the contrary the rapid growth in household and other deposits, both at the large state-owned[1] commercial banks which still dominate the system, as well as at the smaller banks is evidence of ample depositor confidence at present.

Nevertheless, with the ratio of bank deposits to GDP above 150 percent of gross domestic product (GDP)—about three-fifths still concentrated in the four big state-owned banks[2]—sustained household and investor confidence cannot ultimately hinge on the existence or not of a formal deposit insurance system, but rather requires a sustained assurance that the banks are making sound lending decisions. After all, these are banks that slid into an acknowledged 35 percent nonperforming loans to assets (NPL) ratio (before recent recapitalizations). If loss ratios were similar or worse going forward, considering the scale of banking in China, the ability of government to underwrite the losses without damaging side effects (taxation, inflation) could eventually be compromised. Fearing a haircut, large depositors might rationally seek to exit, especially since their existing level of deposits must greatly exceed transactions requirements.

There is no suggestion that any such anxieties are currently present, or that undisclosed losses of the banks could currently be again approaching such worrying levels.[3] Furthermore, most of the larger corporate deposits belong to state-controlled companies, who would likely be constrained from withdrawing. Nevertheless, the fact that a disruptive loss of confidence is not inconceivable underlines the importance of ensuring that insiders' incentives are focused on achieving safe and sound banking.

Up to about 1998, much of the accumulation of losses in China's banking system reflected a quasifiscal imposition on the banking system, as political authorities in effect channeled bank funds to underperforming state-owned enterprises no longer being supported by fiscal resources (Lardy 1998). (At the same time, a sizable number of smaller banks failed for more conventional reasons.)

The degree to which banks will achieve better results from recent and future lending is unclear. Banks are increasingly focused on financial performance and China's top leadership has emphasized the need to get NPL ratios down. Spurred by the energetic new China Banking Regulatory Commission (CBRC), and in preparation for stock market listing and the investment of strategic stakes by foreign institutions, the big banks have indeed reduced their NPLs. But this was largely done not through recoveries, but by write-offs and asset sales, mainly to the government-controlled asset management companies (AMCs).

There have since been numerous suggestions that a new wave of loan losses can be expected in the years ahead. It is providing difficult to avoid losses in certain new types of business, including retail lending. The immense ongoing investment in public infrastructure and in manufacturing capital, much of it bank financed, has caused some observers to forecast a new wave of loan losses emerging if and when these investments cannot be remuneratively employed.[4]

In all of this, we glimpse some of the complexity and ambiguity of the role of governmental entities in Chinese banking. Some agencies or party leaders at the central or provincial level have, both in the past and more recently, encouraged banks to make loans to boost or maintain growth in economic activity. And, although top national decision-makers stepped in decisively to reverse the trend in NPLs, the implementation of this policy by government agencies in the past few years seems to have focused at least as much on the symptom (stock of NPLs on the books of the banks) as on the underlying disease (the propensity to do loss–making banking).

Can the introduction of a new agency for deposit insurance help to clarify this muddy situation, or will it worsen incentives? There is one ray of hope here, in that the new arrangement could serve to limit access of failing banks to the bottomless resources of the central bank, which have often been tapped for meeting the costs of bank rescue. By obliging the agency charged with bank regulation and supervision, and hence with creating and maintaining important elements of the incentive structure for bank insiders, to meet the cost of bank failures itself (rather than simply drawing on the monetary authority), some of the architects of deposit insurance in China may hope to achieve an improved incentive structure among government agencies. However, given the continuing pervasive involvement of government in banking and finance, that hope is likely to be misplaced.

The remainder of the chapter fleshes out this perspective by looking in more detail at China's recent experience. Section 10.2 describes the government's evolving roles in the Chinese banking system—not only as regulator but as owner and through the political process—and its influence on inherited banking losses and depositor confidence. Section 10.3 characterizes the different ways in which depositors have been protected to date, in terms of the techniques used and the past and prospective future sums involved. Section 10.4 turns to the proposed new deposit insurance scheme, contrasting it with the overall strategy that seems to have guided past rescues, and seeking to interpret the authorities' motivation for introducing it now. Section 10.5 concludes.

10.2   Government's Multiple Roles: Owner, Regulator, Loss Generator, Guarantor

Government and politics in China are heavily involved in banking in ways that are not fully transparent or unambiguous. In addition to the conventional roles of regulator and implicit guarantor of banking stability, an even more important dimension of government's involvement has been through ownership and political control, and this has been responsible for heavy loan losses.

10.2.1   Government as Owner and the Political Context

For the past few years, the interaction among banking, government, and politics in China has been evolving radically but slowly, leaving the system still in a curiously ambiguous and intermediate stage of governance. On the one hand, the heritage of the planned economy and its monobank system is vestigial. It is over twenty-five years now since the monobank system was brought to an end, separating the role of central banking from commercial banking; over twenty since agricultural production began to be privatized. Little by little, inherited institutional features of the financial structure that have proved incompatible or problematic within the market economy have been reformed. For instance, in 1998, the branch structure of the central bank—the People's Bank of China (PBC)—was consolidated with each of nine regional branches becoming responsible for several provinces, thereby weakening the tight connection which had previously existed between provincial political leadership and the management at provincial level of what was still at that time not only the monetary authority and lender of last resort, but also the bank regulator.

Yet the direct role of government in the financial system is still a strong one. The degree to which ownership and political control of the banks has been used to allocate loanable funds according to policy rather than market-based goals[5] has diminished, not ceased. Even within provinces, allocation has been based on local goals. Although nominally nationwide legal entities, each of the big banks has operated in a highly decentralized way, and their regional management has been strongly influenced by local governments (Yi 2003).

Despite sizable strategic investments by foreign entities[6] in three of them during 2005–2006, as well as initial public offerings (IPOs) in the Hong Kong and Shanghai markets, central government still controls the four major banks accounting for about three–fifths of the deposits in the system. In addition, lower levels of government control the bulk of the remainder of the banking system—national joint stock banks and city commercial banks (CCBs), and the rural credit cooperative (RCC) network—through indirect ownership stakes. Indeed, only in 2004 did a joint stock bank come under wholly private control.

To be sure, the part privatization process has entailed a complete overhaul of the high-level governance structures of the banks, both the big four and several of the smaller joint stock banks, with some greater clarity as to who exercises the government's ownership role in the case of the big four (cf. Podpiera 2006). The question is whether these will be effective in reaching down to all parts of what are very large organizations that have traditionally resisted central management, retaining considerable autonomy at provincial and city levels (Dobson and Kashyap 2006).

In the case of the state-owned banks the Communist Party still seems to exercise a role in the selection of management, who in practice must have a divided loyalty to the bank as an institution and to their local party organization. This role has been diminished, and recent policy statements emphasize the professionalism as bankers that is expected of party members who have management roles in banks (Wu 2005). But a considerable legacy of the earlier interventionist attitudes undoubtedly remains.

10.2.2   Government as Regulator

As ownership and the population of institutions both evolved, so also has regulation. Banking regulation has been carved out of the PBC since 2003, and the new regulator, CBRC, has taken its place alongside regulators of the securities markets (CSRC) and insurance (CIRC), which had been established five years earlier. In terms of regulatory policy, there has been a clear trend toward liberalization of such aspects as foreign entry and line of business regulation. Nevertheless, the authorities have frequently interrupted, or even reversed, this progress not hesitating to reregulate in response to difficulties or abuses that have arisen. The current set of regulations and supervisory practice should be regarded as provisional and likely to evolve further in unpredictable ways.[7]

The most conspicuous initial feature of CBRC regulation appears to have been a rather single-minded focus of the agency on reducing NPL ratios (Shih 2005). The ratios have indeed declined sharply from about 35 percent at 2000 for the big four banks to about 10 percent by year-end 2005. CBRC seems to have been satisfied to achieve this reduction even though it was mainly done through write-offs and asset sales rather than recoveries by the banks themselves. The apparent emphasis on symptom rather than underlying cause does not augur well for future attention being given to rigorous risk-based supervision. And, while the firm action taken to sanction the numerous cases of managerial fraud and corruption uncovered in the banks in recent years is to be welcomed, the very extent of corruption—rising even to the level of chief executive of one of the big four banks—is also a worrying indication of weak governance throughout the banking system.[8]

10.2.3   Inherited Banking Losses

By the late 1990s, the four big state-owned banks were deeply insolvent if accounted for in accordance with international accounting standards. As later detailed, between 1998 and 2005 measures to boost the capital of the big four banks already amounted to about 30 percent of GDP. In addition, further very sizable injections were being planned.

Much of the accumulated losses have reflected the assumption by banks of quasifiscal responsibilities through the channeling of loans to meet government objectives during the early period of transition (Lardy 1998; Zhou 2004c). For this reason much of the lending by banks in China in the 1990s represented a misallocation of funds in banking terms and likely also in economic terms. The best that can be said of this experience is that, to an extent, these losses may have been a necessary price to pay for a transitional process: most of the old loss–making, state-owned enterprises of the early 1990s have since been drastically pruned and in many cases closed.[9]

Yet, China has grown rapidly, with small and medium-sized firms relying to a remarkable extent, as a recent survey (Dollar et al. 2003) has shown, on retained earnings, loans from family and friends, and foreign direct investment, rather than on bank loans. The latter continue to be disproportionately reserved for state-owned firms, many—though not all—of them lacking dynamism. For example, as recently as 2003, analysts estimated that 17 percent of new loans went to consumers, mainly for mortgages, 10 percent to agriculture, 16 percent to finance infrastructure projects, and the remaining 43 percent to other state-owned enterprises (about one-fifth of that to listed companies).[10]

10.2.4   Depositor Confidence

Considering how widely the loan loss experience and capital deficiencies of the main Chinese banks have been discussed, it is astonishing how deep China's banking system has been over the past decade. Indeed, if one ignores some small offshore financial centers, China has the highest ratio of broad money M2 to gross domestic product.[11] This impression is only slightly exaggerated by the consideration that the near-bank depository sector is relatively small in China. Not only are monetary aggregates a very high fraction of GDP, but these ratios have grown steadily for the past decade.[12] No wonder then that the authorities have been assiduous in ensuring that public confidence in the banking system is not eroded.

And indeed, despite the well-documented costs of the banking losses, the problems of the banks have not been marked by any significant interruptions in the day-to-day functioning of the financial system as a whole. The key here has been the fact that, despite the losses, repayment of deposits with the big state-owned banks that continue to dominate the system has never been in doubt in China.

There have, admittedly, been isolated episodes of depositor panic from time to time. Some of these, in the late 1980s and early 1990s, likely reflected a macroeconomic concern over upticks in the trend of inflation (with surviving folk memories of the massive hyperinflation at the end of the Kuomintang period in the aftermath of World War II), rather than concerns about individual financial firms. Among the macroeconomic measures adopted to calm depositors in the late 1980s were mandated inflation linking of deposit returns for certain household savings accounts.

A wave of insolvencies of small intermediaries in the late 1990s was associated with a new type of depositor fear, namely that the nominal value of their deposits would not be repaid in full. This time, as detailed later, government moved reasonably promptly to ensure that household depositors would not lose their deposits, though institutional depositors were not all indemnified.

In order to understand why the authorities are also opting now to introduce a formal deposit insurance scheme, and how that scheme might affect the failure resolution environment in China, it is essential to understand how failure resolution has been practiced in China up to now.

10.3   China's Approach to Protecting Depositors and Other Claimants

10.3.1   Rescue Techniques in Practice
Multiple failures of depository and other financial institutions have occurred over the past decade in China.

Most of the open failures reflected inexperience or corruption on the part of managers of small intermediaries, and there were also many failures related to bursting property booms in the 1990s (mostly in Southern Chinese provinces).[13] This pattern is familiar from the experience on many liberalizing banking systems worldwide. Several of the earlier closures were preceded by depositor panics.

Less obvious, but larger, failures have come in the large state-owned banks. These were burdened from the mid-1980s with various forms of explicit or implicit policy lending, including to support employment in unprofitable sunset state-owned enterprises. The process of correcting this burden started in the mid-1990s, and capital injections began in 1998.

As has been the case globally, these failures have been dealt with in many different ways. Some interventions have sought to keep the institution as a going concern, some have kept most of the business going through a merger, explicitly or implicitly assisted, and some have involved closure and liquidation.

The channels of financial support used in China mirror those which have been used so often in global financial history that they can be considered standard (cf. Goodhart and Schoenmaker 1995): in addition to liquidity lending by the central bank, there have been forced or encouraged mergers and the explicit use of public funds as a capital injection, or to compensate some of the depositors of an institution that is to be closed.

Mergers   As is well known in China from the failure of Hainan Development Bank,[14] an institution that had initially been formed from the regulatory merger of five trust and investment companies (TICs),[15] combining several weak banks makes a large bank, but not necessarily a strong one. The collapse well illustrates the conventional wisdom that the merger option makes sense only where the acquirer is large or strong, or when the failing bank has appreciable long-term franchise value.[16]

All the same, when there are too many small and poorly run institutions, consolidation of the sector can be desirable. Thus in the past few years, following the failures of the 1990s in this sector, regulatory consolidation and a substantial tightening of rules has reduced the number of TICs from its peak of almost 250 to about seventy and their activities are now much constrained. Likewise the 5,200 urban credit cooperatives (UCCs) of 1994 are being consolidated into about 100 city commercial banks)[17] established on a shareholding basis for this purpose—by 2004, only about 400 UCCs remained in operation.

Consolidation and rehabilitation of the 40,000 or so RCCs, which account for over 10 percent of the banking system, is also in process, and has included mergers of geographically contiguous RCCs into county-level and higher-level RCC unions. Because a failed RCC is often the only intermediary in the region, the authorities have been extremely reluctant to effect closures. Here again financial assistance from the PBC has been employed to give these entities a fresh start (the approach is described in Zhou 2004b), which is an example of explicit recapitalization with public funds.

Capital Injections   Various ways have been found in China for using government entities to inject capital into undercapitalized banks. By purchasing a troubled loan portfolio at values well above what is recoverable, the Chinese AMCs (funded with government promises) have effectively injected substantial values into the big four banks. Another form of capital injection was the acquisition by the state holding company Huijin (a subsidiary of the PBC) of shareholdings in the big banks from 2003. Equity injections were also made by state-owned entities in loss-making institutions that were allowed to continue in operation (such as the case of Everbright TIC in 1996). Special tax concessions that were made in various cases (such as a waiver of sums due) and subsidized loans (recently adopted for the RCC sector) have also entailed a fiscal cost.[18] And it is not only central government that has picked up the ultimate bill. Regional fiscal authorities have also been involved in compensation payments in accordance with the principle established in China whereby provincial and other regional authorities should be responsible for enterprise deposits lost in the failure of intermediaries established under their remit, notably where institutions were actually closed.[19]

Closure   When Chinese intermediaries have been closed, the degree of depositor compensation has differed as between institutional deposits and individual or household deposits. The idea of making such a distinction, which is not common worldwide, likely has some roots in the traditional distinction between enterprise and household financial circuits in the planned economy. But alternative rationalizations are possible as will be discussed later. Whatever the reason, the general principle adopted in China has been to prefer individual (natural person) claims. With some exceptions on a case-by-case basis, especially related to foreign creditors and private enterprises, institutional (legal person) claims have been dealt with on a case-by-case basis.

Role of Central Bank   The PBC has been active in the organization and financing of the rescue of many second- and third-tier institutions in China (TICs, UCCs, and RCCs), as well as securities companies.[20] The much larger mid-2004 purchase (described later) by an AMC of nonperforming assets from two of the state-owned commercial banks, at 50 percent of face value, was fully financed by a loan from the PBC.

In some cases the PBC may have provided the support on its own initiative. To the extent that in some cases it may have made the loans in response to directives from the state council, this can be considered an intrusion on the desirable independence of the PBC in developing monetary policy. Fortunately, the scale of the assistance provided has not in practice been so large as to derail monetary policy goals.[21]

10.3.2 Scale of Recent Injections and of Potential Future Capital Deficiencies

While all categories of intermediary have the potential to present fiscal costs in the event of failure, by far the largest fiscal costs surround the recapitalization of the big four state-owned commercial banks over the past decade. Including the capital injections of 1998,[22] 2004 and 2005, and above market purchases by AMCs of nonperforming loans since 1999, by mid-2005, sums equivalent to roughly CNY3 trillion, or about 30 percent of 2001 GDP, had been injected into these banks alone.[23] Additional sums will need to be provided to the Agricultural Bank of China (ABC), one of the four state-owned commercial banks, which is thought to have been generally in worse shape than the others.

The cleanup of the pre-1999 loan portfolio of the big banks has been quite comprehensive. By the time of its IPO in late 2006, pre-1999 corporate loans amounted to only 5 percent of ICBC's corporate loan book. It is thus from the performance of post-1999 loans that any future loan losses might arise.

Even if banks are now lending more to households and firms not controlled by government it does not follow either that the new lending is sound or that its recoverability is wholly dependent on market conditions. It remains unclear to what extent internal management of the banks has truly refocused lending decisions on profitability as against balance sheet growth and compliance with political goals. For one thing, the ability of the many construction firms and other contractors to different levels of government to repay their bank loans will depend on the financial condition of these governments. Repayment capacity could come into question if current rates of public infrastructure investment prove to be excessive and unsupportable. The over-rapid accumulation of productive capacity in many manufacturing sectors also gives rise to concerns that, where loans have been used to pay for the capital expansion,[24] they may be hard to service, especially if there were a slowing of economic growth. The rapid expansion of consumer credit (credit cards, home mortgage loans) has also caused observers to worry. Nevertheless, banks report low nonperforming rates for new lending.

Naturally enough, the question of whether the recent loan book of the big four banks contains some hidden problems is highly disputed, as witness the debate which followed publication in May 2006 of a flawed estimate by accounting firm Ernst & Young (*China Daily*, 2006). Given the unprecedented nature of the Chinese economic boom, the only fair statement is that no one really knows the true quality of the loan appraisal decisions that have recently been made, and no precise estimate can be made of the likely loan losses that are embedded in the new portfolio and that could lead to a call for further fiscal outlays.

Other parts of the banking system have also experienced solvency problems. In particular, the RCCs are also widely acknowledged to have a large capital deficiency (Zhou 2004b) and certain CCBs are also thought by commentators to be in the same position. In May 2004 provision was made for subsidies or assistance in the amount of over 1 percent of GDP to meet the capital deficiency of the RCCs. It may safely be assumed that further fiscal outlays would be necessary to meet depositors' claims in some of the city commercial banks, too, as well as in insurance and brokerage, though the amount that could be involved is limited by the smaller scale of these institutions.

Note that treatment of the debtors whose obligations were acquired by the AMCs can also represent a bailout to the extent that soft budget constraints are applied. The soft budget problem can be illustrated by the financial restructuring of a borrowing enterprise whose NPLs have been purchased by AMCs. If it receives a debt equity swap by the AMC while still remaining fundamentally unprofitable, this equity injection will strengthen the creditworthiness of the firm, which can thus continue to borrow to cover losses for a considerable interval as it eats its way through the new equity capital. If they are careful, the banks may make such loans without exposing themselves to undue risk, but social welfare declines as value-reducing firms are allowed to remain in business. Case studies from China purport to illustrate this pattern (Steinfeld 2005).[25]

10.4   Plans for a Formal Deposit Insurance Scheme in China

10.4.1   From Implicit to Explicit Deposit Protection in China

Despite the scale of fiscal and quasifiscal outlays to date, it would be a mistake to characterize China's approach to loss allocation as entirely one on which the fiscal authority has always picked up the tab regardless of the circumstances. While there has been a large degree of implicit insurance, it has not been a blanket coverage. Instead, in the case of closures, the central authorities have seen themselves as attempting to place the burden on those who should be held responsible for incurring the losses.

Thus, they have used *central* government or PBC funds to make whole the depositors in insolvent intermediaries controlled by *central* government. But, when the failing intermediary was owned or controlled by a lower level of government, the central authorities have usually insisted that—apart from the claims of individual depositors—claims be dealt with by the sponsoring lower government, thereby reducing the moral hazard.

In this way, the authorities have sought to balance fairness with the need to limit moral hazard and, in the case of state–owned or supervised institutions, to respect a coherent assignment of responsibility.

The major decisions taken in the failures of several small institutions in 1997–1998 provide the key illustration of this policy. All of the banks and nearbanks involved in these failures were owned or sponsored by provincial or lower level governments. It was on these that the cost of compensating individual deposits fell, even though advances were made from central (national) authorities, mainly the PBC, to meet the initial cash needs. The decision in principle that national authorities would not compensate enterprise depositors can be seen as reflecting a caveat emptor view that depositing enterprises ought to have made their own judgments on the creditworthiness of the banks and nearbanks concerned and ought to bear the consequences of their errors or negligence in this regard. Of course, to the extent that these enterprises too were largely owned or sponsored by local governments, the dividing line between fiscal costs and burden-sharing with the nongovernment sector is somewhat blurred. Some of these enterprises may have received injections of funds from their governmental owners under some other rubric. Also, foreign enterprises and some private enterprises were sometimes compensated, reflecting a degree of flexibility in the application of the underlying policy. However, even foreign claimants were hit in the GITIC collapse[26] and there have been cases where enterprises collapsed with job losses as a result of losing their deposits in the failures.

Recent policy announcements about depositor protection imply that the concept of coresponsibility will (under the proposed scheme) be extended to large individual depositors—those with sufficient at stake for them to exercise caution in choosing their depository. Whereas recent Chinese policy has been to protect individual or household deposits in full[27] a recent announcement explicitly limits protection in future by to the first CNY100,000 for individual depositors, while also covering 90 percent of the remainder of any individual's deposits.[28] The figure of CNY100,000 is about twelve times average per capita income in China (or about seven times average per capita *urban* income). Even though enterprise deposits would not necessarily enjoy this level of cover (details of the proposed coverage for enterprises have yet to be announced), it should be noted that such a scheme represents a very high level of coverage, especially in relation to income. Indeed, only Nicaragua and two tiny islands with offshore financial sectors have larger explicit limits on coverage when expressed as a percentage of average income. The typical EU deposit insurance scheme covers only 90 percent of the first EUR20,000—equivalent to less than average per capita income in Europe[29]—and even the notoriously generous U.S. scheme covers only the first US$100,000, or 2.8 times annual per capita income.

The basis for depositor confidence in the big state-owned banks is somewhat different. These entities have been arms of the state. Despite part privatization, there is no doubt that customers still regard their deposits as claims on the state and not merely as a contingent claim on the assets of the banks. Any failure to redeem the deposits would be seen as a default of the state. The heavy loan losses of these banks will be absorbed by some part of society, but if this is the perspective of the depositors they will not see why they should be considered as in the front line when it comes to loss allocation. This perspective also seems to have been accepted in official circles, which have shown no indication of ever considering such an option. Given that China's fiscal position, even after making full provision for banking and other contingent liabilities, seems sustainable over the long run, the case for an alternative approach would be a difficult sell. Over time, if the state's shareholding in the big four banks declines further, the perspective may gradually change, though they are likely to continue to be seen as too-big-to-fail.

10.4.2   The Motivation for and Likely Impact of Formal Deposit Insurance in China

Earlier parts of this chapter have reviewed the background against which the new scheme is being planned. Here we try to infer the rationale that might underlie the introduction of deposit insurance now in China.

Two contrasting theoretical perspectives are useful in considering why deposit insurance might be adopted. The more traditional approach assumes that public policy is designed to achieve public goals. The other approach assumes that policy is driven by private interests.

Given the current policy preoccupations in China, the "public interest" approach does not provide a convincing explanation for why China should want to introduce deposit insurance now. Thus, four main public policy goals have been most often cited worldwide as favoring the introduction of deposit insurance: (1) enhancing financial depth and (2) systemic stability, (3) promotion of more effective banking competition, and (4) reduction of fiscal exposure. Each of these four goals has been suggested for China, too, but it is likely that they do not adequately capture the Chinese authorities' motivation for introducing a scheme. For one thing, recent scholarship has cast doubt on the ability of deposit insurance to deliver such favorable results in the conditions prevailing in many developing countries (cf. Cull, Senbet, and Sorge 2005; Demirgüç-Kunt and Kane 2002). Besides, current Chinese conditions do not suggest that these four are the real policy priorities. For each of the four, a related but different policy goal seems to be receiving greater priority from the authorities at present.

1. Rather than even more banking depth, China needs a relative strengthening of the nonbank financial sector;

2. Instability from depositor panic is not on the immediate horizon, but a strengthening of the governance of banking institutions certainly is;

3. The promotion of new private competitors for the large banks is a worthwhile goal, but dwarfed in importance by the need to reduce the State's ownership role in financial institutions, large and small;

4. While reducing the level of NPLs has certainly been an important goal, reducing the exposure of the PBC in bank failures seems to loom larger in official plans than that of limiting fiscal costs more generally.

Banking Depth vs. Securities Market Development In contrast to the situation in many countries whose plans for deposit insurance have been motivated by a desire to promote confidence in the banking system on a medium-term basis, thereby enhancing overall financial depth, China's banking system is one of the deepest in the world.

Instead, what the Chinese financial system needs is not a bigger banking system but increased diversification of intermediary and financial instrument types, and especially a strengthening of the securities markets and more term finance. It is hard to see the introduction of deposit insurance, especially with such generous ceilings as are now being proposed, doing anything to redress the imbalance between stock market and bank deposit development in China.[30] Also, the selective protection of bank deposits does nothing to encourage small savers to move into longer-term media offered by nonbanks. This inhibits the natural development of term finance.

Stability and Governance As to the potential role of a deposit insurance scheme in helping to stabilize the overall system in a crisis by retaining the confidence of the depositors, this cannot be a strong motivation at present in China, where so much of the banking system is state-owned, and as such enjoying unquestioned backing by the national authorities. Rather than a fear of systemic financial instability, authorities may be motivated to reduce the political fallout of depositor losses in bank failure—for which the euphemism "social stability" is often used in China.

The real challenge in this area facing the Chinese authorities is the need to achieve improved governance of the banks. Advocates of deposit insurance can argue that the establishment of a strong deposit insurance agency, with intervention powers and obligations, can represent an effective administrative tool for early action to curtail the activities of self-serving or poorly governed bank management. With its own funds at stake, such an agency might have internal incentives to move quickly in such circumstances. Also, having signed up to an insurance scheme, shareholders will be on weaker grounds in vexatious appeals to courts against prompt corrective action taken by the insurer. But the powers of the bank regulator CBRC are already extensive and have not so far represented an obstacle to action vis-à-vis small banks. Besides, the use by many countries, notably most European deposit insurers, of the "pay box approach" to deposit insurance which leaves the intervention function in the hands of the supervisory agency suggests that this is not a necessary mechanism.

Instead, potential weakening of market discipline resulting from an extension of formal deposit insurance to even small banks, may outweigh any gain from placing a ceiling on the amount covered. The way in which previous failures have been resolved has left some residual uncertainty in the market about the degree to which institutional depositors and other claimants will be made whole: the new scheme does not necessarily increase large depositors' sense of being at risk.

Competition and the Role of the State   There may be more substance in the idea that at least some of the Chinese authorities wish to help diversify the ownership and reduce concentration in banking. This objective would also be strongly backed by the smaller banks, but it is unclear that they have much political power at present. To the extent that deposit insurance provides greater assurance to small depositors that their savings will be safe in even small private banks, it might seem to promote competition for the large incumbents. But given the continuing ambiguity of the government's role in the financial system and the wider economy, it is not very plausible that in introducing deposit insurance, the government is trying to undermine its own banks.

Fiscal Costs   The Chinese authorities have stated that one of their objectives in formalizing depositor protection is to limit the fiscal exposure to bank failure by defining precisely which bank claimants will be reimbursed. A snag here is the cross-country evidence that fiscal costs are actually higher in countries that opt for a formal protection scheme, except where underlying institutions are quite strong—stronger, it would appear, than in China. Governance indicators for China have not recently been improving—indeed, the composite indicator of governance for China published by the World Bank has remained well below the world average in the past decade and actually declined between 1996 and 2005, to more than half a standard deviation below the world average (Kaufmann, Kraay, and Mastruzzi 2006).

Besides, the fiscal costs already incurred in the big four state-owned banks dwarf anything that might be incurred in the foreseeable future from rescuing the depositors of new private banks. The horse has bolted.

10.4.3   Deposit Insurance and Improved Alignment of Official Incentives

The public interest approach thus has difficulty in explaining why China would wish to adopt deposit insurance now. Recent research has instead emphasized the private interest approach to public policy, highlighting the role of political economy in determining the presence and extent of deposit insurance as well as the approach to banking regulation more generally (cf. Barth, Caprio, and Levine 2006; Kroszner and Strahan 2001; Laeven 2004). In China, the competing interests of different administrative entities and layers of government are likely to be among the most important driving forces.

The introduction of a stand alone deposit insurance scheme can, as will now be argued, be seen as shifting the locus of responsibility for funding the cost of bank failures away from the PBC.

After all, if something is not done, the PBC is likely to be shouldering an ever increasing share of the burden. After all, the current approach for assigning responsibility which, as mentioned previously, has called on the sponsoring government to bear the cost, is breaking down. With a growing number of intermediaries that do not have a controlling government sponsor, the old formula cannot always be applied. Claims of a failing bank without a local government sponsor will likely tend to fall on the PBC, even though it no longer has any role in regulating the bank. The introduction of a funded deposit insurance agency could avert this outcome.

But it's not just a question of shifting the burden. By creating a barrier to the quasiautomatic use of PBC funds, the scheme might possibly bring some greater discipline to the regulatory agencies encouraging them to intervene more promptly in failing institutions. This discipline effect would have a better chance of working if the deposit insurer and the primary regulator were the same entity.

However, this envisaged incentive mechanism might not work very well. After all, the PBC is still likely to be tapped as soon as insurance agency funds run out.

10.5   Concluding Remarks

Over the past few years, fear of financial instability or of the related social instability has slowed or deferred reforms that would be desirable to ensure a system better geared to providing the financial services needed by China to support sustained and broadbased economic growth. In addition, unlimited compensation for household depositors and for all claimants of state-owned banks has placed a substantial—albeit somewhat hidden—burden on the fiscal accounts.

Steps are being taken to correct the situation. Not only have NPL stocks been reduced through write-offs and asset sales, but internal governance changes and managerial action have been adopted with a view to reducing the flow of new nonperforming loans at the big four state-owned banks and to improving the financial performance of the banks more generally.

The key policy challenges are inextricably linked to the interpenetration of state agencies and financial intermediaries and markets. For the longer term, the sound development of banking and finance in China clearly needs a clearer dividing line between the role of banks (including those that are directly and indirectly controlled by central or other levels of government) as financially autonomous and profit-seeking intermediaries on the one hand and the wider economic and social role of the state on the other. Improved incentives for state agencies involved either in regulation or ownership of financial institutions will be an important part of this process. This need is at least partly recognized by the authorities. Gradually the state is divesting itself of shareholdings in the banking system, though full privatization is still not on the horizon.

Despite the many warning signs, the authorities' partial success in coming this far in the transition from the planned economy without experiencing an open financial crisis, or a burst of hyperinflation (albeit at the cost of assuming a heavy fiscal burden and a sizable misallocation of loanable funds away from the more dynamic segments of the economy) makes it conceivable that their gradualist and unorthodox approach to institutional reform in the financial sector could perform better than is suggested by experience in other countries to date.

The authorities wisely refrained from introducing deposit insurance in the early years of banking sector reform. But now they are proposing to take what must be considered a calculated risk in formalizing a deposit insurance scheme in the face of cross-country evidence that such schemes fail to achieve the expected reduction in crisis frequency and cost unless the general institutional environment is stronger than it appears to be yet in China.

The degree of coresponsibility now proposed for individual depositors is very low, and the proposed ceiling to coverage is very high.

Inasmuch as it could reduce the open–ended role of the central bank PBC in funding rescues, introduction of a formal deposit insurance

scheme could conceivably reduce fiscal costs. But to do this, the responsibility for the insurance payout would need to be assigned to the primary regulator—the CBRC for banks. Even then, deposit insurance alone may be too weak an instrument to do much in this direction. International experience suggests that it will not work.

More generally, the weak and deteriorating scores, by international standards, in indicators of governance in China suggest that the preconditions for moving safely to a formal deposit insurance system are simply not present.

Because China's banking system is so large, the costs could be high if the gamble of introducing insurance does not pay off.

Acknowledgments

I would like to thank Aslı Demirgüç-Kunt, Luc Laeven, Khalid Mirza, David Scott, Wang Jun, Xie Ping, Yi Gang, Zhang Wei, and Zhang Xin for helpful suggestions or comments. However, all opinions expressed are those of the author alone.

Notes

1. As used here, the term "state-owned" refers to entities directly owned central agencies of the Chinese government.

2. Over 97 percent of the banking system is directly or indirectly owned by some level of government.

3. Even the exaggerated loss estimates suggested by Ernst and Young in a 2006 report, subsequently withdrawn, would not be sufficient to generate the kinds of pressure being considered here.

4. Managerial corruption has also been a problem, as evidenced by thousands of officials who have been sanctioned, up to and including the chief executive of one of the big four banks.

5. Well illustrated by econometric analysis of the interprovincial flow of funds (Boyreau-Debray 2003; Boyreau-Debray and Wei 2004; Podpiera 2006), and documented by a variety of surveys (cf. Dobson and Kashyap 2006 for some examples).

6. Foreign investors are still limited to an aggregate of no more than 25 percent of the equity of any bank.

7. Examples here are the restriction on banks participating in most securities markets (a restriction imposed in response to imprudent lending for such purposes by some banks) and the restriction on the formation of financial or industrial-financial conglomerates (seen as presenting special risks because of the difficulty the supervisors have in obtaining sufficient information on the whole group for adequate prudential supervision). Despite this latter restriction, there are such conglomerates in China, some fully authorized

(in a grandfathering), such as Everbright, some subsisting in a legal grey area, such as the failed D'Long group (for a journalistic account of the complex but revealing failure of the latter see the report in the financial periodical Caijing: http://caijing.hexun.com/english/2004/040805/040805delong.htm.

8. As recently as March 2005, as CCB was being prepared for part privatization, bank chairman Zhang Enzhao, resigned amid allegations of corruption (http://caijing.hexun.com/english/detail.aspx?issue=167&id=1205725). No fewer than 58,000 responsible officials in two state banks alone were sanctioned for abuses according to reports of a speech by PBC Deputy Governor Guo, reported in SCMP, March 8, 2005. Senior bank officials have been executed for fraud (four cases are detailed in http://www.chinadaily.com.cn/english/doc/2004-09/15/content_374453.htm; other death penalties have been subject to appeal; see http://www.bjreview.com.cn/En-2005/05-34-e/people-34.htm).

9. The use of growing deposit resources to insulate politically influential segments of the economy, notably the state-owned enterprise sector, from collapsing under the pressure of wider economic reforms, can be seen as an illustration of a wider pattern in Chinese economic reform, whereby interim institutional and policy reforms were designed to perform the dual function of making the reform incentive compatible for those in positions of power facilitating while facilitating economic efficiency improvements (Qian 2003).

10. Goldman Sachs 2004. Note, however, that the official formal ownership categories are no longer considered reliable indicators of effective nongovernment control (Gregory, Tenev, and Wagle 2000). Many of the firms theoretically controlled by government are in practice controlled by their management (Zhou 2004c). Non-state-controlled exporting firms tend to rely heavily on foreign direct investment (Huang 2004).

11. Despite the major upward revision in the official estimate of the level of 2004 GDP announced in December 2005. Where not otherwise specified, the data reported in this chapter is taken from the websites of the chief financial authorities.

12. Before the data revision mentioned in note 3 was announced, the ratio of M2 to GDP seemed to have doubled in ten years. Revisions to GDP for earlier years have not yet been released; it is likely that the growth rate of the M2/GDP ratio was slightly lower.

13. More recently, brokerage firms have also gotten into difficulties not only because of insufficient trading volumes and depressed market prices, but because they speculated with clients' funds.

14. This institution was closed in 1998, less than three years after its formation, and after additionally absorbing twenty-eight local urban credit cooperatives. The PBC had provided CNY3 billion in liquidity support before closure (Xie 1999; Liu 1999; Yang, Chun, and Xie 2002).

15. Sponsored mainly by different level of government and state–owned enterprises as a kind of freewheeling universal bank designed to raise funds for the sponsor's needs (including making property and equity investments), TICs emerged first in the 1980s.

16. The same may be said of encouraging a bank to buy a weak securities or insurance firm.That is not to deny that allowing universal banking may provide some protection against crises (Barth, Caprio, and Levine 2006).

17. Together they account for 6 percent of the banking system. Some of these have grown quite large, such as the CCB of Kunming, which has a presence in all the major urban centers of Yunnan province. Only two have so far been permitted to operate in more than one province: Beijing in Tianjin and Shanghai in Ningbo. The CCBs are to be

distinguished from the twelve nationwide or regional joint stock banks (of which five are listed on the Shanghai exchange), and which account for 16 percent of the system.

18. China Construction Bank's IPO prospectus reports sizable reliefs of this type.

19. Between 1997 and 2001, one regional bank, five TICs (including the very large China Agricultural Trust and Investment Company, January 1997, and the Guangdong International Trust and Investment Company (GITIC), October 1998—each of them with more than CNY30 billion in liabilities, 304 urban credit cooperatives (147 of them in Guangdong province alone after 1999) and eighteen RCCs were actually closed (Wu 2001). Mention should also be made of the largely unregulated network of Rural Credit Foundations (RCFs), operating under collective control mainly at township level, which grew strongly from the mid-1980s—to the point where they had more than CNY100 billion in deposits. The sector was comprehensively intervened in 1999 following the failure of a several large RCFs in Chongqing and Sichuan. Most of the better performing RCFs were absorbed by RCCs; the others were closed and, to the extent that they had insufficient funds, their deposit liabilities to households fell on local governments, on the logic that it was these who had authorized the creation of RCFs (Cheng, Findlay, and Watson 2003).

20. Even as recently as June 2005, the PBC agreed to rescue brokerage firms that were in difficulty. The sums can be large; media reports put the estimated deficiency of just one of these brokerage firms, the state-owned Galaxy, at over CNY5 billion.

21. The financial independence of the PBC could also be compromised by such activities inasmuch as this independence depends on having a largely interest bearing asset side of the balance sheet. To the extent that bailouts are matched by the accumulation of nonperforming or notional assets in lieu of interest-bearing ones, this erodes the net income of the central bank.

22. This was a thirty-year bond with coupon way above market at 7.2 percent. As of November 2004 the coupon was lowered (by decision of the Standing Committee of the National People's Congress) to 2.25 percent and will float with the one-year deposit rate.

23. The main amounts are: (1) CNY270 billion capital injection of 1998; (2) The 1999/2001 AMC purchases of loans from the main banks amounted to CNY1.4 trillion; (3) The 2003 injection of US$45 billion into two banks (apparently in return for further NPLs) equals CNY370 billion; (4) CNY280 billion of loans was bought from the same two banks in mid-2004 at 50 percent of face value by one of the AMCs (Cinda), financed with a loan from the PBC; (5) In April 2005 a further sum of US$15 billion was injected into ICBC, and in the following two months, bad loans amounting to RMB705 billion were transferred to AMCs at close to face value; together these ICBC transactions come to CNY830 billion. Let us take the 2001 GDP of CNY10 trillion (this figure may be subject to upward revision) as a somewhat arbitrary but convenient reference point, given that most of the losses to be noted had likely accrued by then or earlier. Then the CNY3 trillion total of transactions (1)–(5) is equivalent to 30 percent of GDP. These are gross figures and it should be acknowledged that there has been some recovery on the bad loans transferred to AMCs: by March 2006, with more than two-thirds of the original AMC transfer having been disposed of, CNY210 billion had been recovered (of which CNY181 billion in cash). (CNY is the international symbol for the Chinese yuan; the currency is also known as renminbi (RMB). From 1994 to 2005, a fixed rate of US$1 = CNY 8.28 was in effect; a modest appreciation has occurred since then.)

24. Though much has been financed by retained earnings, with little pressure in particular on profitable state-owned firms to pay dividends (cf. Kuijs 2005).

25. It may be questioned just how independent China's AMCs are from the state-owned banks with which they have each been associated considering that the president of each bank was appointed Communist Party secretary of the corresponding AMC (Fung et al. 2004).

26. Individual depositors in GITIC were compensated by local government as to the face value of their deposit, but not for interest; in addition, a large fraction of the foreign liabilities of GITIC were excluded from the benefiting from the liquidation as the borrowing had not been properly authorized (Zhu 1999; Fedelino and Singh 2004).

27. For an interesting account of a 2003 scheme to exploit the full coverage of individual deposits and to defraud the PBC by taking control of a small financial intermediary and creating bogus individual household deposits before driving the intermediary into liquidarion, see Caijing magazine: http://caijing.hexun.com/english/2004/040620/040620Stockbrokers.htm.

28. There is to be no ceiling in respect of individual saving deposits and clients' securities transactions settlement funds. The "Guidelines on Acquisition of Individual Claims and Clients' Securities Transactions Settlement Funds," were announced in November 2004. According to the announcement, funds to meet these disbursements are to be advanced by the PBC, with any eventual deficiency to be made up out of the resources of planned explicit depositor protection schemes. Protection for the insurance and securities markets was recently being put in place. A regulation creating a scheme for insurance policyholders was issued by the CIRC in January 2005, and an investor compensation fund (covering depositors at insolvent securities brokerage firms), with initial capital funding from public resources of over RMB6 billion was launched in September 2005.

29. A few EU countries offer much more generous schemes, for example, Italy, where maximum coverage per depositor is over €100,000.

30. Despite the rescue as mentioned of a handful of market intermediaries. Media discussion of possible equity market support schemes has not been confirmed.

References

Barth, James, Gerard Caprio, and Ross Levine. 2006. *Rethinking Bank Regulation: 'til Angels Govern*. New York and Cambridge: Cambridge University Press.

Boyreau-Debray, Genevieve. 2003. Financial Intermediation and Growth: Chinese Style. Policy Research Working Paper no. 3027. The World Bank, Washington, D.C.

Boyreau-Debray, Genevieve, and Shang-Jin Wei. 2004. Can China Grow Faster? A Diagnosis on the Fragmentation of the Domestic Capital Market. Working Paper no. 04/76. International Monetary Fund, Washington, D.C.

Chang, Enjiang, Christopher Findlay, and Andrew Watson. 2003. Institutional Innovation without Regulation: The Collapse of Rural Credit Foundations and Lessons for Further Financial Reforms. In *Rural Financial Markets in China*, ed. C. Findlay, A. Watson, Cheng Enjiang, and Zhu Gang, 89–104. Canberra: ANU Asia Pacific Press.

Cull, Robert, Lemma Senbet, and Marco Sorge. 2005. Deposit Insurance and Financial Development. *Journal of Money, Credit and Banking* 37 (1): 43–82.

Demirgüç-Kunt, Aslı, and Edward Kane. 2002. Deposit Insurance around the World: Where Does It Work?" *Journal of Economic Perspectives* 16: 175–195.

Demirgüç-Kunt, Aslı, Edward J. Kane, and Luc Laeven. 2006. Deposit Insurance Design and Implementation: Policy Lessons from Research and Practice. Policy Research Paper no. 3969. The World Bank, Washington, D.C.

Dobson, Wendy, and Anil K. Kashyap. 2006. The Contradiction in China's Gradualist Banking Reforms. *Brooking Papers on Economic Activity* (Fall): 103–148.

Dollar, David, Mary Hallward-Driemeier, Anqing Shi, Scott Wallsten, Shuilin Wang, and Lixin Colin Xu. 2003. Improving the Investment Climate in China. Mimeo., The World Bank, Washington D.C.

Fedelino, Annalisa, and Raju Jan Singh. 2004. Medium-Term Fiscal Challenges. Occasional Paper no. 232, 29–35. International Monetary Fund, Washington, D.C.

Fung, Ben, Jason George, Stefan Hohl, and Guonan Ma. 2004. Public Asset Management Companies in East Asia. FSI Paper no. 3, Financial Stability Institute, Basel.

Goldman Sachs. 2004. China Banks: Loan Growth. Mimeo., Goldman Sachs (January 26).

Goodhart, Charles, and Dirk Schoenmaker. 1995. Should the Functions of Monetary Policy and Banking Supervision Be Separated?" *Oxford Economic Papers* 47 (4): 539–560.

Gregory, Neil, Stoyan Tenev,and Dileep Wagle. 2000. *China's Emerging Private Enterprises.* Washington, D.C.: International Finance Corporation.

Huang, Yasheng. 2004. Why More May Be Actually Less: Financial Biases and Labor-Intensive FDI in China. Mimeo., Massachusetts Institute of Technology.

Kaufmann, Daniel, Aart Kraay, and Massimo Mastruzzi. 2006. Governance Matters V: Governance Indicators for 1996–2005. Mimeo., The World Bank Institute, Washington, D.C.

Kroszner, Randall S., and Philip Strahan. 2001. Obstacles to Optimal Policy: The Interplay of Politics and Economics in Shaping Bank Supervision and Regulation Reforms. In *Prudential Supervision: What Works and What Doesn't*, ed. Frederick S. Mishkin, 233–273. Chicago: University of Chicago Press.

Kuijs, Louis. 2005. Investment and Saving in China. Policy Research Working Paper no. 3633, The World Bank, Washington, D.C.

Laeven, Luc. 2004. The Political Economy of Deposit Insurance. *Journal of Financial Services Research* 26 (3): 201–224.

Lardy, Nicholas R. 1998. *China's Unfinished Economic Revolution.* Washington, D.C.: Brookings Institution.

Liu, Shiyu. 1999. China's Experience in Small and Medium Financial Institution Resolution. BIS Policy Paper no. 7, Bank for International Settlements, Basel.

Podpiera, Richard. 2006. Progress in China's Banking Sector Reform: Has Bank Behavior Changed? Working Paper no. 06/71, International Monetary Fund, Washington, D.C.

Qian, Yingyi. 2003. How Reform Worked in China. In *In Search of Prosperity*, ed. Dani Rodrik, 297–333. Princeton: Princeton University Press.

Shih, Victor. 2005. China's Uphill Battle for Stronger Banks. *Far Eastern Economic Review* (November 21): 37–40.

Steinfeld, Edward S. 2005. Government Failure or Market Failure: China's Debt-Equity Swaps. In *Financial Sector Reform in China*, ed. Yasheng Huang, Anthony Saich, and Edward S. Steinfeld, 50–66. Cambridge: Harvard University Press.

Wu, Xiaoling, ed. 2001. *Almanac of China's Finance and Banking 2001*. Beijing.

Wu, Xiaoling. 2005. Conditions and Environment for Improving Corporate Governance Structure of China's Financial Enterprises. Address to the China International Finance Development Forum, April 16.

Xie, Ping. 1999. Bank Restructuring in China. BIS Policy Paper no. 6, Bank for International Settlements, Basel.

Yang, Wonkeun, Sun Eae Chun, and Zhigang Xie. 2002. Introducing Deposit Insurance System in China: A Comparative Study from Korean Experience. In *Overcoming Financial Crisis: Financial Reform in Asia*. Proceedings of the 3rd KDIC International Financial Symposium, October 25, 2002.

Yi, Gang. 2003. Changes in China Capital Market. Paper presented at the World Bank/ DRC Workshop on National Market Integration (September).

Zhou, Xiaochuan. 2004b. Some Reflections on Rural Financial Reform. Speech at the Conference of the Chinese Economists Society, Beijing, China (June 20).

Zhou, Xiaochuan. 2004c. Improve Legal System and Financial Ecology. Speech at the Forum of 50 Chinese Economists, Beijing (December 2).

Zhu, Jun. 1999. Closure of Financial Institutions in China. In Strengthening the Banking System in China: Issues and Experience. BIS Policy Paper no. 7, Bank for International Settlements, Basel.

IV   Deposit Insurance: Database

11 Deposit Insurance around the World: A Comprehensive Database

Aslı Demirgüç-Kunt, Edward Kane, Baybars Karacaovali, and Luc Laeven

11.1 Introduction

This chapter presents and discusses a new deposit insurance database that updates an earlier one constructed in 1999 by Demirgüç-Kunt and Sobaci (2001) and extends it in several important dimensions.

This new comprehensive database includes fourteen countries that have adopted deposit insurance schemes since 1999[1] and identifies twelve other countries[2] that had adopted deposit insurance as of 1999 but do not appear in Demirgüç-Kunt and Sobaci 2001 due to lack of data. Apart from the use of various country sources, we have carried out surveys directed to officials of deposit insurance institutions, central banks, and related government officials around the world. The other important extension is to develop an historical time series (rather than data for year-end 1999 only) for several key variables, including deposit insurance coverage, coverage ratios, and coinsurance. Additional measures include the level of coinsurance requirements, percentage of the value of deposit covered, and whether the payments are per depositor or per depositor per account. Finally, the dataset incorporates part of the survey data relevant for deposit insurance provided by Barth, Caprio, and Levine (2004).[3]

Deposit insurance is used by governments in hopes of assuring the stability of banking systems and protecting bank depositors from incurring large losses due to bank failures. Almost all countries have de facto financial safety nets in place that combine explicit and implicit deposit insurance, bank regulation and supervision, central bank lender of last resort facilities, and procedures for resolving bank insolvencies. Although explicit deposit insurance is gaining in popularity among policymakers, its desirability is challenged by concerns about moral hazard problems and excessive risk taking by banks (see, e.g., Demirgüç-Kunt and Kane 2002).

This chapter aims to facilitate additional research on the effects of deposit insurance design on different banking outcomes (e.g., Demirgüç-Kunt and Huizinga 2004; Demirgüç-Kunt and Detragiache 2002; Laeven 2004) by providing detailed data on features of individual deposit insurance schemes in an empirically usable format. We present the salient features of the data in detail with countries grouped according to income level and geographical region.

The chapter is organized as follows. Section 11.2 discusses the adoption of deposit insurance around the world and Section 11.3 describes the main database. Section 11.4 discusses main features of the deposit insurance schemes and Section 11.5 concludes.

11.2   Deposit Insurance Adoption

As Demirgüç-Kunt, Kane, and Laeven (2005) point out, every country has a de facto implicit deposit insurance scheme (IDIS) in place since governments are pressed for relief whenever systemic banking distress breaks out. If an explicit deposit insurance scheme (EDIS) does not exist, we classify the country as offering implicit deposit insurance.

Figure 11.1 provides the number of countries with EDIS and IDIS in our sample of 181 countries based on their income level, and table 11.1 lists their names. Figure 11.2 and table 11.2 provide similar information for middle and low-income countries where the countries are grouped according to their geographical region. As of 2003, eighty-eight countries adopted EDIS, whereas the remaining ninety-three countries in our sample are considered to have IDIS (table 11.1 and figure 11.1).

As shown in table 1.2, the adoption of EDIS rises with income level; 16.39 percent of low income countries have an EDIS, whereas the ratio goes up to 60.71 percent for upper middle income and to 75 percent for high income countries. When the proportion of countries with EDIS is computed based on the dollar value of their GDP, hence how large their economies are, the proportions rise to 96.35 percent for high income countries and to 78.11 percent for low income countries. The proportions based on GDP per capita are similar to the ones based on the number of countries.

Among the middle- and low-income countries, the occurrence of EDIS is higher in Europe and Central Asia (74.07 percent) and Latin America and Caribbean (66.67 percent), and it is the lowest in sub-

Panel A: Explicit deposit insurance

Number of countries

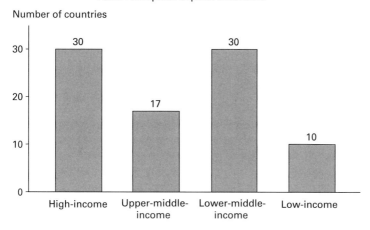

Panel B: Implicit deposit insurance

Number of countries

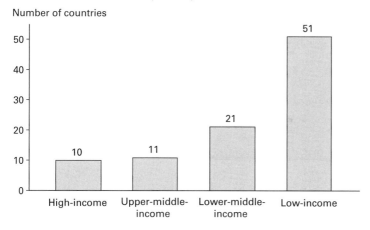

Figure 11.1
Adoption of deposit insurance around the world by income level (as of 2003)

Saharan Africa (10.87 percent). The occurrence rates go up to approximately 98 percent for both European and Central Asian and Latin American and Caribbean countries when proportions are based on GDP.

The United States is the first in history to adopt a national EDIS. Its scheme dates from 1934—a year marked by a severe banking crisis.[4] This adoption was followed in the 1960s by nine other countries and the trend has been dramatically upward, especially since the 1980s.

A. Demirgüç-Kunt, E. Kane, B. Karacaovali, and L. Laeven

Table 11.1
Adoption of deposit insurance around the world by income level (years of establishment/revision in parentheses and number of countries by group in brackets, as of 2003)

Panel A: Explicit deposit insurance

High-income countries [30]

Austria (1979/1996)	France (1980/1986/1999)	Korea (1996)	Spain (1977/1996)
Bahamas (1999)	Germany (1966/1969/1998)	Liechtenstein (1992/2003)	Sweden (1996)
Bahrain (1993)	Greece (1995/2000)	Luxembourg (1989)	Switzerland (1984/1993)
Belgium (1974/1995/1998)	Iceland (1985/1996)	Malta (2003)	Taiwan (1985)
Canada (1967)	Ireland (1989/1995)	Netherlands (1978/1996/1998)	United Kingdom (1982/1995)
Cyprus (2000)	Isle of Man (1991)	Norway (1961/1997)	United States (1934/1991)
Denmark (1987/1995)	Italy (1987/1996)	Portugal (1992/1995)	
Finland (1969/1992/1998)	Japan (1971)	Slovenia (2001)	

Upper-middle-income countries [17]

Argentina (1979/1995)	Hungary (1993)	Mexico (1986/1990/1999)	Uruguay (2002)
Chile (1986)	Latvia (1998)	Oman (1995)	Venezuela (1985/2001)
Croatia (1997)	Lebanon (1967)	Poland (1995)	
Czech Republic (1994)	Lithuania (1996)	Slovak Republic (1996/2001)	
Estonia (1998)	Malaysia (1998)	Trinidad and Tobago (1986)	

Lower-middle-income countries [30]

Albania (2002)	Colombia (1985)	Kazakhstan (1999/2003)	Russia (2003)
Algeria (1997)	Dominican Republic (1962)	Macedonia (1996/2000/2002)	Serbia and Montenegro (2001)
Belarus (1996/1998/2000/2001/2004)	Ecuador (1998)	Marshall Islands (1975)	Sri Lanka (1987)
	El Salvador (1999)	Micronesia (1963)	Thailand (1997)

Bolivia (2001)	Guatemala (1999)	Paraguay (2003)	Turkey (1983/2000)
Bosnia and Herzegovina (1998)	Honduras (1999)	Peru (1991)	Turkmenistan (2000)
Brazil (1995/2002)	Jamaica (1998)	Philippines (1963)	Ukraine (1998)
Bulgaria (1996/1998/2001/2002)	Jordan (2000)	Romania (1996)	

Low-income countries [10]

Bangladesh (1984)	Kenya (1988)	Tanzania (1994)	Zimbabwe (2003)
India (1961)	Nicaragua (2001)	Uganda (1994)	
Indonesia (1998)	Nigeria (1988/1989)	Vietnam (2000)	

Panel B: Implicit deposit insurance

High-income countries [10]

Australia	Brunei	Israel	New Zealand	Singapore
Barbados	Hong Kong	Kuwait	Qatar	United Arab Emirates

Upper-middle-income countries [11]

Belize	Costa Rica	Grenada	Mauritius	Saudi Arabia	St. Lucia
Botswana	Gabon	Libya	Panama	Seychelles	

Lower-middle-income countries [21]

Armenia	Djibouti	Iran	Morocco	Swaziland	Western Samoa
Cape Verde	Egypt	Iraq	Namibia	Syria	
China	Fiji	Kiribati	South Africa	Tunisia	
Cuba	Guyana	Maldives	Suriname	Vanuatu	

Table 11.1
(continued)

Panel B: Implicit deposit insurance

Low-income countries [51]

Afghanistan	Central African Republic	Ghana	Malawi	Pakistan	Tajikistan
Angola	Chad	Guinea	Mali	Papua New Guinea	Togo
Azerbaijan	Comoro Islands	Guinea-Bissau	Mauritania	Republic of Congo	Uzbekistan
Benin	Côte d'Ivoire	Haiti	Moldova	Rwanda	Yemen
Bhutan	Equatorial Guinea	Kyrgyz Republic	Mongolia	Senegal	Zaire
Burkina Faso	Eritrea	Laos	Mozambique	Sierra Leone	Zambia
Burundi	Ethiopia	Lesotho	Myanmar	Solomon Islands	
Cambodia	Gambia	Liberia	Nepal	Somalia	
Cameroon	Georgia	Madagascar	Niger	Sudan	

Panel A: Explicit deposit insurance

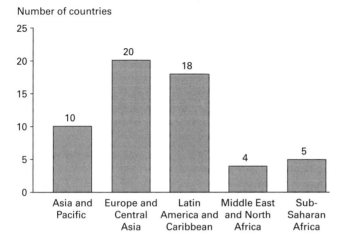

Panel B: Implicit deposit insurance

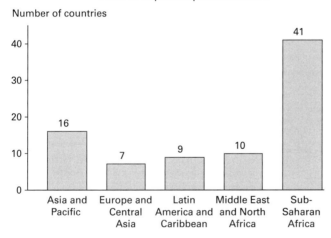

Figure 11.2
Adoption of deposit insurance around the world by region (as of 2003)
Note: High-income countries are excluded from the analysis.

Table 11.2
Adoption of deposit insurance around the world by region as of 2003 (years of establishment/revision in parentheses and number of countries by group in brackets, as of 2003)

Panel A: Explicit deposit insurance

Asia and Pacific [10]

Bangladesh (1984)	Malaysia (1998)	Philippines (1963)	Vietnam (2000)
India (1961)	Marshall Islands (1975)	Sri Lanka (1987)	
Indonesia (1998)	Micronesia (1963)	Thailand (1997)	

Europe and Central Asia [20]

Albania (2002)	Czech Republic (1994)	Lithuania (1996)	Serbia and Montenegro (2001)
Belarus (1996/1998/2000/2001/2004)	Estonia (1998)	Macedonia (1996/2000/2002)	Slovak Republic (1996/2001)
Bosnia and Herzegovina (1998)	Hungary (1993)	Poland (1995)	Turkey (1983/2000)
Bulgaria (1996/1998/2001/2002)	Kazakhstan (1999/2003)	Romania (1996)	Turkmenistan (2000)
Croatia (1997)	Latvia (1998)	Russia (2003)	Ukraine (1998)

Latin America and Caribbean [18]

Argentina (1979/1995)	Dominican Republic (1962)	Jamaica (1998)	Trinidad and Tobago (1986)
Bolivia (2001)	Ecuador (1998)	Mexico (1986/1990/1999)	Uruguay (2002)
Brazil (1995/2002)	El Salvador (1999)	Nicaragua (2001)	Venezuela (1985/2001)
Chile (1986)	Guatemala (1999)	Paraguay (2003)	
Colombia (1985)	Honduras (1999)	Peru (1991)	

Middle East and North Africa [4]

Algeria (1997)	Jordan (2000)	Lebanon (1967)	Oman (1995)

Sub-Saharan Africa [5]

Kenya (1988)	Tanzania (1994)	Zimbabwe (2003)
Nigeria (1988/1989)	Uganda (1994)	

Panel B: Implicit deposit insurance

Asia and Pacific [16]

Afghanistan	China	Laos	Myanmar	Papua New Guinea	Western Samoa
Bhutan	Fiji	Maldives	Nepal	Solomon Islands	
Cambodia	Kiribati	Mongolia	Pakistan	Vanuatu	

Europe and Central Asia [7]

Armenia	Georgia	Moldova	Uzbekistan
Azerbaijan	Kyrgyz Republic	Tajikistan	

Latin America and Caribbean [9]

Belize	Cuba	Guyana	Panama	Suriname
Costa Rica	Grenada	Haiti	St. Lucia	

Middle East and North Africa [10]

Djibouti	Iran	Libya	Saudi Arabia	Tunisia
Egypt	Iraq	Morocco	Syria	Yemen

Sub-Saharan Africa [41]

Angola	Central African Republic	Gabon	Madagascar	Niger	South Africa
Benin	Chad	Gambia	Malawi	Republic of Congo	Sudan
Botswana	Comoro Islands	Ghana	Mali	Rwanda	Swaziland
Burkina Faso	Côte d'Ivoire	Guinea	Mauritania	Senegal	Togo
Burundi	Equatorial Guinea	Guinea-Bissau	Mauritius	Seychelles	Zaire
Cameroon	Eritrea	Lesotho	Mozambique	Sierra Leone	Zambia
Cape Verde	Ethiopia	Liberia	Namibia	Somalia	

Note: Figures exclude high-income countries.

The total of eighty-eight countries reached in 2003, quadruples the 1984 figure. In 1994, deposit insurance became the standard for the newly created single banking market of the European Union (EU). Until the 1990s the EDISs prevailed and kept building mostly in high income countries, but beginning in 1995 we observe a special surge to EDISs in lower-middle-income countries. This is partly driven by the Eastern and Central European transition economies which eventually became or are expected to become EU members, although EDISs remain prevalent in Latin American and Caribbean countries as well, as EDIS came to be labeled as accepted best practice in advice given to the developing countries (Folkerts-Landau and Lindgren 1998; Garcia 1999).

11.3   The Database

The database builds on Demirgüç-Kunt and Sobaci (2001). Much of that database was constructed from the survey results of an International Monetary Fund working paper (Garcia 1999) and earlier sources such as Kyei (1995) and Talley and Mas (1990) and augmented from specific country sources. We extend and improve this database by drawing on other country and online sources as well as a survey of deposit insurers carried out by the International Association of Deposit Insurers in 2002–2003. One of the main improvements is the introduction of historical data on coverage and coinsurance, introducing a time series dimension to the data. The main cross-country part of the database comprises readily usable data for empirical and statistical analysis where most variables are coded as indicators along with explanatory details.

The electronic version of the full dataset is available online (http:// econ.worldbank.org/programs/finance under Datasets), where the coverage ratio data span 1960 to 2003 for all countries. We will periodically update the database and post it on this website. In the next few sections we describe the dataset and define the variables included we also discuss the main features of explicit deposit insurance systems around the world.

11.3.1   Explicit versus Implicit Deposit Insurance

EDISs differ from IDISs due to their reliance on formal regulation authorized by such statutes as central bank law or banking law, or by a country's constitution. The relevant laws establish the main ingredients of the EDIS including the beginning date, coverage limits, how (if any) they are going to be funded, and how bank failures will be resolved.

If deposit insurance is not so authorized, we assume that the DIS is implicit relying on the observation that every country establishes a de facto insurance system for banks.

The variable *Type* denotes the form of the deposit insurance— explicit or implicit—present in each country. The variable takes the value of one for countries with EDIS, and zero otherwise. The variable *Date enacted/Revised* provides the year in which an EDIS was first enacted along with the year in which the system was later revised, if applicable.

11.3.2   Coverage

EDISs vary in their extent and amount of coverage. EDISs also differ in the types of deposits and institutions they apply to. For example, countries which intend to protect their payments systems only, limit the guarantee of EDISs to deposits with commercial banks and other depository institutions that provide payment transactions. On the other hand, some EDISs may extend guarantees to other types of institutions such as savings banks, if they embrace a wider set of objectives.

. Some countries have tailored different EDISs to the features of different types of institutions. Usually, there exists one EDIS for commercial banks and another for other deposit taking institutions. For example, Japan, France, Germany, and Norway have two separate EDISs, and Spain has three. For countries that have more than one EDIS, the database provides information on the EDIS for commercial banks only.

Depending on the objective of the EDIS, the coverage varies across different types of deposits. Foreign deposits of domestic banks, domestic deposits of foreign banks, interbank deposits, and deposits denominated in foreign currencies are not covered under most EDISs. The database provides information on the coverage for interbank deposits, and deposits denominated in foreign currency.

Foreign Currency Deposit Coverage   The variable *Foreign currencies* takes the value one for systems that cover deposits in foreign currency, and zero otherwise. However, some EDISs are restrictive in the set of foreign currencies they cover. For instance, Hungary extends coverage to deposits denominated in EURO or currencies of other OECD countries. This variable takes the value one for such countries as well.

Table 11.3
Explicit deposit insurance schemes which extend coverage to interbank deposits by income level (as of 2003)

High-income	Upper-middle-income	Lower-middle-income	Low-income
Canada	Lebanon	Bosnia and Herzegovina	Kenya
United States		Colombia	Nigeria
		Guatemala	Tanzania
		Honduras	
		Marshall Islands	
		Micronesia	
		Philippines	
		Thailand	

Interbank Deposit Coverage The EDISs seldom cover interbank deposits since unlike small depositors, banks are perceived to have enough resources to monitor other banks. Thus, extending coverage to interbank deposits could reduce bank incentives to supervise one another, which promises to undermine market discipline. Countries with interbank deposit coverage are listed in table 11.3 and grouped by income level. The only two high income countries with this feature are Canada and the United States. Interestingly, some eight lower middle income countries also provide it (table 11.3).

In the database, the variable *Interbank deposits* takes the value one for EDISs that extend coverage to interbank deposits and zero otherwise.

Amount of Coverage The amount of coverage matters since it directly affects the market discipline exerted by depositors. If the coverage is low, then better and more reliable banks will be preferred by depositors. On the other hand, very low coverage conflicts with the goal of protecting small depositors who lack the resources to evaluate the soundness of banks. At the other extreme, very high coverage limits could inhibit any form of monitoring on the depositors' end and downplay market discipline. Coverage ratios of one to two times GDP per capita are generally considered appropriate. However, as illustrated in figure 11.3, coverage ratios often go beyond this limit in practice.

The variable *Coverage limit as of 2003* details the amount of coverage and coinsurance. More specifically, the provided information includes

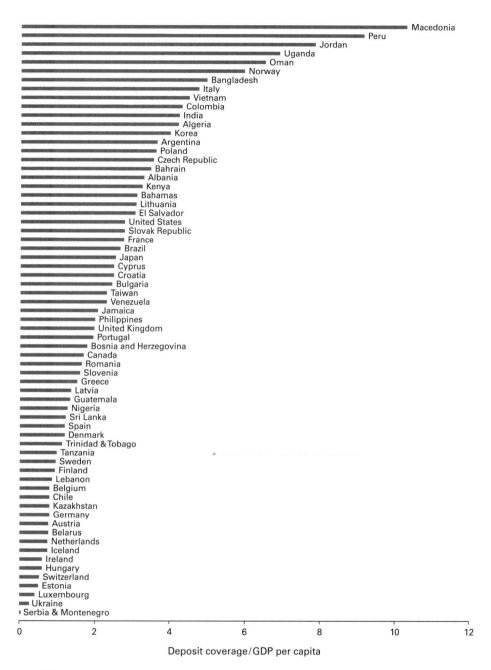

Figure 11.3
Ratios of deposit coverage to GDP per capita in selected countries, 2002

Table 11.4
Explicit deposit insurance schemes with coinsurance by income level (coinsurance requirements in parentheses, as of 2003)

High-income	Upper-middle-income	Lower-middle-income
Austria (10 percent)	Chile (10 percent)	Albania (15 percent)
Belgium (10 percent)	Czech Republic (10 percent)	Belarus (20 percent)
Cyprus (10 percent)	Estonia (10 percent)	Bolivia (50 percent)
Germany (10 percent)	Lithuania (10 percent)	Colombia (25 percent)
Ireland (10 percent)	Oman (25 percent)	Macedonia (10 percent)
Isle of Man (25 percent)	Poland (10 percent)	Russia (50 percent)
Luxembourg (10 percent)	Slovak Republic (10 percent)	
United Kingdom (10 percent)		

the currency in which the coverage is reported, the coverage limit, and whether it entails full coverage; the percentage of the deposits covered if coinsurance exists and the structure of coinsurance. *Coverage limit as of 2003 in US$* expresses the coverage limit in U.S. dollars.

Some countries provide unlimited coverage, usually in response to a banking crisis. For example, in 2003 the Dominican Republic, Indonesia, Malaysia, Thailand, Turkey, and Turkmenistan had full guarantees in place. Similarly, other countries, such as Ecuador, Japan, and Mexico, had full coverage in the past, was and revoked it after their crises seemed to abate.

Coinsurance   Coinsurance mechanisms require depositors to bear part of the cost in case of a banking failure. The aim is to get depositors to make more prudent bank choices in their deposit decision. As of 2003 twenty-one EDISs had coinsurance. Table 11.4 lists these countries and the coinsurance requirement by depositors for each country. Coinsurance does not exist in low-income countries but its use rises with a country's income level (table 11.4).

The variable *Coinsurance* takes the value of one if the country requires a coinsurance, and is zero otherwise. *Coinsurance percentage* states the percentage of the deposit amount that a depositor would lose in the case of a bank failure.

Extent of Coverage   The EDISs differ in terms of the extent of their coverage as well. In most countries, the coverage is per depositor, which means that the sum of deposits per depositor is protected up to the applicable limit. However, some countries provide protection per depositor per account making the level of coverage higher for persons with multiple accounts. The variable *Payment* takes the value one if the protection is per depositor and zero if it applies per depositor per account.

Coverage Distribution We observe varying degrees of deposit values being covered in different EDISs across the world. The variable *Percentage of deposit value covered* provides the extent of total coverage as a share of total deposit value in each country. This variable takes the maximum value of 100 percent for countries that provide full coverage and is less than 100 percent for the rest, which averages around 48 percent.

11.3.3 Funding
EDISs can be either funded or unfunded. In funded systems, member institutions need to make periodic contributions to the fund, which is then used as the main source for paying out depositors during bank failures. A minority of countries (mainly belonging to the high-income category) unfunded systems exist in which members have to contribute to the fund after the failure. Chile is an exception, in that the government is the sole contributor of the fund. As of 2003, only fourteen countries[5] out of eighty-eight had unfunded EDISs and eleven of these countries are in Europe.

Premiums The variable *Annual premiums* provides information on the premiums required as a percentage of the base. The database also indicates whether the premium involves a variable or fixed rate and whether it is risk-based.

Assessment bases for premiums vary across systems. Premiums are generally based on deposits and insured deposits. However, some systems are based on domestic or all obligations of the banks. This is denoted by the variable *Premium or assessment base*.

When premiums vary with the riskiness of the assessment base, they are classified as risk-adjusted premiums. As of 1995, only the United States had adopted risk-adjusted premiums. Since then, the number of countries with risk-adjusted premiums has risen to twenty (see table 11.5 for the complete list of countries with risk-adjusted premiums). The variable *Risk-adjusted premiums* takes the value one if premiums are risk-adjusted, and zero otherwise.

Table 11.5
Explicit deposit insurance schemes with risk-adjusted premiums by income level (as of 2003)

High-income	Upper-middle-income	Lower-middle-income
Finland	Argentina	Belarus
Italy	Hungary	Bolivia
Portugal	Uruguay	Bulgaria
Sweden		El Salvador
Taiwan		Kazakhstan
United States		Macedonia
		Marshall Islands
		Micronesia
		Peru
		Romania
		Turkey

Funding Source, Administration, and Membership   Public funding may be available to supplement the premiums contributed by banks. Public funds may take the form of initial contributions, of losses absorbed ex post by the government, or central bank loans. In this case, funding comes from both private and public sources. The variable labeled *Source of funding* takes the value of two if the EDIS is funded by the government only, zero if funded privately only, and zero if jointly funded.

The variable *Administration* takes on three values: 1 if the administration of the fund is official, 2 if it is joint, and 3 if it is private. If the EDIS of a country is administered by its central bank, it is considered to have an official administration. Moreover, some privately administered institutions have limited authorities. For example, in Italy and Croatia some decisions need central bank approval, hence the EDISs of these countries are considered to have a joint administration in the database.

Finally, the variable *Membership* takes the value one if membership in the fund is compulsory and zero if it is voluntary. The majority of countries have compulsory membership; only ten percent of them operate a voluntary system.[6]

11.3.4   Bank Failure Resolution
We also incorporate survey results on deposit insurance and bank failure resolution from the Barth, Caprio, and Levine database (2004) on

banking regulation and supervision. These variables are coded as follows: (1) *Does the deposit insurance authority make the decision to intervene a bank?* The answer "Yes" is coded with one and "No" with zero; (2) *Does the deposit insurance authority have the legal power to cancel or revoke deposit insurance for any participating bank?* The answer "Yes" is coded with one and "No" with zero; (3) *As part of failure resolution, how many banks closed or merged in the last five years?* The number of banks is reported; (4) *Were depositors wholly compensated (to the extent of legal protection) the last time a bank failed?* The answer "Yes" is coded with one and "No" with zero; (5) *On average, how long does it take to pay depositors in full?* The number of months is reported; (6) *What was the longest that depositors had to wait in the last five years?* The number of months is reported; (7) *Were any deposits not explicitly covered by deposit insurance at the time of the failure compensated when the bank failed (excluding funds later paid out in liquidation procedures)?* The answer "Yes" is coded with one and "No" with zero; (8) *Can the deposit insurance agency/fund take legal action against bank directors or other bank officials?* The answer "Yes" is coded with one and "No" with zero; (9) *Has the deposit insurance agency/ fund ever taken legal action against bank directors or other bank officials?* The answer "Yes" is coded with 1 and "No" with 0; and (10) *Are nonresidents treated differently than residents with respect to deposit insurance scheme coverage?* The answer "Yes" is coded with 1 and "No" with 0. All of these data are for the year 2003.

11.3.5 Time Series: Coverage Limits, Coinsurance, and Coverage Ratios

The database also includes time series data for coinsurance and coverage limits, specifically the limits and the coinsurance requirements since the year of EDIS adoption and the revisions to them over time. The amount of coverage is seen to vary across different schemes. They are also adjusted through time to account for inflation as well as changing economic conditions. The database provides the coverage limits, the currency they are measured in, and the coinsurance percentages.

Finally, the database provides ratios of coverage amounts to GDP per capita and deposits per capita. All elements of these ratios are expressed in local currency. The sample years span 1960 to 2003 in the main database online. The underlying data—that is, GDP per capita, total deposits, population, and coverage amounts—are also reported.

11.4   Main Features of the Deposit Insurance Schemes around the World

The main features of the schemes are summarized in table 1.3, where countries are grouped based on their income level. Foreign currency deposit coverage is prevalent in 76 percent of the countries; whereas it is observed in 57 percent of the low income countries and only 25 percent of the low and middle income countries located in Middle East and North Africa. Extension of coverage to interbank deposits is not very common, amounting to only thirteen out of eighty countries (16 percent) with data for this variable. It is mostly observed in lower-middle- and low-income countries (29 percent in each), and among them mostly in the Asia and Pacific region (57 percent of them). Coinsurance is not required by low income countries and is otherwise required by about a third of the countries. Among the middle income countries, it is most prevalent in the Middle East and North Africa. Most countries, 79 percent in total, calculate the coverage on a per depositor (per institution) basis.

Almost all schemes are permanently funded except the ones in the high income category, where 37 percent of them have no permanent fund and contributions are usually called upon, if deemed necessary, on an ex post basis. Premiums are not risk-adjusted in the low income category and it is also uncommon in other categories where only 23 percent of the countries employ this feature. Membership to the schemes is compulsory in 90 percent of the countries. Outliers lie in the Asia and Pacific Region, where 50 percent of the group show voluntary membership. Funding is predominantly provided jointly from private and public resources, in 63 percent of the countries. Only Chile has a sole public funding, but in most countries government at least provides the initial capital. Sole private funding is more widespread in the high income category, where half of them operate a privately funded system. The schemes are mostly administered officially (60 percent), followed by joint administration (26 percent). Private administration is highest in the high income category, where 23 percent of the group operate a privately administered system.

11.5   Conclusion

Our comprehensive database provides detailed information on the deposit insurance schemes across the world as of 2003. It improves in four ways over the Demirgüç-Kunt and Sobaci (2001) cross-country database. First, the database identifies fourteen countries that have adopted deposit insurance since 1999 and includes twelve other countries with DISs as of 1999 that were not covered before. Second, the database uses various country sources and targeted surveys of individual country deposit insurance agencies and related officials to complement and further detail on the original data. Third, this dataset adds historical time series data, on the values of deposit insurance coverage amounts, coinsurance, and coverage ratios since the inception of the first nationwide scheme by the United States in 1934. Fourth, new variables are incorporated, including the level of coinsurance requirements, the percentage of the value of deposits covered, and whether the protection is denominated per depositor or per depositor per account.

The data developed here are part of a broader research project in understanding and characterizing the design, and implementation of deposit insurance as analyzed in chapter 3. It is hoped that this analysis will stimulate further research on the effect of deposit insurance on the links between financial development, financial stability, fragility, and market discipline. We provide the data in an empirically usable format to make it easier for other researchers and to contribute to this growing literature.

Acknowledgments

We are very grateful to Guillermo Noguera for providing excellent research assistance and to numerous colleagues at the World Bank, the International Association of Deposit Insurers, and officials of deposit insurance agencies, ministries of finance, and central banks around the world for providing input for the deposit insurance database.

Notes

1. The new adopters are Albania (2002), Bolivia (2001), Cyprus (2000), Jordan (2000), Malta (2003), Nicaragua (2001), Paraguay (2003), Russia (2003), Serbia and Montenegro (2001), Slovenia (2001), Turkmenistan (2000), Vietnam (2000), Uruguay (2002), and Zimbabwe (2002) where the adoption years are indicated in parentheses.

2. These countries are Algeria, Bahamas, Belarus, Bosnia and Herzegovina, Guatemala, Honduras, Indonesia, Isle of Man, Kazakhstan, Liechtenstein, Malaysia, and Thailand.

3. This database is available at http://econ.worldbank.org/programs/finance under Datasets.

4. In Norway there was a guarantee fund for savings banks with voluntary membership in 1921 which became obligatory in 1924, whereas a guarantee fund for commercial banks was first introduced in 1938 (Gerdrup 2003). However, Norway's guarantee fund is not considered a pure deposit insurance scheme so it had no official explicit deposit insurance until 1961.

5. Countries with unfunded EDISs are Austria, Bahrain, Chile, France, Gibraltar, Isle of Man, Italy, Liechtenstein, Luxembourg, Netherlands, Slovenia, Switzerland, Thailand, and United Kingdom.

6. Membership is voluntary in the following countries: the Dominican Republic, Kazakhstan, Marshall Islands, Micronesia, Sri Lanka, Switzerland, and Taiwan.

References

Barth, James R., Gerard Caprio, and Ross Levine. 2004. The Regulation and Supervision of Banks around the World: A New Database. 2003 version and update, Washington, D.C.: World Bank.

Demirgüç-Kunt, Aslı, and Enrica Detragiache. 2002. Does Deposit Insurance Increase Banking System Stability? An Empirical Investigation. *Journal of Monetary Economics* 49 (7): 1373–1406.

Demirgüç-Kunt, Aslı, and Harry Huizinga. 2004. Market Discipline and Deposit Insurance. *Journal of Monetary Economics* 51 (2): 375–399.

Demirgüç-Kunt, Aslı, and Edward Kane. 2002. Deposit Insurance around the World: Where Does it Work? *Journal of Economic Perspectives* 16: 175–195.

Demirgüç-Kunt, Aslı, Edward Kane, and Luc Laeven. 2005. Determinants of Deposit-Insurance Adoption and Design. Mimeo., The World Bank, Washington, D.C.

Demirgüç-Kunt, Aslı, and Tolga Sobaci. 2001. A New Development Database: Deposit Insurance around the World. *World Bank Economic Review* 15: 481–490.

Folkerts-Landau, David, and Carl-Johan Lindgren. 1998. Toward a Framework for Financial Stability. Mimeo., International Monetary Fund, Washington, D.C.

Garcia, Gillian. 1999. Deposit Insurance: Actual and Best Practices. Working Paper no. 99/54, International Monetary Fund, Washington, D.C.

Gerdrup, Karsten R. 2003. Three Episodes of Financial Fragility in Norway since the 1890s. BIS Working Paper no. 142, Bank for International Settlements, Basel.

Kyei, Alexander. 1995. Deposit Protection Arrangements: A Comparative Study. IMF Working Paper no. 95/134, International Monetary Fund, Washington, D.C.

Laeven, Luc. 2004. The Political Economy of Deposit Insurance. *Journal of Financial Services Research* 26 (3): 201–224.

Talley, Samuel H., and Ignacio Mas. 1990. Deposit Insurance in Developing Countries. Policy Research Working Paper no. 548, The World Bank, Washington, D.C.

Index